Undesired Revolution

Studies in
Critical Social Sciences

Series Editor
David Fasenfest (*York University, Canada*)

Editorial Board
Eduardo Bonilla-Silva (*Duke University*)
Chris Chase-Dunn (*University of California–Riverside*)
William Carroll (*University of Victoria*)
Raewyn Connell (*University of Sydney*)
Kimberlé W. Crenshaw (*University of California, Los Angeles/
Columbia University*)
Raju Das (*York University*)
Heidi Gottfried (*Wayne State University*)
Karin Gottschall (*University of Bremen*)
Alfredo Saad-Filho (*King's College London*)
Chizuko Ueno (*University of Tokyo*)
Sylvia Walby (*Lancaster University*)

VOLUME 263

The titles published in this series are listed at *brill.com/scss*

Undesired Revolution

The Arab Uprising in Egypt: A Three Level Analysis

By

Ahmed M. Abozaid

BRILL

LEIDEN | BOSTON

Cover illustration: "No language II" 2018. © Darya Tsymbalyuk. Used with kind permission.

The Library of Congress Cataloging-in-Publication Data is available online at https://catalog.loc.gov
LC record available at https://lccn.loc.gov/2023027761

Typeface for the Latin, Greek, and Cyrillic scripts: "Brill". See and download: brill.com/brill-typeface.

ISSN 1573-4234
ISBN 978-90-04-68132-3 (hardback)
ISBN 978-90-04-68133-0 (e-book)
DOI 10.1163/9789004681330

Copyright 2023 by Ahmed M. Abozaid. Published by Koninklijke Brill NV, Leiden, The Netherlands.
Koninklijke Brill NV incorporates the imprints Brill, Brill Nijhoff, Brill Schöningh, Brill Fink, Brill mentis, Brill Wageningen Academic, Vandenhoeck & Ruprecht, Böhlau and V&R unipress.
Koninklijke Brill NV reserves the right to protect this publication against unauthorized use. Requests for re-use and/or translations must be addressed to Koninklijke Brill NV via brill.com or copyright.com.

This book is printed on acid-free paper and produced in a sustainable manner.

To Darya

Contents

Acknowledgments XI
List of Illustrations and Tables XIV

Introduction
Arab Uprising in Ten: Studying Change from Inside/Outside 1
  1   The Post Arab Uprising(s) Chaos: What Went Wrong? 8
  2   The Arab Uprising and the Prolonged Crisis of the Arab States 9
  3   Book Structure 11

1 Revolutions That Have Not Been Theorized
International Relations and Change in the Arab World 16
  1   Structural Change in International Politics since the End of the Cold War 19
  2   Critical School and Change 23
  3   Critical International Relations Theories and the Arab Uprising(s) 28
  4   Political Identity 32
  5   The Failure of Neoliberal Policies 33
  6   Political Will 35
  7   Arab Uprising and IR Theories: An Encounter 36
      7.1 *Cognitive Fallacy* 39
      7.2 *Eurocentric Fallacy* 42
      7.3 *Modernity/Enlightenment Fallacy* 43
      7.4 *Monologic Fallacy* 44
      7.5 *Pedagogical Fallacy* 48
  8   The [Mis]representation and [Mis]location of the Arab World in the Field of IR 49
  9   Knowledge Production of IR in the Arabic Speaking World 52
  10   The Ahistorical Perspective of IR in the Arab World 56
  11   The Fallacies of Applying IR Theories to the Study of the Arab World 57

2 No Revolution
Why as-Ṣaʿīdiyya Did Not Really Revolt 59
  1   Saʿid: Identity and Politics 61
  2   Doing Ethnography in Upper Egypt 65
  3   Reflexivity/Limitations 76

4   Peasants and Rural Societies: An Overview   81
  5   as-Ṣaʿīdiyya, al-fellaheen, and the 2011 Uprising   84
  6   Findings   94
  7   Abu-Qurqas Case Study   96
  8   Conclusion   104

3 **Incomplete Revolution**
  The Determinations of Post-revolution Egyptian Foreign Policy   113
  1   Introduction   113
  2   Theories of International Relations and Revolution   114
  3   Revolution and Foreign Policy   115
  4   The Determinations of Egyptian Foreign Policy after the Arab Uprisings   120
       4.1   *The Nature of the Revolution*   121
       4.2   *Regional and International Changes*   123
       4.3   *Global Public Opinion Orientations*   125
  5   Domestic Policy and Post-revolution Foreign Policy   128
       5.1   *National Choices*   128
       5.2   *National Performance*   129
       5.3   *Domestic Policy*   130
       5.4   *Regime Type*   132
       5.5   *Civil-Military Relations*   133
       5.6   *Public Participation*   134
       5.7   *National Strategy*   135

4 **Counterrevolution**
  Egypt-Gulf Relations after the Arab Uprising   138
  1   Introduction   138
  2   Revolution and War and Peace   140
       2.1   *The Nature of Revolutionary Organizations and Ideologies*   142
       2.2   *Domestic Repercussions of Internal Changes*   143
       2.3   *The Type of Revolutionary Regimes and Leadership*   144
  3   Revolution from the Perspective of 'Balance of Values' Theory   147
       3.1   *Security Concerns*   149
       3.2   *Threat Perception*   150
       3.3   *Misperception and Miscalculations*   151
       3.4   *Foreign Aid*   151
       3.5   *Stability Concerns*   152
  4   Regional Balance of Power in the Middle East after the Arab Uprisings   155

- 5 Between Morsi and Sisi: Regime Change and Egypt-GCC Relations 158
  - 5.1 *Locally* 158
  - 5.2 *Regionally* 159
- 6 Egypt–GCC Relations Issues 160
- 7 Bilateral Relations 161
- 8 The GCC and the Arab Uprising in Egypt 162
- 9 Egypt and Saudi Arabia 163
- 10 Economic Aid 166
- 11 Political Support 167
- 12 Regional Stability 168
- 13 Conclusion 169

5 Undesired Revolution
Power Transition in the Arab World 171
- 1 Structural Realism and International Relations of the GCC Countries 174
- 2 The Characteristics of the Arabian Gulf Regional System 175
- 3 The Small States in the Arabian Gulf: an Outline 179
- 4 How to Study Small States: A Historical Sociology Perspective 184
- 5 Historical Sociology and the Rise of Small Arab Gulf States 186
- 6 A Three-Level Model 189
- 7 Welcome to "The Khaleeji Age" 196
- 8 The Pillars of the GCC Rise 199
- 9 The Aspects of the GCC Rise 200
- 10 The Objectives of the GCC Rise 204
- 11 Challenges and Obstacles to the GCC Rise 205
- 12 Great Expectations? 207

Conclusion
Much Ado about Nothing: [Eurocentric] Theories of International Relations and the Study of Arab Uprisings 213
- 1 Towards New Imagination: On Decolonizing the Study of the Arab World 216

Bibliography 223
Index 254

Acknowledgments

Unequivocally, I owe everything to *Ummi w' Abboyia* (my mother and father), Sayyidah and Mohamed. My mother, this miraculous superwoman of my life, erased words such as impossible, defeat, and give up from my daily-life dictionary. My father, one of the strongest working men I know, did not spare anything, despite the hardship and the poverty we suffered for many years, like millions of *Sa'îdi* families. This magnificent couple, who can hardly read or write, never stopped supporting, loving, and encouraging me unconditionally, until I joined the world's best universities. Likewise, I am grateful and in constant debt to my sisters and brothers, Souad, Fatima, Abdelrahman, Medhat, Amer, and to all my nieces and nephews, for the love and encouragement that made me keep doing what I am doing here as in my previous works.

The infinite debt of gratitude on my shoulders goes to Darya (*Dasha*) Tsymbalyuk; without her love, kindness, passion, and existence next to me I cannot do much. Only god knows how much I owe her for this book and for a great deal more. Further, for the constant support (and prayers) of Victoria and Anatoly Tsymbalyuk in Kyiv, despite the unbearable and factious life condition caused by the Russian colonization and invasion of Ukraine that occurred in February 2022.

I am hugely indebted to the encouragement and generosity of many friends and mentors for their insightful comments. I am deeply grateful to all friends in Egypt for everything they are doing for me that makes me able to move forward, and even to survive. I will be forever grateful for their inspirational thoughts, support, and love. For those who I am proud to call friends; they were (and still are) very kind and humane to give me infinite support, encouragement, and insightful conversations and mentorship over and over. Abdelrahman Abozaid (BOLLA), Ahmed Mahmoud (3s4), Ahmed Fayez, Mayada Madbouly, Islam Melba, Mahienour El-Masry, Noha Kamal, Kholoud Said Amer, ALy El-Reggal, Hatim Nassif, Mohamed Muftah (Ta7), Abdelrahman Mahmoud, Mohamed Abou-Zied, Ismail Alexandrani, Amal Bachiri, Laila Said, Amr Ismaeil, Dina El-Khawaga, Nasser Rabat, Eid Mohamed, Yasser Elway, Mourad Diani, Fatima Alzubairi, Mira El-Hussein, Abdullah Baabood, Madonna Kalousian, Maryam Al-Hajri, Moomen Sallam, Khalil Al-Anani, Abeer Rabei, Makieh Nadjar, Marwa Dawdy, Tasniem Anwar, Amal Kamel Hamada, Rabha Seif Allam, Hanaa Ebeid, Lujain Al-Meligy, and Nicola Pratt. They are, above all, great human beings, and kind souls. Beside their constant love and care, their insightful comments, conversations, and thoughts are scattered all over the book, as well as my other works.

I am blessed with the friendship and companionship of Hana Ebid, Mohamed Al-Saif, Mohamad Mahdi Berjaoui, Henny Ziai, Mohamed Al-Shmar, Yumna El-Serafy, and Hanna Al-Taher. Also, I am deeply grateful for all love, generosity, and inspirational spirits of our amazing "APSAMENA Cohort". My dear friends Abdulla Moaswes, Parichehr Kazemi, and Sara El-Masry. Our lovely summer long walks, conversations, and smoking shisha and drinks in Amman's streets and Beirut's corniche gave me strength and made me optimistic about our common future as young Middle Eastern scholars, despite all despair and defeatism that surrounded us, at home and abroad. We met by accident in other Arab capitals, where we have had very tense and deep overnight conversations and discussions, and at the same time, enjoyed our lives, and shared mutual dreams, food, love, respect, and support, and we still do. Meeting with all these beautiful minds and hearts always reminds me that we have not been defeated yet.

Likewise, I would like to thank my friends who were kind enough to read and comment on the first drafts of the manuscript, repeatedly. I am in great debt especially to Cassandra Humble, Hassan Baig, Nadia Giannelou, Ainhoa Arroyo, and Mustafa Khedewi. From the University of St Andrews, I am grateful to Pietro Esposito, Chloe O'Rourke, Giulia Borrini, Thomas Reid, Ellie Crabtree, Chaeyoung Young, Tony Lang, Bruce Hoffman, Jasmine Gani, Karin Fierke, and Pinar Bilgin for their constant support and encouragement. I am also grateful for the generosity, support, and hospitality I received from the Joyces (Joyce Walsh and Joyce Lapeyre), and Clive and Dorothy Sneddon. Also, I would like to express gratitude to my professors in the Department of Politics & International Relations at the University of Aberdeen, Eva Herschinger, James Wyllie, Ritu Vij, Samantha May, and Tom Bentley. From University of Southampton, a special thanks are dedicated to Professor Russell Bentley. I am deeply touched and grateful for his mentorship, friendship, and continued support. Also, my gratitude for Gillian Kennedy, Jonathan Havercroft, and John Glenn.

I also want to thank my students at St Andrews's School of International Relations and at Southampton's Department of Politics and International Relations–where this book was completed–for their kindness and for their inspirational souls. In the last few years, I was lucky to have many brilliant students who were always inspiring, challenging, and supportive. I am grateful for insightful questions, discussions, and conversations with Alan Zamayoa Romero, Thomas Vilinskis, David Penny, Olivia Mills, Danielle Ogbechie, Charlotte Evans, Miles Butler, Elise Thomson, Chloe Agius, Cerys Rogers and others whose names I am afraid I forget, but I will never forget their kindness, and provocative conversations, and questions. I learned so much from them.

Also, I would like to express my gratitude to the late Kenneth Waltz (1924-2013) for his short comments and responses to a fresh postgraduate Egyptian student who barely spoke and wrote English at the time. A few months after the Arab Uprising of 2011 in Egypt when I was formulating the idea for this book, as a big fan of Ken's works, I decided to share with him a rough draft of the chapters on realism and revolutions, foreign policy in the post-revolution periods, and theories of IR in the Global South. Ken was unimaginably cordial and humble for someone globally considered a demigod in the field of International Relations. Ken sent me several profound notes and comments that not only made me rewrite the chapters but also reconstruct my way of thinking and perceptions–which were often pessimistically hyper-realistic views at the time–about foreign relations and the global prospects and repercussions of the regional situation in the MENA region. I kept exchanging several personal emails with him. After a while, I received an unexpected gift from Ken: a signed copy of his most prominent book, *Theory of International Politics*, with a very tender and supportive inscription for a young scholar from a village in Upper Egypt, who had the audacity–perhaps recklessness too–not only to challenge his theory but also send these critiques to him. I was so naive, yet unprecedentedly lucky (and deeply grateful for my naiveté) at the same time. Ken, you great and humble scholar, wherever you are now, may your soul rest in peace and prosperity.

From Brill, I would like to express my deep gratitude to Prof. David Fasenfest, the Studies in Critical Social Sciences series editor, who was enthusiastic about the project. Also, I am grateful to Debbie deWit, Judy Pereira, and Christine Hededam. Some parts of this book were published in *Middle Eastern Studies Journal* (vol. 57, No. 6, 2021), *Journal of Rising Powers and Global Governance* (vol. 1, No. 2, 2020), and *Athens Journal of Social Sciences* (vol. 8, No. 2, 2021). I am deeply grateful to Helen Kedourie, Ali Murat Kurşun, Afrodete Papanikou, and to the anonymous reviewers of the journals for their insightful comments, and to Taylor & Francis, Athens Institute for Education and Research, and Rising Powers in Global Governance Project for permission to reproduce them here. Also, I am deeply grateful to Darya Tsymbalyuk for her generosity and for allowing me to use her painting.

Finally, I would like to dedicate this book to all friends and strangers, young and old, martyrs and livings, who marched to Tahrir Square(s) everywhere, chanting and demanding *"Aish, Horreya, Adala Egtema'eya"* [Bread, Liberty, and Social Justice], and to those who still believe in the possibility of change, fighting for a better future anywhere, and justice for all. To the memory of all Arab Uprisings martyrs, may your souls rest in peace, and your sacrifices not be in vain.

Illustrations and Tables

Figures

1.1 GDELT project map of global protests 1979–2015   30
3.1 Relationship between revolution and war according to Walt   121
5.1 The rise of the small state: three levels model   191
5.2 Materialist dialectics of change   192
5.3 Systematic process of small states' rise   192

Maps

2.1 The location of Al-Minya governorate   68
2.2 Map of al-Fikriyya city   68
2.3 Map of Munshaʻiat al-Fikriyya   71

Photos

2.1 The city of al-Fikriyya   69
2.2 The village of Munshaʻiat al-Fikriyya   70
2.3 hajaʼh Wasfa   72
2.4 hajaʼh Sayyidah   73
2.5 Meeting with some interviewees inside their homes (2011–2012)   73
2.6 Some of the interviewees carrying out their everyday activities at al-Gheit   74
2.7 Changing urban landscape before and after 2011 around al-Fikriyya city   75
2.8 The slogan of the 'No more marginalization of Saʻid' campaign   107
2.9 A copy of the petition addressed to the members of the Fifty's Committee to end the marginalization against as-Saʻidiyya   109

Tables

3.1 Wars and revolution (1789–1979)   117
4.1 GCC countries by GDP per capita (by US dollar) (2013–2014)   159
5.1 Mobilization type in small Arab Gulf States   194

Introduction

Arab Uprising in Ten: Studying Change from Inside/Outside

After more than a decade since the eruption of the so-called Arab Uprisings, this study claims that the body of scholarly engagement with such unprecedented events through the dominant Western International Relations (IR) theories is still substantially inadequate. Most of these theories, including the critical theory of IR, have discussed, engaged with, analyzed, and interpreted the events as "the Arab Uprisings", a term usually perceived by critical Middle Eastern experts to be orientalist, troubling, totally inappropriate, and implying a passive phenomenon. Such neglect reveals a strong and enduring egoistic Western perspective that simply places emphasis on the preservation of the status quo, ensuring protection of the interests of Western and neoliberal elites and the robustness of counterrevolutionary regimes. On the other hand, writings and scholarship that reflexively engage with and represent authentic Arab views, interests, and prospects have been scarce, if not entirely missing.

The aim of this book is to critically examine the fundamental arguments and propositions of the main research agenda of critical theory in the field of IR, with reference to the study of change in the international arena and the Arab Uprisings in particular. Moreover, this book reveals the limitations of dominant Western International Relations for studying the Arab Uprisings that overemphasis the systematic and external factors in the study of revolutions and regional transformations. It shows instead that focusing on three levels analysis, that encompasses varied domestic social forces and non-state actors, as well as semi-political and socio-economic transformations on national scale, side by side with regional and international changes, can establish new ways of reading both domestic politics and the foreign relations of post-revolutionary Middle East countries such as Egypt, towards non-revolutionary states such as Saudi Arabia, Qatar, UAE, and Gulf Cooperation Council (GCC) countries.

Using this empirical research and local IR scholarship from the region, which is not usually discussed or considered, the book presents a critical account of why democratic revolutions have failed, how counterrevolutions and authoritarianism have fortified, and why revolutions will once again experience a resurgence in such a turbulent region. In doing so, it emancipates international politics, Middle Eastern studies, and foreign policy from the Western hegemonic cognitive approaches and introduces a different contribution from outside the West. This new approach embraces open dialogues with other forms of knowledge and envisions new forms of more inclusive and pluralistic political theories.

It also transforms international relations to become a tool of achieving people's goals in ending fear and oppression and expanding freedom and justice beyond sovereign territories. Interestingly, this perspective (emancipation-based perspective) is done not only by the state but through other non-state actors, such as individuals, social movements, and civil society organizations, which could help in the scholarly efforts that aim to establish a "people-centric model" that does not recognize the separation between the internal and external sphere of the state's actions.

To be clear, in the book, as a scholar in International Relations and International Security, in the first place I am interested in the view to the Arab Uprising from the field of IR. There is significant and enormous discussion and debate on revolution, change, and social change from comparative politics, Sociology, democratization, revolutionary theory, authoritarian resilience, and other fields. However, there is – on the other hand, a considerable scarcity of studying revolution from International Relations theories, especially when it comes to the Arab Uprising. Even the current scholarships on the Arab Uprising, it is overwhelmingly policy-oriented and security-stability nexus. Accordingly, since I wanted to discuss and present a new perspective and away from the dichotomies that characterize the dominant IR scholarship, the main focus of the book was not to explain the drivers and trajectories of the revolutions in the first place, but to bring the discussion on Arab Uprising to the contributions from IR, and vice-versa.

In the mainstream IR theories, there was no significant engagement from the mainstream IR theorists and Middle Eastern Studies in the West with the Arab Uprising revolutions, the same way they did with the 1968 revolutions, 1989 revolutions, or the so-called 'waves of democracy' from IR perspectives.[1] Most of the discussion was either about individual cases, foreign policy, security implications, etc., but not the theoretical debate. This is the main argument/debate I tried to engage with in this book. My rethinking was dedicated to different questions, different aspects, and different positionality and methodological choices. By focusing on the International Relations theories perspective, level analysis approach, and understudied cases, allows me to examine the case of Egyptian revolution, and its development, overlapping, and impact (away from policy-oriented, security implications, ideological, and identity politic discussions, etc.) in a different manner. Therefore, the book chooses to focus on the Arab Uprising in Egypt from bottom-up perspective. This three-level analysis looks first on certain social transformations that took

---

[1] e.g., Walt 1987, Halliday 1999; Maoz 1996.

place domestically (the case of Upper Egypt), then zooming-out to understand the determinations of Egypt foreign policy and its trajectories in the post-revolution period, especially–thirdly–in defining the orientations and repercussions of these transformations (domestically and regionally alsike) on its foreign relations towards the Arabian Gulf countries in particular, as a case to examine my argument.

This book substantially engages with the scholarly literature of different IR theories that have been produced during the last ten years regarding the Arab Uprisings and changes in the Arab World and beyond, with particular emphasis on mainstream Western positivist IR theories (i.e., Realism, Liberalism, and Constructivism) as well as critical theory applications, especially those of the Frankfurt School and the Habermasian project, and their employment in the study of the Middle East and the changes that have taken place over the last decade. The purpose is to detect and reveal these theories' fallacies, deficiencies, disconnection from (and even contestation of) reality, and likewise to point to what went wrong with what were once perceived as promising alternative theoretical approaches.

Specifically, the discussion in this book demonstrates that the theses of IR theories in general, and specifically the dominant ones are not only controversial but also contradictory and even fictitious. This book elucidates that these are not just "misleading", "biased" and "orientalist", but also promote a "pseudo-scientific" argument – as the late Edward Said described dominant Western theories – of the Middle East and their ontological and epistemological fallacies concerning political existence. Nevertheless, these theses are still crucial for understanding "large-scale" changes in world politics, especially in the Western hemisphere.

By critically comparing the literature that has been produced since 2011 on the Arab Uprisings, this book finds that these studies have been biased and politically prejudiced against non-Western cultures, ethics, and religions. The book explores such prejudices by focusing on the concept of "structural change" in international politics, on the one hand, and current developments in the Arab World and Greater Middle East since the outbreak of the Arab Uprising, on the other. Unfortunately, this topic has rarely been discussed or investigated. Most publications on the subject have either appeared in peer-reviewed journals with an emphasis on IR theory, security studies, and Middle Eastern Studies, or in chapters in edited collections. In fact, it is very difficult (as far as I know) to find books in English dedicated to the study of the Arab Uprising and the theory of International Relations in general, especially from critical perspective. Further, the works on this topic approach it but neither extensively engage with it from the standpoint that this manuscript adopts, nor share the latter's view and position. These works discuss the Arab Uprising from the perspective of dominant International Relations theories (Realism, Neoliberalism, and Constructivism) but not from that of radical approaches (i.e., Critical or Postcolonial theories); overall, they provide an international view, rather than theoretical investigation, of the Arab Uprisings.

For instance, almost four decades since its emergence, the critical theory of IR has achieved several goals that help to push forward the debate in the field. According to Andrew Linklater,[2] the main achievements of the critical theory of IR can be summarized as follows:

(1) Critical theory still adheres to the challenges posed to epistemological positivism (rationalism), since its proponents continue to believe that knowledge does not arise from the neutral engagement of the subject with objective reality; on the contrary, it reflects pre-existing social purposes and interests.

(2) Challenging the position that current social structures are unchanging, Critical theory, in contrast, supports the claim that structural inequities of power and wealth are in principle changeable. Furthermore, it stresses the notion of emancipation, according to which the possibility of transforming these social orders and ending the fundamental forms of social exclusion could be realized despite the epistemological position that defends a much more contemplative account.

(3) Despite acknowledging the undeniable contribution and influence of Marx and Marxists on the critical school, it tries to overcome the inherent weaknesses of Marxism that stress the notion of class struggle as the fundamental form of social exclusion. Instead, it perceives the modes of production as the fundamental determinant of the conflict in society and throughout history.

(4) In the face of several forms of global (and local) exclusion, so-called International Critical Theory rejects and challenges the unjustified forms of exclusion. Alternatively, it calls on us to judge social arrangements by their ability to embrace open dialogues with everyone, and to envision new forms of a more inclusive political community.

Other scholars indicate that the main achievement of critical theory in the field of IR since its emergence in the 1980s was to expose the deep relation

---

2 Linklater 1996, 1998.

between the mainstream approaches of IR theory (specifically neorealism, rational-choice, and neoliberal institutionalism) and the dominant interests they served in world politics: i.e., the maintenance of a bipolar system and the manifestation of American preponderance, possessive individualism, and world capitalism.[3] Likewise, Critical International Relations (CIR), and later Critical Theory of International Relations (CTIR), sought to expose the consequential shortcomings of the predominant traditional theories by continuously challenging and questioning the fundamental postulates of the extremely-positivist field.[4] For instance, Jim George indicated that one of the clear achievements of CIR is that its direct ontological and epistemological criticism of positivism, rationalism and structuralism made it possible to rethink IR by enabling a broader thinking space and supporting efforts to develop alternative conceptions of the international that are sensitive to history and to the sociological understanding of the international.[5]

Nevertheless, both critical theory of IR and the critical IR theory still suffer from several deficiencies and fallacies, which I will articulate and highlight in Chapter 1, with special emphasis on the critical IR theories that did not get enough attention comparing with the mainstream IR theories. For instance, after years of notable expansion, the intellectual space that the Frankfurt School-inspired theorists have traditionally occupied is declining in prominence and losing vitality.[6] According to Schmid, after occupying a significant space within scholarly debates during the 1980s and 1990s, critical theory (including both the Neo-Gramscian and the Habermasian projects) appears today decidedly out of fashion, increasingly fragmented, lacking in practical relevance, operating within very specific orientations, and with theoretical, rather than more generalist, political interests in focus.[7] A quick cross-referencing of the leading critical database, platforms, journals, and critical books since 2010 shows that there are very few applications of such theoretical ideas to the case study of the Arab Uprisings (or other Global South cases). Sadly, one study noted that between 2011 to 2016, critical IR journals (e.g., *International Political Sociology*, *Millennium*, *International Studies*, and *Alternatives: Global, Local, Political*), have shown little direct interest in the Arab Uprising, but considerable interest in issues that range across the problematic of uprisings, interventions, and conflicts in the Middle East/North Africa (MENA) region.[8] Interestingly though,

---

3 Brincat 2018.
4 Silva 2005.
5 George 1989; Yalvaç 2015.
6 Schmid 2018; Dunne, Kurki and Smith 2013.
7 Kurki 2012: 130–137.
8 Bustos 2017: 52.

even those studies that address the Arab Uprising were noticeably devoid of interrogation and/or investigation of the genesis of the causes and topics that created the Arab Uprising intifadas in the first place, and of how to resist the resurgence of resilient authoritarianism and counter-revolutionary forces that crucially seek to abort the emancipation project that the Arab Uprising hoped to carry out.

To a large extent, these studies can be assimilated with neorealism and neo-liberalism studies, in which positivist research focused on the outcomes, consequences, and repercussions of the Arab Uprising on issues such as security policies, immigration, responsibility to protect (R2P), the Israeli occupation and in general to the processes of neoliberal globalization.[9] Therefore, as several scholars pointed out, due to its heavy emphasis on the external critique, the "dysfunctional side effects" of capitalism, and intrusions on other subsystems, critical theory (especially the Habermasian version) has come to oscillate between the empty radicalism of its procedural utopia and the practical resignation demanded by its social and political analysis.[10] Not only that, but the positivists themselves intensely criticized the so-called emancipation-based critical theory. After more than twenty-five years, several of these objections are still valid and consistently heard. For instance, the neoliberal institutionalists accused critical theory of being preoccupied with agenda-setting and meta-theoretical reflection, but unwilling or unable to produce substantive work in International Relations. Moreover, the "reflectivist" paradigms lacked a coherent research agenda that could structure their contribution to the discipline, and by implication provide real knowledge.[11] At the same time, several Neorealist scholars claimed that critical International Relations theory had failed to deliver much in the way of empirical research.[12]

Therefore, in order to understand the current wave of democratization in the Arab World – regardless of the setbacks that have occurred – the book indicates that scholars should be moving away from the positivist (state-centric) perspectives that define International Relations and foreign policy in terms of the pursuit of "national" interests, which sovereign states define in terms of power, and towards a more critical approach that places human beings at the center of analysis. Interestingly, this is done not only by the state but through other non-state actors, such as individuals, social movements, and civil society organizations. The emancipation of international politics and foreign policy

---

9   Ibid.
10 Ibid.
11 Keohane 1998.
12 Mearsheimer 1995; Price and Reus-Smit 1998.

projects aims to create and establish a "people-centric model" that does not recognize the separation between the internal and external spheres of the state's actions.

In fact, we live in a (global) system that constantly operates so as to silence other (non)Western voices and make their contributions invisible. According to Grada Kilomba, mainstream (Western) academia has never had an interest in non-Western knowledges because it is embedded in white-narcissistic societies.[13] Therefore, this book seeks to introduce knowledge from outside the West and give it a voice, a space, along with the opportunity to express and represent itself. By presenting an encounter with and an understanding of these areas, away from the dominant Western knowledge, the book contributes to the efforts of freeing knowledge (as a subject) from Western epistemic domination and its arguments and statements on the East. Likewise, the study strives to initiate and establish a dialogue and conversation between the different forms and types of knowledge, both Western and non-Western, which could unpack and dissolve the dominant monistic (monological) model of knowledge to move towards a genuinely pluralistic model. Finally, it contributes to the efforts to decolonize the field of Middle Eastern studies, departing from the Anglo-Saxon domination that has entirely controlled the production of knowledge about the region and its peoples since the establishment of the field following the Second World War.

In other words, the aims of this book are as follows:

(1) Understanding the wave of democratization and radical change in the Arab World – regardless of the setbacks that have occurred – this study indicates that scholars should be moving away from the positivist (state-centric) perspectives that define International Relations and foreign policy in terms of the pursuit of "national" interests, which sovereign states define with reference to power, and towards a critical approach that places citizens at the center of analysis.

(2) Presenting a critical and radical reappraisal of the dominant IR theories, with the aim of emancipating fields such as international politics, Middle Eastern studies, and foreign policy projects, from Western hegemonic cognitive approaches, and to introduce a contrasting contribution from outside the West, thus embracing the calls to establish open dialogue with other forms of knowledge and

---

13 Kilomba 2010; Smith 2012.

to envision new forms of more inclusive and pluralistic political theory.

(3) Transforming International Relations into a tool for achieving people's ends through ending fear and oppression and expanding freedom and justice beyond sovereign territories. In other words, this book is on International Relation as if the people matter. Interestingly, this emancipation-based perspective is adopted not only by the state but also by non-state actors, such as individuals, social movements, and civil society organizations, which could support scholarly efforts to establish a "people-centric model". i.e., from bottom-up.

1 The Post Arab Uprising(s) Chaos: What Went Wrong?

Many leading orthodox Middle Eastern experts believe that the dynamic that drives regional powers to destructive proxy conflicts consists of fears of resurgent domestic uprisings, Iranian power, and US abandonment, alongside the insatiable desires and aspirations to take advantage of weakened states and the condition of international disarray. These dynamics are what led some experts to label this new situation in the region as "fundamentally one of disorder".[14] The problem with this argument is that the situation it describes is not new at all; likewise, that it overlooks one of the main causes of conflict in the Middle East, which is the GCC countries' regional leadership ambitions. Only a few studies refer to or highlight the role of Qatari- Emirati (and Saudi) regional competition in this instability. These counterrevolutionary countries were (and still are) a part of the problem of, not the solution to, this regional chaos and instability due to their miscalculated and misguided interventionistic foreign policies.

Apart from the re-emergence of popular uprisings, and the strategic and political situation in the area since the US withdrawal from Iraq after 2008, the region witnessed an intensive and raging confrontation between Saudi Arabia (and its allies in the Gulf region) and the larger Sunni Middle East. Likewise, the threats to weak states were always present, especially in places like Sudan, Yemen, Somalia, and Iraq. The Failed States Index cited these as among the most fragile states in the region since 2008.[15] The new feature is that the Arab

---

14 Lynch 2018: 117.
15 Foreign Policy, The Failed States Index 2009, 2010, 2011, 2012; The Fragile States Index 2019, 2020, 2021.

Uprising was the final nail in the coffin of these states, paving the way for the current chaotic and messy situation in the region.

For instance, Lynch discussed these results as if they were the cause of the same problem, which, it is argued, is inaccurate or at least unconvincing. For instance, when he reviewed the 2015 US decision to withdraw from the region (the "pivot to East Asia") and the nuclear agreement with Iran later, he did not link it with the deep-rooted and intense crisis caused by the conflict between Iran on the one hand, and Israel, Saudi Arabia, Egypt, and other GCC monarchies on the other. This approach seems absurd and reductionist. Likewise, Lynch did not discuss the influence of the Saudi Israeli pressure to pull the US away from Iran.[16] The likelihood of war between Iran and Israel that Lynch pointed to was not a result of the withdrawal from the nuclear deal, but of Israeli existential fears and sense of hazard not only from Iranian bombs but also from the emergence of any other power in the Middle East that might seek to acquire weapons of mass destruction.

The other crucial element determining the future of the Middle East region is the rise of competitive and revisionist Small Gulf States, i.e., the UAE, Qatar, Oman, and Kuwait. For decades, these states had enjoyed conditions of significant prosperity, stability, and economic growth, which increased their political and diplomatic influence and reach. These conditions led to claims by several experts and scholars that this was the kind of change that would transform the future of the region.

2 The Arab Uprising and the Prolonged Crisis of the Arab States

Since the outbreak of the so-called Arab Uprising in 2011, the regional system in the Middle East has been in flux. Under these new circumstances, the status quo starts to unravel, and a new order is being imposed, accompanied by new regional dynamics and security arrangements. Nevertheless, although the number of studies that discussed, engaged with, and analyzed the post-revolutionary strategic situation in the Middle East region grew tremendously, unfortunately, most of these studies did not provide a relevant and extensive explanation of the "real" situation in the region. Instead of asking the ontological question of "who caused or created the recent quagmire and chaos in the Middle East?" scholars like Marc Lynch – and others – took it as guaranteed that this was not the case here. In his last book, *The New Arab War*, Lynch

---

16   Guzansky, 2014; Ulrichsen, 2016; Totten, 2016; Ramani, 2017.

presumed that this was a pre-given situation, and the important goal was to know how to deal with the challenges and threats the United States (and maybe the other great powers, or even the international community) were facing in the Middle East.[17] This study argues that the main challenge to the United States and even to Arab society itself is the "Arab State", not the Arab Uprising or even Terrorism.

One of the contradictions of Arab politics is its continuity in the face of the changing environment that surrounds Arab states. Some scholars claim that there are new patterns of behavior and power relations in the current structure of the Middle East. "For a moment, it looked as if the old Middle Eastern order was coming to an end and a new and better one was taking its place. But things quickly fell apart. Some states collapsed under the pressure and devolved into civil war; others found ways to muddle through and regain control over their societies".[18] From that author's perspective, this is the manifestation of what he called "the new Arab order". For many reasons this is inaccurate.

What happened in the region after 2011 was not "new" insofar as it was an "adjustment" in the tools and means of solving or managing the conflicts in the region, rather than in the ends or objectives that the US and its allies were trying to achieve. Most of the studies falsely claim that to find a way to deal with this situation, the United States needs first to characterize and outline the current structure of the region. On the contrary, this study believes that the underlying cause of the current crisis finds its roots in the competition and rivalry over leadership, either inside the Gulf area or throughout the Arab World in general. Therefore, it argues that to understand the current situation in the region, it is urgently necessary to deconstruct it, by questioning and illuminating the factors that created this chaos in the first place. If we jump from asking "Who causes what?" to "How to deal with it?" or "What is going on?" we will remain stuck in a vicious cycle of policy-oriented scholarship and kept trapped in what I call security-stability nexus logic of studying the Middle East and the Global South in general.

First, regarding the dysfunction of the Arab states, this is not new. Many studies showed that the Middle East had been on the brink of collapse and chaos for decades. Second, the so-called new chaotic conditions are also nothing new. Looking back to what happened in Iraq, Lebanon in the early 2000s or Yemen in the late 1990s, we see that non-state actors like Hezbollah, Al-Qaida, and Houthi had already had their controlled territories, years before the

---

17   Lynch 2016, 2018.
18   Lynch 2018: 116.

emergence of what was known as the Islamic State (IS). In Egypt from the late eighties up to the mid-nineties, Al-Jama'ah al-Islamiyyah also expanded their power in large territories in Upper Egypt and later in Sinai. Therefore, these conditions are not new. Thirdly, the Arab States had been in a deeply dysfunctional state since the early 1980s.

Scholars (Arab and Western) from the far right to the far left wrote about the crisis of the Arab State.[19] A leading political scientist, A. Hilal Dessouki, wrote in 2008: "this is the end of the Arab regional system, and the alternative is either fragmentation or penetration".[20] This is the result of a deep-rooted crisis, caused – in the first place – by the neoliberal policies coercively imposed by the US and the IMF. Therefore, it was the substantial American and Western support for authoritarian regimes in the region, not the Arab Uprisings which were a further result of these misleading policies, that was the main cause of the chaotic situation in the region.[21]

What created the muddled situation after the Arab Uprisings was the US and Western reluctance to support the popular-civic upheavals, and the conflicting and inconsistent intervention strategies of the Gulf countries in the region's disputes and internal conflicts. Instead of pushing forward the democratic movement in the region, the US administration chose to support authoritarian regimes in line with an illusory "Authoritarian-stability nexus" which had been proved useless since the outbreak of the Islamic revolution in 1979. Under the threat and fear of losing its overseas interests, the Arab World again fell into the hands of repressive dictatorships and backward radical and violent groups such as the Islamic State in Iraq and Syria (ISIS). In sum, both the US and Western European powers ended up by losing both its interests and its values.[22]

3   Book Structure

The book has two main objectives. The first engages with the mainstream IR theories regarding the study of revolution, change, and the study of Arab Uprisings. It examines the scholarly literature of different Western IR theories that have been produced during the last ten years on the Arab Uprisings to highlight their fallacies and deficiencies as well as their disconnection from

---

19   Mossad and Youssef 2009; Luciani 2015; Guazzone 2012; Susser 2009; Owen 2012; Ayubi 1995.
20   Dessouki 2008 2015; Mattar and Dessouki 1982.
21   Gause 2011: 81–84 85–90; Taleb and Blyth 2011; Hicks 2015; Burns 2018.
22   Gause 2011: 81–82; Walt 2011, 2016; Cook 2018; Luce 2018.

reality. The book also points at what went wrong with the alternative theoretical approaches that were once perceived as promising. By engaging with the mainstream theories from postcolonial and decolonizing perspectives the book finds that this literature was biased and politically prejudiced against non-Western cultural, ethnic, or religious inspirations and forms of knowledge. The second objective covers the ethnographic research in light of Egypt's revolution to explain the implicit causes of the failure of the Arab Uprising in Egypt on three levels, i.e., the individuals, the state, and system levels of analysis. It is based on over 10 years of fieldwork, ethnography, and empirical research in several Arab countries including Egypt, Jordan, the GCC countries, Yemen, and other Arab countries. This included interviews with more than 250 people, most of whom were from marginalized and excluded communities and who have not yet been examined.

Chapter One indicates the most chronic critiques of and prolonged objections to both the mainstream Western Positivism IR theories surrounding the study of the Arab Uprisings. By interrogating these dominant and mainstream theories, and aiming to reveal and detect their fallacies, deficiencies, disconnection from (and even contestation of) reality – similarly pointing to what went wrong with a theoretical approach that was once perceived as a promising alternative to positivist and problem-solving theories– the chapter identifies nine main deficiencies: the cognitive (ontological and epistemological) fallacy, the Eurocentric-Capitalism fallacy, the Modernity-Enlightenment foundations fallacy, the fallacy of the monologic (not dialogical) nature of both positivist and normative and communicative turns in IR, the Pedagogical fallacy of teaching and studying IR in the MENA region, the de-positionality and selectivity fallacy, the statism and militarization fallacy, the urbanism and privileged fallacy, and the falsifications fallacy.

Chapter Two discusses the reasons behind the absence of revolution in the large, marginalized, and excluded part of Egypt known as Sa'îd (Upper Egypt). The purpose of this chapter is to investigate and inspect the causes that prevented the marginalized and isolated society of Sa'îd from rebelling against Mubarak's authoritarian regime, as the North had done. Here I seek to present a different interpretation of as-Sa'îdiyya's attitudes towards the 2011 uprising, moving away from the Manichean "glorification" vs "ignominy", or "celebration" vs "contempt" narrative that dominated the study of the roles of Sa'îd and as-Sa'îdiyya in the 2011 Arab uprising. My research, based on interviews, participant observation and ethnographic investigation conducted with more than fifty women and men, articulates the behavior of peasants as political actors in this time of turmoil. While most sociological and anthropological studies of revolutions concentrate on cities and urban areas, this chapter focuses on a small town, Madinat Al-Fikriyya, and village, Munsha'iat Al-Fikriyya, in the Al-Minya governate in Upper Egypt. Therefore, to understand the role of as-Sa'îdiyya in the 2011 uprising, the chapter suggests three conceptual changes to this convention – firstly, by putting peasant communities within sociopolitical and socioeconomic contexts; secondly, by concentrating on understanding the dynamics of state-society relations; and lastly, by exploring the role of the security establishment and levels of penetration into the society, in that order.

Chapter Three analyses the changes in Egypt's foreign policy orientations and tendencies in the post-Arab Uprising period in the light of dominant IR theories (i.e., Realism, Liberalism, and Constructivism). The focal point here is to engage with the theoretical debate on the idea that the foreign policies of any country are nothing but a reflection of current transformations within the local political situation (e.g., the nature of the political system, the quality of the ruling elite, the party system, the role of public opinion, political ideology, political culture, and political participation, etc.). In other words, any quantitative or qualitative changes affecting the nature of the local system are accompanied by changes related to the nature of the foreign policy. The main argument of this chapter is that transformations at a unit level (i.e., state, or political system) that occur because of revolution and regime change, etc. will have a crucial impact on both foreign policy and regional and international interactions. The extent of positioning and influence of these domestic transformations depends on revolutionary states' geopolitical position in the regional environment on the one hand, and its centrality and significance for regional coalitions and global balance of power considerations on the other. With special emphasis on revolutions that take place within medium and small powers of the Global South, such as Egypt, the chapter reveals the constitutive role of domestic transformations and the part they play in shaping and (re)shaping relations between nation-states, at times of both peace and war. At the same time, the chapter analyses the impact of a unit-level variable such as revolutions, on system-level variables, that is, on the structure of foreign policies and interactions with both regional and international orders.

Chapter Four explores how shortly after it prevails, revolutions tend to reject the opposing parties' behavior, but the "socialization" process and the crucial impact of 'unit-level' variables and needs force the new revolutionary regime to deal with all countries on the same foundations of international politics: interests and mutual gains. Based on the discussion outlined in Chapter 3, I will discuss the post-revolution Egyptian foreign policy based on five main determinations, which arguably will shape GCC foreign policies (i.e., security concerns, threat perception, misperception and miscalculation, foreign aid, stability concerns). At the same time, these factors explain the correlation between revolution and instability and the tensions between revolutionary regimes and their non-revolutionary (conservative) neighbors. This chapter first discusses the debate on the correlation between revolution, and the state of regional war and peace. Secondly, the behavior of revolutionary regimes (i.e., Egypt between 2011 and 2013) towards non-revolutionary and counterrevolutionary regimes (i.e., Gulf monarchies), through the lens of balance of power and balance of threat theories. The second parts discuss the behavior from the perspective of non-revolutionary regimes (With Egypt who represent the revolutionary regime and the GCC countries that represent non-revolutionary camp). Especially with the significant alert and transformation of balance of power dynamics and condition in the MENA region that occurred because of the rise of small rich and rich oil-exporting monarchies in the Arabian Gulf region which will be discussed separately in Chapter 5.

Chapter Five examines the case of a change on the regional and transregional level, as manifested in the rise of the small Arabian Gulf States, and the relationship between these emerging and rising regional powers with traditional yet declining regional powers such as Egypt. The chapter indicates that the change process in international relations has two separate dimensions: process and outcome, which will yield different causal and historical accounts for each event. In terms of outcome, it refers to "the result of changes that may lead to either continuity or a complete breakdown and the creation of a new order". This term indicates whether forms of change and turbulence events suggest the birth of a new order or the persistent endurance of institutions. In terms of process, a slow-moving casual process of change may occur suddenly or gradually and can be termed incremental or cumulative. This chapter argues that the same analogy could apply to the case of a change in the Persian Gulf. In order to understand the rise of small states in the region (as a form of change), it could be useful to emphasize sudden disruptive mechanisms that occurred in the region such as the Gulf Wars of 1980–88, 1990, and 2003, Saudi Iranian rivalry, and the power transition in the broader Middle East over the last three decades. Similarly, we can understand this process by arguing that it did not happen suddenly, but as a cumulative product of many incremental changes that took place within these small states, along with the changes taking place in the regional and international contexts during the same period. Further, the chapter explains Egypt-Gulf relations in the light of Emirati and Qatari expansion and interventionist policies.

The concluding chapter, in order to understand the current wave of democratization in the Arab World – regardless of the setbacks that have occurred – indicates that IR and Middle Eastern scholars should move away from the positivist (state-centric) perspectives that define international relations and foreign policy in terms of the pursuit of "national" interests, which is defined in terms of power by sovereign states, and towards a more critical approach that places human beings at the center of analysis. A critical perspective, in turn, claims that International Relations should become a tool for achieving people's ends through ending fear and oppression and expanding freedom and justice beyond sovereign territories. In conjunction with the emancipatory inclinations of the Arab Uprising waves between 2011 and 2021, scholars need to keep pace with the movement and the demands of the public so that it is possible not only to reduce the frequency and intensity of unrest and insecurity, but also – and most importantly, improve the living conditions of millions of impoverished, excluded, and suppressed citizens. Interestingly, this is done not only by the state but through other non-state actors, such as individuals, social movements, and civil society organizations. Emancipatory international politics and foreign policy projects aim to create and establish a "people-centric model" that does not recognize the separation between the internal and external spheres of the state's actions.

CHAPTER 1

Revolutions That Have Not Been Theorized

International Relations and Change in the Arab World

This chapter problematizes the concept of change in the international order and in the sub-regional context in particular, exploring overlaps between material-ideational forms of power and the dynamics of regional shift, rather than maintaining the conventional claim that these forms represent entirely distinct types of engines of change. To address this lacuna, the thesis will adopt Aseema Sinha's definition of change in international politics as "a shift in three dimensions: power or interests, ideas, and institutions". According to Sinha, international change can be revealed through "shifts in global power distributions, changes in the ideological commitments by nations and non-state actors, and reorientations in the workings of institutions or the creation of new institutions, defined broadly to include regimes or informal rules and norms".[1]

How should we model the process of change? According to Vincent, the predominance of a punctuated equilibrium model in IR theory means that many important international concepts rely on a static understanding or equilibrium of discrete situations, such as World Wars I and II, the Cold War, and now the post-Cold War era.[2] Others believe that the dead weight of tradition causes the theory of International Relations to give priority and advantage to static over dynamic analysis, and to over-emphasize continuity at the expense of change.[3] It is clear now that the main purpose of many of these theories was to articulate the elements of a situation, such as anarchy, the balance of power, polarity, etc. In such accounts, there is a strong assumption of system stability and self-reinforcing elements.[4]

Therefore, given this theoretical conservatism (if not anti-change) and worship of stability within Western-dominated IR academic circles, it is not surprising that there is no theory of international social change, as witness strategic studies and its overwhelming tendency to emphasize the security of

---

1 Sinha 2018: 197.
2 Vincent 1983: 64.
3 Gilpin 1981: 4; Buzan and Jones 1981: 2; Holsti et al. 1980: XVII.
4 Vincent 1983: 63.

the status quo and revisionist states.[5] According to Nazli Choucri, this problem is embodied in the nature of Political Science itself. Comparing economics with Political Science, Choucri argued, "Economists are more rigorous in both theory and method but focus almost exclusively on static or comparatively static relations. Political scientists are to a large extent, concerned with institutional and historical change, but their theories are generally vague".[6]

The over-emphasis on "disruptive change" has rendered invisible other pathways of change that could be and have been as transformative, such as incremental and gradual changes seen in the global emergence of populism, the life cycle of norms, and how norms change, which are still outside the theoretical debate on International Relations.[7] The mission of constructing a theory of change demands the import of several key concepts and methods of historical analysis from other disciplines. Dialogue with other theories and fields such as Comparative Politcs and Historical Sociology could make it possible to offer an analytical typology that directs attention to the process of change in addition to the outcome of change.[8]

Sinha tries to construct a more rigorous typology of international change by differentiating between three forms/types of change: gradual and incremental change versus disruptive change, process versus outcome, and path dependence.[9] She suggests that this typology is "intended to help researchers analyze a broader set of events and transitions and to analyze the conventional change conjunctures (end of the Cold War for example) through the lens of slow-moving change".[10]

A change process in international relations has two separate dimensions: process and outcome, which will yield different causal and historical accounts for each event. In terms of outcome, it refers to "the result of changes that may lead to either continuity or a complete breakdown and the creation of a new order".[11] This term tells us whether forms of change and turbulent events suggest that a new order was born, or that the endurance of institutions persisted. In terms of process, a slow-moving, casual process of change may occur suddenly or gradually and can be termed incremental or cumulative.[12]

---

5   Buzan and Jones 1981: 87, 155–172.
6   Choucri 1980: 103.
7   Sinha 2018: 196.
8   Ibid.
9   ibid: 198.
10 ibid: 196.
11 ibid: 199.
12 Streeck and Thelen 2005; Pierson 2003.

One example of the incremental process is globalization and technological change. These events, on the one hand, are gradual processes that have unfolded through many endogenous developments, rather than an exogenous global shift; on the other hand, they have "transformed the context, the forms, and the actors of international relations" in an incremental way.[13] Others have pointed to what is called "threshold effects" that differentiate between incremental and sudden processes. According to Pierson, when threshold effects are salient, "historical process moves slowly" and when this process reaches "a critical threshold or tipping point" then it "triggers major changes" in the system.[14] However, there is no clarification as to which type of incremental change may be evident in the major eras and periods of change.[15]

Regarding cumulative change, events such as the rise of China and other great powers is an excellent example. The rise of these great powers and their incentive to enter global institutions and expand their international reach did not happen suddenly but was a cumulative outcome of many incremental (political and economic) changes, within both the domestic context and the regional and global contexts.[16]

The same analogy could apply to the case of change in the MENA region and in the Persian Gulf region specifically. To understand the rise of small states in the region (as a form of change), it could be useful to emphasize the sudden disruptive mechanisms that have occurred in the region, such as the Gulf Wars of 1980–88, 1990, and 2003, the Saudi Iranian rivalry, and the power transition in the broader Middle East in the last three decades. Likewise, we can understand this process by arguing that it did not happen suddenly, but as a cumulative product of many incremental changes that took place within these small states, as well as the changes that took place in the regional and international contexts during the same period.

It may be important to recognize the differences (whether in process or outcome) between violent or peaceful, systemic, or incremental change.[17] Basically, students of international relations and foreign policy need to pay more attention to the way "transformative changes can happen one step at a time",[18] which could justify the importance of certain incremental and partial changes that take place within significant and noteworthy small states (such

---

13 Sindjoun 2001: 220.
14 Pierson 2003: 182.
15 Sinha 2018: 199.
16 ibid: 200.
17 ibid: 198.
18 Streeck and Thelen 2005.

as oil-exporting Arab Gulf States) or on the unit level. Unfortunately, the static nature of IR theory has pushed many scholars to proclaim that "IR theory needs a more well-developed theory of dynamic change".[19] In fact, one of the main flaws of the dominant IR theories is that they explain change by "privileging revolutionary and large-scale systemic factors originating from global levels", to the neglect of other forms and levels of change.[20] Realism stresses that if a change in international politics is not "radical, discontinuous, violent and far-reaching", then it is not worth paying attention to.[21]

Therefore, it is important to mention that this book is interested in studying the process of change more than its outcomes. Likewise, this book will not investigate the systemic forms of change, but instead will focus on what Sinha called the overlooked, invisible, and other equally important mechanisms and pathways of change in world politics, especially those which occur at units-level among small powers.[22] This book completely diverges from Realist studies of change in world politics that discuss the case and conditions of great powers on the systemic level of analysis and stress their expansion strategies. Instead, it places emphasis on middle powers and small states, and forms of change at unit and regional levels of analysis in particular. Furthermore, the book tries explaining the Emirates' expansion and interventionist policies, despite its small size and capabilities, as a form of violent change on the unit-level rather than on the system level.

1 Structural Change in International Politics since the End of the Cold War

Since the creation of modern Eurocentric international system in the sixteenth century, there have been a few transformative moments that changed the rules and the structure of international politics: for example, the transformation from the medieval to the modern world through with the rise of European empires such as Portuguese, Spanish, and Dutch empires since early 1500s, the establishment of nation-states, the rise of Napoleon at the end of the 18th century, the British hegemony in the 19th century, the First World War (1914–1919), the Second World War (1939–1945), and last but not least the end of the Cold War and the nonviolent disintegration of the former Soviet

---

19 Sinha 2018: 199.
20 ibid: 196.
21 Campbell 2004.
22 Sinha 2018: 201.

Union (1917–1989). On the other hand, there were many critical moments that changed the course and the nature of events and interactions at the regional level, but they were not radical enough to be considered "structural changes" in international politics, as they did not have the same effects on a global level. These critical moments included the fall of the Spanish empire, the rise of Prussia in the mid-19th century, the fall of the Ottoman empire, the terror attack on the United States on September 11th, 2001, and the Arab Uprising.

What are the factors that cause one event rather than another to be considered or perceived as a structural change? Is it a perspective? Or are there indicators that can identify the differences? How have these events changed the rules and the structures of international politics, and to what extent do they affect global security issues? Here, I argue that the standards by which to distinguish between structural changes and other changes in the international system are the scale of change and the degree of threat that the change poses to global security.

According to Neorealism, which tries to understand the rapidly changing world by focusing on great power behavior, with categories of analysis that emphasize continuity and change,[23] structural (or systemic) change in international politics happens only when there are certain types of events happening in the international order. According to Neorealist thinkers, the most important factors in the process of international political change are the differences or uneven growth of power among states and the imbalance of capabilities between great powers, which cause "structural changes" in the international system.[24]

Alexander Johnston defines structural change in international politics as: "these developments that have an important bearing on issues such as the nature, prevalence, and intensity of conflict in international relations and specific topics like arms control and disarmaments ... and questions the content and conduct of foreign policies on a wide range of factors, from the major western states and everywhere".[25] In order to measure and identify this kind of change, Johnston defines three decisive elements of structural change: 1) status of change in the contemporary distribution of powers among nation-states, which imposes a rough-and-ready framework of freedom and constraints, of dominance and dependence; 2) the changes in the pattern of rules, understanding, and institutions, in and through which relations are conducted; and 3) changes in the pattern of values, assumptions, and perceptions

---

23 Katzenstein 1990.
24 Waltz 1979; Gilpin 1981.
25 Johnston 1990: 45.

through which states (and other actors) interpret the distribution of power and the pattern of rules and understandings.

Based on that definition, and on a review of recent political developments in the world post-1989 and post-2001 in terms of distribution of power, along with the framework of rules and pattern of values, we can figure out which type of developments are considered structural changes, and thus had the greatest impact on the world order, and other changes that did not have the same impacts on global security issues. Further, we can understand the position of Islam and Muslims (as an international actor) and how this position affects their status and the perception of them as a threat to world order, as it is put and represented on their behalf via theories such as "clash of civilizations".

According to the previous definition of structural change in international politics, only the end of the Cold War is considered a type of "great event" that changed the rules and structures of the international system. The end of the Cold War changed the rules and structure of the global security landscape. With the nonviolent dismantling of the former Soviet Union there was no bipolar international structure anymore, the international system was transformed to become unipolar with one "lonely" superpower at the top,[26] and the gap in the balance of capabilities between the United States and other great powers evidently expanded in favor of the former. At the same time, there was a structural change in the pattern of values and the norms that determine the relationship between great powers. With the triumph of capitalism and the failure of socialism, there was no more capitalist-socialist conflict. The ideological global conflict had transformed to an economic and technological conflict between Western and Northern developed nations and the nations of the developing Global South.

Instead of arguing about which events constitute structural change and which do not, this study discusses the implications of these two events on global security issues. Firstly, it seeks to measure their impact on world security issues, and to check whether there are more effects from one or the other. For example, while the destruction of the Twin Towers has nothing to do with the rise of China, the re-emergence of Russia as a revisionist power, or the rise of the other emerging powers (i.e., Brazil, India, South Africa, and others), it had a huge impact on regions like the Middle East and the Islamic World, while the end of the Cold War had uneven and mixed impacts on almost all the world's regions and conflicts.

---

26   Huntington 1999.

Secondly, while the Cold War was a conflict between two giant nuclear superpowers, the terrorist attacks on the United States are seen as having provoked a defensive reaction by the United States against a foreign attack on its soil by non-state actors, and despite the narrow impact of these attacks on international order and global security issues in general, they led to the outbreak of a global war on terror, especially in the greater Middle East, and against poor and weak countries like Afghanistan, Iraq, Yemen, and other countries. Hence, the terrorist attacks on New York and Washington had and will continue to have a huge impact on the future of global security conditions.

Thirdly, while the end of the Cold War in 1989 ended the ideological conflict between the West and the Soviet Union, it did not settle or end conflicts in the Third World countries. On the contrary, the domination policies of the United States towards countries like Iraq and Afghanistan created new enemies, not only against American policies, but also against the whole of Western society.[27] The transnational terrorist Islamic groups became the new threat to the world order, peace, and security. This new kind of threat may be considered less dangerous than the Soviet or even the Sino-Russian threat to the West, but nowadays it is being held up as the leading threat to global security.

This threat did not exist before the terrorist attacks against the United States. The defenders of "clash of civilizations" discourse argue that, while the end of the Cold War terminated the ideological foundations of the global rivalry between the West and the East, the terrorist attacks recreated ideological clashes on the global scale once again, by leading to a declaration of war on Islam and Muslim people (at least as the US-led war on terror is perceived by Muslim people). This kind of ideological conflict can spark the beginning of a global-religious war (a Crusade or Holy War) between Christianity and Islam – not necessarily, as Samuel Huntington predicted three decades earlier, but as a political and nationalistic conflict created by the aggressive and hostile imperialist policies of the United States and some Western powers towards Islamic countries around the world.

Finally, while the end of the Cold War had a massive impact on almost the whole global order compared with the narrow geographical and geostrategic impacts of the September 11 attacks, the growing scale of globalization and the increasing influence of technological tools, transnational movements, and groups (non-state actors), the privatization of warfare, and the diffusion and transition of world power make these small impacts important. For example, the revolutions of the Arab Uprising, and perhaps the earlier outbreak of

---

27   Rashid 2000.

the Green Movement in Iran 2009, have led to the spread of global protest movements against neoliberalism, authoritarian regimes, economic inequality, unfair distribution of wealth, and the failure of national governments, due to production among political elites, to provide enough economic and social security to meet the basic needs of its own citizens. These protests have ranged from Tunisia to Cairo, then across the Mediterranean to Athens, to Rome, Madrid, London, Paris, to Kyiv, and other cities in Eastern Europe across the Atlantic to the headquarters of neoliberalism in New York's Wall Street, and thence to Washington D.C., the capital of neo-imperialism. The proliferation of this culture and movement is considered the most recognizable evidence of how domestic changes can turn into a regional storm and then into a global tsunami that threatens the foundations, rules, values, and bases of the modern international order.

To sum up, there is no doubt that the end of the Cold War was considered the biggest and most important change in the international system since the end of the Second World War in 1945. It still has impacts on regions like Europe, Asia, Eurasia, and others. Nevertheless, with the increasing influence of non-state actors, the diffusion of power among/within great powers, and the greater complexity and integration (economic, technological, and social) of world society, the small or non-structural changes (like the September terrorist attacks, the War on Terror, and the Arab Uprising) could have the same influence as big world changes like the end of the Cold War, not only by creating conventional threats to global security conditions, but also by creating a new kind of global transformation and threat. As Kissinger argued in 2009: "We have never had so many transformations occur at the same time in so many different parts of the world and made globally accessible via communications".[28]

2   Critical School and Change

The first task in evaluating whether critical theory has been successful is to measure the extent to which its presence and engagement in the ongoing mainstream debates within a certain field or research pool is significant. In the field of IR, one prominent study concludes that "various forms of 'critical theory' ... constitute the main theoretical alternatives within the discipline".[29] Rengger and Thirkell-White observed that several, varied sorts of elements of

---

28   Kissinger 2009.
29   Rengger and Thirkell-White 2007: 4–5.

critical theory had become notably lodged within the ivory tower of the robust, analytical, and still heavily "scientific" American academic cycles.[30]

Another test of success is the extent to which a theory reflects, relates, and is committed to the topic/s it investigates and examines. In the case of the Arab Uprisings, the core issue was and still is the search for freedom and emancipation. The massive numbers of ordinary people, from Tunisia, Egypt, Libya, Syria, Yemen, Bahrain in 2011 to Sudan, Algeria, Lebanon in 2019 and 2021, who marched in the streets and public squares, were not claiming or demanding security, stability or R2P as positivist approaches maintain; instead, they shouted out for freedom and emancipation from fear, need, and exclusion. In this regard, critical theory incorporates a wide range of approaches which emphasize the idea of emancipation, defined in terms of freeing people from the modern state and economic system and anticipating how the world could be reordered and transformed, rather than merely explaining it, as Marx stated. In fact, bringing critical theory (as an emancipation-seeking theory) back into the field of IR, Ashley and Walker argued, would enable those who were "exiled" or "excluded" from International Relations to start speaking their own language.[31] For example, in the field of security studies, comparison of orthodox security studies with Critical Security Studies (CSS) shows that, while the former is immune to moral progress, seeking mainly to find a solution to urgent "global" security concerns, especially those that address the system of nation-states, and to maintain the status quo, the latter, by contrast, presents a challenge to the mainstream of International Relations by undermining claims that the strategic realm is a realm apart. CSS seeks to engage traditional thinking about the meaning and practices of security with the aim of emancipating "those who are made insecure by the prevailing order".[32]

In fact, the Critical school does not neglect or underestimate the significance of security challenges and other forms of violent challenge facing nation-states and people. But rather than adopting the problem-solving style of analysis, it concentrates on the genesis and structural origins, measures, methods and modes, discourses and practices that have created and established these threats and challenges in the first place. In other words, it seeks to understand threats, not to explain them. Moreover, for the critical school, it is not enough to understand and trace the origins of harm and displacement in the world; rather, it is necessary to use that understanding to reach fairer

---

30 ibid: 9.
31 Ashley and Walker 1990: 259.
32 Wyn Jones 1999: 118; Wyn Jones 2001; Fierke 2007; Shapcott 2008: 334–335.

security arrangements that do not neglect oppressed people's claims to basic rights.[33] Therefore, it is no wonder that the main critical projects in IR, those of Cox, Linklater, and other critical theorists, are united in their political inquiry by an explicitly emancipatory purpose. They aim at uncovering the potential for a fairer system of global relations, which would result from already existing principles, practices and communities that expand human rights and prevent harm to strangers.[34]

In contrast, the positivist theories (i.e., Realism and Liberalism) concentrate on material structures in explaining and interpreting International Relations and foreign policies. They focus on power (realism) and interests (liberalism) and take as inevitable the anarchic character of international structures and the formulation process of the nation-state (as the main actor). As such, the chance to adjust or modify this order is quite limited. By contrast, Critical theory sees international and foreign policy as a historical phenomenon, shaped by social forces and intersubjective social structures such as norms, values, ideas, images, language, discourse, and common meaning.[35]

For instance, Robert Cox explained the historical structures of hegemony in terms of three constitutive levels: state forms, social forces, and world orders. These levels are a result of the struggle between rival structures, and notably, of diverse historical contexts producing a specific configuration of social forces, states, and their interrelationship that would resonate as a particular world order.[36] While the initial level (state forms) covers the state/society complexes, it is crucial to point out that the diverse state forms and structures that specific societies develop are derived from the configuration of material capacities, ideas, and institutions that is specific to a complex state/society.[37] The second level contains the organization of production which reflects or expresses the observed transformations in the genesis, strengthening, or decline of specific social forces. For example, in the prevailing form of the capitalist system, the social forces associated with the real economy, as opposed to financial markets, have been weakened in favor of strengthening private investors and corporations.[38] The third level is the world orders that constitute the forces determining the way states interact. Cox argues convincingly that the correlations between these levels are not unilineal but reciprocal. For instance, he

---

33   Ferreira 2015.
34   ibid.
35   Cox 1986; Linklater 1990; Weber 2001; Abadi 2008.
36   Silva 2005.
37   Cox 1987, 1995.
38   ibid; Silva 2005.

believes that state forms affect the development of social forces by the types of domination they exert to enhance the interests of one class at the expense of another. Likewise, he claims that transnational social forces have influenced states through the world structure, as evidenced by the reflections of nineteenth-century expansive capitalism, or the proliferation of globalization since the second half of the twentieth century, affecting the development of state structures in the center and the periphery, and movement from the North into the South.[39]

According to this perspective, in relation to the Arab Uprisings, one can argue that Cox was correct when he perceptively referred to the way the struggles and resistance against hegemonic "global" structures will emerge at first within national societies, since the historical bloc of the working classes is still nationally organized, but could grow and expand into the transnational territories due to economic and social globalization leading to the internationalization of production and thence to the formation of a new class of transnational labor. By civil society, Gramsci meant "the network of institutions and practices of society that enjoy the relative autonomy of the state, through which groups and individuals are organized, represented and expressed".[40] This network of institutions represents the essence of what he called a "historical bloc", referring to the relations between the material base (infrastructure) and the political-ideological practices that support a certain order. Accordingly, the change arises when civil society challenges the hegemonic structure; then the possibilities for transformation emerge when the notion of counter-hegemony at the heart of civil society starts to challenge the ruling elites and prevailing order, thus comprising the search for or formulation of an alternative historical bloc.[41]

The Critical school attacks the deliberate separation between facts and values that realism emphasizes, arguing that realism neglects the social genesis and content of these facts. This means that realism is not interested in the question of whether the theory should help to liberate people from oppression and deprivation, and so suppresses meaningful engagement with the open-ended possibilities of social and political change. Despite the fact that most scholars and students of international relations and foreign policy tend to employ mainstream positivist theories to explain and explore the nature and behaviors of foreign policy, these theories suffer from many shortcomings

---

39 Cox 1995; Silva 2005.
40 Silva 2005.
41 Murphy 1990: 25–46; Murphy 1994; Gramsci 2011; Cox 1987.

and misconceptions when dealing with topics like revolution, revolutionary foreign policy, and the actions of Third World countries. This suggests that IR scholars must not only reconsider the nature of the state itself, but also re-examine and interrogate the motivations behind these states' actions in the first place.[42] Several studies have argued that positivist theories (such as classical and structural realism) are not appropriate approaches to the study of the Global South's foreign policies and post-revolutionary external behavior. The reason is that these theories lack the appropriate knowledge for explaining the behaviors of other non-Western countries which do not share their history, culture, and values, and neglect several essential variables that construct and formulate state behavior in the Global South.[43]

Realism (classical and structural) largely focuses on analyzing the behaviors and actions of great "Western" powers and gives little attention to small "non-Western", developing states, such as the Middle Eastern countries. Moreover, realism is a static theory. It assumes that all units (states) in IR (nation-states in particular) are essentially identical and act in an identical manner in pursuit of their self-interest.[44] According to this view, states seek to achieve the same objectives and adopt the same policies in doing so. Realism wrongly claims that all political entities are "power-oriented" actors who solely pursue selfish, materialistic interests. Thus, it neglects the influence of non-material structures and sources of power, such as ideology, identity, religion, revolutions, etc., and underestimates their independence and contribution in shaping a nation-state's external behavior. Furthermore, realism is a unilateral, inevitable, and closed-ended theoretical framework. As a "traditional" theory, in Horkheimer's definition, realism relies on an instrumental, rational-choice approach and a forceful separation between facts and values, based on a pre-given and unexamined definition of social reality.[45] By neglecting topics like revolution, emancipation, global citizenship (cosmopolitan) governance and social movements, realism has failed to engage with the open-ended possibilities of social and political change and emancipation projects that aim to liberate humanity from any kind of hegemony, oppression, and deprivation.

---

42 Mastanduno, Lake and Ikenberry 1989; Keohane 1969; Elman 1995; Hinnebusch 2015; Bayat 2010, 2017.
43 Smith 2002; Elman 1995.
44 Waltz 1979: 54.
45 Hopgood and Horkheimer 1992.

3   Critical International Relations Theories and the Arab Uprising(s)

In international affairs, moments at certain historical junctures such as the end of the Cold War and the onset of the "unipolar moment" represented a new window of opportunity for a new normative tendency in IR theory.[46] According to David Schmid, as a result of the fall of the Soviet Union, combined with the apparent waning of national borders and traditional power politics and the unstoppable global economic restructuring and expansion of worldwide communications, plus a victorious liberal-democratic order and an emerging regime of human rights protection, that very realm of international politics that had long appeared blocked, impervious to change and devoid of emancipatory possibilities suddenly appeared open to new normative theorizations.[47] Likewise, this study argues that a juncture moment such as the Arab Uprising, despite the underestimation of its effects and impact on world politics,[48] could open new possibilities and inspiration to the critical theory of International Relations, particularly if we consider the popular intifadas of the Arab People as an integral segment of larger anti-capitalist, anti-neoliberal, and anti-hegemonic resistance movements, having greater global reach.[49]

In this case, after almost a decade of the Arab Uprising, critical IR scholars should analyze and understand it as a chain of global resistance movements that started to appear in the early 2000s with the US invasion of Iraq in 2003 and the global-scale opposition to and demonstrations against the war; the Color Revolutions in former Soviet countries in 2003–2006; the economic and financial crisis of 2008; the 2009 Green movement in Iran; the ongoing Democratic-led protests in several Latin American countries from 2018; the "Occupy Wall Street" movement of 2011; the Catalonian-Spanish protests of 2011; Iran's protests in 2018 and 2022; global climate change rallies beginning in 2019; the Arab Uprising 2.0 of 2019; Hong Kong protests of 2014 and 2019; and other forms of micro-level protest and micro-narratives of resistance against the global and local systems of power and domination (e.g., women's rights movements, students protests, anti-elections protests, and environmental protests). In sum, the Arab Uprising, using Cox's words, reflects a manifestation of

---

46   Beardsworth 2011; Calhoun 2004: 887.
47   Schmid 2018.
48   Katz 2014; Onar 2015; Lynch and Ryan 2017; Bush 2017; Valbjørn 2017.
49   Abul-Magd 2013.

the so-called global civil society revolution against systems of global domination[50] (see Figure 1.1).

The GDELT (Global Database of Events, Language and Tone) Project map contradicts and opposes all positivist theses, whether the neorealist arguments on the stability of the international "unipolar" order,[51] or the neoliberal institutionalist and constructivist arguments on the proliferation and stability of democratic societies, and the correlation between liberal-modern norms and stability and prosperity.[52] In contrast to these false arguments, for decades the global system has vulcanized and fueled resistance and rejection movements against the neoliberal and imperialist order of domination.

Regarding the Arab Uprising, according to Rafael Bustos:

> while neo-realists tend not to focus on the Arab Uprising itself but rather on the possible threats that derive from it (an increase in Jihadism, nuclear proliferation, etc.) and their consequences for alliances and US interests, critical theorists reverse the analysis and locate it in the economic causes and implications of armed interventions (e.g. neoliberalism, distribution of markets, the military leverage of US hegemony) as well as the social processes of vigilance and control that are associated with the 'security obsession' (e.g. census elaboration, detention centers, massive espionage, 'biopolitics', etc.).[53]

The Arab Uprising broke out ten years ago, but CIR did not appropriately address or engage with it. As of 2020, there were few studies that tried to explain and investigate the causes, consequences, and outcomes of the Arab Uprising, although these Intifadas could find their genesis in the early writings of Frankfurt School scholars of the 1940s and 1950s. CIR could provide a more rigorous and lucid understanding of the Arab Uprising by focusing on the socio-political dynamics of authoritarianism, Neo-Gramscian studies on the role of hegemony and the power structure within the global political economy order, and the role of social forces (such as ideas, ideologies, institutions, processes, and material capabilities) in determining the frameworks

---

50 For more details and data see Mass Mobilization Project: https://massmobilization.github.io/about.html Also see Al-Jazeera: https://www.aljazeera.com/news/2021/3/30/mapping-major-protests-around-the-world.
51 Brooks and Wohlforth 2002 2008; Wohlforth 1999 Krauthammer 1990/91 2002/3; Ikenberry 2001; Ikenberry Mastanduno and Wohlforth 2011.
52 Huntington 1991; Fukuyama 1992; Pinker 2018, 2011.
53 Bustos 2017: 53.

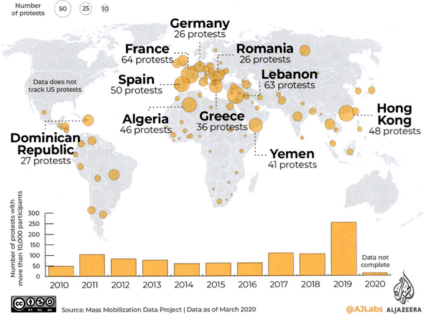

FIGURE 1.1 GDELT project map of global protests 1979–2015
SOURCE: MAPPING GLOBAL PROTESTS REDUX. AVAILABLE AT: HTTP://DATA
.GDELTPROJECT.ORG/BLOG/MAPPING-GLOBAL-PROTESTS-REDUX/PROTE
STS-EVENTV1-MONTHLY-1979-2015.GIF [ACCESSED DECEMBER 30, 2019]
SOURCE: HTTPS://WWW.ALJAZEERA.COM/NEWS/2021/3/30/MAPPING-MAJOR
-PROTESTS-AROUND-THE-WORLD

of individual and collective action. Likewise, the motivations and the reasons behind the outbreaks of the Arab Uprisings could be traced through the writings of Habermas and Linklater, such as those on the discursive power of democratic norms, values, and promoting the global rule of law through dialogue and deliberation to enhance people's participation in political institutions that boost democratization, human rights, equality, and justice.[54]

For instance, regarding the Egyptian coup d'état, disturbances in Syria and Libya, the riots in Persian Gulf countries and intervention in Yemen, Libya, and Syria, for critical theorists (neo-Marxists and neo-Gramscians in particular) these represent proof of a hypocritical US/EU discourse that cannot hide market greed and the crisis of the transnational financial and capitalist classes. At the same time, these events reflect the profound crisis of the Arab nation-states. Critical scholars such as Eric Hobsbawm, Tariq Ali, Samir Amin, Hamid Dabashi, Gilbert Achcar, Noam Chomsky, Kees Van der Pijl and others[55] have argued that the way the US tolerated the crushing of the riots at the hands of the Gulf security forces (in Bahrain and Yemen), with Saudi Arabia and the UAE at the head, and in Egypt, Syria, Sudan by the military juntas, reveals the double standards of the leading capitalist power.[56] For example, in 2013 Tariq Ali wrote: "If the Arab uprisings began as indigenous revolts against corrupt police states and social deprivation, they were rapidly internationalized as western powers and regional neighbors entered the fray".[57]

Moreover, others believe that the Arab Uprisings do not represent any fundamental change on the global scale and have not substantially altered North-South relationships. Furthermore, Ali argues that compared with Latin American revolutions in the earlier decade (the 2000s), the upheavals in several Arab countries have not produced true revolutions that have replaced elites or been capable of slowing down neoliberalism and breaking with their foreign partners, mainly because of the actions of the US, EU, and their allies in the region.[58] Such claims led other critics to argue that critical theorists tend to extol and amplify the role of external actors to the point of becoming, in some cases, close to conspiracy theories.[59] Misleadingly, critical theorists – according to these criticisms – were wrong to look at the autonomy and decision-making will of internal actors in quite a limited way, unless they produced revolutions,

---

54   Cox 1983 1986; Linklater 1990; Habermas 1996; Gill 2003; Roach 2013.
55   Amin 2016 ; Chomsky 2012 ; Dabashi 2012 ; Achcar 2016, 2013 ; Van der Pijl 2011.
56   Bustos 2017: 51.
57   Ali 2013: 64.
58   Ali 2013; Amin 2011, 2016.
59   Bustos 2017: 53.

and underscore the importance of transnational economic, financial, and military factors, and their interaction as determinants of international policy.[60]

In general, the critical studies of the Arab Uprisings (especially the CIR and the Habermasian-based studies) could be summarized within four main categories. According to Stephan Roach, to explain the Arab Uprising from the view of CIR, some critical theorists suggested focusing on four political and social dynamics of these uprisings.[61] These dynamics are the political identity and consciousness of the Arab peoples, the failure of neoliberal policies, the political will to instantiate the rule of law, and the role of social media.

4 Political Identity

The Arab Uprising was a crucial moment in the revival of a collective Arab political identity after decades of political hibernation. For CIR scholars, identity has provided a common framework for the solidarity that dictators had sought to suppress.[62] The latest Arab Uprising movement was not identical to the movements of pan-Arabism of the 1950s and 1960s; in fact, it was the opposite. In the 1950s and 1960s, leaders like Nasser, Saddam Hussein, and Assad employed sentiments of collective identity to achieve false regional unity and national independence from colonial and imperial powers through domestic mobilization and development, as well as nonalignment and external solidarity with other Third World countries.

While the pan-Arabism moment of collective identity completely overlooked the demands of democratization, the rule of law, and human rights, the later wave was genuinely about democracy, freedom, and human rights. In other words, the post-independence moment of collective identity was directed against external enemies, such as imperialist and capitalist powers, while the Arab Uprising was directed towards local enemies (the authoritarian regimes and their pawns). Likewise, while the pan-Arabism moment supported the interests of the ruling regimes/elites, the Arab Uprising moment, on the contrary, was an action by the people against internal dictators, and sought to achieve public goods and objectives such as establishing a new democratic regime, enhancing the rule of law, and respecting human rights,[63]

---

60 Ali 2013; Van der Pijl 2013.
61 Roach 2013: 181.
62 ibid.
63 Ibid; Gause 2011.

either through revolution or, as Foucault insisted, incitement to "cut-off the king's head".[64]

In this context, pan-Arabism was a liberation attempt that did not seek to free Arab citizens from domestic authoritarian structures. In contrast, the Arab Uprising is considered an emancipatory attempt that tried (in Richard Ashley's words) to secure people's freedom from all kinds of constraints, relations of domination, and conditions of distorted communication and understanding that deny humans the capacity to shape their future through full will and consciousness.[65]

5 The Failure of Neoliberal Policies

Any attempt to understand and explain the Arab Uprising and post-revolution policies of the Middle East must address the failure of neoliberal policies. Neoliberalist assumptions about the relationship between the liberalization of political and economic regimes on the one hand, and democratization and stability on the other, proved misleading. Even with the enormous amount of economic aid, political support, and military assistance from Western powers (especially from the United States, European Union, and the GCC countries) to these regimes, they failed to liberate and achieve stability and democratization. The reasons for this ineffectiveness revolve around several economic and socio-political factors. On the economic level, these were primarily the massive levels of corruption, the continuation of the deficit in the balance of payments, the deterioration of developmental conditions, and the lack of strong industrial productivity. On the socio-political level, we see the systematic violation of basic human rights and the spread of torture, the blocking of the political sphere and the unwillingness of the growing number of super-wealthy elites to support the authoritarian regime.[66]

During the last five decades, and particularly after the setback of the pan-Arab ideology and defeat in the Six-Day War of 1967 with Israel, the authoritarian Arab regimes began exchanging political freedom for economic liberalization. Most of these regimes abandoned socialist ideologies and adopted restricted versions of capitalism and a liberalized economic system without fully democratizing their political systems. These regimes adopted corrupt models such

---

64   Foucault 1980: 121.
65   Ashley 1981: 227.
66   Gause 2011: 86; Roach 2013; Goldstone 2011.

as "sovereign democracy", "managed democracy", "Islamic constitutionalism", and "adaptive authoritarianism" and other hybrid concepts.[67]

For many critical theorists, especially neo-Gramscians, the failure to materialize the alliance between these authoritarian regimes and the wealthy elites was not an isolated or insignificant event.[68] For them, this was more than a clash-of-interests between the two blocs. It reflected the changing norms, values, power dynamics, and the nature of social forces in Arab societies. Neo-Gramscians such as Achcar, Van der Pijl, Gill and others argue that the real reason behind the failure to establish such an alliance was the inability of the regimes to enhance and legitimize elite control, especially in the economic field. This was compounded by the rising historic bloc of unemployed, marginalized workers and students who united to counteract elite control.[69]

Eventually, nevertheless, these attempts failed for many reasons. Firstly, the failure was due to the absence of political freedom, which prevented the process of systemic liberalization from succeeding in the long term. Like their predecessors, the second generation of Arab dictators were also anti-democratic leaders. There was no effective oversight, and the rule of law was restricted, leading to a marked increase in grievances, the violation of the social contract, and a fundamental over-stating of the Arab states.[70] Secondly, these regimes were still steeped in rampant corruption. In most Arab countries, the reforms were unable to fight and confront organized crime and the deeply corrupted elites.[71] Thirdly, both the people and the economic elites viewed these liberalization attempts unfavorably. The absence of social considerations in economic policies led to neglect of people's demands, and this inability to satisfy their basic needs drove them to rebel. Moreover, these policies were biased and intransigent, which caused the poverty rates in several Arab Uprising countries (i.e., Yemen, Egypt, Tunisia, Sudan, and others) to increase in real terms.[72] The burgeoning super-wealthy elites were unwilling to support the authoritarian regime, which prevented the materialization of the economic alliance between the new wealthy elite and the ruling bloc.[73]

---

67 Rutherford 2008; Zakaria 2007.
68 Roach 2013: 181.
69 ibid.
70 Ayubi 1995; Owen 2012.
71 Roach 2013.
72 UNDP 2000, 2010, 2015, 2019.
73 Gause 2011: 86; Roach 2013.

6 Political Will

Since the creation of the modern Arab states in the late 1940s and beginning of the 1950s, these countries have gained their independence from Western Imperial powers; however, the Arab peoples never gained their autonomy from authoritarian regimes, both external and internal. The Arab people continuously suffered from a lack of freedom and low standards of living. Indeed, much of what is known as "the Arab Uprising countries" including Egypt, Libya, Yemen, Syria, and Tunisia, were at the bottom of the UN Human Development Index, World Bank development indicators and Freedom House reports. Due to the non-democratic political system, corrupt economic system, and overstated nature of these Arab countries over the last three decades, the citizens of these countries revolted against their governments in order to emancipate themselves from fear, poverty, torture, and dependency. The massive numbers of protestors who marched in the streets and public squares were seeking freedom, integrity, justice, and equality.[74]

Many Western countries believed that, despite the people's desire for democratization and the rule of law, the authoritarian governments represented the best opportunity to liberalize the Arab regimes, enhance stability, and protect Western interests in the region.[75] However, historical experience shows that the strategy of authoritarian stability proves to be short-lived and incapable of guaranteeing or sustaining stability and security in the region.[76]

Firstly, historical records show that Western powers cannot buy stability by selling out other peoples' freedom in the long run. After three decades of support for Mubarak's regime, the United States failed to prevent the outbreak of the revolution, not only in Egypt but in other allied countries across the region as well. These revolutions proved that this kind of realpolitik policy was based on unrealistic assumptions.[77]

Secondly, the assumption that supporting unpopular authoritarian regimes could serve the interests of the Western powers proved to be false. Therefore, authoritarian allies became a strategic burden, as their domestic policies sowed the seeds of future upheaval and promoted hostility towards these Western powers and their interests in the region.[78]

---

[74] Ismail 2012; Kandil 2012.
[75] Roach 2013.
[76] Gause 2011.
[77] Keck 2012.
[78] Gause 2011; Katzenstein and Keohane 2006.

Third, the assumption that Arab and Muslim culture is incompatible with democracy, or that there is an Arab exceptionalism working against democracy and liberalism also proved to be inaccurate. The Arab Uprising moment showed that Arab societies are no different from others who seek freedom and democracy. The claim that the durability and robustness of authoritarianism in the Arab World caused the region to miss the previous waves of democratization was a myth. Most of the Arab citizens in countries like Tunisia, Egypt, Yemen, Syria, Libya, Bahrain, and elsewhere rebelled against these authoritarian regimes, demanding freedom, justice, and equality.[79]

The critical assumption as to the discursive power of people's inclination to instantiate the rule of law, democratic norms, values, processes, and promotion of the global rule of law through dialogue and deliberation was more appropriate and relevant in explaining the Arab Uprising. It also refutes the myth of pre-given and unexamined (realist and liberal) conceptions of the social reality of the Arab World, such as the authoritarian-stability nexus and Arab exceptionalism.[80]

7   Arab Uprising and IR Theories: An Encounter

IR theories continue to neglect the causes and consequences of revolutions despite their importance vis-à-vis state behavior (unit level) and the international structure (system level). Traditionally, revolutions cause radical changes and intersect with fundamental issues in international politics, such as war, violence, balance of power, security, stability, cooperation, identity, oppression, and emancipation. Nevertheless, major theories of International Relations (i.e., Realism, Neoliberalism, Constructivism, and the Critical school) still give little attention to the study of such revolutions.[81]

For instance, what drives and determine states' foreign policy in a post-revolution period? Is it national interests, security considerations, emancipatory trends, or all the above? The Neorealism school argues that due to the fear of revolution, the spread of instability, and the rise of extremist groups, non-revolutionary countries always try to contain the revolution within their borders, either by counterbalancing it (through allies) or confronting it.[82]

---

79   Bellin 2012.
80   Habermas 1996; Linklater 1990; Horkheimer 1992; Diamond 2010; El-Hamalawy 2011; Wittes 2008.
81   Walt 1997; Holsti 1992; Halliday 1997; Goldstone 1997; Roach 2013.
82   Walt 1997.

Furthermore, other studies,[83] show that there is an additional, "friendly" strategy employed by these countries, designed to attempt to assist the revolutionary regimes in overcoming social and economic crises. These strategies are employed to contain the conflict as much as possible and prevent its escalation.

Positivist theories of foreign policy do not take resistance and social movements into account. Neorealism, for instance, ignores the effects of nonmaterial elements, i.e., norms, values, emancipation claims, political identities, the aspirations of Arab peoples, socioeconomic changes, the failure of economic policies, the political will to establish the rule of law, and social media networks. By emphasizing these elements and others, critical theory provides a wider, more comprehensive, and accurate explanation, not only of the foreign policy of revolutionary and non-revolutionary countries, but also of the construction and formulation of domestic policy and how it determines foreign policy, and vice-versa.

Neorealist theory, for example, argues that, because of the fear caused by the expansion of revolutions and the subsequent instability, non-revolutionary countries often try to contain revolutions beyond their borders, either by counterbalancing them or by joining the bandwagon. However, different studies show that other non-revolutionary countries have employed varied strategies aimed at assisting states undergoing a revolution by overcoming their social and economic struggles. Ultimately, the vicissitudes that have occurred because of the Arab Uprisings cannot be disentangled from the wider context of the global political economy and globalization.[84]

In Chapter 1, I elucidate why the positivist and traditional research agenda of hard-core neorealist and neoliberal approaches, which are profoundly focused on security considerations (interests, survival, and regime stability) on the one hand, and on the prospects of democratization, liberalization and regional functional integration, on the other, have prevailed over the post-positivist emancipatory agenda of critical theory on IR in the MENA region, in contrast with the general wisdom that dominates the field of Middle Eastern studies in the West.[85] The starting point is to mark the difference between revolutions that succeed in removing the political regime and replacing it with a new one, and those that fail to replace it. In the former, the differences between the pre- and post-revolution periods become clear, while in the latter, these differences are unclear and cloudy, so that it becomes difficult (if not impossible) to observe or show the differences between the situational conditions before and

---

83   Goldstone 2011.
84   Talani 2014.
85   Keck 2012.

after the revolution. Under these conditions, realists start to re-examine outmoded philosophical topics, and engage in outdated debates over questions such as: Why did the revolution occur? or What is the revolution?

Despite the current backlash against the popular Intifada that occurred in the Middle East at the end of 2010 and the beginning of 2011, no one can deny that the Arab Uprising was an attempt to deconstruct authoritarian structures in the Middle East through an emancipatory project of Arab citizens that ultimately failed. By emancipation, I mean what Ken Booth defined as "the freeing of people (as individuals and groups) from those physical and human constraints which stop them carrying out what they would freely choose to do".[86] When Arab citizens rebel against their authoritarian regimes, as well as against foreign (regional and international) supremacy and intervention in their internal affairs, these regimes and powers regard these revolutions as threats to their security and interests. In order to protect and preserve their interests and security, they seek to spoil, foil, and vanquish these revolutions with many tools and means, including foreign aid, military intervention, political manipulation, and economic sanctions. In sum, since 2011 there have been two conflicting tendencies in the Middle East: the cult and resurgence of the authoritarian state, and the emancipatory movements of the people.

For many reasons, these emancipatory projects were never completed. Such "incomplete revolutions" failed to achieve people's goals and hopes. The main reason for this failure was the presence of traditional and reactionary authoritarian regimes, either within the revolutionary countries or in neighboring ones. The domestic regimes, or the so-called "counterrevolutionary forces", deterred the people from achieving the rule of civil and democratic governments and fair and just institutions that would respect their rights and enhance their freedoms. The other major reason behind the failure of the Arab Uprisings was the status quo-upholding conservative regimes and monarchies, especially the Gulf Cooperation Council (GCC) countries, who prevented the revolutionary countries from becoming free, independent, and sovereign. These monarchies considered such popular uprisings as a threat to the region, putting at risk their security, stability, prosperity and even survival. For example, because of the Arab Uprising, GCC countries are facing a new kind of threat that is considered the most dangerous since the fall of Saddam's regime in 2003. In the aftermath of the Arab Uprising, the popular Intifada reached Bahrain and Oman in the middle of 2011, the Islamic State in Iraq and Syria (ISIS) rose violently in Syria and Iraq, and the regional landscape became more chaotic and violent. These

---

86   Booth 1991: 319.

challenges forced GCC countries to focus their foreign policy orientations and approach on dealing with regional crises and conflict.

Theoretically speaking, instead of trying to contain or prevent the spread of the revolutions, as neorealism argues, these countries in fact acted in contrast to this expectation. They intervened deeply in the affected countries to stave off the revolutionary fervor, buttress their decaying institutions, and delay the attempt to reconstruct society and emancipate the population from the authoritarian regimes that had monopolized power since the creation of the modern Arab states following World War II. While neorealism has ignored the effects of non-material elements, the aspirations of the Arab peoples, socio-economic changes, the failure of economic policies, the political will to establish the rule of law, and social media networks, critical theory's emphasis on these elements (and others) provides a wider, more comprehensive, and accurate explanation. These explanations not only elucidate the foreign policy of the GCC countries towards countries like Egypt, but also can answer the questions of why emancipatory attempts fail, and how small states act in the international system – all questions which neorealism cannot answer.

Theories such as Neoliberalism and Constructivism argue that the growing impact of interdependence, globalization, the spread of democratic, liberal ideas and human rights principles, shared collective norms, values, and identities among Arab societies drive countries to concentrate on improving living standards, expanding freedom and democratization. In addition, these forces drive them to enhance cooperation as opposed to mere self-interest through the mobilization of national resources for defense objectives.[87]

Now, I review the most persistent critiques of and prolonged objections to the critical projects in the field of IR (and the mainstream positivist theories alike to a larger extent), concentrating on the case of the Arab Uprisings. By interrogating the Neo-Gramscian and Habermasian IR projects, the study has identified eight main deficiencies: Epistemic Fallacy; Eurocentric Fallacy; Modernity/Enlightenment Fallacy; Monologic Fallacy; Pedagogical Fallacy; Selectivity & Positionality Fallacy; Statism & Militarization Fallacy; Urbanism & Privileged Fallacy.

7.1 Cognitive Fallacy

There have been several criticisms of the Coxian critical project, one of them being that it is cognitively insignificant. For instance, from a Marxist perspective, Benno Teschke claimed that Robert Cox did not add anything new to the

---

87 Moravcsik 2008.

critical school of IR since some of his constitutive concepts (such as structures of accumulation) were not originated or developed by Cox himself, but rather were adapted from Marx's modes of production. Also, Teschke claims that, despite his assertion that he was questioning the origins of knowledge concerning International Relations, Cox did not completely follow his own suggestions when investigating the development of capitalism in a pre-constituted state system. Cox did not question the conditions and circumstances of the formation of capitalist structures, especially outside Europe, which prevented him from fully understanding the main dynamics of several modes of the non-European capitalist system.[88] Moreover, John Hobson indicated that Cox's project was considered inherently Eurocentric.[89] Cox's failure to explain the geographical expansion of capitalism from the West to the East renders his approach a prisoner of European modernity and historical experience, thus placing Cox's project among other (positivist and post-post-positivist) IR research programs that suffer from the triple fallacies of ahistoricism, chronofetishism and tempocentrism.[90]

Likewise, the main problem with Habermas's theory of communicative action and its applications in the field of IR is that it is an attempt to combine practical and emancipatory interests, and in the end, fails to accomplish either of these two goals. This failure reflects both an ontological and an epistemological fallacy, even though Habermas himself proposes that knowledge is related to the idea of interests.[91] By interests, Habermas meant two different types: the technical/practical interests that seek to understand and control the environment, and the emancipatory interests that seek to change, rather than to understand other factors.[92] Therefore, claiming that a certain theory is seeking to combine both interests under one umbrella is just preposterous and spurious since they are ontologically and epistemologically contradictory.

In addition, from a postcolonial perspective, when it comes to the case of the Arab Uprisings, Linklater's project (and the Habermasian project in general) suffers from further genuine deficiencies and fallacies. For instance, Linklater starts his model from different epistemological (if not ontological) backgrounds. He assumes and stresses the nature of Western Liberal societies as embodying democracy and civic culture, essential components of what he called a universal political community based on dialogue and communicative

---

88   Teschke 2008: 173–175.
89   Hobson 2007.
90   Hobson 2002: 6–15; Hobson Lawson and Rosenberg 2010: 3361–3363.
91   Habermas 1992.
92   Habermas 2001.

activity. In contrast, Arab authorities/states (not societies)[93] has different social, economic, and political bases. The Arab World is a tribal, patriarchal, authoritarian system of power. Seen apart from orientalist, exceptionalist and positivist perspectives on the Arab World and the Islamic Middle East in general, this region structurally diverges from Western values and norms. It has different types of communicative and verbal civic association that do not necessarily contradict or reverse the Western-Liberal norms that Linklater

---

93 Despite theoretical and methodological restrictions in Western comparative politics and political systems scholarship – that I am aware of – regarding the definition of the state, authority, political systems, regimes, etc., that are identified and recognized as distinct political and theoretical terms, in Arabic, scholars use terms such as "state", "authority", and "regime" as synonyms (state = authority) to refer to the complex of security–police apparatuses of the Arab states. Yet, while I acknowledge the intersections between the two concepts, this thesis uses them as distinct terms. In particular, the thesis concentrates on analyzing not the administrative, institutional, regulatory, or bureaucratic features of the state, but rather the security and policing features of the authority, and the highly politicized and securitized embodiment of Sharia-based discourse. In principle, this terminological choice accords with the long tradition in Arabic scholarship, whereby the words *dawla* (state), and *sulta* (authority) are normally used to refer to high-power, coercive, and repressive political bodies. Moreover, according to prominent Arab political scientist Ghassan Salamé, in the postcolonial and contemporary Arab World there is an intersection of the definitions and perceptions of the state, authority, regimes, and governments. Indeed, the intertwined condition of state and ruler is striking. Throughout the last five decades, we have seen how Arab rulers have become the living embodiment of power, authority, order, and the state combined. Heads of Arab states such as Hosni Mubarak, Ali Saleh, Bashar al-Assad, and Qaddafi have explicitly and publicly announced on TV "It's either me or chaos", "It's either me or civil war", or "I am the state", to prevent citizens from revolting against the ruling ʿasabiyat and dynasties that sought to inherit power in false-parliamentary republics. These concepts were not only mixed or overlapping; rather they were fused together, either in the person of the ruler, the family, or the ʿasabiyya, which monopolizes power completely, as it was during the Islamicate period, or in Janissaries and praetorians ʿasabiyat such as the Mamlūki era. Furthermore, other scholars have argued that sometimes ʿasabiyat have become greater than the authority and the state put together. According to Salamé, the overstating of modern ʿasabiyat has facilitated its requisition of absolute power and authority, in a way empowered the ʿasabiyat to absorb the state itself, and not only its monopoly on violence. Indeed, the domination of military ʿasabiyat over the whole country in a post-colonial state became a phenomenon standing "over the state", as Yezid Sayigh and others remind us, while the state turned into "a military society", to borrow Anwar Abd al-Malik's famous book title. The hegemonic status of a group of officers (and the security and military apparatuses in general) and their penetration of the society, the state, and politics in many Arab countries, have reached unparalleled levels in modern times (cf.; Abdel-Malek 1968; Sayigh 2012, 2019; Abdalla 1990, 1988; Hammad 1990; Makiya 1998; Seurat 2012; Springborg 2018; Salamé 2019: 12–19; Ayubi 1995: 203–207; Saad-ullah 2003:7–15; Al-Jabri 1971; Hinnebusch 1985; Ibrahim [2000] 2011; Owen 2012.).

exclusively depends on in his project. Such ontological and epistemological prejudices make his project reductionist and do not represent other cultures' values and norms, as universal projects should do.[94]

7.2 *Eurocentric Fallacy*

It was not only critical International Relations theory that was accused of Eurocentrism; the early Frankfurt School sociological works were, according to Brincat, "problematically confined to the examination of Euro and state-centric possibilities for emancipation".[95] In fact, despite all efforts of the so-called anti-colonial, universal, pluralistic, and global conversation projects, several leading critical scholars like John Hobson and others believe that the explanations and elucidations of the critical school still suffer from a Eurocentric bias which it purports and needed to leave behind.[96] Further, to overcome this shortcoming, the critical school needs to rethink its approach and attempt to develop a truly global, more open, post-Western International Relations, instituting a different kind of universalism and cosmopolitanism based on an inclusive perspective that concentrates on empowering the oppressed Global South rather than the powerful and rich North.[97]

The Habermasian project suffers from the same fallacy. While this critical direction emphasizes its profound cosmopolitan and universal tendencies in order to differentiate itself from the dominant Western IR theories, one of the main common criticisms of it is that it is Eurocentric, since most of its concepts, ideas, and norms (especially notions of emancipation, dialogue, communicative action, etc.) actually originate from and are products of European modernity and enlightenment, which are culturally specific, reflecting only the values of the European enlightenment. According to this skeptical perspective, such deficiencies would lead to a problematic universalism that threatens to assimilate and legislate out of existence all significant differences.[98]

Furthermore, while many critical theorists believe that the so-called Habermasian-Linklaterian critical project which involves "building a global community that institutionalizes respect for the harm principle and grants all human beings the right to express their concerns and fears about injury, vulnerability, and suffering"[99] comes closer than ever to the universal model,[100]

---

94   Said 1994; Fierke and Jabri 2019; Acharya 2018; Acharya and Buzan 2019.
95   Brincat 2012: 219.
96   Hobson 2012, 2011; Yalvaç 2015.
97   Jabri 2013; Fierke and Jabri 2019.
98   Hopgood 2000; Inayatullah and Blaney 2004; Fierke and Jabari 2019.
99   Linklater and Suganami 2006: 277.
100 Shapcott 2008: 339–340.

critics disagree with such claims. They argue that, paradoxically, while it claimed to be universal, in essence this project is built on modern and enlightenment European ideas and notions such as human rights, institutions, and international law. In addition, while this project tried to identify avenues for greater inclusion in international and global decision-making, it did not articulate how to overcome the structural inequality of power between the democratic North and Global South, which is considered the fundamental obstacle to remedying the "varieties of avoidable human suffering" that characterize current global relationships.[101]

7.3   Modernity/Enlightenment Fallacy

One of the main criticisms of Linklater's communicative-based model is that it neglected the concept of the uneven, multilinear, and interactive nature of social development, and thus failed to specifically address the "material prerequisites" (e.g., the substantive levels of political, economic, racial, and gender equality) for "the force of the better argument" to be effective in a dialogic community and "detach" emancipatory practices from the "material and social" relations of capitalism.[102] When such concepts are ignored, it is impossible to imagine a dialogue, but rather suggests a form of uneven and mixed development reflecting the Eurocentric bias in Linklater's model.[103] According to Alexander Anievas, Linklater's model "merely states a Euro-centric 'inside-out' bias by attributing the West's development of higher levels of rationalization and morality to its unique ability to learn and borrow from other cultures".[104] Indeed, such criticism makes Linklater's project seem to be an "uncritical political project" or even one difficult to distinguish from other positivist IR analyses such as neoliberalism and Constructivism.[105]

Like Habermas, Andrew Linklater starts his project based on a genuine faith in the so-called condition of "democratic peace" that had been established in the Western hemisphere since the end of the Second World War. In the so-called "Long Peace" order, there are no conflicts or military confrontations between the Western powers, who rely deeply on non-coercive methods of interaction "only" with each other and their "democratic" non-Western allies. Linklater was completely silent about the conflictual characteristics of several Global South regions such as the Middle East; likewise, about the role of

---

101   ibid: 340–341.
102   Anievas 2010: 154.
103   Rosenberg 2006; Yalvaç 2015.
104   Anievas 2010: 153.
105   ibid: 155; Yalvaç 2015.

Western powers in sustaining and fueling these conflicts for decades, and how such intervention has diminished and aborted the possibilities of creating a perpetual condition of dialogue and peace in the region. Instead, Linklater, like others, blames so-called non-democratic values and norms, and the way these communities contradict Western norms. He suggests that Arabs may need to abandon such values and notions, as they are considered the main obstacle to the creation of the so-called dialogical global community. Such chronofetishism and tempocentrism (to use Hobson's words, referring to a form of ahistoricism in which the present is thought to be explicable by looking only at current causal variables), according to which European notions and norms such as democracy and dialogue stand as a constant structural condition, rendering the international sphere an apparently continuous, almost static realm, makes Linklater seem not only "uncritical" but also "neoliberal", "neoconservative" or even "orientalist".[106]

According to Hobson, such chronofetishist perspectives, which rest on the assumption that the present can be adequately explained only by examining the present, and thus inherently indicate either bracketing or ignoring the past, create three illusions. First, there is the reification illusion, whereby the present is effectively "sealed off" from the past, making it appear as a static, self-constituting, autonomous, and reified entity, and so obscuring its historical socio-temporal context. Second, there is the naturalization illusion, whereby the present is effectively naturalized on the basis that it emerged "spontaneously", thus obscuring the historical processes of social power and identity/social exclusion, and the norms that constitute the present. Finally, there is the immutability illusion, whereby the present is eternalized because it is deemed to be natural and resistant to structural change, thus obscuring the processes that reconstitute the present as an immanent order of change.[107]

7.4 Monologic Fallacy

The Habermasian-Linklaterian model of communicative actions and global political community that is based on dialogue and intersubjective understanding between societies on grounds of supposedly widely accepted universal norms and values, suffers from several shortcomings. For instance, Yalvaç pointed out that Linklater's model neglects the significant power differential in international society which makes negotiation and consensus difficult to achieve. Also, Linklater's model is noticeably ambiguous and abstract as to

---

[106] Hobson 2002; Hobden and Hobson 2010.
[107] Hobson 2002: 6.

what he meant by the type of political activities required for the formation of a universal communication community.[108] Moreover, it is not clear whether "the discourse ethic" is "always the best, or only, means for achieving transformation, or emancipation in general".[109]

Linklater ignored the role and impact of uneven development conditions between the West and the rest of the world, which creates what I called the "monologic" model of global communicative actions, in which the Western democratic societies initiate and conduct dialogue within and among themselves, and not with others. In other words, the so-called Habermasian communicative action in global politics is a conversation with the self, in front of the mirror, not with others. In fact, the communicative and normative critical project deliberately (despite the Marxist background of both Habermas and Linklater) omitted to take into consideration the effects of sociopolitically and socioeconomically underdeveloped conditions in the Arab World and the rest of the Global South. Likewise, it overlooked the long historical (and still ongoing) experience of state repression, violence, systematic exclusion, human rights violations, crushing of civil society organizations, blocking of public space, and elimination of any foreseen possibilities of dialogue and non-coercive verbal interactions.

Political repression and uneven economic development not only represent the main elements crushing the civic culture that embraced dialogue and the democratic communities emerging in the Arab World and other regions in the Global South, as the Welfare and democratic culture did in post-1945 Europe and the West in general. It also makes the dialogue between the North and the Global South semi-impossible, since Linklater and other scholars did not acknowledge and recognize other non-Western cultures and norms, or the absence of certain structural conditions from such models. Overall, this is a deeply ahistorical perspective, from which the so-called "universal" for Linklater and Habermas becomes only the West (or democratic societies), and the so-called history of global ideas only reflects and represents the history of Western modernity and enlightenment notions, as in the projects of the other positivist scholars whom he criticizes.[110]

Instead of calling for change in the international structures of inequality and injustice that inhibit sincere and genuine global conversation and dialogue, Habermas supports the calls of revisionist approaches that aim to "fix" these structures. By arguing thus, Habermas not only misunderstands the

---

108 Yalvaç 2015.
109 Eckersley 2008: 353.
110 Hobson 2002.

fundamental crisis of the global society and dysfunctional global order, but he also misdiagnoses and misidentifies the factors that are aborting attempts to establish the successful global/universal dialogue project which Linklater had heralded.

For example, in order to deal with the problem of the democratic deficit of supranational institutions, which is not being filled by some form of transnational democratic process,[111] or replaced with other radical alternatives, due to the persistent weakness of cosmopolitan solidarity that makes it difficult for the conventional model of democratic sovereignty based on a collective, self-legislative body to be "scaled-up" beyond the national or regional level,[112] Habermas advocated replacing the existing dysfunctional global system with what he called a more nuanced and realistic model of a "decentered world society as a multilevel system" that builds on and reforms existing global institutions.[113] However, paradoxically misdiagnosing the real crisis of the current dysfunctional global system, Habermas was misled into foolishly indicating that the alternative world society was nothing but the same unfit and deteriorated European Union. Habermas believes that, despite the existential crisis of the EU (not only because of Brexit, but also because of conditions following the *financial* crisis of 2008), it still constitutes a suitable example of politics following the lead of the market in constructing supranational political agencies,[114] whereby the "democratic" and institutional bodies will play a veritable "civilizing role" of providing a "test" of the "will and capability of citizens, of political elites and the mass media".[115] Moreover, Habermas claims that the existence of the EU represents "a point of departure for the development of a transnational network of regimes that together could pursue a world domestic policy, even in the absence of a world government".[116] With the completion of the Brexit deal, the consistent rise of ultra-right-wing parties inside Europe and across the Atlantic on the one hand, and the increasing power, domestically and internationally, of fascist and hyper-nationalist regimes in countries like India, Russia, and China, the Habermasian bet on an undermined Europe to save the world is just another mirage, if not a nightmare.

Principally, this methodological orientation and positionality was chosen for several reasons: (1) to explore how Arab academia and intelligentsia

---

111 Habermas 2015: 52.
112 Fine and Smith 2003: 473–475; Schmid 2018.
113 Habermas 2006: 135–136; Schmid 2018.
114 Habermas 1998: 123.
115 Habermas 2012: 11–12.
116 Habermas 2003: 96; Schmid 2018.

(and in the Global South in general) think and discuss their problems, and to respond to the allegations that such knowledge was outdated and imitative of European thought at best, particularly of French, English, and German philosophy;[117] (2) to compare Arabic knowledge and perceptions regarding the study of certain phenomena such as states, authority, legitimacy, and violence with Western knowledge and sources; (3) to examine the investigations presented by classical Arab scholars on these phenomena, and their impacts on the formation and establishment of states' discourse and practices, while tracing the manifestations and articulations of these discourses and practices in contemporary Arab political thought; (4) to introduce knowledge from outside the West, and give it a voice and opportunity to express and represent itself; (5) to present an encounter with and understanding of these areas apart from the dominant Western knowledge, which could contribute to the effort to (6) free knowledge (as a subject) from Western epistemic domination and its arguments and statements on the East; (7) to initiate and establish a dialogue and conversation between the different forms and types of knowledge, whether Western or non-Western, which could unpack and dissolve the dominant monistic (monological) model of knowledge and move towards a genuinely pluralistic model; and finally, (8) to contribute to efforts to decolonize the field of Middle Eastern studies from the Anglo-Saxon domination that had entirely controlled the process of producing knowledge about the region and its peoples since the establishment of the discipline after the Second World War.[118]

This unilateral, monologic, Eurocentric nature of the mainstream of IR theories and Middle Eastern studies makes it false, not genuine in its objectives since it did not recognize and acknowledge the forms and types of knowledge that had been produced by non-Western societies. In fact, not only is it false to claim that we (Arabs, Muslims, and others) did not produce and add knowledge to the world, or indeed that we did not speak; on the contrary, this claim fundamentally stems from the fact that we live in a (global) system that constantly pushes towards the silencing of other (non)Western voices and making their contributions invisible, according to Grada Kilomba, who believes that mainstream (Western) academia never took care of (and never cared about) this problem (i.e., exploring and including non-Western knowledges) because of living in white-narcissistic societies that do not want to deal with it.[119] Nevertheless, for the sake of objectivity, and despite historical evidence, indications, and experiences that asserted and admitted the presence of tyranny

---

117 Ayubi 1989, 1993; Lauri 1981, 1990.
118 Dabashi 2012; Schayegh and Di-Capua 2020; Keskin 2018; Alkadry 2002.
119 Kilomba 2010.

and excessive use of violence (both material and symbolic) in dealing with the Global South countries, most scholars significantly neglected such critical issues for decades.

By addressing (and challenging) these impediments, will give other forms of knowledge the opportunity to represent and express themselves, as well as countering allegations that there is no 'Arabic' knowledge, or that natives and non-Europeans cannot think[120] – which is considered a form of 'epistemic' violence and suppression of other narratives that challenge Western knowledge – in the hope of initiating a global conversation between these contending perspectives.

7.5 *Pedagogical Fallacy*

This deficiency is as old as the establishment of both International Relations and Middle Eastern Studies disciplines in the Western academia. It is too big to be summarize here; however, I will concentrate on one of the most recent scholarships that discuss this issue, i.e., teaching International Relations in the Middle East. In December 2020, the *International Studies Perspectives* journal (which is published and sponsored by the International Studies Association, ISA) has published a very rich forum which evaluates methods used in teaching International Relations (IR) in the Arab World (Darwich 2021). Nine scholars, eight of whom are Arabs, and the whole comprising seven men and two women, contributed to the publication. The forum also was funded by the British Academy Writing Workshops grant (£18,340) according to the editor Dr May Darwich website. I will discuss this forum as an example of how mainstream Western academics perceived the status of the IR field in the Arab World, and how they discuss, analyze, and teach international politics in the region. Overall, the discussion provided a substantive evaluation that encourages constructive engagement and reflexivity. However, while the contributors to the forum claim to critique dominant Anglo-Saxon IR theories, there is nevertheless a blind acceptance of Western methodologies. Having mentioned some Arab names (e.g., Korany, Abu Al-Fadl, Badran, Amin, and others), the authors seem to be convinced that there has been a remarkable lack of knowledge in the region. I find this claim flawed and believe it shows the authors' lack of involvement with the region and its scholarly work.

Myself, I come from Egypt and studied IR in a public university in Upper Egypt in the early 2000s (University of Assiut), where both IR and Political Science were taught mainly in Arabic. I also taught IR in Egypt and the UAE.

---

120   Moyo and Mutsvario 2018; Dabashi 2015; Mamdani 1996; Spivak 1988; Alatas 1977.

Finally, since 2017 I have studied and taught IR in the UK, where I obtained a MSc and a PhD in International Relations. As a form of embodied knowledge, I build upon my experiences as a student and a teacher to challenge claims presented in the forum.

Besides the fallacies mentioned above, I present three main pedagogical critiques. The first is related to the issue of representation and positionality; the second is regarding knowledge production in the field of IR in the Arab World; the third critique is about the ahistorical interpretation of teaching IR. While acknowledging the negative impact that authoritarian political and pedagogical regimes have had on the discipline,[121] I argue that the constitutive (ontological, epistemological, and methodological) foundations of Euromodernism and Eurocentric IR theories play a significant role in impeding the movement of theories. Collectively, these factors lead to the failure of the project of decolonizing IR in the Middle East as well as elsewhere in the Global South correspondingly.

8   The [Mis]representation and [Mis]location of the Arab World in the Field of IR

The forum did not feature a discussion of the problem of representation and the absence of Arab perspectives within canonical academic journals and other influential publications, which do not have a strong enough intention to genuinely engage with non-Western forms of knowledge. As a result of what Stephen Walt once called "social networking", scholars from outside the Anglo-Saxon world do not have access to the same English-language journals and book publishers that dominate global distribution systems.[122] A quick survey of the contributors to such journals as *International Security*, *International Organization*, *American Journal of Political Science*, *European Journal of International Relations*, etc. reveals the scale of the problem, as there are found in them very few authors from the Arab World or the Global South in general (if ever). In the last two years, since the beginning of the Black Lives Matter movement, the situation has slightly changed.[123] While Sayed Alatas famously deconstructed the myth of "the Lazy Native", there is still a prejudice that non-Western scholars lack the cognitive and methodological skills

---

121   ibid: 23, 25.
122   Walt 2011.
123   Howell and Richter-Montpetit 2020; Shilliam 2020; Sabaratnam 2020; Zvobgo and Loken 2020; Henderson 2013; Le Melle 2009.

needed to publish in these journals or to add value to the field. The ugly truth is that many journals do not welcome other perspectives unless they are written in "perfect" English (even if by non-native speakers) and in accordance with "Western", "scientific" standards, and well-established "traditions" within each subfield or research program (i.e., Realism, Liberalism, Constructivism, and even Critical School).

The Eurocentric IR field has been built upon Eurocentric ontology, epistemology, and methodologies. Its foundations are not global; on the contrary they are based on biased notions of (Western) European enlightenment, modernization, Westphalianism, and capitalism, and even on racism, Robert Vitalis having rigorously and provocatively revealed the racial, segregated, and white genesis of the canonical Anglo-Saxon IR discipline which the authors of the forum celebrated, promoted, and embraced as the ideal pedagogical methodology.[124] Furthermore, Robbie Shilliam equally reveals the racist, Eurocentric, and imperialist discriminatory ontological, epistemic, and methodological constitutive foundations of the whole Politics (i.e., Political Sciences) discipline and its sub-fields (i.e., Political Theory, Political Behavior, Comparative Politics, and International Relations).[125]

The unilateral, monologic, colonial, and Eurocentric nature of the mainstream IR theories and Middle Eastern studies shows how genuine the objectives of these fields are since they do not acknowledge other forms of knowledge(s) produced outside the West. We live in a (global) system that constantly pushes toward silencing other non-Western voices and rendering their contributions invisible.

Most of the contributors to the forum (except for Amira Abou Samra) have lived, studied, and worked in the West or in one of the Western-oriented (American and Anglo-Saxon in particular) universities planted in the region. Likewise, most of the authors (except for Morten Valbjørn) belong to the region and are native speakers of Arabic. However, their methodologies are Eurocentric. Most of the "Arab" authors in the forum (again except for Abou Samra) have not published in Arabic, since Western and European academia does not recognize publications in Arabic (even if they are peer-reviewed). This means that publishing in Arabic is seen as insignificant and meaningless for an academic career in the West, a view which in turn reveals an explicit prejudice of Western academia against non-Western knowledges.

---

[124] Vitalis 2015.
[125] Shilliam 2021.

Furthermore, some of the contributors sometimes subtly and sometimes crudely defend Western and Anglo-Saxon teaching methodologies,[126] on the pretext that IR is an American science.[127] Although this argument is outdated, they still encourage privileging of these methodologies. There is also a pedagogical bias towards Western knowledge as superior. As a result, other forms of knowledge are not given the same space and attention in the forum as Western knowledge.[128] The authors intended, on the one hand, to criticize and dismantle the mainstream methodology, and on the other hand, to enhance the "Global IR" turn. However, the forum clearly failed to do so. Shockingly, the forum never mentioned the term "decoloniality".

Moreover, there is a lack of a reflection on positionality among the authors, regarding their gender (most are men), their class, or their affiliation. The piece gives an impression of representing perspectives of the Arab people, but most of the authors' other publications are in English only. It is surprising to me that I could not find any publications in Arabic, which would bring the "missing" theories and "absent" methodologies the authors are concerned with into the space of Arabic language, thus showing willingness to rebalance and adjust perceived deficiencies. Therefore, just like the native scholars they criticize, the authors themselves share the blame for the existence of these deficiencies. Instead of making sure to circulate their "original knowledges" in the Arab World, they chose to perform the "negative critique". While the "negative critique" stops at highlighting what is absent and wrong, without effectively engaging in efforts to solve the problems, the "positive critique" seeks to offer epistemological "hybrid" alternatives pedagogical approaches, or a "third space" to use Homi Bhabha's term,[129] and constructive engagement that works on bridging these gaps and providing new possibilities.

The forum seems to be preoccupied with addressing the West (and its funding bodies and research institutions) not the East or the Global South. This is not a dialogical (between the West and the Rest) turn, it is a monologue (within the West only). Such tendencies do not genuinely engage with the marginalized. They do not resist the Western pedagogical hegemony that systematically displaces and ignores non-Western perspectives outside the canon. Above all, they certainly do not attempt to develop pedagogical alternatives with which to teach and study IR in the region.

---

126 Darwich 2021: 7, 26.
127 Hoffman 1977.
128 Cox 1992; Dabashi 2015.
129 Bhabha 1994.

9   Knowledge Production of IR in the Arabic Speaking World

One of the problems the forum discussed was the absence of authentic Arabic IR scholarship that could be used to enhance the quality of teaching of the discipline in the region. According to several contributors, there are visible difficulties in finding sources in Arabic, which "adds to the challenges of engaging students with mainstream IR theories".[130] According to AlBloshi:

> Professors often rely on relatively outdated Arabic textbooks or translated books that do not cover the current state of the art in the subject. Few scholars in Kuwait (or in the Arab World) write textbooks, as they are discouraged by the promotion system at KU that does not count textbooks as academic achievements. Due to the lack of academic sources in Arabic and considering the limited resources and time that academics in the Arab world often grapple with, professors just rely on a few available sources; one among them is the translated Arabic version of the Penguin Dictionary of International Relations.[131]

Likewise, some authors stated that the translation of theoretical and "scientific" concepts was poor, even if the evidence for it came from a non-academic book review.[132] These claims come from a reductionist reading of the history of the field in the region (which I discuss in detail in the next section) and a lack of familiarity with literature and Arabic translations of "Western" and Anglo-Saxon classics in IR and Political Science. To mention a few examples, Hans Morgenthau's seminal book *Politics Among Nations* (1947) was translated into Arabic by Khairy Hammad in 1964; Karl Deutsch's *The Analysis of International Relations* (1968) was translated into Arabic and reviewed by an Egyptian scholar of international organizations and international law, the late Prof. Ezzeldin Fouda in 1982; Dougherty and Pfaltzgraff's *The Contending Theories of International Relations* (1971) was translated into Arabic by a Jordanian IR scholar, Walled Abdelhai, in 1995. With regard to terminologies, Ali Hilal Dessouki reviewed a translation (1993) of Robert Dahl's *Modern Political Analysis* (1991), and since then it has seen more than five editions. Moreover, there are translations of Waltz's *Man, the State and War* (2013),

---

130   Darwich 2021: 7, 21, 23.
131   ibid: 23.
132   ibid: 21.

Wendt's *Social Theory of International Politics* (2006), Nye's *Soft Power* (2007), *The Future of Power* (2015) and other books, Gilpin's *War and Change* (2009) and *International Political Economy* (2004), Mearsheimer's *The Tragedy of Great Power Politics* (2012), Kennedy's *The Rise and Fall of Great Powers* (1993), and works of Samuel Huntington, Francis Fukuyama, and others. Translation into Arabic also encompasses, outside the authors' awareness, several classical critical IR textbooks: for example, Baylis, Owens, and Smith's *The Globalization of World Politics* (2004), Dunne, Kurki, and Smith's *International Relations Theories: Discipline and Diversity* (2016), and Burchill, Linklater, and Devetak's *Theories of International Relations* (2014) among other texts. It is surprising that these contributions and efforts were overlooked by the forum authors. There needs to be a more rigorous and in-depth historical and chronological investigation of the field of IR in the region.

Moreover, the active role played by online platforms run by academics, such as the Algerian Encyclopedia of Political Science, was also neglected. These informal platforms represent a "third space" for both scholars and students in the region, creating a place of exchange between dominant Western and "native" orthodox traditions. They play a crucial role in translation and dissemination of Western academic works, albeit without a copyright.

With a significant degree of confidence, I believe that there is plenty of original scholarship in IR (and Political Science in general) written in Arabic. These texts are no less insightful or rigorous than the Western and Anglo-Saxon texts I studied in two of the top British schools of International Relations. Unfortunately, none of the Arabic texts were mentioned by the contributors to the forum, so let me list some names as examples. I begin with the classics, widely recognized and well-read across the Arab World: Boutros-Ghali's *On Political Science* (1966), *International Organizations* (1974) and *International Law* (1978), Ismail Sabri Makled's *Theories of International Relations* (1993, 2018) and *Theories of Foreign Policy* (2013), Ali Hilal Dessouki and Jamil Matar's *Arab Regional System* (1982), Ahmed Youssef's *Arab-Arab Conflicts* (1988), Hassan Bakr Hassan's *Theories of International Relations* (2004) and *Crisis Management and Conflict Resolution* (2005), Mohamed El Sayed Selim's *Foreign Policy Analysis* (1996) and *IR Theories in the 19th and the 20th Centuries* (2002), Nazih Ayubi's *Over-stating the Arab State* (1995), Muhammad al-Sayed Saeed's *The Arab Regional System* (1992) and *Multinational Corporations* (1986), Hassanein Tawfiq Ibrahim's *Arab Political Regimes* (2003) and *Political Violence in the Arab Political Systems* (1992), Abdulkhaliq Abdullah's *The Gulf Regional System* (1998), Mohamed Al Romaihi's *Oil and International Relations* (1995), and even the contested work of Nadia Mustafa and the rest of "Egyptian School"[133] scholarship.[134]

Furthermore, there is also literature on political philosophy and political thought written in Arabic; for instance, Houria Tawfiq Mujahid, Azmi Bishara, Abid al-Jabri, Khaldoun al-Naqib, Abdullah Laroui, Muhammad Al-Ansari, Halim Barakat, Saad Eddin Ibrahim, Mona Abul-Fadl, and Sari Hanafi, as well as Burhan Ghalioun in Sociology. It is surprising that none of these authors were considered, because of either ignorance or invisible bias towards Western scholarship.

In addition to the classic texts listed above, there is a generation of scholars who either studied or worked in the West and returned to the region. After they came back, they wrote, taught, and translated Anglo-Saxon IR texts into Arabic. Among these scholars are Hala Saudi, Mustapha Kamel Al-Sayyid (Egypt). Abdul-Jalil Al-Marhoun (Bahrain), Ahmed Ali Salem (Egypt/UAE), Abdullah Al-Otaibi (Saudi Arabia), who translated Alex Wendt's work into Arabic (2006), Hassan Hajj Ali (Sudan), Abdullah Al-Shaji (Kuwait), Adnan Hayajneh (Jordan) and others.

The participants' lack of familiarity with recent developments in the field of IR that took place in the region after the Arab Uprisings is also striking. There was no discussion of what I call "the new generation" of Arab IR scholars. Since 2010, several Arab countries (e.g., Egypt, Syria, Algeria, and the Arab Gulf States) have witnessed a youth-led "cognitive" bulge in fields such as Sociology, Political Science, and IR. In an unprecedented manner, these young scholars managed to push the debate on the study of IR forward, inclining me to claim, optimistically and naively, that in the next decade, Arab scholars will make a notable contribution to the field of IR in general and to Middle Eastern Studies in particular, either in Arabic or in other languages. This includes the writings of, to name a few, Eman Rajab, Sally Khalifa, Shaimaa Magued, Tasniem Anwar (Egypt), Moutaz Alkheder and Hamza Al-Mustafa (Syria), Wafa Alsayed (Bahrain), Fatemah Alzubairi (Kuwait) Anwar Farag (Iraq), Houcine Chougrani and Zaynab El-Bernoussi (Morocco), Mekia Nedjar, Sid Goudjili and Mohamed

---

133   The so-called "Egyptian School" that Abou Samra claimed never received recognition from the remaining IR scholars either within or without the Arab World. In fact, most of the Egyptian and Arab scholars disagree with their ontological and epistemological foundations. The scholarship of this small group of academics (based in the Faculty of Economics and Political Science Cairo University) lacks sufficient consensus on what they called the Islamization of knowledge and International Relations. On the contrary these "pseudo" claims have been widely questioned and criticized by most Arab scholars.
134   Darwich 2021: 14.

Hamchi (Algeria), Haya Al-Noaimi and Aisha Alrashdi (Qatar), and many others.

The forum also ignored remarkable and increasingly numerous contributions made by several peer-reviewed Arabic journals such as the *Arab Journal of Political Science, Al-Mustaqbal Al-Arabi, Arab Journal of Sociology* (Lebanon), *Al Siyassa Al Dawliya* [International Politics] (published since 1968), *Journal of Democracy* (under the editorial supervision of Hana Ebid), *Strategic Studies* (under the editorial supervision of Mohamed Fayz Farahat (Egypt)), *Journal of Social Sciences* (Kuwait) (published since 1993), *Journal of Political Science* (Iraq), *Siyasaat Arabia* [Arab Politics] (Qatar), *Journal of Social Affairs* (UAE) (published since 1982), *Journal of Strategic Research* (Bahrain) and numerous others that add significant value and original scholarship to the field of IR in Arabic. The forum mentioned only one of these journals, Siyasaat Arabia,[135] while the rest of these platforms did not receive the recognition they deserve.

Likewise, even though two of the interviewees came from Algeria, the forum did not highlight the considerable developments that the country had witnessed in the past decade. Several Algerian "public" universities have seen a flourishing turn in both teaching and publishing in IR. Since 2011, I have counted more than 15 new refereed journals in the field of IR and international studies published by Algerian universities. Surprisingly, though, the forum does not mention that one of the interviewees, Goudjili, works as editor-in-chief of one of these promising new journals, *Mura'jat al-dirasat al-dawliya (International Studies Review)*, which in fact could be a great opportunity to include an insightful perspective on the field in this country. This is just another opportunity missed by the forum. Moreover, regarding pedagogical standards in the region, a quick look at scholarly theses and newly published literature indicates the originality of these works and tells us a lot about the standards and quality of IR teaching in the region. For instance, two of the three interviewees, Goudjili and Hamchi, finished their PhDs recently, and their work–their theses are available online–was acknowledged across the region. Both Goudjili and Hamchi graduated from Algerian universities, but the forum did not mention this crucial piece of information. Consequently, if the opinions of these Arab scholars are trusted when evaluating standards of the field in the region (according to one of the contributors),[136] this contradicts the forum's claim as to the backwardness of the field and the standards of IR teaching.

---

135   ibid: 22.
136   ibid: 20–22.

Finally, no attention has been given to another visible development in the region, namely the increasing number of Political Science and IR colleges and departments, in terms of understanding the crucial expansion taking place in pedagogy.

10   The Ahistorical Perspective of IR in the Arab World

In addition to what has already been discussed, most of the forum's content lacked a clear historical framework and reflection on the diversity of pedagogical schools in the Arab World. Except for Saddiki,[137] and a very short reference to the impact of different colonial and postcolonial histories on the institutional context in which the teaching takes place,[138] there was no discussion of the emergence of the Political Science and IR fields in the region (e.g., contexts, founders, major trends, and stages gone through by the field). Political Science has been taught and researched in the Arab World for almost seventy years. It is important to bear in mind that the "Western" field of IR celebrated its 100-year anniversary just two years ago (1919–2019). The first Arab college of Political Science was founded in Cairo in 1959, around the same year that the college of Political Science was founded in Baghdad. Prior to that, in 1952 the Institute of Arab Research and Studies (IARS), the first institution to teach and research IR in the region, was established as the first specialized Arab academy within the framework of the Arab League. Most interestingly, in 1968 a department of Political Science was established in the University of Assiut, an isolated, marginalized, and impoverished region of Upper Egypt. Many other Arab countries established faculties of Political Science soon after gaining independence. Since the early 1970s, countries like Syria, Tunisia, Kuwait, Saudi Arabia, Morocco, Lebanon, and others sequentially established such faculties. Nowadays, there is no single Arab country that does not have at least one faculty of Political Science. I counted more than fifty departments of Political Science and IR in the Arab World. Thus, the field has a considerable history and range, in contrast with the perceptions created by the forum.

The standards of these colleges certainly vary for many reasons, not least of which are the robust authoritarian and repressive regimes of most Arab countries. These regimes are notorious for their extreme brutality, especially regarding civil liberties and human rights (e.g., freedom of expression, freedom of the

---

137   ibid: 16.
138   ibid: 7.

press, academic freedom, and access to information). Hence, many scholars and journalists have been systematically arrested, forcibly disappeared, and even ruthlessly assassinated because of their work.[139]

Moreover, the forum did not refer to the role played by the Al-Ahram Center for Political and Strategic Studies, established in 1968 in Cairo. Many prominent IR scholars either worked or are still working there; to name just a few: Boutros Boutros-Ghali, Ali Hilal Dessouki, Anwar Abd al-Malik, Syed Yassin, Bahgat Korany, Abdel Moneim Said, Abdel Moneim Al-Mashat, and Saad Ibrahim. Since the late 1960s these scholars have had a crucial role in the dissemination of IR theories within the region, especially in such subfields as regionalism, foreign policy analysis, security studies, and comparative politics.

11 The Fallacies of Applying IR Theories to the Study of the Arab World

The key cause of the problem discussed by the forum is neither the absence of reliable sources nor the methods of teaching and studying IR in the Arab World, as most of the contributors stated. The forum portrayed the pedagogical crisis in the Arab World as a problem of Arab scholars. Such problematic and contested claims remind me of "The Lazy Natives" to use Alatas's phrase,[140] or to borrow Dabashi's title Can Non-Europeans Think?,[141] and their weak knowledge and reliance on poor translations and outdated sources. I believe the main reasons for the crisis (besides the authoritarian characteristics of both political and pedagogical systems) are inherited fallacies of Western IR disciplines, such as Eurocentrism, Modernity and Enlightenment foundations, and monologic and exclusive characteristics. Therefore, I call for a radical critique and decolonizing of these ontological, epistemological, and methodological flaws. The following section questions some of inaccuracies regarding the study of the Arab World, which were neither discussed nor analyzed appropriately in the forum.

One of the forum's participants wondered "How can the 'non-West' to a larger extent become a 'producer of knowledge' rather than being only an 'object of knowledge', and how can insights from different places be connected in a genuinely international debate?"[142] This is a problematic question. First

---

139 Abozaid 2022.
140 Alatas 1977.
141 Dabashi 2015.
142 Darwich 2021: 8.

of all, it presumes that no knowledge has been contributed by Arab scholars to the field of IR. Secondly, it uncritically embraces prejudiced foundations of the Eurocentric field of IR. Almost all the contributors recognized that the field is centered around Western methodologies and forms of knowledge, yet instead of challenging this fallacy, the authors chose to co-opt it, to "feed into mainstream theoretical debates" in Salloukh's words,[143] and criticize it from within, despite the fact that "the approaches in these textbooks seemed disconnected from their lives and everyday politics around them".[144] However, to use the words of Audre Lorde: "the master's tools will never dismantle the master's house". No wonder the project of decolonizing IR methodologies and pedagogy was not mentioned in the forum.[145]

Finally, let me dismantle some of the fallacies of Western IR theories regarding the study of the Arab World, of which I highlight at least nine. Here, I apply Jackson's two-orders critique. The first-order critique reveals that any discourse is grounded on several highly contestable sets of assumptions and knowledge practices. The second-order critique discloses the ways in which the discourse functions politically to naturalize and legitimize certain forms of knowledge and political practices.[146] Without this critique our understanding of the defects that characterize the study and teaching of IR theories in the Arab World (and elsewhere, with some reservations) will be incomplete.

Moreover, one of the contributors expresses one of the commonest false claims: that the Critical Project of studying IR and the Middle East represents a better and more inclusive alternative to the Anglo-Saxon canonical IR theories (i.e., Realism, Liberalism, and Constructivism).[147] Contrary to this view, I claim that the two main projects of the Critical School (i.e., the Neo-Gramscian/Coxian and Habermasian projects), and the dominant theories of IR share the same fallacies. Therefore, neither of them represents an acceptable alternative to the study of the Arab World or the Global South in general. The solution I am suggesting is a radical decolonization of the field of International Relations, or what I call "Inside/outside decoloniality".

---

143 ibid.
144 ibid: 26.
145 Smith 1999; Jones 2006; Taylor 2012; Mignolo 2012; Mignolo and Walsh 2018; Wane and Todd 2018.
146 Jackson 2008: 383.
147 Darwich 2021: 5–7 10–13.

CHAPTER 2

No Revolution

Why as-Ṣaʿīdiyya Did Not Really Revolt

> What Revolution or Kha'rah [bullshit] you are talking about? Taking part in what? You ask us why no one acted here [in a Saʿidi city], as if you do not know the truth. We can barely feed and educate our children. Kosom Hosni Mubarak [F**k Mubarak] and Kosom el-hokoma [F**k the government]. They never cared about us here.[1]

∴

As political and social agents, the designation of peasants oscillates between two contradictory framings. This perspective identifies them as a 'sack of potatoes', the 'steam of revolution', 'docile' or 'piston box' agents. Overall, the study of peasant societies is widely acknowledged to be ambiguous. This contradictory framing makes it difficult to investigate the relationships between peasant societies and politically charged phenomena, such as revolutions, away from a Manichean perspective. Even though most of Egyptian cities had participated in the popular 2011 Arab uprising, most of as Saʿid did not.[2] In fact, many towns, and villages in Saʿid are still isolated from politics despite the social, economic, and educational changes which occurred in Egypt throughout the last five or six decades. The reasons for this are still unrevealed. Consequently, this chapter aims to shed light on the causes which prevented the people of as-Saʿidiyya from rebelling, or at least participating, in the 2011 Arab uprising with the rest of Egypt.

The purpose of this chapter is to investigate and inspect the causes that prevented the (marginalized and isolated) society of Saʿid[3] from rebelling against President Mubarak's authoritarian regime, as the North did. Here I seek to

---

[1] An interview with a Saʿidi man (3 February 2011).
[2] For the purposes of decolonizing terminologies, the chapter introduces the Arabic name for Upper Egypt that the locals use: Saʿid.
[3] For the purposes of decolonizing terminologies, the chapter introduces the Arabic name for Upper Egypt that the locals use: Saʿid.

© AHMED M. ABOZAID, 2023 | DOI:10.1163/9789004681330_004

present different interpretation of as-Saʿidiyya's attitudes toward the 2011 uprising away from the Manichean 'glorification' versus 'ignominy', or 'celebrating' v. 'contempt' narrative that dominated the study of the Saʿid and as-Saʿidiyya role in the 2011 Arab uprising. My research is based on interviews, participant observation and ethnographic investigation which articulates the behavior of peasants as political actors in this time of turmoil. While most sociological and anthropological studies of revolutions concentrate on cities and urban areas, this chapter focuses on a small town, Madinat Al-Fikriyya, and village, Munshaʿiat Al-Fikriyya in Al-Minya governate in Upper Egypt. Therefore, to understand the role of as-Saʿidiyya in the 2011 uprising, the chapter suggests three conceptual changes to this convention. Firstly, by putting peasantry communities within socio-political and socio-economic contexts; secondly by concentrating on understanding the dynamics of state-society relations, and lastly, exploring the role of security establishment and levels of penetration into the society in order.

Drawing on ethnographic interviews and participant observation, I propose that despite the people of as-Saʿidiyya's struggle against President Mubarak's policy for decades, they did not participate in the first wave of the Arab uprising in 2011. However, after the removal of Hosni Mubarak on 12 February 2011, they joined the nationwide political uprising. The causes which deterred as-Saʿidiyya from rebelling against Mubarak in January were neither the psychological nature of the peasants nor the spread of modernity and urbanization. This chapter argues that while the revolution was a socially manifested phenomenon, to understand why the as-Saʿidiyya people were more inclined to initial docility, we need an in-depth analysis of the social structure and power relations within that society and its relations with the Egyptian state. Furthermore, this chapter also indicates the presence of certain socio-political and socio-economic impediments in the Saʿid which were created and normalized by state institutions, and which resulted in the absence of revolt (but not necessarily resistance) in the region. If these constraints are removed, rebellion against an authoritarian regime occurs.

The chapter seeks to find whether a deterioration of socio-economic and socio-political conditions in Saʿid contributed to their refraining from participating in the 2011 Arab uprising. According to Robert Garr, the conditions have been profoundly deteriorative over the past five or six decades and, if we believe the claims, are correlative to poverty and destitution and the ultimate inclination toward rebellion.[4] Why then, despite this causal link, did most of

---

4 Runciman 1966; Gurr 1970; Obadele 1978; Scott 1979; Cherkaoui 2001; Yazbak 2000; Kazemi 1980; Eckstein 1982; Power Madsen and Morton 2020.

the Saʿid not rebel against Mubarak's regime, like the northern part of the country, especially in the urban centers? The answer this chapter suggests, based on ethnography, interviews, and fieldwork in one city and one village in Al-Minya governorate, is that this for several reasons. The most obvious reason is the iron security grip, the securitization of the public and private spheres, the domination of the state and its apparatuses (security and police in particular) over the society in Saʿid. Likewise, the systemic marginalization and exclusionary policies of civil society and the public participation. Moreover, the hatred of politics and refraining from participating in public activities because of the bitter and repressive experience of counterterrorism in the 1980s and 1990s. Finally, because of the prevailing subjugation that defined state-society relations in Upper Egypt throughout the last four decades of the last century,[5] which terrorized as-Saʿidiyya and freezes any form of rebellion or revolt against the central authority.

To clarify this mystification, the chapter first outlines the fundamental features of Saʿidi society in Egypt, and its relationship to the 2011 Arab uprising, by engaging with the literature discussed. Secondly, I outline the research design and the limitation of the fieldwork and ethnographic fieldwork conducted in Al-Minya governorate, inside one city (Madinat al-Fikriyya) and village (Munshaʿiat al-Fikriyya) during the period from January 2011 until August 2015. Thirdly, the chapter discusses the literature pertaining to the relationship between peasant and rural societies, political events, and revolution. The fourth part of the study encompasses the analysis and presents the main findings and result of the ethnographic fieldwork and interviews. In conclusion, I tried to draw upon its findings and the lessons learned from what happened after the 2013 coup to understand the recent developments in Upper Egypt (from September 2020) by highlighting the changes that took place inside the Saʿidi community over the five years from the end of the study, especially regarding the resurgence of rebellion against the authorities after the release of law no. 1 of 2020, known as the Construction Violations Reconciliation Law. These changes indicate that Saʿidi people are more inclined to rebel when the unjust policies of the authorities threaten their main livelihood, i.e., the land.

1   Saʿid: Identity and Politics

For centuries, because of the overwhelming prevalence of poverty, illiteracy, and marginalization the words 'saʿid', 'saʿidi', and 'as-Saʿidiyya' have been used

---

5 Abozaid 2022.

to identify the people of Upper Egypt to differentiate them from other groups. In the collective perception and popular discourse, the word 'as-Sa'idiyya' also derogatively signifies stupidity, naivety and bluntness combined with poverty and underdevelopment.[6] Because of its peasantry and predominantly rural character, where 75 per cent of its people live in rural areas,[7] the Sa'id always suffered from exclusion and neglect from the central government and the colonial centers (especially Cairo and Alexandria) in the North.[8] According to the World Bank, although Sa'id has only 40 per cent of Egypt's population, it is where 80 per cent of severe poverty is concentrated. Moreover, the illiteracy rate for young Sa'idis is higher than the national average, with illiteracy rates for women more than twice those of men.[9]

The dominant (public and formal alike) discourse refers to Sa'idi people as being 'stupid', 'dirty', and 'ignorant'. Such allegations indicate a negative bias of northern Egyptians against the south. This bias alludes to a collective memory whereby the fragmentation of Egyptian identity is based on structures of geographical belonging.[10] This reflects arrogance, prejudice, classism, and

---

6   Miller 2004; Abu-Lughod 2012 2007.
7   The World Bank 2012.
8   Tantawi 2003; Al-Masry al-youm 2009.
9   The World Bank 2012; Maghazi 2013.
10 One of the recent glaring examples of prejudice and intolerance towards as-Sa'idiyya happened in August/September 2020. The minister of transportation [Marshall] Kamel Wazir announced that the government was intending to build a $1.5 billion railway station in Bashteel (southern part of Greater Cairo) between 2020 and 2025. This project has been under consideration since 2015. The pretext of building the new station was to 'eas[e] the congestion and crowding in both downtown Cairo and Giza' mainly caused by the people of Upper Egypt. Sa'idi trains were supposed to arrive at the new station instead of *Mahatet Masr* (Ramses' Station) thus forcing as-Sa'idiyya to travel an extra 25–40 minutes outside the capital to be able to catch trains home. In Egypt everything is centred around Cairo and the construction of a new station outside the downtown would mean an extra challenge to millions of as-Sa'idiyya who visit work and study in the capital and the north. The news about the new station was received with rage and condemnation from the people of Upper Egypt. For instance, Muhammad Salim a member of the parliament from Aswan objected to the minister's decision. Many Sa'idi people posted videos on social media platforms especially Facebook, YouTube and Tik-Tok, in which they expressed anger frustration and rejection of prejudice and discrimination against them. In most of these videos people threatened the minister and Sisi with a rebellion if they prevented as-Sa'idiyya from entering Cairo. Clearly the people of Upper Egypt interpreted the reason for building a new station as an attempt to prevent them from coming to the capital. After controversy and objections on social media and in newspapers the minister of transportation was forced to apologize for any kind of expressed prejudice or racism against as-Sa'idiyya. See: Amer 2015; Malla 2020; YouTube 2020; Al-Husseini 2020; Ghazal

discrimination of the North towards the people of the Southern Egypt, which is rooted in the cultural memory of division between the North and the South.

> Peasants in Egypt and throughout the world have been held to strange standards: observers have expected either everything or nothing from them. They have been portrayed alternatively as so patient and resigned as to bear any injustice or as so full of revolutionary wrath and solidarity as to bring any unjust system crashing down. Such high and low expectations have combined to obscure their actual political activity.[11]

For a long time, due to a combination of geographical, economic, political, and cultural factors, Saʿid had been combined with an extensively traditional societal structure.[12] Traditional in this context refers to the dominant discourse on Saʿidi identity while as-Saʿidiyya emphasizes traditional cultural values, norms, institutions, and societal practices. These cultural traits include honor, revenge, dignity, family, heritage (*asl*), and a rigid social hierarchy, and signifies the widespread disparities within Saʿid society compared to other local societies, such as Nubians, Bedouins, peasants and farmers of the Delta.[13] Consequently, the Saʿid is recognized, not only as a regional geographic location, but also as a symbol of identity.

According to Catherine Miller, the Saʿidi identity is a historical and situational process of affiliation and categorization (the 'We-group' versus the 'they-group').[14] For example, the Saʿid has always been neglected by the central Egyptian and colonial authorities of the North.[15] This has been primarily because of its peasantry and rural characteristics as mentioned above.

2020; After finishing the first draft of this chapter another case of prejudice and discrimination against as-Saʿidiyya erupted. This time it started with a TV presenter called Tamer Amin. In his programme akher al nahar that aired on 18 February 2021 Amin insulted the people and particularly the women of Upper Egypt and their habits customs and social behaviors. Amin described as-Saʿidiyya as 'mut'khalefeen' and 'weskheen' (backward and dirty). After a storm of protest on social media then on television channels newspapers and the parliament as well Amin was suspended his TV program was 'temporarily' terminated and The Supreme Council for Media Regulation announced that Amin was to be investigated. A week later Amin made a public apology for his shameful and prejudiced behavior. El-Sayed and Soliman 2021; Egypt Today 2021.

11   Brown 1990: 1.
12   Miller 2004: 26.
13   ibid.
14   ibid: 25.
15   Al-Masry al-youm 2009.

One of the most common mistakes among Egyptian and foreign researchers alike is they tend to deal with Upper Egypt as a unified bloc or entity from southern Giza to northern Sudan. This inaccuracy needs to be reviewed in-depth, recognizing the region's differences of language, culture, urbanization, dialects, customs, and traditions, as well as cuisine and costumes. For instance, most scholars incorrectly persist in associating fellaheen with as-Sa'idiyya as if they were one social community.[16] This is not accurate. If most of as-Sa'idiyya are peasants because they live an agrarian lifestyle, fellaheen of the Delta are not as-Sa'idiyya. In other words, while most of as-Sa'idiyya are rural, fellaheen are urban. Labelling as-Sa'idiyya as '*fellaheen*', which refers to the rural North and the Delta, eliminates several social and cultural attributes which distinguish this local community from other constituents of Egyptian society. Sa'id consists of more than farmers and peasants. It also includes large ethnic groups including Nubians, Arabs, Bedouins, al-jmaseh, al-Halab, al-Bajah. When the urban centers (Cairo and Alexandria in particular) refer to the peripheries in Sa'id and the Delta by calling them 'al-Fellaheen', they are perpetrating a kind of discrimination, based on geographical and class affiliation. This behavior represents a reproduction of colonial and imperial discourses which were practiced against 'Ahl al-balad' [the natives] by the Mamlūks, Ottomans, and the British colonial authorities, and now by the westernized, neoliberal elites.

As for their roles in revolts and attitudes towards popular uprisings, the historical impressions of the as-Sa'idiyya's attitude have divided them into two main camps. The first camp supports the revolution and the other opposes it.[17] While exploring the attitudes towards the 2011 uprising, I found that within these two main camps there were three strands of opinion. The first group was the largest one. It included those who are unsympathetic to the uprising and not interested in politics at all. The second group consisted of people who were against the uprising and had a negative view of it. This group considered the protests and Tahrir Square's demonstrators to be a conspiracy against the country or spies and fifth column as the national television channels and the official discourse describe them. Finally, the third group was the minority who supported the uprising. It consisted of young, educated (mostly to university level) people who lived, worked, and studied, in the North or outside their

---

16   The prominent example is Blackman [1927] 2000.
17   Adams 1957; Goldberg 1992; Brown 1990.

Saʿidi cities. This perception is a product of an ingrained process of social distortion and negative framing.

2   Doing Ethnography in Upper Egypt

This ethnographic study takes the form of social research which has specific criteria. For example, the research has a primary emphasis on exploring the nature of particular social phenomena, rather than setting out to test a specific hypothesis. Secondly, it tends to work mostly with 'unconstructed' or un-coded data at the point of data collection in term of a closed set of analytic categories. Thirdly, it investigates a small number of cases in detail. Finally, it analyses data involving explicit interpretation on the meaning and the function of human actions.[18] Likewise, the product of this research primarily takes the form of verbal descriptions and explanations, with quantifiable and statistical analysis playing a secondary role at most.[19] Ethnographic methods are usually applied to cross-discipline purposes, including in fields such as Sociology, Anthropology, Education, Health and Social Policy, Human Geography, Organization Studies and Cultural Studies.

The study's research design is based on Joseph Maxwell's five component interactive model of qualitative research design.[20] This model integrates all components (purpose, the conceptual context, research questions, methods and techniques and validity) closely tied to each other, rather than being linked in a linear or cycle sequence, which allows for the clear representation of a two-way relationship of influence.[21] The interactive nature of this model allows the researcher to engage in designing their own study and even creating a design of particular qualitative project(s). Also, it enables the researcher to change in interaction with the situation in which the study is conducted, rather than being a fixed determinant of research practice.[22]

A case study with data collection was conducted mainly through an individual, face-to-face, verbal, unconstructed, and interchange ethnographic interview and participant observation.[23] I used this interviewing method for the

---

18   Atkinson and Hammersley 1998: 248.
19   ibid.
20   Maxwell 2005, 1996.
21   Maxwell 2005: 5.
22   ibid: 7–8.
23   Fontana and Frey 1994: 361.

purpose of producing data for academic analysis and to understand individual and group perspectives. However, I mostly relied on the former because it affords greater breadth articulation than the other types of interviews (structured, group, and gendered interviews) given its quantitative nature.[24]

The differences between unconstructed ethnographic interviews and participant observation are still controversial. Some studies do not differentiate between the two methods and point out that 'the two [methods] go hand in hand, and [much] of the data gathered in participant observation come[s] from informal interviewing in the field'.[25] Other studies, however, distinguish between these styles based on the interviewer's influence, personal feelings, and intervention in determining the answers of the respondents and the meaning of the responses.[26] For Andrea Fontana and James Frey, the difference between structured and unstructured interviews is that 'the former aims at capturing precise data of the codable nature in order to explain behavior within pre-structured categories, whereas the latter is used in an attempt to understand the complex behavior of members of society without imposing any prior categorization that may limit the field of inquiry'.[27]

The unstructured, in-depth ethnographic interview method is important for several reasons. It allows the establishment of human-to-human relations with the respondents and the desire to understand rather than explain. Likewise, it also contributes to expanding the ability to understand and articulate the interviewees' culture, language, and way of life.[28]

This chapter challenges the dominant studies about the political and social behavior of the people of Sa'id, especially regarding their attitudes toward the 2011 Arab uprising. Dominant political discourse still ascribes the Sa'id and as-Sa'idiyya communities as being a passive, and counterrevolutionary force that undermined the revolution.[29] It is based on my ethnographic fieldwork, comprising over fifty interviews in a Sa'idi city and village at Al-Minya governorate. The interviews were conducted from February 2011 to August 2015. This chapter found a general trend of people feeling marginalized and which had generated political apathy across the region. This led to a lack of participation in the 2011 Arab uprising.[30] In fact, in the words of one of the Sa'idi

---

24 ibid: 365.
25 Lofland 1971 cited by Fontana and Frey: 265.
26 Janesick 1994
27 Fontana and Frey 2005: 706.
28 Spradley 1979 cited by Fontana and Frey: 366.
29 Al-Iskandarani 2013; Aboul Gheit 2012.
30 Al-Aswany 2015b.

people (Sharshoub Hamam) commenting on the situation after the revolution, for most as-Sa'idiyya, the fear of starving is a more serious concern than instability.[31]

In contrast, other studies glorify as-Sa'idiyya as a whole and portray them as fundamental actors of the revolution, thereby overestimating their contributions.[32] Finally, this chapter aims to set the foundation for future investigation into the political and social behavior of a semi-peasant and semi-urban (hybrid) society like Sa'id in such a way as to be as unbiased as possible and to refrain from underestimating their contributions and sacrifices during the 2011 Arab uprising.

My experience in belonging, and participating, in the uprising, meant I wanted to study the reasons why the Sa'idi people did not rebel against Mubarak's regime. In order to do so, I chose to conduct the ethnographic interviews in Al-Minya governorate (see Map 2.1) and within the small Sa'idi city, al-Fikriyah (see Photo 2.1 and Map 2.2), and a village called Munsha'iat al-Fikriyya or Mansheyat al-Fikriyah (see Photo 2.2, and Map 2.3). The city and village were chosen as an ethnographic site for several reasons. The most obvious reason is the securitization of public and private spheres and the domination by the state over the society in Sa'id. Likewise, the systemic exclusionary policies of civil society and public participation. Finally, the distrust in politics, due to the bitter and repressive experiences of counterterrorism in the 1980s and 1990s, bred reluctance to participate in political activities. Finally, due to the oppression which defined state-society relations in as-Sa'idiyya of the last forty years,[33] as-Sa'idiyya was terrorized and deterred from any form of rebellion against the central authority.

This chapter is based on more than fifty interviews, and half of them are with women for the purposes of equality and fair representation of women. Even if it would be false to project the outcomes of this chapter onto the whole of Sa'idi society, the interviews, nonetheless, provide us with a valuable snapshot, an insider's perspective of as-Sa'idiyya between 2011 to 2015 and perceptions of the social mobilization and revolt in the region. The age of the interviewees ranged from 18 to 70 years old. However, due to the limitation of words, I have chosen a random sample which reflects participants of various gender, age, and educational, economic, and professional backgrounds for the purpose of diversity and inclusion. Of this selection, three interviewees

---

31 YouTube 2016. As expected, after publishing the video Sharshoub was arrested.
32 Abu-Lughod 2012; Abul-Magd 2013; El-Nour 2015; Al-Aswany 2015a.
33 Abozaid 2020a.

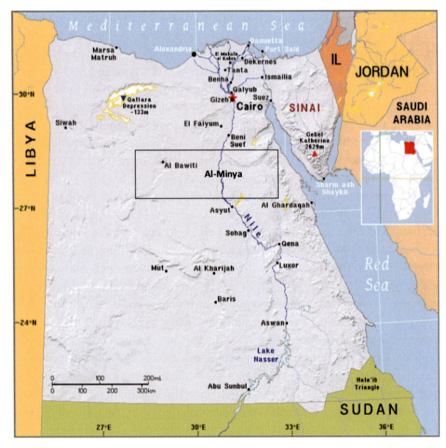

MAP 2.1   The location of Al-Minya governorate

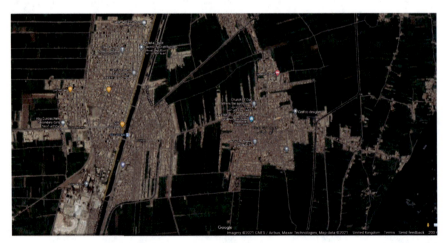

MAP 2.2   Map of al-Fikriyya city
SOURCE: GOOGLE MAPS (2021). AVAILABLE AT: HTTPS://WWW.GOOGLE.CO
.UK/MAPS/@27.9278739,30.83231,2603M/DATA=!3M1!1E3 (ACCESSED 3
JAN. 2021)

PHOTO 2.1 The city of al-Fikriyya

PHOTO 2.2   The village of Munshaʿiat al-Fikriyya

were women (Wasfa 75, Sayyidah 48, and Souad 27) and five were men (Ragab 35, Mohamed, Abdo 18, Hassan 26, Asfour 31). The interviews were conducted in a semi-structured and open-ended way to give the interviewees the opportunity to steer the conversation through several topics related to the 2011

NO REVOLUTION: WHY AS-ṢAʿĪDIYYA DID NOT REALLY REVOLT

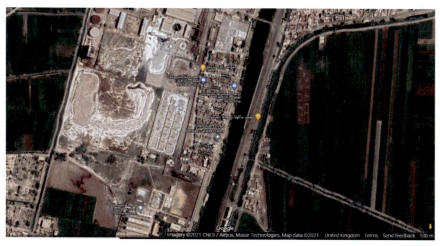

MAP 2.3   Map of Munshaʿiat al-Fikriyya
Note: The arrows point at the sugarcane factory known as al-Fawreyka.
SOURCE: GOOGLE MAPS (2021). AVAILABLE AT: HTTPS://WWW.GOOGLE.CO.UK
/MAPS/@27.9202286,30.8179104,713M/DATA=!3M1!1E3 (ACCESSED 3 JAN. 2021)

Arab uprising and to raise topics I had neglected to take into consideration. I asked the interviewees general questions about their reactions and attitudes toward the uprising, including the reasons they did not participate, and finally about the future of coming revolution or opposition actions. I was mainly interested in discussing and understanding their political and social behavior regarding the uprising, and political mobilization in Egypt from January 2011 to the end of August 2015.

The interviewees were informed verbally about the aim of the study and asked to answer only the questions they felt comfortable with. All interviewees agreed to participate after I provided them (separately) with a brief about the topic of the study. Participants also agreed to the use of their 'first' names in the study. Some of the interviews were conducted in private locations, such as inside the interviewees' houses (see Photos 2.3, 2.4 and 2.5), while others were conducted at al-Gheit (the land) (see Photo 2.6), and at coffeehouses where men, exclusively, spend their evening time smoking shisha, playing dominoes, and watching WWE on television.[34]

---

34   WWE refers to World Wrestling Entertainment, Inc., an American integrated media, and entertainment company that is primarily known for professional wrestling competitions.

PHOTO 2.3   haja'h Wasfa

Some of the interviewees cannot read or write (Wasfa, Ragab, Mohamed and Sayyidah) so they did not sign the consent form. However, I read it for them, and they agreed to participate in the interviews. The rest of the participants read and signed the consent form, after I translated it into Arabic and electronically forwarded it to them (via Facebook and WhatsApp) to sign, as a requirement of this chapter.

I am from the same city and village as all participants, who asked me about my family and relatives. This was their way to demonstrate the relationship with me, the author. This initial relationship helped me to establish a rapport with the interviewees and gain their trust. Alongside the interviews, I will also use the autobiographic method of sharing my personal experiences of the uprising and a recognition of the village's traditional cultural values, norms, and social practices. Moreover, I also understand and speak the local dialect which gives me insight to the social and political environment, thereby enhancing my communication and trust with the interviewees.[35]

Throughout this ethnographic study, I noticed unexpected changes and indications I had not experienced before when I was living in this city and my family living in the village. I noticed numerous changes in the urban landscape of al-Fikriyya city and surround. Spaces for agriculture have been erased by illegal construction sites that rapidly expanded after the fall of Mubarak in 2011 (see Photo 2.7). Moreover, new forms of communication and access to information (smart phones, social media) have developed. I cannot confirm

---

35   Miller 2004: 27–29; Adams 1957: 225–228.

NO REVOLUTION: WHY AS-ṢA'ĪDIYYA DID NOT REALLY REVOLT 73

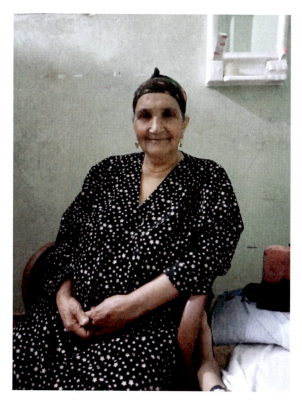

PHOTO 2.4   haja'h Sayyidah

PHOTO 2.5   Meeting with some interviewees inside their homes (2011–2012)

PHOTO 2.6   Some of the interviewees carrying out their everyday activities at al-Gheit

if these changes in communication dynamics are permanent or temporary. I also observed the rapid changes which have occurred regarding state-society relations in Sa'id during the 2011 post-revolution period, compared with the pre-revolution era. These changes are a direct result of increased development and mobilization in Sa'id over the last three decades. For example, the spread of schools, educational institutions and universities during this period have expanded the extent of political and societal participation among young Sa'idi citizens. Likewise, these transformations are a manifestation of revolutionary 'Information and Communications Technology', ICT (i.e., the internet, mobile phones, and satellite television), which were implemented and backed by Ahmed Nazif's governments (1994–2011). According to Krishna Ghimire:

> In recent decades, it is evident that young people have become more educated, more mobile, and more knowledgeable about wider events than the previous generation. Young people are agile and less burdened by family responsibilities, thereby making it easier for them to get involved in social actions and movements. Naturally, not all of the activities in which young people are involved need be revolutionary.[36]

---

36   Ghimire 2002: 36.

NO REVOLUTION: WHY AS-ṢA'ĪDIYYA DID NOT REALLY REVOLT

PHOTO 2.7   Changing urban landscape before and after 2011 around al-Fikriyya city

3 Reflexivity/Limitations

At the outset, it is crucial to elaborate that this chapter's main emphasis is on as-Saʿidiyya who live in Upper Egypt not those who live in the North (i.e., Cairo, Alexandria, and other cities). While the latter participated in the 2011 revolution as several studies articulated, this chapter is profoundly interested in investigating the political and social attitudes of those living in Saʿid and revealing the reasons behind their not taking part in the revolution. Having said that, the chapter is not occupied with the questions of whether Saʿid and as-Saʿidiyya participated in the 2011 revolution or whether what happened in Saʿid (i.e., local demonstrations, the spontaneous, popular initiatives, public and community participation actions) were genuine actions of revolution, resistance, or a form of the everyday life and categorial struggles.

I believe such questions are not only superficial or disingenuous, but also reflect prejudiced and judgmental perspectives that prohibit us from understanding the latent and inherited structural restrictions that prevent as-Saʿidiyya from rebelling against systemic injustice and exclusion. However, scholars who discussed Saʿid's role in the revolution failed to identify the overlap between the concepts, which causes misinterpretations. Hence, in this chapter I highlight the divergences between what J. C. Scott called 'organized resistance' (i.e., revolutionary actions) and 'everyday life resistance' (i.e., infrapolitics) in the context of rural and peasant societies such as Saʿid. While 'organized resistance' refers to actions such as rebellions, oppositional campaigns, or demonstrations,[37] the concept of 'everyday life resistance' addresses subversive ways in which subalterns act in their everyday lives; or in other words resistance that is not formally organized.[38] In other words, while the political struggle is aiming to remove the regime and change the structure of power that produced these economic and social conditions that contribute to decrease living standards, development levels and political mobilization open the public sphere and create a new democratic and just regime.

Scott challenged mainstream (positivist) approaches of studying resistance that often focus on visible historic 'events' such as organized rebellions or collective action while overlooking subtle but powerful forms of 'everyday resistance'. He researched peasant societies and their ways of responding to domination and repression, focusing not on observable acts of rebellion but on forms of cultural resistance and non-cooperation that are employed over

---

37 Scott 1985, 1989.
38 Lilja, Baaz, Schulz and Vinthagen 2017: 44.

time through the course of persistent servitude.[39] For Scott, resistance is a subtle form of contesting 'public transcripts' by making use of prescribed roles and language to resist the abuse of power through 'rumor, gossip, disguises, linguistic tricks, metaphors, euphemisms, folktales, ritual gestures, anonymity'.[40] These methods are particularly effective in situations where violence is used to maintain the status quo, allowing 'a veiled discourse of dignity and self-assertion within the public transcript ... in which ideological resistance is disguised, muted and veiled for safety's sake'.[41] As Nathan Brown accurately states, 'peasants have often conveyed resentment and resistance instead of patience or wrath'.[42]

> Most of the political life of subordinate groups is to be found neither in the overt collective defiance of powerholders nor in complete hegemonic compliance, but in the vast territory between these two polar opposites.[43]

Overall, to differentiate between 'organized resistance' and other forms of 'everyday resistance', Scott demonstrates how peasant rebellions are rather uncommon and unexpected, and often do not have a profound impact. The forms of 'everyday resistance' require little coordination or planning and are employed by both individuals and groups to resist without directly confronting or challenging elite central norms. According to Mikael Baaz, Mona Lilja, and Stellan Vinthagen, he looks at what he called the infrapolitics, or the less visible, everyday forms of resistance such as foot-dragging, evasion, false compliance, pilfering, feigned ignorance, slander, and sabotage, which he studied in rural and factory settings, and also among the middle class and elites (for instance through tax evasion or conscription), but particularly among rural people who are physically dispersed and less politically organized than urban populations.[44]

The methodological choices of this chapter do not neglect the role of reflexivity. These methods interlink with other tools, such as autobiography and auto-analysis, and with methodological and epistemic positionalities and choices such as 'Decolonizing Methodologies', 'Subaltern Studies', and 'People's History'.[45] Such tendencies aim to avoid 'foreigner', 'outsider', 'observer' and

---

39   Scott 1985: 133–135.
40   ibid: 137; Scott 1992.
41   Scott 1985: 137.
42   Brown 1990: 1.
43   Scott 1985: 136.
44   Lilja, Baaz, Schulz and Vinthagen 2017: 42–43; Baaz, Lilja and Vinthagen 2018: 69–70.
45   Smith 2012; Spivak 1988; Zinn 1980.

'authenticity' claims and other invisible cognitive biases, in favor of other 'from within' interpretations. The latter propositions do not claim to be superior, rather they claim to be more conscious and complementing of the amalgam of material practices and forms of language and knowledge that frame and (re)constitute the social structures and psychological life inside certain communities.

Such complex methodology is familiar with local history, social challenges and struggles and its contexts, complex social networks and relationships between demographics, familial and sectarian affiliations. Likewise, it acknowledges the complexity of positionality researchers face.[46]

Being from Saʿid myself, I have experienced some of the challenges, as have other people in the region. For the purposes of this chapter, I used participant observation, autobiographical and auto-analytical methods, reflecting on my positionality and relation to the field. I perceive reflexivity as the process of a continual internal dialogue and critical self-evaluation of researcher's positionality as well as active acknowledgement and explicit recognition that this position may affect the research process and outcome,[47] in which the researchers (1) acknowledge and recognize themselves as a part of the research, (2) take responsibility for their own situatedness within the research,(3) self-monitor the impact of their biases, beliefs, and experiences on their research, and (4) acknowledge the effect that it may have on the setting, participants, questions asked, data collected, and data interpretations.[48] Reflexivity not only makes researchers aware of an analytic focus (subject), but it also turns the researchers' lens back onto themselves (the self) to recognize their relationship to the field of study, and the other (object) that attends to the ways that cultural practices involve consciousness and commentary on themselves.[49]

More importantly, it allows us to unearth the challenges experienced by underprivileged, marginalized, oppressed, and socially excluded societies, who are located outside the purview of this chapter's research interests and general academic (both local and foreign) agenda. Nevertheless, this research does not claim to represent them or speak on their behalf. In addition, the chapter aims to understand these communities, based upon the knowledge of the lifeworld of these communities, without shipping away the so-called 'authenticity', drafting away, or abandoning the cognitive and disciplined methodology. In fact, while I recognize my biases and acknowledge solidarity with the Saʿid

---

46 Naples and Sachs 2000; Finefter-Rosenbluh 2017.
47 Pillow 2003: 220.
48 Berger 2015: 220–21; Finlay 1998.
49 Berger 2015.

community in the case study (which I do not try to deny), I endeavored not to allow them to influence my analysis.

Finally, in an ontological sense, academics must recognize their audiences and distribute content in an appropriate manner. For example, are we writing for purely academic purposes, for donor institutions and policy makers, or to further represent the communities we study? Most importantly, researchers should reflect on how they are writing and their positionality. For example, researchers who belong to the Global South should be aware of their epistemological and methodological choices. Likewise, academia and journals should be encouraged to support critical investigations which aim to broaden non-western perspectives and raise awareness of euro-centric positions. In the case of this chapter, eastern cultures share distinct histories from mainstream western experiences. This chapter hopes to contribute to a growing body of southern academic literature representing common experiences in contrast to western perspectives of non-western political phenomena, such as the 2011 Arab uprising.

Researchers need to renounce their privileged positions inside the ivory tower of academia and engage with the 'real' world, the lifeworld to use Habermas's terms, in more ethical and committed ways. This means actively challenging structures of domination, techniques of subjugation and exclusion of marginalized and underprivileged groups. Moreover, as mentioned before, most studies on the 2011 uprising focused on the cities of Luxor and Aswan and overlooked other peripheral locations like the Red Sea and al-Wadi al-Gadeed governorates. Neglecting the peripheries contributes to their further marginalization and othering. Therefore, researchers should shift their focus away from urban centers such as Cairo, Alexandria, Luxor, and others which are seen more easily accessible, both in terms of logistics and perceived cultural differences, and be encouraged to explore understudied and marginalized localities and communities.

As for this chapter, I was fortunate to be able to engage with the field of research without any complications, where the people were welcoming and cooperative. Substantially, Saʿid is known as a conservative region and people are particularly cautious when speaking with strangers. Their vocabulary and heavy dialects are varied and difficult to understand for outsiders and even for some Egyptians.[50] Despite this, during the interviews the participants were very cooperative and clear in answering my questions. Unexpectedly, the answers of the interviewees were critical of the state's policies in Upper

---

50   Miller 2004.

Egypt, which was unusual prior to 2011. Nevertheless, this familiarity with the research field was not enough to know how the people of both Munshaʿiat al-Fikriyya village and al-Fikriyya city think, and how their self-identity differs between generations, genders, social classes, religious beliefs, educational background, and personal experiences. This chapter also takes into account the role of social media, and the local structure of power and traditions which contribute to the construction of social and political behavior.[51]

I was surprised to learn that participation in the uprising did not necessarily mean that someone was progressive or pro-revolution. The young people engaging in social movements and civil activities were working within state and regime frameworks which did not encourage free public participation. Instead, their participation was primarily for clientelist purposes that aimed at gaining financial and political self-interest objectives, and not public goods. Similarly, the young Saʿidi youth expressed generally negative opinions of available youth centers which lacked equipment and catered only to men, and in which the local authorities offered little in the way of cultural or educational activities.[52]

While the numbers of non-governmental organizations (NGOs) and civil society organizations has increased significantly over the last 25 years (there are now more than 50,000 NGOs in Egypt, according to President Sisi), they are only there as a slogan. According to Ray Bush, 'exist[s] in anything other than as a slogan used by the Government of Egypt to curry favor from the donor community'.[53] Civil society had been employed in Egypt as a tool to construct and institutionalize state practices by the government with the aim of enhancing loyalty to, and boosting solidarity within, the ruling party and the state. However, this manipulation has increased the mobilization, recruitment, and popular support for rival political factions (like the Muslim Brotherhood, al-Wafd, the Coptic Church).

> Many youth and their representative organizations are commonly manipulated by the regime to show that they are enthusiastically supporting the civil society sector. Youth and youth organizations are utilized to vehicle the party policy of the ruling National Democratic Party (NDP) and to boost good opinions of President Mubarak. They are thus expected to play an active role in promoting official doctrine, helping to recruit new members, mobilizing voters, and holding meetings.[54]

---

51 Adams 1957: 36.
52 The World Bank 2012.
53 Bush 2001: 2.
54 Ghimire 2002: 59.

In sum, while the 2011 revolution was an example of organized resistance, the peasants' and as-Saʿidiyya activities are an example of everyday life struggles/resistance. Although the differences between these two kinds of socio-political behavior are very small, it is still important to reveal the difference to understand the drastic apathy and indifference of Saʿidi people toward participation not only in the revolution, but in public life in general. According to World Bank reports, young Saʿidi people have the lowest level of civic engagement in Egypt, with less than five per cent in the country, and only three per cent in Upper Egypt belonging to social, artistic, or political groups.

4   Peasants and Rural Societies: An Overview

Peasants suffer not only from political marginalization but also from social oppression. They have been labelled as 'a class of low classness' compared to other classes.[55] Often synonymous with rural societies, peasants are usually characterized as 'parochial, traditional and fatalistic, resigned to their situations and largely incapable of effective collective action'.[56] There is a dominant Manichean perception of peasants which frames them as 'ignorant' and 'inscrutable'.[57] However, according to Eric Hobsbawm, there is not enough historical evidence to support an argument that links peasants with large-scale revolts or uprisings.[58] Even when peasants engage in wider revolutionary actions, the reasons behind this participation are always due to external forces, i.e., natural, economic, political, or ideological.[59]

The literature on the topic of this chapter revolves around three main subjects. The first is the study of peasants and rural societies, then the political and social behavior of peasants, and finally the study of Saʿid as the focal point of this chapter. Peasants, as a community or even as a class, in Egypt have been neglected for a long time, especially in fields such as Political Science and Middle Eastern studies.[60] Likewise, the study of rural society and the traditions of popular rural protests and political action, especially in complex societies such as the Middle East, are still 'ill-served' in comparison with other regions such as Europe, Asia, and Africa.[61] The Middle East societies turned out to be

---

55 Shanin 1966; Bush 2002.
56 Brynen 1991: 410.
57 Brown 1990 chapters 1 and 3.
58 Hobsbawm 1973: 9.
59 ibid.
60 ibid: 5; Brown 1990: 210.
61 Magagna 1991: 920–921.

a 'genuine anomaly' to generate sustained traditions of these kinds of actions that demand more investigation.[62]

Other studies consider peasants to be a subordinate class which infrequently rebels or revolts against the regimes, structures, or laws that repress them. Instead, they tend to work within the system to minimize disadvantages. This has led some authors to conclude that, 'the peasantry is a political nullity unless organized and led by outsiders'.[63] Further accounts portray peasants as latent rural revolutionaries ready to be spurred to political upheaval.[64] Even where peasants rebelled or started a revolutionary movement, instances of which were few and far between according to Scott, most of these revolutions were brutally crushed.[65]

Instances where these revolts have been successful have resulted in a greater, more dominant state apparatus gaining power over the peasantry which has ultimately suppressed them more effectively than the previous regime they rebelled against. The reason behind such behavior, according to Rex Brynen, is that it is rare for peasants to risk and engage in confrontation with the authorities over taxes, cropping patterns, development policies or new laws. They are likely to, instead, hedge or 'nibble away' at such policies through attitudes of noncompliance, foot-dragging, deception, desertion, pilfering and other quixotic action.[66]

In contrast to the prevailing narrative which stresses the passive, nonviolent and even pusillanimous nature of the peasants, other studies have found that not all peasants and rural societies were passive or nonviolent. These studies show that rural societies in countries like Egypt (either in the North (al-Delta) or in the South (Sa'id)) maintain deeply imbedded behaviors of collective and popular resistance to all forms of power, as I shall elaborate upon later.[67]

For instance, Indian peasants have a long tradition of armed uprisings, both against the British occupation or the pre-modern Moghul government. According to Kathleen Gough, for more than 200 years peasants in all the major regions have risen repeatedly against landlords, government revenue agents, police, and military forces.[68] Academics, including Chalmers Johnson and others, have focused on 'peasant nationalism', which emphasizes the

---

62   ibid.
63   Scott 1985: xv.
64   Brynen 1991: 410.
65   Scott 1985: xvi.
66   ibid: xvi; Brynen 1991.
67   ibid; Brown 1990; Magagna 1991: 921.
68   Gough 1974; Vishwanath 1990.

importance of the Japanese invasion for rural mobilization in China.[69] Other studies have discussed Chinese peasant rebellions, which aimed to replace the official history written by Confucian historiographers. This aim was embodied in Mao Tse-tung's belief that claimed, 'the ruthless economic exploitations and political oppression of the peasantry by the landlord class forced the peasants to rise repeatedly in revolt against its rule'.[70]

Studies have also been conducted on Brazilian present revolts. During the 1950s, the so-called Peasant Leagues rebelled against the semi-colonial government, objecting to the relationship between Brazilian ruling elites and the US. This relationship conspired to oppress the working class by forcing rural workers to produce cash crops instead of food for native consumption and refusing to develop land which could not support those crops. Seeking emancipation from these hegemonic structures, the Peasant Leagues leader, Francisco Julião's used violent revolutionary rhetoric in a way that made the rest of the political actors (i.e., communists and workers movement) worry about retaliation from the military and police, and US intervention.[71]

Lastly, studies of revolutions in Africa have discussed the methods and circumstances which could transform peasantries into grass root movements of revolutions in places like Mozambique and Tanzania. where the divided and demoralized 'sack of potatoes' peasants turn to being the 'steam of revolution'. Allen Isaacman's study for instance explored the circumstances and conditions under which peasants abandoned their 'carelessness and fragmentation' to become revolutionary actors.[72] In comparison to these case studies, the overall historical experience of Egyptian peasants shows that these rebellions, which were not passive or nonviolent all the time, seemed to be directed against the state; or more particularly, against its local agents who tried to enforce adverse decisions which directly affected their survival.

In the case of Egypt, 'Egypt's rural people struggled to defend their vision of a moral order that was endangered by the destabilizing and arbitrary interruption of powerful outsiders whose understanding of agrarian reality seems to have been woefully limited',[73] according to Victor Magagna. Likewise, Nathan Brown argues that the rural protests in Egypt during the 1919 uprising were neither revolutionary nor a classical Marxist class struggle.[74] In Brown's opinion,

---

69   Perry 1978; Johnson 1962.
70   cited by Wakeman 1977.
71   Welch 2009 2006; Wiarda and Wiarda 1967.
72   Isaacman 1990; Saul 1974.
73   Magagna 1991: 922.
74   Brown 1990: 9–11.

these protests were reactionary or represented the defense of a sphere of popular autonomy against the claims of 'modernizing' elites.[75] According to Brown, during both 1882 'Urabi revolt and 1919 revolution peasants resorted to the same weapons they had always used – that is, the generally little-noticed forms of atomistic and communal actions.[76]

However, other studies show that the rural clashes with the British in 1882 and 1919 were violent, in which the Egypt's peasants often engaged in direct confrontation in pursuit of their goals.[77] For example, in 1919 protesters from the cities of Dairut, Assiut governorate, Mallawi and Dayr-Mawas, al-Minya governorate, all located in Sa'id, attacked the train no. 89 that was going from Aswan to Cairo to deliver army food supplements and equipment to British military forces in the North.[78] They toppled the train and killed seven British commissioned officers and several soldiers.[79] After independence, 18 March (the day these events took place in 1919) has become the national day of al-Minya governorate.

Finally, Saker El-Nour argues that what incited the peasants in more than 1,000 Egyptian village to rebel against Mubarak's regime in 1997/1998 was primarily the application of the 1992 tenancy law. This law had a devastating impact on over one million rural families, by jeopardizing their main source of work and food security according to Reem Saad. The peasants' act of resistance against that law represented 'a crucial turning point in the relationship of citizens to the state during the Mubarak era'.[80] For the first time since Mubarak rose to power in 1981, between October 1997 and May 1998, the police killed twenty-three peasants, injured more than 750 citizens, and arrested over 2,500 others. During this reign of intimidation, most peasants faced intimidation, illegal detention, and torture by the police forces.[81]

5   as-Ṣa'īdiyya, al-fellaheen, and the 2011 Uprising

Overall, there is considerable literature on the actors of the 2011 Arab uprising in Egypt. For example, in her work, *Egypt's Long Revolution*, Maha Abdelrahman discussed the roles of multiple actors in the 2011 revolution

---

75   Magagna 1991: 922.
76   Brown 1990: 209.
77   ibid: 15; Magagna 1991: 923.
78   Goldberg 1992: 262.
79   ibid: 274–276. Badrawi 1981; Anderson 2017; 'Ashmawi 2001; al-Rafi'I 1946.
80   Saad 2016; El-Nour 2015.
81   El-Nour 2015: 202.

against Mubarak's regime, among which are academics, judges, workers, farmers, and 'almost everybody else'. Abdelrahman demonstrated that the revolution did not start with Tahrir, but rather originated through continuous forms of protests, activism and opposition activities that had existed since the 1990s.[82] In addition, several studies emphasize the role of feminism and the feminist movement against the persecution and intimidation suffered by Egyptian women at the hands of the authorities. Furthermore, they elaborate on how women resisted this violence.[83]

Nadine Abdullah, Ahmed Tohamy, and others investigated the role of youth movements and youth activism during the uprising and the aftermath.[84] Other studies have shed light on the role of other groups such as workers,[85] trade unions and professional syndicates,[86] farmers in the Delta,[87] urban mobility groups,[88] the Church and the Copts (Roy 2016; Yaqoub 2012; Samir 2013), the Sinai and other marginalized communities (Alexandrani 2016). Other studies concentrated on additional 'ethnic' groups, such as Nubians. Drawing upon oral history, ethnography, and interview methods, Mayada Madbouly revealed the growth of Nubian activism in the post 2011 period, especially regarding 'the right of return', 'collective memory', identity, and other denied cultural rights, which were results of official forced displacement policies and postcolonial repression in the name of national unification and development (Madbouly 2019, 2021).

As for Upper Egypt, despite its long history of struggles against the central authorities and the colonial powers, the number of studies that discuss or investigate its role in these revolutions (and in the 2011 uprising in particular) are strikingly insignificant. While this chapter is not trying to trace the history of civil unrest in Upper Egypt, however, it is primarily concerned with the correlations between the social, economic, and political contexts of rural and peasantry unrest in modern Egypt, and the momentum of the 2011 Arab uprising in Upper Egypt.

For decades, the common consensus among scholars about Sa'id was that it suffered from many enduring problems as outlined here: 1) declining levels of

---

82   Abdelrahman 2014.
83   Hammad 2017; Hafez 2014a 2014b; Abaza 2013.
84   Abdalla 2016a; Tohamy 2016.
85   Abdalla and Wolff 2019; Abdalla 2016b.
86   Alexander and Bassiouny 2014.
87   Woertz 2017; Ayeb and Bush 2019 2014; Bush 2011; De Lellis 2019; Ayeb 2010.
88   Stadnicki 2016.

tourism, 2) the absence of development efforts, 3) the government's failure to compensate as-Sa'idiyya for losing their incomes as a result of the sharp decline of tourism revenues, 4) continuing neglect of Sa'id's situation regarding security, employment, education, government corruption and criminal violations, 5) the arrogance of central authority (i.e., Cairo) in dealing with the demands of Sa'idi society concerning the improvement of educational and health services, 6) lack of understanding regarding regional developmental and subsistence needs, 7) the continuation of systematic marginalization of the as-Sa'idiyya in the media, 8) inherent national political under-representation, 9) bias against intellectual, cultural and artistic production in the media compared with the north, and 10) failure to allow historical and cultural rights of ethnic groups such as Nubian people and others who have been affected by the policies of the Egyptian state for decades.[89]

In addition, historically Sa'id as a region have a bad reputation of being at 'the margins of power and wealth' which forced large numbers of its population, especially young people, to migrate in search of better jobs. They escaped to the north of Egypt or to neighboring countries, such as Libya, the Gulf States, or to European countries.[90] Lila Abu-Lughod argues that life in marginalized Upper Egypt is deeply affected by tough circumstances, such as devastating economic and social policies, the excessive use of force, and the arbitrary power of the police.[91]

Besides, another aspect which, in my opinion, could help us understand the diverse attitudes and behaviors of Egyptians toward the 2011 Arab uprising in Sa'id is the structure of power within the region. Illuminating the authoritarian nature of the Egyptian state could help us in deciphering the enigma of as-Sa'idiyya's political and social behaviors as well as their capability to resist and challenge power and authorities.

> The different experiences of the villagers in authoritarian and equalitarian institutions determine many of their differences in values and techniques. Their different attitudes toward the conflict between these institutions affect their interpretation and implementation of communications from within and without the village.[92]

---

89 The World Bank 2012; Hamzawy 2013a, 2013b.
90 Abu-Lughod 2012: 22; Bush and Ayeb 2012.
91 Abu-Lughod 2012: 21.
92 Adams 1957: 231–32.

Thus, from the eighteenth century, there is a correlation between increased violence and draconian oppression practiced by the Egyptian state, on the one hand, and the desire for rebellion by civil society on the other. Most of these uprisings resulted from state violence and the excessive use of force against as-Sa'idiyya's rights and the coercive acquisition of their lands.[93] However, other studies challenge the claims and argue that in the late nineteenth and early twentieth centuries, peasants did not initiate revolutions (which often was not of their own making) but participated in them, when 'they could safely become involved'.[94] I believe that to a considerable extent such attitudes persisted until the outbreak of the Arab Uprising.

In the postcolonial period, authorities' fear of rebellion of any form inclined them to react with excessive violence against any movements challenging the regime. This occurred during the Sadat and Mubarak periods. During the latter, Egypt reached the brink of civil war because of the resurgence of Islamic militant groups, especially in the south of the country (Sa'id) early on, and then in the rest of the country.[95]

Consequently, the so-called Egypt's 'war on terror' in the 1980s and 1990s.[96] has caused the people of Upper Egypt to suffer due to the repressive and arbitrary power held by the police, state officials and the Army.[97] I still remember in the mid-1990s when a $200,000 al-moddara'h (an armored fighting vehicle) came to my village to terrorize the locals and destroy sugar cane farms, under the guise of looking for terrorists. Many of the young men arrested were my friends, neighbors, and classmates, who were forcibly and illegally imprisoned for a long time, although they were also minors.[98]

In conclusion, studies on rural and peasant societies have focused on topics such as structure of rural production; the relationship of rural villages to agrarian markets; state capacity and repression; rational choice and the pursuit of individual self-interest; and the existence of a peasant class.[99] Some studies also explored the dynamics of social behavior within these societies, the role of education, development, technology, and social media over the collective

---

93 Abul-Magd 2013; Lawson 1981.
94 Brown 1990: 210.
95 Ajami 1995; Reed 1993; Alterman 2000; Bradley 2008; Osman 2010.
96 Egyptian media called the counterterrorism and counterinsurgency that took place in Upper Egypt in the 1990s the 'war on terror'. In this context, I am not referring to the "global war on terror" that initiated by the US and its allies after the attacks of September 11th, 2001.
97 Abu-Lughod 2012: 23.
98 Abozaid 2022: 211–215.
99 Brynen 1991: 410.

action of the peasants and rural groups, especially in the Global South, and particularly in the Middle East. I also note that there is no empirical evidence to support the arguments presented in the Modernization school of thought surrounding developing countries and peasant societies, link the Sa'id community. Nonetheless, there are many studies that associate the improvement of economic and developmental conditions in Egypt, with the expanding political and social transformation among rural communities. For example, according to Richard Adams, the time after the 1952 coup saw development levels[100] increase across Egypt, including the marginalized rural regions of Upper Egypt.[101] He argued that:

> Within rural areas, as the population of young people grows, education is spreading and the means of communication and transport are improving, and there is no reason why social mobilization, with considerable participation by youth, should not occur in rural settings as well.[102]

Likewise, Nathan Brown argued that 'the removal of constraints that existed on political activity thus allowed peasants to pursue local grievances in ways that would not otherwise have been possible'.[103] The removal of these constraints during 'Urabi's revolt of 1882 and the 1919 uprising encouraged rural populations to volunteer and support the rebels by attacking local and foreign moneylenders and landowners (feudalist class) to effect political turmoil, rather than as a sign of political and social mobilization.[104] However, the historical record shows that it was a result of resistance (from both Fellaheen and as-Sa'idiyya) against Turkish and British despotism, and the Saraya (the palace). Magagna and other studies indicate that the peasant protests in the 1919 nationalist uprising were not a result of threatening starvation or the effect of war-induced inflation, but rather were a result of political and social mobilization.

> The idea that the peasants went hungry may seem strange, for in 1919 they still produced a considerable portion of their food and the rebellion's slogans spoke of nationalism, not food shortages.[105]

---

100 By development Adams meant 'changes in three central criteria over time: a decrease in poverty: a decrease in inequality: and an increase in productivity (land and labor)'. Adams 1985: 715; Adams 2000: 272–73.
101 Adams 1985: 705.
102 Ghimire 2002: 32.
103 Brown 1990 cited in Brynen 1991: 411.
104 Magagna 1991.
105 Goldberg 1992: 262.

Based on this perception, it is possible to understand how the post-colonial state subdued the peasants and Sa'idi society for at least two decades following independence. To understand the transformations that took place in Sa'id in the post-independence period, it is necessary to analyze a set of variables which transform the social and economic map of Upper Egypt.[106] These variables include: 1) the effects of the oil boom in the 1970s, and the massive migration of the Sa'idi people to other Arab countries, i.e., the Arab Gulf States, Iraq, Libya, and other countries; 2) the expansion of the middle class which emerged during Nasser's era (1952–1970) which established a new education system paving the path for social transformation and class mobilization; 3) the emergence of the technocrats or the so-called tabaqet al-mou'zafeen (employees' class) which provided opportunities for Sa'idi people to join Egypt's bureaucratic institutions;[107] 4) the empowering of the working class, which witnessed a tremendous growth due to national infrastructure projects (e.g., the High Dam 1960–1970) and development planning policies initiated by Egypt in the mid-1950s and 1960s. During this period, the state established hundreds of industrial complexes in sectors like the sugar cane industry, which preserved agricultural products, aluminum, natural gas, marble, limestone, and quarries. These projects employed hundreds of thousands of workers, and greatly contributed to modernizing the lives of tens of thousands of peasants and poor as-Sa'idiyya;[108] 5) enacting laws of agrarian reform and the abolition of feudalism which profoundly improved the standard of living for hundreds of thousands of the destitute and poor, and re-distributed wealth which reduced the rate of poverty in most Upper Egypt regions; 6) The revival of militant and extremist religious discourse after the defeat of the Nasserite project in the 1967 war, which heralded the gradual abandonment of state development in the 1970s, due to the open-door policy and liberalization of the economy[109]; and 7) the resurgence of marginalization polices toward Upper Egypt.

---

106 Ismail 2011.
107 Ayubi 1991.
108 The most comprehensive reflection (if not the only one) on the processes of modernizing Sa'id is Abdul-Rahman al-Abnoudi's epic poem jawabat Heraji al-kot al-'amel fi al-sed al-'a'li [The letters of Heraji Al-kot, the Worker in the High Dam]. The poem is structured as a correspondence between a Sa'idi farmer Heraji al-Kot and his wife Fatimah Ahmed Abdul-Ghafar, after he left his village to join the project of building the high dam in Aswan. In the poem, al-Abnoudi captures the essence of radical changes experienced by Heraji and his family as they live through a decade of Nasserist 'modernization' (1960–1970). Al-Abnoudi 2017.
109 Ayubi 1995.

The role of religion and religious discourse is also a factor in whether a rural society will rebel. As mentioned above, Sa'id is a conservative, rural, and state-dominated space, where the state, represented by both al-Azhar and al-awqaf (Islamic Endowments), controls the mosques and the creation of religious discourse. This promotes the cult of the state and the obligation to obey and be loyal to the state. This factor had been widely neglected,[110] although in a 'Muslim' country like Egypt, the relationship between Islam and rural protests, either in accelerating and constraining, or legitimatizing and criminalizing such protests, is considered a 'fruitful topic with substantial implications for comparative politics'.[111]

Furthermore, the religious factor has a crucial effect in both fueling and accelerating a revolution or curbing it and alienating protestors in the eyes of the public. However, the role of religion in the Sa'id revolution still lacks critical academic analysis. In the case of Upper Egypt for example, by religion and religiosity, I refer to the social and popular discourses and practices, either for Muslims or Copts. In other words, in a social, political, economic, and cultural environment, such as the Sa'idi society, it is easy to imagine the kind of socio-economic and socio-political roles that religion, specifically religious institutions, are expected to play under almost complete security control and domination over the public sphere. The religious discourse in Sa'id (away from official platforms) is deeply reactionary, racist, and sectarian. In fact, two directorates of Upper Egypt (i.e., Assiut and al-Minya) were the birthplace of takfiri groups in Egypt. Likewise, the biggest internal challenge that faced Egypt in the postcolonial period was religious and social upheaval in Upper Egypt in the 1970s and 1980s. This unrest was driven by poor and marginalized Sa'idi cities such as Mallawi, Abu Qurqas (where this study was conducted), and Dairut. According to several local and international observers, these areas were labelled the 'the epicenter of tension' and 'the capital[s] of Islamic terror in the world'.[112]

Such religious discourse, along with other variables including state-owned mass media tools such as television and radio, could elucidate the secrets behind radio silence that afflicted most Sa'idi cities and villages, not only during the time of the 2011 Arab uprising, but also during the last several decades. In Upper Egypt, the mosque/church were saying that revolution and rebellion against the ruler is religiously forbidden and sinful activities. Mass media tools portrayed revolution, demonstration, revolutionaries as khawana'h ('traitors'),

---

110   Al-Anani 2016.
111   Magagna 1991: 923.
112   *The Washington Post* 1985, quoted in Bakr 1999.

a'daa al-watan ('enemies of the country'). Likewise, police and security institutions repressed and killed protesters in the streets. Consequently, the political behavior of as-Sa'idiyya was shaped, I argue, fundamentally via the official media platforms which fed them with information. In light of the state's semi-control over the media, as well as the number of media outlets and platforms (television, radio, and the press) available, on the one hand, and due to the dominating socio-political and socio-economic conditions in Upper Egypt on the other hand, political attitudes for the time, although unacceptable, were completely logical and understandable.[113]

Since 2013, Egyptian authorities have actively restricted the freedom of the media and public expression. With almost a quarter of the population unable to read or write (18 million are illiterate), (national) television, has been the main source of information, education, and entertainment for most of the population for decades. Nonetheless, from the mid-2000s, al-wasla (a monthly subscription, ranging between half a dollar and one US dollar), emerged in a group of Arab and Egyptian entertainment and news satellite TV channels. Usually, this group of channels includes between 10 and 20 stations (such as Al-Jazeera, Al-Arabiya, Al-Jazeera Sport, Rotana Cinema, Rotana Zaman, Nile Cinema, Songs Channels, WWE Wrestling Channels, and several religious and Salafi TV channels). However, the popular networks are a group of illegal services providing information and entertainment to 32 per cent of Egypt's poorest; this outreach increased the level of awareness and public knowledge in almost every village in the country but did not show the extent to which the uprising mobilized and encouraged people to overthrow the authorities.[114] This explains the inclination of most as-Sa'idiyya (and most regions of Egypt in fact) to support the state and the old regime, and fear of the revolution (and not participating in it). The Sa'idi people receive only one view if they care to listen or wanted to lend their interest. For most of them, life is home, al-Gheit [the land], the local markets, and the mosque/church. Unless these transformations or changes that take place in the country do not (directly) alert them or affect their modest lifeworld, they simply do not care at all.[115]

Such a perspective is contradicted by another Sa'idi scholar. In a series of op-eds about politics and revolution in Upper Egypt published after the 2011 revolution, Amr Hamzawy argued that the claims about how Sa'idi is deserting and does not care about political issues are incorrect. In his view, these views are based on illusions and myths. For instance, the overwhelming prejudice

---

113 Abozaid 2014.
114 Abozaid 2022.
115 Abozaid 2014.

and false claims that what determines voting behaviors and trends of the elections in Upper Egypt is based on providing the necessities of life (the myth of sugar and oil bribe) or the embodied influence of the politicization of religion (the one-dimension citizen myth) where the public consciousness in Saʿid is formed basically in/by mosques, or in response to sectarian impulses. In return, Hamzawy argues that many of the governorates of Upper Egypt (especially Luxor and Aswan) enjoy and are characterized by the existence of high levels of political and public awareness, and these perceptions are much deeper than being reduced to the vocabulary of indigence, the politicization of religion, or/and sectarianism claims.[116]

In exchange for this 'reductionist' view, Hamzawy proposes a different approach to understanding the conditions of Upper Egypt, which consists in grasping its political and historical specificities, and the role of the central authority. In his opinion, the Saʿidi citizen, 'after long periods of marginalization and exclusion by the central authority, does not trust it and does not expect justice, equality or development from it'.[117] The crucial variable behind the continuation of such historical attitudes towards the central authority is the hydraulic nature of the nation-state in Egypt (i.e., the centrality of the Nile), where the prime function of the state is to discipline and organize both the river and the citizens for the sake of irrigation and agriculture and secure a minimum level of security to managing everyday life and public affairs.[118] Likewise, the riverine nature of the state is what explains the wide traditional influence of the tribalism and large families in Saʿid, which have a long history of working with the authorities as a buffer zone between the state and the citizens. Traditionally, these families played a crucial role in forming public opinion and awareness among the vast majority of the ordinary as-Saʿidiyya, albeit in opposition to the central authority and whoever controls it historically. In return, the state maintained its ties with these families, provided protection services and expressed the interests of their members, to control and guarantee the loyalty of Saʿidi society.

Regarding the participation in opposition activities and engaging in the nationwide protesting and revolutionary rhythm of 2011 and the aftermath, there are two profoundly contradictory perspectives. The first strand believed that Upper Egypt appeared to play a very minor role in the 25 January revolution.[119] On the other hand, most studies confirm the claims that Saʿidi people

---

116   Hamzawy 2013b, 2013c.
117   Hamzawy 2013a.
118   Hamzawy 2013c; Ayubi 1989; Hamdan 1967.
119   The World Bank 2012.

(especially the youth) did participate in the events of the revolution, whether in Cairo or in Upper Egypt. The authors supported their arguments with ample evidence confirming the presence of demonstrations, protests, attacks on security directorates and police stations, initiated and organized resistance actions, whether in public spaces or on digital and cyberspace in deeply remote and deprived Izab, Kafuor, Nejou'h (villages), in Beni Suef, al-Minya, Assiut, Sohag, Qina, Luxor and Aswan, and even in marginalized and remote cities such as al-Wadi al-Gadeed.[120] Yet, other writings opposed and doubt this narrative.[121]

In fact, I agree with El-Nour that looking to the Arab Uprising either as an instant analysis without a historical perspective or configured into a specific form embodied by the occupation of central city-public-squares, is an insignificant and reductionist perspective. According to El-Nour, this kind of analogy 'negates other forms [of protesting and opposition], not deeming them to be integral to the framework of the revolution, even though they were, during other historical periods'.[122]

Based on that, El-Nour claimed that the peasants' and as-Sa'idiyya participation in the revolution was essential if we see the 2011 uprising as a historical process (devenir) that had been developing since the 1970s, 1980s and 1990s. He also argues that the Sa'idi people took part in the revolution of 2011 like other Egyptians. Correctly, he pointed out that as-Sa'idiyya were in Tahrir Square during the 25 January Revolution, and they obviously declared their identity.

According to many eyewitnesses (including the author) during the 18 days of demonstrations in Tahrir Square, there were several tents and assembly points for as-Sa'idiyya, and these tents carried the name of their cities. In addition, there is consensus over the widespread support for the 25 January uprising among young people in Sa'id, which was manifested in a series of local demonstrations, and an unprecedented surge in spontaneous, popular initiatives, such as efforts to clean the streets and the establishment of new community alliances.[123] Furthermore, El-Nour claimed that the behavior of peasants and as-Sa'idiyya during the revolution and in the post-Mubarak era can be described as an example of what Asef Bayat called 'social non-movements', where a group of people 'lack ideological leadership and organizational structure; neither do they have a goal to overthrow the existing system', but when they 'feel that there is an opportunity, it is likely that they will carry out

---

120   Abu Al-Magd 2013; El-Nour 2015; Wagner 2011; Saad 2018.
121   Alexandrani 2013; Abozaid 2014; Aboul Gheit 2012.
122   El-Nour 2015: 206.
123   The World Bank 2012; Al-Aswany 2015; Ismail 2011.

organized group protests, or merge into a broader social and political mobilization'.[124] For El-Nour and others, this was how the as-Saʿidiyya, and rural small farmers behaved during the 2011 revolt and its aftermath.

The problem with that analysis and other writings is that it still cannot illuminate why the Saʿidi people did not participate in the protesting activities before the regime fell.[125] El-Nour stresses the 'revolutionary' activities in the post-Mubarak period, but not during the first wave of the uprising that took place between 25 January and 12 February 2011, and his analysis did not contain much about why the Saʿidi people did not rebel before the fall of the regime. During the first wave of the 2011 revolution, there was a remarkable absence of big protesting activities in the largest Saʿidi cities such as Assiut, Sohag, Qina, Aswan and al-Minya, where this study was conducted.

Additionally, El-Nour (and other writers) compulsorily mixed between categorical and public political protesting activities. The peasants' and small farmers' resistance against Mubarak's regime were a partial struggle against authoritarian regimes; but in the end this kind of struggle was for sectional and private interests or objectives directly related to the peasants, not to the whole society. The small farmers' struggle in Egypt and in Upper Egypt in particular, according to El-Nour himself and based on data gathered by Al-Ard [the Land] Center for Human Rights, after two years of the 2011 revolution, '95% of the demands of the small farmers protesting were mostly related to a shortage of resources, the greatest of which were land, water and fertilizers.[126]' Consequently, as mentioned above, while the political struggle is aiming to remove the regime and change the structure of power that produced these economic and social conditions that contribute to decreasing the living standards, development levels and political mobilization open the public sphere and create a new democratic and just regime.

6   Findings

Uprisings in Egypt, Tunisia, Libya, and other Arab countries following from the 2011uprising, were defined as revolts against authoritarian regimes and political, social, and economic exclusion. In Egypt, the gap between the North and South is striking. According to the World Bank, the top five poorest governorates and poorest 1,000 villages are almost all concentrated in three directorates

---

124   Abu-Lughod 2012: 23; Bayat 2009.
125   Abu-Lughod 2012; Saad 2011.
126   El-Nour 2015: 205.

of Upper Egypt (al-Minya, Assiut, and Sohag).[127] Moreover, although the official unemployment rate is 16 per cent, in actuality almost 70 per cent of young people and educated women are jobless. Most young, uneducated women are also unemployed.[128] In addition, the rate of illiteracy is higher than the rest of the Egyptian republic. While the national rate in 2017 was around 26 per cent i.e., 18 million, the rate of illiteracy in Sa'id was higher than the Delta and the North. According to the Central Agency for Public Mobilization and Statistics (CAPMS), al-Minya was at the top of the list with a rate of 37.2 per cent, and 35.9 per cent in Beni Suef. Assiut and Fayoum maintained 34 per cent illiteracy, while Aswan and Luxor achieved the lowest percentage of literacy out of the total population (19 per cent).[129] Nonetheless, despite high levels of illiteracy, unemployment, disenfranchisement, and intimidation among the youth in Upper Egypt and across the region in general, it is surprising that the majority of Sa'idi citizens did not participate in the 2011 uprising to improve their conditions.

Authoritarianism and political, social, and economic exclusion in Upper Egypt were not only the result of governmental policies but also of Egyptian civil and political culture. According to political scientist, Amr Hamzawy:

> The neglect of successive governments in Upper Egypt has led to the loss of confidence in the central authority and in those who control it. Traditionally, political parties and forces have ignored Upper Egypt. They only appear during election seasons, with a sole aim of obtaining the voices of big groups and families.[130]

In fact, after the 2011 uprising, most of these political organizations confined themselves to electoral propaganda and the establishment of party headquarters. They did not convey their positions via programmed either to raise awareness, enhance political culture, or to represent the needs of Upper Egypt. This apathy led the Sa'idi people to say, 'both liberal and left parties are not much different from the religious right [i.e., the Muslim Brotherhood and the Salafists]' (emphasis added).[131] In Sa'id, political parties dealt with the people's grievances in opportunist and exploitative ways. They perceived Sa'id primarily as a 'voting bloc', rather than as human beings. In addition, as-Sa'idiyya's

---

127 The World Bank 2012.
128 ibid.
129 ibid; Akhbar al-yom 2020.
130 Hamzawy 2013a.
131 ibid.

confidence in the political process steadily declined as politicians were perceived as people who made false promises and followed a fake agenda, despite the demands and crises of Upper Egypt being quite evident.[132]

Key literature exploring the 2011 Arab uprising emphasizes the role of Egyptian youth in the urban rebellion.[133] According to experts, this metanarrative was deliberately constructed with the aim of hiding the true protagonists behind the uprising.[134] There is significant evidence that the uprising was in fact a multi-generational rebellion which took place at the periphery. This theory is supported through the writings of American anthropologist, Jessica Winegar, who dictated her own experience as a demonstrator in Tahrir Square in January 2011:

> I saw countless older men and women, some quite old and in wheelchairs or with canes. They walked with their spouses, and/or children and in many cases grandchildren. Some of the mothers and grandmothers ululated, also, in Tahrir, Alexandria, Damanhur, Suez, and other cities, one can find prodemocracy demonstrators in their late 60s and 70s.[135]

This account disproves the assumption that emphasized presenting the 2011 Arab uprising as a Cairoian (Cairo-based) Intifada. There was a media bias for people who gathered in Tahrir Square, neglecting most of the population who were not in Squares, especially in Sa'idi cities.[136]

7 Abu-Qurqas Case Study

Analysis conducted of al-Fikriyya city and Munsha'iat Al-Fikriyya village provides a more balanced explanation for why the people of Upper Egypt did not join the 2011 Arab uprising on 25 January. These locations are a part of the 6,100 square kilometers which make up Abu-Qurqas city, locations almost 285 kilometers south of Cairo.

According to the Central Agency for Public Mobilization and Statistics (CAPMS) report (2016) this city consists around 48 villages, with more than half-million inhabitants (around 605,000). The village of Munsha'iat al-Fikriyya

---

132 ibid.
133 Alexandrani 2013; Winegar 2012.
134 Al-Aswany 2015.
135 Winegar 2011.
136 Abu-Lughod 2012: 21.

consisted of around 500–600 households, and around 3,000–3,500 of the 74,794 for the whole al-Fikriyya city.[137] As shown on Google Maps (see Maps 2.2 and 2.3), it is a semi-rural location, where sugarcane, beets, wheat, and corn farms surround the village, together with a semi-urban and industrial area because of the presence of the sugarcane industrial factory Al-Fawreyka[138] (established 1897) that employs 1500–2000 workers, almost 1 kilometer away from the city.

Apart from militant Islamic rebellions in late 1970 to the mid-1990s, the city of al-Fikriyya has had almost no manifestations of resistance or revolt (either everyday life resistance or organized resistance). Focusing on the role of Said peasants and examining the data presented by Brown, I counted that between 1882–1952 out of more than 110 communal actions, only 22 per cent (25 activities) took place in Sa'id's provinces. Most of these activities happened in Qina, and only 5 per cent (6 activities) took place in al-Minya. However, most of the clashes listed by Brown related to issues of land, crops, and disputes with local authorities (i.e., 'Umdah, Khufara') over violations and abusive behaviors, which do not constitute organized political resistance, to use Scott's term. The only known political actions during that time, though oddly not mentioned by Brown, were the attack on the British train in March 1919 at Dayr-Mawas city and other events that took place in al-Fikriyya city and nearby villages, Brown did however list the May 1926 attack by Ittihad's candidate on a rally organized by the Wafdist candidate. Five hundred residents from the village of Safay (3–5 kilometers south of al-Fikriyya), led by the 'Umda and guards of Safay, participated in attacking the rally and the house of the 'Umda of Al-Fikriyya. The police arrested over 100 from both sides.[139]

Several studies indicate that there are certain indicators which show that there was widespread support for the 25 January uprising among young people in Sa'id, which is undergoing a 'youth bulge', where more than half the population is under the age of 29, and one third are between the ages of 15 and 29.[140] The young Sa'idi (mostly men) established a series of local demonstrations and spontaneous, popular initiatives, such as efforts to protect the banks, stores, churches and clean the streets.[141] However, contrary to popular belief,

---

137 CAPMAS 2016.
138 This word finds its origin in the French word fabrique (factory) and has been modified into al-fawreyka. This village has been known for decades as ezbet al-fawreyka (the Fabrique's village) because of its geographical proximity to the factory.
139 Brown 1990:134–36.
140 The World Bank 2012.
141 ibid: 40–41; Abu-Lughod 2012.

there was no demonstrations inside the city of al-Fikriyya and the nearby villages, although the organized resistance and protest activities appeared after the fall of Mubarak.

When I asked the interviewees about what they thought the reasons for the lack of demonstrations in al-Fikriyya city and Munshaʿiat al-Fikriyya village were, one interviewee (Sayyidah) said, 'I do not know what revolution is. All I want is for my kids to find jobs instead of sitting at home or in coffee shops, I want them to get married and have families.' This statement supported by another interviewee's claim, about how getting married and establishing a family is considered one of the central roles of young people in Egyptian society, as well as a key challenge for young people and their families in Upper Egypt.[142]

A third participant (Mohamed) said, 'What revolution? We are struggling to survive, and the government treats us very badly. We must focus on survival, to get enough food and money to raise our kids.' Finally, interviewee Ragab added that for as-Saʿidiyya, 'To participate or not, this is not the question. Nothing has changed here since my childhood. Life is very hard and expensive now. We just want to be able to live and find a decent job that provides for food, things for the kids and for us. Since Nasser [Jamal Abdul-Nasser] no one cared about Saʿid or as-Saʿidiyya. Revolution or not, Upper Egypt will be the same, there is no justice, no equality, no fairness for the poor people that live here. We struggle more than anyone else in this country, and no one cares.' This statement reflects the argument that peasants' '[e]veryday forms of resistance make no headlines.'[143]

Interestingly, the mystification perception that as-Saʿidiyya are just sacks of potatoes and obedient has prevailed for more than a century (since the revolution of the 1840s) until it was interrupted during the Nasser era of the 1950s and 1960s. There is a romantic narrative alongside this perception, purported to be by the famous Saʿidi poet, Abd al-Rahman al-Abnoudi. According to this narrative, for centuries the Saʿidi people were buried in their trench until Nasser seized power. Then, the as-Saʿidiyya left their trenches to support him, despite his fatal faults. The reason this narrative has prevailed is because the people felt Nasser belonged to them, respected them, and treated them with dignity. This was in direct contrast to how the people were treated by the Mamlūks, Turkish and British authorities. Nasser's attitude and policies toward as-Saʿidiyya explain why many ordinary Saʿidi people kept his picture in their houses and

---

142 Abu-Lughod 2012: 22.
143 Scott 1985: xvii.

treated it like an icon of a saint. In other words, as-Saʿidiyya, like most impoverished regions, sympathized and supported the post-independence state (while still authoritarian in essence) for the following reasons: 1) President Gamal Abdel Nasser was of Saʿidi origin, and the people celebrated the head of the state as being 'one of them'; 2) significant social and agricultural transformations of Upper Egypt occurred, perhaps for the first time in the region's history; and lastly 3) the uprising provided opportunities for the people of Upper Egypt including education, civil governance, and a higher standard of living.

This nationalist statement is supported by Richard Adam's study, published in 1985, where he referenced an eyewitness account which remarked, 'You have come to study rural development, ya 'ustaz? Maybe then you should pick another village, there has been no development here.[144]' The interviewee's description of how unmotivated people were in protesting against the government was consistent with what Ghimire argued about a common theme of populations striving for survival by seeking access to sustainable labor markets in countries like Egypt, Brazil, and Nepal.

In Upper Egypt regions, the lack the support of a private sector and the poor quality of education and civic nepotism has led to high levels of unemployment.[145]

> Most of these young people are among those who constitute the bottom of the socio-economic ladder and find themselves confronting various forms of exploitation, violence and manipulation by individuals, groups and classes wielding political and economic power. Thus, young people need to deal with day-to-day as well as structured physical, political, and economic insecurity and exploitation, with the prime issue being how to negotiate secured access to vital means of production, wages and working conditions with their employers, and to consolidate the gains made.[146]

As part of my auto-ethnographic study, I asked one young woman (Souad) whether she had participated in the revolution or not. She said:

> I did not participate in the revolution, but I supported it from day one. Here, if you are a woman, you cannot go outside the village or the city without the company of or permission from your family, and if like me, you are a married woman, I cannot leave the house without my husband's

---

144   Ibid: 705.
145   The World Bank 2012.
146   Ghimire 2002: 31.

permission. As for me, I wanted to participate in the revolution because I studied history at the university and I hated Mubarak's regime, but again [remember] you are in Sa'id. Women are not independent, they are not allowed to take part in politics or public issues, away from their city or home. Some of my girlfriends from other cities and from the north participated in the revolution of 2011. Here the traditions and the family are very restricting, in their eyes, I should only care about my children and house, not politics or revolution.

This description highlights the many kinds of restrictions women face living under the conservative patriarchy of Upper Egypt society. This is reflected by the World Bank's statistic that in Sa'id, around 40 per cent of young women are jobless, including most uneducated young women.[147] According to Ghimire:

> Young women are even more discriminated against when it comes to access to education and inheritance of household economic resources, as well as in their ability to influence overall household decision-making processes.[148]

A contrasting perspective offered is that of the interviewee, Wasfa, who remarked, 'This [uprising] is a good thing because in the past many people were in jail unjustly, and now they are free.' Such a statement shows that the catalyst for the 2011 uprising was social injustice and poverty. Wasfa also added, 'The government was hurting our guys for many years during Mubarak's time and the police was very brutal. The revolution was good because he [Mubarak] is removed and is in prison now [2012] together with many other corrupt people. But we wish that the revolution made things cheaper. People here are very poor ya 'ustaz.'

From the pool of young men, I interviewed for this study, their opinions on the uprising were ambivalent. On the one hand, interviewee Asfour said, 'I think the revolution in general is a good thing. Mubarak and the ruling party members and the police were very bad, corrupt and stole everything. Most of the people here [in Upper Egypt] cannot find good opportunities for jobs and education, compared with Cairo or Alexandria. I hope things will change, but I am not optimistic.'

---

147 The World Bank 2012.
148 Ghimire 2002: 32.

In contrast, his friend Hassan said, 'The revolution was bad for me and for many of my friends, and I think for everyone here. I am a tourist guide, or I used to work like that until the revolution happened in January 2011. Since then, almost all my friends and myself (who are not only from Upper Egypt, but also from the North part he added) lost our jobs and we have become unemployed for almost two years since the revolution. The chaos and insecurity in the country damaged the tourism business in the whole country.'

These two accounts demonstrate that while the 2011 uprising is generally acknowledged as a positive transformation, several interviewees contest this perception. In fact, there was a lot of concern about the future among young people and those who work in the private sector and as 'um'al al-Yawmiya (temporary workers or day labor). It is worth mentioning here that tourism is a major source of income across Egypt, including the Upper Egypt regions of Aswan, Luxor, Aswan and al-Minya. According to the CAPMS data on tourism, about 14.7 million tourists visited Egypt in 2010, generating revenues of approximately US$12.5 billion. These numbers decreased considerably in 2011 to 9.8 million tourists and related revenue of $8.8 billion, before rising again in late 2012 to 11.5 million tourists and $9.9 billion. However, with the growing atmosphere of civil unrest following the 2013 military coup, political and social instability has significantly weakened Egypt's tourism sector in particular: tourist revenue for 2013 dropped to $5.9 billion, and again to $7.5 billion in 2014, before recording Egypt's lowest revenue in a decade, with $6 billion in 2015. Tourism revenue did not fully recover to 2011 levels until 2019, when it reached $12.6 billion.[149]

As demonstrated above, Egyptian tourism revenue from 2013–2019 suffered because of political and social unrest across the country. This was also reflected in revenue studies conducted in the al-Minya governorate (266 kilometers south of Cairo) and the Luxor governorate (656 kilometers south of Cairo) Both governorates relied mainly on tourism revenues to fund public initiatives, and when foreigners were evacuated from Egypt and many cancelled their trips, there were no tourists. This resulted in many people becoming unemployed.[150] However, contrary to Abu-Lughod, my ethnographic interviews showed that there was no evidence to support her argument that claimed, 'and it was not just what happened in Tahrir Square; in every village and every hamlet of every village was another square like Tahrir'. In contrast, in the first three days of the revolution (25 to 28 January 2011) before I left the

---

149 Al-Arabiya 2020; Akhbar al-yom 2016; Al-Assema'h Center for Economic Research and Studies 2019; Sky News 2013; Shawky 2011.
150 Abu-Lughod 2012: 24–25.

city to join the protests in Tahrir Square, I did not observe any signs of uprising. My interviews confirmed later that there were no protests until Mubarak resigned on 12 February 2011.

I asked my interviewees whether they knew anyone from their city or village who had participated in the revolution. Sayyidah said, 'One of my sons went to Tahrir Square in 2011', and when I asked her about her reaction to their decision she said, 'I was very worried. If I knew he was going to the square, I would have stopped him.' In a follow-up interview, Sayyidah told us that she 'was very proud of her son because he was one of the few people in the village that went to the maidan.' Likewise, interviewee Hassan said about the 2011 protest in Tahrir Square: 'I did not participate. We did not have any protests during the eighteen days of the revolution in the whole city, but I did participate in checkpoints improvised by self-organized civilians that guard our own people from thugs and thieves. I was not the only one that volunteered at checkpoints, almost everyone I know did.' This sentiment concurred with other attitudes of Upper Egyptians towards the revolution in different cities and villages in Sa'id, as Anna Roussillon's 2014 documentary *Je suis le peuple* (I am the People) demonstrated. The documentary follows the story of a Sa'idi family in a Luxor village from 2009/2010 to 2014 and documents the changing political attitudes as the events of the revolution and its aftermath are unfolding.[151] Such activities and actions were considered by academics as forms of participation in the 2011 uprising. Despite strong consensus in the literature, I disagree with these claims that such practices and behaviors represent a revolutionary momentum against the central authority.

Interviewee Hassan added that '[W]e also, me and number of my friends, created a Facebook page called Shabab Abu-Qurqas (the young people of Abu-Qorqas) which encouraged people to change, develop the city and not to tolerate corrupt officials and members of Mubarak's party al-hizb al-watani (National Democratic Party).' This kind of behavior coincides with the behavior of other young people in the Upper Egypt region after the removal of Mubarak in 2011, as Abu-Lughod noticed.

> People across Egypt seem to be using different languages for their activism as well. In al-Tayeb's village, the youth speak the moral language of responsibility, selfless- ness and community welfare, the struggle against corruption and self-interest. It is a strong language of social morality,

---

151 Roussillon 2014.

not of rights. They do not speak of democracy, but in tackling problems directly and personally, they are living it.[152]

Finally, I asked the interviewees whether they believe that the people of Upper Egypt will witness or participate in any future uprising and why. Mohamed, one of the interviewees, said, 'No, people in our village did not even protest demanding more jobs like everyone else did in this country. Only a few young people speak out and ask for change. Everyone knows here that only money can change things. I have seven sons and daughters, five of them are workers in Khaleeji countries (the Gulf), trying to make a living and support their families. Life here is very difficult and politics is not important for us.'

Abdo, the youngest interviewee, disagreed, saying, 'Yes, after Mubarak left, I know many of my friends went to Cairo and participated in the demonstrations on Fridays, especially the one organized by the Muslim Brotherhood and Islamic movements. Personally, I did not participate because my family did not let me go to the demonstration out of fear that I get arrested or killed by the police.' Abdo's response agreed with the findings of other studies. According to the World Bank, prior to 25 January 2011, young people in Upper Egypt were forcefully discouraged from civic engagement by a combination of parental opinion, state policies and harassment by security forces.[153]

Another interviewee, Asfour, stated, 'some people will participate of course. After 2011, some people in our city [truck drivers, peasants, and schoolteachers] start to organize themselves and protest unfair treatment by the police. Others demand work opportunities in the nearby sugarcane factory because this is their town and they [believe] they should have an advantage to be hired over strangers from other cities. These actions tried to change conditions of young people who cannot find a job here. It was unusual and had not happened before 2011. In the past no one dared to speak out or protest because the police would immediately throw them into jail for years, as it happened with al-jama'ah al-Islamiyyah when we were young [in the 1980s and 1990s], if you remember.'

Finally, another interviewee, Wasfa, said, 'Yes. After Mubarak leaves, we should change, and everyone looks for his [or her] rights. People need to change and be more active and positive.' She added, 'I am an old woman, but after the revolution I went to every election and take my daughters and my

---

152   Abu-Lughod 2012: 25.
153   The World Bank 2012.

grandsons with me to vote. Before 2011 I did not do that because I did not like Mubarak'.

8   Conclusion

This chapter has attempted to interrogate the proposition of why as-Sa'idiyya did not revolt during the 2011 Arab uprising. It explored the reasons behind why they did participate in protests after the fall of Mubarak in February 2011, when the people engaged in various forms of resistance to change the regime (*isqat al-nizam*). This chapter opposes the perceptions and propositions presented by several scholars relating to the role of Upper Egypt in the 2011 Arab uprising. While these accounts heavily insist that as-Sa'idiyya did revolt against Mubarak's regime, I indicated that the actions carried out by as-Sa'idiyya cannot be considered revolutionary. Rather, they should be interpreted as acts of civic engagement in Egypt's public arena. Despite scholarship suggesting that prolonged socio-economic crises trigger rebellions, Upper Egypt was not a significant player in the 2011 uprising. The reason for this is either the ruthless intimidation and repression of the region by the security apparatuses, or high reliance on public sector jobs and the lack of a private sector, as well as the poor quality of the education, nepotism, and corruption in the region.

My personal observations throughout this chapter were of strong feelings of bitterness among all participants, regardless of age, gender, educational background, and profession, directed at the Egyptian government. They told me this came from their experiences of poverty, marginalization, and excessive use of force by the central authority when putting down the uprising in the years following 2011. Likewise, I found that delayed economic and social development, including food and housing shortages, late marriage, and high unemployment, were the most frequent topics discussed during my interviews. This revealed to me the increasing pressure people face living in Upper Egypt and how concerned the population are with surviving in a region where there are high illiteracy, social disorganization, and dense population growth.

This chapter identified four main reasons for this behavior. Firstly, people feared security organizations, such as the police, and arrest. Secondly, there was a strong apathy toward regional and national political affairs. Thirdly, people were preoccupied with making a living in the face of a severe decline in household income. Lastly, there was a strong distrust of central authorities which paralyzed the region from taking any real action to alleviate their marginalization and oppression. Most importantly, the study found that the behavior of the police and security apparatuses in particular toward local communities had a significant impact on the socio-political attitudes of the population towards the regime or the state's institutions. A comparative analysis of other Saʿidi societies, such as Qina, Luxor and Aswan, found that the experiences of Saʿidi cities and villages with police intimidation were distinct from the experience of other areas, such as al-Minya and Assiut. The latter (besides Sohag) were the lowest three Saʿidi governorates which participated in the revolution among the eight governorates of Saʿid. Both al-Minya and Assiut have a vicious history of state brutality going back to the 1970s, which created an atmosphere of fear in these regions. I did, however, find that there were no genuine antirevolutionary sentiments among the Saʿidi people, as many academic studies tried to construct and downplay the role of as-Saʿidiyya during the 2011 uprising.[154] Further research should be done into the relationship between state violence, the central authority, and social mobilization to determine which socio-political and socio-economic structures, modes and conditions could accelerate or restrain social change and the transformation of marginalized communities such as Upper Egypt.

Overall, I emphasize the importance of economic and security analysis in determining the behavior of peasant societies. However, despite evidence of relative deprivation in the city and the village, the interviews contradict similar academic literature which reluctantly links poverty and deprivation to the 2011 Arab uprising. Surprisingly, I claim that – based on ethnography and fieldwork interviews – poverty was not the (only) instigator in people joining the uprising. Moreover, the proliferation of information and communications technology (ICT) (such as computers, laptops, smartphones) has had a crucial impact on the level of political awareness and participation in the region. Access to al-Wasla and purchase of low-price satellite dishes and other technologies were made possible by the flow of financial transfers and remittances of Egyptian workers in the Khaleeji countries.[155] During the four-year period of this study, there were about 5 major political events which took place in Egypt, including presidential and parliamentary elections and constitutional referendums. Of note was that my interviewees spoke about these events in an enthusiastic and vigorous way and did not appear to be shy about which candidates they supported. Before 2011, such visible support of the Muslim Brotherhood was unusual behavior.

The removal of constraints that prevented the people of Upper Egypt from rebelling could facilitate social and political mobilization in Saʿid. Expectedly,

---

154 El-Nour 2015; Bush 2002; Ayeb and Bush 2019.
155 Abu-Lughod 2007.

when repressive police and security forces, the deep state's institutions and other constraints temporarily disappeared following the fall of Mubarak, the people of Upper Egypt felt encouraged to engage in the revolutionary momentum. For instance, in the first free election after the revolution, Upper Egypt was the biggest supporter of President Morsi (the first civil-elected president) who, at that time, was associated with the revolution camp and opposed the candidate of counterrevolution Ahmed Shafiq. The level of participation in the election in Sa'id (and in most of Egypt in general) was unprecedented.

After 2013, when the army re-seized the power through a popular-backed coup, the old constraints were re-established in an even more brutal form. The new military regime started to repress the Sa'id once again, this time for the region's support of the Muslim Brotherhood candidate, as well as for the daring attempt to challenge what is known as the deep state or the police state. In return, in September 2013, a group of Sa'idi activists from Aswan initiated a campaign against systematic marginalization of the Sa'id. The campaign called la le-tahmeesh al-Sa'id (no more marginalization of Sa'id) (see Photo 2.8) objected to the absence of representatives from Upper Egypt in the so-called lajnat al-khamseen (the fifty's committee) that was appointed to rewrite the constitution.[156] The activists encouraged as-Sa'idiyya to sign a petition (see Photo 2.9) addressed to the members of the committee and requesting the end of the marginalization of Upper Egypt and negligence of its demands (Ahmed and Malik 2013). Sadly, as expected, the campaign did not have the desired impact.

Unfortunately, the vibrant revival was quickly repressed. After 2014, when the army re-seized power through a popular-backed coup, the old contenders reclaimed power and even became vastly more robust and repressive than before. The new regime seems to believe that Upper Egypt is the 'stronghold' of the Muslim Brotherhood and deals with it based on that false perception. The resurgence 'defeated' security and police apparatuses started to repress the Sa'id once again for its support for the Muslim Brotherhood presidential candidate, as it did with the Islamists and Salafists candidates which guaranteed and secured their majority in the 2011–2012 parliamentary election, where the Muslim Brotherhood and Salafists swept and dominated more than 80 per cent of the seats (356 of 498 seats) in the first free elections held after the revolution.[157] The new regimes punished Sa'id for daring to challenge the so-called

---

[156] Ali 2013a, 2013b.
[157] France24 2012.

PHOTO 2.8　The slogan of the 'No more marginalization of Saʿid' campaign
SOURCE: HTTPS://WWW.FACEBOOK.COM/LA.TAHMESH.ELSAED/ (POSTED ON 9 SEPTEMBER 2020)

'deep state' or 'police state' that despised and repressed as-Saʿidiyya for centuries, and still humiliates them.

Moreover, scholars should be aware of misrepresenting the Upper Egypt region as a single bloc or unified entity. However, this suggestion does not negate the existence of commonalities between parts of the said region. These include shared customs, geographical proximity, and continuity of governance as well as a dependence on agricultural lifestyles. These commonalities were demonstrated by Saker El-Nour who argued that the so-called tenancy law of 1992 unified the Egyptian peasants (al-fellaheen and as-Saʿidiyya alike) in protesting the law which was designed to disenfranchise them from their farms.[158]

158　Daily News Egypt 2020.

Likewise, interestingly the releasing of law no. 1 of 2020, known as the Construction Violations Reconciliation Law represents strong evidence of such claims. This example demonstrates Sa'id's ability to act as a unified bloc to a large extent as well as the significance of shared agricultural lands in everyday as-Sa'idiyya life. Finally, the people show through their protests that they are willing to challenge authority to retain control of their land.

For instance, while this chapter was under review, despite the state of emergency caused by the COVID-19 pandemic, protests spread across Upper Egypt for the first time since 2011, in reaction to the Construction Violations Reconciliation Law. In October 2020, inside the city of al-Awamiyah, Luxor, residents of the city clashed with security forces after a resident was assaulted during the arrest of his brother who was protesting the law. The man (his name is Aweys al-Rawi) was killed by the police forces. The police then started shooting and setting off bombs which resulted in residents attacking the police in retaliation. A fortnight after al-Rawi's death, the city of al-Awamiyah witnessed demonstrations against police brutality, the land law, and general standard of living. Several cities and villages in Sa'id witnessed a similar protest. The confrontations between the police and residents became nationally focused following online content of the protests. Furthermore, there was a strong solidarity between social media platforms and protestors, to the extent that some activists started a Twitter hashtag (#George_Floyd_of_Egypt) comparing (despite the different historical and sociopolitical context) the treatment of

السادة أعضاء لجنة الخمسين،

نظراً للإهمال الذي عاني منه الصعيد طوال الحقب السابقة، وغياب خطط تنمية عادلة عنه على مدار عقود كاملة، وما أدى له ذلك من تراجع لدور الصعيد وقيمته، وما تسبب فيه ذلك من معاناة للصعيد ولمصر كلها، نطالب بوضع نصوص دستورية صريحة تلزم الدولة بالعمل على تنمية وتطوير الصعيد وتخصيص نسب عادلة له في خطط التنمية.

	المحافظة/المركز		الإسم الرباعي
	التليفون (إن وجد)		الرقم القومي

التوقيع: ....

حملة لا تهميش الصعيد

شارك في وضع مادة في الدستور لتنمية الصعيد؛ شارك في تحسين مستقبل أبناءك

NO REVOLUTION: WHY AS-ṢAʿĪDIYYA DID NOT REALLY REVOLT

بيان من حملة لا لتهميش الصعيد

بخصوص مؤتمر مصر المستقبل لدعم الاقتصاد المصري

يعقد في الفترة من ١٣ إلي ١٥ مارس من العام الجاري المؤتمر الدولي لدعم الاقتصاد المصري و كالعادة يأتي مكان انعقاد المؤتمر بمدينة شرم الشيخ ، و ليس بأي محافظة أو مدينة بصعيد مصر كما هو الحال في كل الفاعليات الدولية بل و الوطنية مع كون الصعيد الأولي بالأمر لما يعانية من ضعف الأوضاع الأقتصادية و المعيشية به

و لكن مع ذلك نطالب القائمين علي المؤتمر النظر بعين الاعتبار لصعيد مصر لرفع ما يقع علية من ظلم و تهميش متواصل ، مع توافر كافة الأمكانات التي تجعل الصعيد منطقة واعدة و قابلة لأحتضان أغلب المشاريع التنموية و الأستثمارية من أيدي عاملة و مساحات متوفرة لإنشاء المصانع و المشاريع بكافة أشكالها شريطة أن تتواجد أرادة سياسية حقيقية لتذليل العقبات التي تواجة فرص الأستثمار بصعيد مصر و نطالب بمحور خاص بتنمية الصعيد في المؤتمر يوضح فرص الاستثمار وخططها و ان نذكر بمحور الباز في الصحراء الغربية وخط سكة حديدية جديد موازي و خطوط عرضيه من شرق الي غرب البلاد وعكسها . هذا و علينا إن نحرص علي أن لا يكون الوضع كالسابق حيث ان الصعيد يتواجد به رسميا أكثر من ٣٥ منطقة و مدينة صناعية من الفيوم حتي أسوان لا تتعدي نسبة التشغيل الفعلي بها ال ٢٠٪ حيث أن معظم تلك المناطق و المدن الصناعية شبة مهجورة و تفتقر لأغلب الأساسيات المطلوبة لأتمام تشغيلها .

وأننا اذ نطالب بذلك فطبقا للمادة المادة رقم (٢٣٦) من الدستور المصري المقر باستفتاء عام ٢٠١٤ التي نصت علي : « **تكفل الدولة وضع وتنفيذ خطة للتنمية الاقتصادية، والعمرانية الشاملة للمناطق الحدودية والمحرومة، ومنها الصعيد وسيناء، ومطروح ومناطق النوبة، وذلك بمشاركة أهلها فى مشروعات التنمية وفى أولوية الاستفادة منها، مع مراعاة الأنماط الثقافية والبيئية للمجتمع المحلي، خلال عشر سنوات من تاريخ العمل بهذا الدستور، وذلك على النحو الذى ينظمه القانون. وتعمل الدولة على وضع وتنفيذ مشروعات تعيد سكان النوبة إلي مناطقهم الأصلية وتنميتها خلال عشر سنوات، وذلك على النحو الذى ينظمه القانون**

نوجة الحكومة المصرية و القائمين علي المؤتمر بوضع الصعيد نصب أعينهم في أولويات التنمية و إيجاد نصيب عادل و حقيقي له في المكاسب العائدة علي الأقتصاد المصري كنتاج لهذا المؤتمر لما يستحق الصعيد من رفع حالته و مواجهة تهميشة المتوالي و نحن اذ نطالب الحكومة بعدم أغفال الصعيد واستمرار تهميشه في مؤتمر التنمية فأننا نعرض عقد لقاء مفتوح مع رئيس الوزراء او من ينوب عنه بأعضاء الحملة من مختلف محافظات الصعيد لمناقشة رؤيتنا وتصورنا لسد الفجوة في التنمية والية مشاركة اهل الصعيد وانحسار تهميش طال لعقود كثيرة ولازلنا نذكر بما نبهنا به من قبل ان استمرار هذا التعامل مع هذا الجزء من الوطن سيكون أحد العوامل السلبية لأي تصور لتنمية شاملة للوطن او لجعله في الصفوف الأمامية نتمني أن يمثل لنا هذا المؤتمر بارقة أمل للصعيد و أهلة . و أن يكون نواة و بداية لتنمية حقيقية تكون خطوة في سبيل إلغاء تهميش الصعيد

حملة لا لتهميش الصعيد

PHOTO 2.9 A copy of the petition addressed to the members of the Fifty's Committee to end the marginalization against as-Saʿidiyya
SOURCE: HTTPS://WWW.FACEBOOK.COM/LA.TAHMESH.ELSAED/PHOTOS/A.545536235499982/555164794537126/?TYPE=3&THEATER (POSTED ON 3 OCTOBER 2020)

men like al-Rawi to the murder of George Floyd, whose murder on the hands of the police was a catalyst for the Black Lives Matter movement.[159]

During my return trips to Egypt following 2015 I noticed that the common behaviors of anger and frustration continued to grow. For example, I noticed a clear change in the language used by interviewees to express their anger at economic and political conditions. The inclination to use s'ab al-deen (sinful cursing by using forbidden religious words) became increasingly common among lower socio-economic groups of men to express their anger at the state of local unemployment, poverty, and rising inflation. This kind of irreverence for the Egyptian central authority was unusual both before the 2011 revolution and after.

This chapter argues that it would be useful for future studies to explore more comparable interviews on the themes of protest and social mobilization in the Sa'id region. By trying to interview groups with different variables, such as age, gender, class, and religion, it would be possible to investigate how these identities affect regional political attitudes. Moreover, future studies which draw upon this chapter's findings would allow me to focus my future enquiries on the topics raised in the interviews with the aim of drawing a comparison between results across other Sa'idi cities and villages.[160] Moreover, I am intending to strengthen my knowledge of Sa'idi society, and investigating the genesis of the identity construction process, state-society relations, and the role of social and power structures. In addition, exploring the dialectic relationships (from below) between the Authority (i.e., security, police, military, and other disciplinary apparatuses) and the citizens, penetration of the society by these apparatuses, and the role of ideological, discursive, and pedagogical techniques and apparatus, in Antonio Gramsci's words, that exists in symbiosis with the oppressive apparatus of the state.[161] Also, I aim to expand my understanding and to pave the way for these isolated, peripheral societies, to reveal what is hidden and unsaid about political behavior in modern Egypt in the light of the fact that focus and concerns about these kinds of societies is still insignificant. Further investigation into dialectic relationships between the state and citizens is needed to understand the articulation between these concepts and show the methods of displacement evident in Sa'id and other local communities.

---

159 Egypt Watch 2020; Matta 2020; Italian News 2020.
160 Abu-Lughod 2012.
161 Gramsci 1957: 80–83; Buci-Glucksmann 1980: 357–61.

Furthermore, academics working to understand social marginalization in the Middle East should be aware of any western-centric unconscious bias within their research. This chapter's focus of Upper Egypt's social, economic, and political relationship with power demonstrates how such societies are not represented in mainstream academia. Despite being inhabited by more than thirty different ethnic, communal, and religious groups (such as al-jmaseh, al-Halab, al-Bajah, and other invisible communities), Upper Egypt, and other subaltern communities, are an under-represented area of study. Academics must acknowledge the presence of subaltern communities within the meta narrative and strive to fairly represent them in future literature.

In fact, the problem is not only representation or recognition but also getting rid of the clichés that characterize area studies. For instance, these fields suffer from several deficiencies such as the tendencies toward unification, distortion, and acquisition of small communities and forcible annexation of them under colonial, hegemonic, and politically loaded frames. While these regions include varied ethnicities, religions, nationals, races, groups, nations, these imposed (from above) academic, research, and political-charged frameworks tend to integrate and homogenize these different communities under one illusory and imaginary umbrella based on shared religious, national, languages.[162] Likewise, these frameworks are genuinely ignoring the fundamental differences not only between de-homogenized states and societies but also within a singular country (such as Upper Egypt and Nubia in Egypt, and Kurds, Yazidis, Assyrian, Turkmen, and Chaldean–Syriac communities in Iraq among other examples).

Interestingly, such tendencies are not exclusive or limited to Middle Eastern studies; it affects other areas studies of the Global South such as Eastern Europe, which are studied as a part of the so-called Slavic, East European, and Eurasian Studies, Latin America, which is traditionally studied as a part of Spanish or Portuguese studies. Under this framework, Latin American societies, the Caribbean, and other societies are treated mainly as a part of 'colonial' Spanish culture. Overall, these contested 'macro' frameworks are too broad,

---

162 Most of academic and research programs and frameworks in the West and elsewhere imprecisely unit regions such as the Middle East, Central Asia, Caucasus, North Africa, and other culturally and ethnically distinct communities under one umbrella called the Greater Middle East that extend from the boundaries of India in the East to the Atlantic beaches in the West. Likewise, other programs that encompass distinct societies and diverse cultures under anomaly frameworks such as Oriental Studies or Oriental and African Studies.

ambiguous, and problematic, in which local (micro) communities, native, and indigenous communities are lost and have been coercively integrated and unified. This causes several tensions, ruptures, and systematic epistemic and moral contestation. These epistemic impositions need to be seriously and openly addressed, encountered, and remediated.

CHAPTER 3

Incomplete Revolution

The Determinations of Post-revolution Egyptian Foreign Policy

1 Introduction

One may wonder the reason behind the interest in studying revolution. Overall, there are two answers to this question. From the theoretical point of view, revolutions are important to clarify how the transformations that taking place within states and their institutions can have an influence on the international arena, especially the neighboring states. Likewise, the study of revolutions explores the impact of organizational factors and the changing external behavior of institutions as a result of changes within states' foreign political policies. On a practical level, studying the effects of revolution and its evolution gives a better understanding of the orientations of decision-makers inside states (revolutionary and non-revolutionary alike) that seek better ways and adequate policies to deal with these new revolutionary conditions, and to preserve their security and stability from threats and dangers to which they are confronted because of the sudden and radical changes.

This chapter aims at revealing the effect of some aspects of internal changes such as a revolution that takes place within the social and local political structure affecting its policy towards different international institutions on the international level. The focal point of the chapter is to engage with the theoretical debate on that the foreign policies of any country are nothing but a reflection of the current transformations within the local political situation (e.g., the nature of the political system, the quality of the ruling elite, party system, role of the public opinion, political ideology, political culture, and political participation, etc.). In other words, any quantitative or qualitative changes affecting the nature of the local system are accompanied by changes related to the nature of the foreign policy. In addition, the chapter examines the transformations caused by revolutions on neighboring countries' attitudes especially when it related to war and peace. The author noticed that there is a sort of consensus among both scholars and politicians about the interlink between the eruption of revolutions and the increasing tendencies of involving in wars and armed conflicts between revolutionary countries and their neighbors. To investigate that, the chapter compares the pre-revolution situations and attitudes with the post-revolution ones and assessing the revolution impacts on these conditions that affect the orientations and tendencies of the domestic system and on regional order in general.

The main argument of this chapter claiming that transformations at a unit-level (i.e., state, and political system) that occur because of revolution and regime change, etc., will have a crucial impact on both foreign policy and regional and international interactions. The extent of positioning and influence of these domestic transformations depend on revolutionary states' geopolitical position in the regional environment on the one hand, and its centrality and significance for regional coalitions and global balance of power considerations on the other hand.

In detail, this chapter critically engages the continuous debate between the three dominant schools of thought in International Relations (i.e., Realism, Liberalism, and Constructivism) regarding revolutions, radical changes, and their impacts on both international and regional orders, with special emphasis on revolutions that take place within middle and small powers from the Global South such as Egypt. In particular, and by mainly engages with Stephen Walt's *Revolution and War*, this chapter emphasizes the constitutive role of domestic transformations and the role it plays in shaping and (re)shaping the relations between nation-states both at times of peace and war. On the other hand, the chapter analyses the impact of a unit-level variable such as revolutions, on system-level variables, i.e., on the structure of foreign policies and interactions on both regional and international orders.

2 Theories of International Relations and Revolution

This section critically engages with the continuous debate between the three dominant schools of thought in International Relations (i.e., Realism, Liberalism, and Constructivism) regarding revolutions and their impacts on both international and regional orders, with special emphasis on those that take place within middle and small powers from the Global South. In particular, this chapter emphasizes the constitutive role of domestic transformations and the role it plays in shaping and (re)shaping the relations between nation-states both in times of peace and war. On the other hand, the chapter analyses the impact of a unit-level variable such as revolutions, on system-level variables, i.e., on the structure of foreign policies and interactions on both regional and international orders. Finally, in light of prior theoretical debate, the chapter presents a comprehensive analytical framework to understand Egypt's volatile foreign policy in the post-revolution period based on the so-called Realist Constructivism.

3 Revolution and Foreign Policy

Despite their importance, revolutions are an understudied area of International Relations, particularly regarding their influence on foreign policy.[1] Limited research into the connection between foreign policy and revolution in nation states signifies a noteworthy gap in IR literature in this area.[2] One reason for this gap stems from a lack of big contemporary revolutions to study.

Stephen Walt argues that revolution constitutes a threat to regional powers because of their ability to mobiles the masses and change political regimes. Either through the possibility of revolution expansion beyond its national territories, or due to the weakness of the new revolutionary regimes which often lead to regional instability or the eruption of wars. This phenomenon of revolutionary countries leads to increased power and capabilities outside their borders as well as threatened neighboring countries seeking to limit their expansionist actions by engaging in war with them.[3] In fact, while most unites are keen to preserve the status-quo, revolutionary countries are revisionists which means they seek to challenge status-quo conditions by redistributing state capabilities to tilt the balance of power in their favor. Due to their revisionist nature, revolutionary states tend to inspire suspicion of most units.

The fear revolution inspires emerges from the fact that revolutions aim to recruit supporters and sympathizers by claiming the following: (1) that they can change the old regime and replace it with a new one constructed on new ideas and values; (2) that the revolutionary regime will promote the interests and aspiration of the majority, not the few; and (3) that the likelihood of achieving regime change is high.[4] These claims lead revolutionary regimes to export their principles and ideologies and assert that their values have a global reach (universal) and can be applied over all societies. For instance, some revolutionary extremists (as Bolsheviks or Islamists) occasionally refute the idea of sovereign nation-state itself–as the essence of the modern international system–and call for abolishing the state-system and to establish a global revolutionary society based on these trans regional ideologies.[5]

Unlike Walt, Kenneth Waltz argues that the constraints and pressures imposed by the system limits the behavior of revolutionary countries. Waltz

---

1 Maoz 1996; Goldstone 2008; Goldstone and Opp 1993 Goldstone, Gurr and Moshiri 1991; Walt 1997.
2 Walt 1992:321–322.
3 ibid, p. 335.
4 ibid, p. 336.
5 ibid, p. 339.

claimed that even revisionist states seek to socialize[6] with the world order in the hope that external pressures will force them to adopt calculated policies in order to protect the security and the stability of the revolutionary regime and state against threats and challenges posed by global and regional environments. Many of the problems that revolutionary regimes encounter stem from a lack of trust in the intention, capabilities, and probabilities of expansion of the revolutionary ideology.[7] By showing their good intentions, the relationship between revolutionary and non-revolutionary states becomes "business as usual", where every actor can develop and regulate its policies.[8] According to Walt, despite their rejection of traditional goals of the state and questioning the legitimacy of the old regime, revolutionary regimes still tend to dominate the state apparatuses. By succeed in doing so, they become a part of the Geopolitical arena and accordingly will be subject to the constraints, pressures, and opportunities imposed on them, like the structural theory like neorealism predicted.[9]

The ability of a revolutionary state to resist external international norms is measured by its success in delivering domestic objectives during the transfer of power. In other words, realists claimed that if the transfer of power is smooth, key revolutionary ideology will be established and disseminated internationally. According to this logic, revolutionary leaders concentrate on political ideology which make them more aware of the obstacles and flaws of their revolutionary ideology. Hence, they will behave in a controlled manner, the same way other countries behave.[10] Meaning, if there is a struggle for power, instead of emphasizing on political ideology, revolutionary regimes should seek to gaining more military support and sowing favors to boost mass domestic loyalty of the revolution's ideology in the first place.

Studies show that there is a strong link between the way revolutionary changes occur and the tendency for such regimes to become involved in armed conflicts with other states or avoid it. If revolutions are peaceful, studies show revolutionary regimes tended to adopt non-hostile foreign policies. Conversely, revolutions achieved through violence tend to adopt aggressive foreign policies and are more likely to engage in armed conflict with other actors.[11]

---

6 By state socialization, I am referring to the process by which revolutionary regimes provide and exchange information in response to each other's actions.
7 Waltz 1979: 127–28.
8 ibid, p. 197; Walt 1992: 361.
9 Walt 1992: 332.
10 ibid, p. 339.
11 Maoz and Abdolali 1989.

TABLE 3.1   Wars and revolution (1789–1979)

Revolution	Post-revolutionary war
France (1789)	Austria-Hungary, Prussia Spain, England (1792–93)
Mexico (1910)	[U.S. intervention (1916)]
	Allied intervention (1919)
Russia (1917)	Poland (1920)
Turkey (1919)	Greece (1920)
	Korean War (1950)
China (1949)	Tibet (1950)
Cuba (1959)	Bay of Pigs invasion (1961)
Ethiopia (1974)	Somalia (1978)
Cambodia/Kampuchea (1975)	Vietnamese invasion (1979)
Iran (1978)	Iraq (1980)
Nicaragua (1979)	United States (1981)

SOURCE: WALT 1992: 325

There is overwhelming consensus among scholars that revolutions are linked with instability. Yet, most of these studies are unclear about the actors that initiate these disturbances, its trajectories, interests, or whom it targeting?

In his study on the link between regime types and international conflict, Zeev Maoz concluded that states that go through revolutionary experiences (which he defined as changing the regime by using force) are more inclined to engage in wars following the revolution. Historical record of international conflicts shows that, from the French Revolution of 1789 to the Revolution in Nicaragua in 1979, eight out of every 10 wars fought have occurred between revolutionary countries and their neighbors within the first five years of the occurrence of the revolutions (see Table 3.1).

This confirms the dominant claim that revolutions make wars. The same conclusion can be applied to countries who go through political regime change.[12] Indeed, on a domestic level, revolutions often have dire internal repercussions and present a great risk to opposition social forces. Under the chaotic conditions following the fall of the old regime, many citizens and

---

12   Maoz 1989.

public institutions come under imminent threat from the new regime. Until the new regime consolidates its power, domestic struggles are often settled violently by means of a zero-sum equation, where the winner takes all.[13] A limitation in Maoz's argument, however, is that he doesn't explain how regime change is directly linked to war. Likewise, the role of revolutionary states in these wars is still ambiguous.[14]

Revolutionary ideologies are mostly based on criticizing the status-quo and aimed at finding better alternatives for those in power. In short, these ideologies are the catalyst to empowering resistance groups to act to change the corrupted regime and reassert the efforts of redistributing power and wealth within society. To achieve these outcomes, revolutionary ideologies lean on three main pillars: the old regime is evil, the old regime is impeding reforms, the notion that the triumph of the revolution is inevitable, and lastly, the revolution has global impact.[15] The manifestations of this ideological shift are reflected in the revolutionary states' foreign policy towards their neighbors and other great powers, achieved by alerting the relationship between states in different directions. Most of the time, revolutionary regimes increase aggressive perceptions and mutual suspicions and mistrust. Rarely does it improve and expand the level of rapprochement and cooperation among states.

Overall, according to Stephen Walt, the impact and exacerbation of the revolution on interstates relation can be determined in four variables: overestimating the sense of danger, underestimating other states sense of vulnerability, the pernicious influence of exiles, the loss of expertise that accompanies a revolution.[16]

Overestimating the sense of danger: Revolutionary regimes tend to exaggerate the sense of threat imposed by other states. This tendency emerges from the difficulty of measuring state's capabilities in the post-revolution periods which could encourage both sides to maximize and inflate their military capabilities. More importantly, the perception of vulnerability and fragility increases the fear that revolutions will spread beyond their national borders or will easily yield to the pressures imposed by counterrevolutionary forces. Mainly, for political and military reasons, revolutions are more prone to maximize the mutual feeling of danger on the one hand, and windows of opportunity to get rid of these threats and menace on the other hand. Either way,

---

13 Walt 1992: 334.
14 ibid, p. 333.
15 ibid, p. 337.
16 ibid.

the sense of insecurity increases the tension and make the possibility of war higher than before.[17]

Underestimating other states sense of vulnerability: Apart from difficulties of restructuring post-revolution society, revolutionary regimes continuously face serious domestic opposition which threatens their existence in a way that makes these regimes very sensitive and often exaggerating in responding to threats. Despite this sense of vulnerability, revolutionary regimes tend to portray themselves and act as if 'everything is under control'. To encounter their rivals, revolutionary regimes overestimate their power to defeat domestic counterrevolutionary forces and stop foreign interventions.[18] Likewise, neighboring countries fear the devastating repercussions of deteriorating conditions of revolutionary states countries. The fears of the proliferation of chaos, instability, and spill-over could contagion other countries to an extent of increase the tension between the neighbors, especially if these threats jeopardize domestic and regional stability. Threats such as terrorist groups, the possession of sophisticated arms, adopting aggressive ideology, etc., can cause mass forcible displacement to other states' borders. In globalized world, eventually, these developments add to the burdens on neighboring governments which also threaten their security and increase mutual tension and suspicions.

The pernicious influence of exiles: Revolutions usually force a considerable portion of the population, who does not share their ideology and values, to flee out. In return, under the fear of seeking to re-seize and eager to return to power, those who support the old regime and intimidated by the revolution tend to settle in countries which sympathize with their cause and preoccupations, and eager to assist those exiles and opposition orchestrating a counter-revolution to achieve these goals, exiled groups seek to tarnish the image of the revolutionary regime by demonize it. This strategy operates in collaboration with both domestic and external supporters in the media, decision-making institutions, and other state apparatuses that shape public opinion.[19] In return, revolutionary regimes see these activities and strategies as being provocatively hostile which requires, in return, a harsh response to regimes that host those opponents.

The loss of expertise that accompanies a revolution: The lack of a skilled and intelligent revolutionary elite that can run the country's affairs successfully, is an inevitable result of the systematic exclusion of the intellectual and political

---

17   ibid, p. 348.
18   ibid, p. 345.
19   ibid, p. 346.

elite who used to work or have a close links with the old regime and revolution's potential rivals.[20] Revolutions tend to perceive the old elite as a "fifth column" that must be ousted. This is a double-edged sword, however, where the revolutionary regime will lose experts and leaders who had a connection with the old regime. Likewise, when radical, extremist, and stubborn revolutionary leaders have access to power, they allow their dogmatic and hostile ideological ideas to have a crucial role in constructing and agenda setting and policymaking. Consequently, those hardline politicians and experts create more crisis and tension with other regional and international partners more than helping the revolutionary regime to either socialize and adapting to international order, or successfully and efficiently running the country.[21]

4 The Determinations of Egyptian Foreign Policy after the Arab Uprisings

In case the revolution failed, no one cannot deny the power of both realism and neorealism explanations in defining the future trends and orientations of the post-revolution foreign policy. In fact, most of the challenges previously discussed were security-based which dominate the process of foreign policy decision-making. These challenges include: (1) revolution which increases the risk of war as it exaggerates the of sense of threats between revolutionary states and their rivals; (2) revolution encourages all parties to believe that the use of military force as a way to confront these threats is easy; (3) revolution increases the probabilities of miscalculation which therefore slipping into wars; (4) revolution magnifies the level of threat posed by others; (5) revolution increases the reciprocal sense of vulnerability which pushes states toward balancing against the source of danger or bandwagon together to minimize the level of danger and threat (see Figure 3.1).

The developments that took place in Egypt and the Middle East after 2013 urge us to claim that these fears are likely to grow because of the factors detailed below.

---

20   ibid, p. 347.
21   The example of Mustafa El-Feki's candidacy to be the General-Secretary of the Arab League after the Arab Uprisings is a good manifestation of such claim. After 2011 revolution, the so-called Egyptian revolutionary government nominated El-Feki for this sensitive position after the step-down of Amr Moussa. The Egyptian request was refused by several Arabian Gulf States because of El-Feki's hostile attitudes and opinion about them. This refusal led to a short crisis in Egypt-GCC relations shortly after the revolution of 2011.

INCOMPLETE REVOLUTION 121

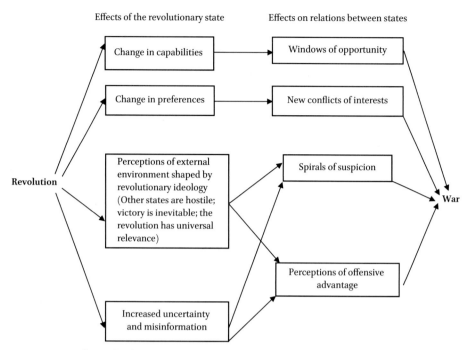

FIGURE 3.1　Relationship between revolution and war according to Walt
SOURCE: WALT 1997: 44

4.1   *The Nature of the Revolution*

The predominant conception of revolution looks almost exclusively through the lens of violent change of the political regime or by causing radical change in the structure of the society through violent means. However, other revolutions did not depend on violence to make this change. For instance, the Egyptian revolution of 2011 was a peaceful protest which succeeded in removing the old, corrupted regime in eighteen days, and sought to construct a new system, without relying on mass violence between the revolutionaries and other social forces.

Such essential differences between the Arab Uprisings revolution and traditional revolutions make it difficult to predict the developments that take place at the domestic level. For instance, while such developments could lead countries like Tunisia and Egypt to present an unprecedented model of revolutionary transformation if they succeed in escaping the tendency for revenge on remaining former regime figures. In return, if the revolutions failed to peacefully transit power and establish a democratic system or replaced the regime with a counterrevolution or a coup d'état, as what happened in Egypt in 2013, the future tendencies (domestically and externally) of revolutionary actions will be consonant with realist predictions. In which violence, aggression, and repression control the behavior of the counterrevolutionary regimes toward their adversaries, at home and abroad alike.

Revolutionary elites: Most of the revolutions throughout modern history had clear leadership determine their ideas, principles, and sacrifices for the sake of unique moments, have contributed to mobilize the people and incite them to rebel against authoritarian regimes. These elites have a philosophy regarding both the necessity of dismantling the old regime and replacing it with a better regime that is based on revolutionary ideology and ethical principles. The revolutionary leadership claims that the status quo regime is the worst, and its fall is imminent, the victory of the revolutionaries is inevitable, and that the revolutionary leaders have better future for most of the people, although the historical record shows that after seizing power and control, revolutionary leadership tend to take the completely opposite directions than originally planned. Having said that, the Arab Uprising revolutions were without leadership (yet were planned) which means there was no hierarchical leadership structure. These revolutions were in essence a "people's revolution". The new generation of well-educated, Arab youth (with modern and innovation narratives, techniques, style, and ideas) was the one that ignited the people's revolution without leadership or guidance, ideology, or theorizing. The Arab Uprisings were primarily (and even naively) sought towards freedom, regardless the nature of the regime (Islamic or liberal) which will replace the despotic regime that has been overthrown.

Such leaderless revolutions caused wide ambiguity and indecision among scholars of Middle East and IR as well. These scholars did not know who are the leaders they are talking about? What are their ideas, principles, and ideologies that enable them to understand the nature of the transformations taking place across the region, and therefore predict the future orientations of decision makers of the new revolutionary regimes? In fact, cynically, most of the scholars were unable to differentiate between the media figures and the real forces on the ground, or the legitimate voice of the revolution. All these questions remained without an answer, which in turn led to equivocation, inconsistency, and overall uncertainty that characterized the foreign policy of the US, EU, and the rest of great powers towards the Arab revolutions. However, with the success of orchestrated counterrevolutions and coup d'états in countries like Egypt, Libya, Yemen, Sudan, and the persistence of the old regimes in Syria, Algeria, Bahrain, etc., realists and neorealists presented exceedingly efficient explanations than other theoretical propositions.

4.2   Regional and International Changes

As mentioned earlier, regional challenges and threats are usually considered the biggest obstacles facing revolutions. The milieu that surrounded the French Revolution in 1789, the Bolshevik Revolution in 1917, the Egyptian Revolution of 1952, the Cuban Revolution of 1959, the Iranian Revolution of 1979, were mostly hostile towards the revolutionary regimes. These atmospheres often led to instability and the outbreak of armed conflicts between revolutionary countries and their neighbors in the first few years following regime change. Several studies found that of ten wars which took place between 1789–1979, eight began between revolutionary states and their neighbors, while the rest were indirectly linked with revolutionary regimes.[22] The developments which took place in the Middle East shortly after Arab Uprisings confirm realistic propositions. Indeed, most of the ongoing armed conflicts, low-tense warfare confrontations in the region since 2011 took place within revolutionary states. These confrontations were either between revolutionary and insurgent movements and their allies on the one hand, and the counterrevolutionary forces, the old regimes, and their allies on the other hand.

Traditionally, status-quo powers reject [revisionist] revolutionary regimes that challenge global conditions such as the balance of power, alliance formation, and security arrangements, established by these great powers to preserve their interests. Indeed, revolutionaries look at present conditions (whether at home or at the global one) as the primary reason behind their belief in the necessity of abolishing their domestic regimes. They believe that the removal of these regimes would enable their domestic revolutions to disseminate ideologies and principles on the basis that they reject the continuation of present global power relations and structures which they believe take advantage of weaker states.

In this scenario, these global powers continue not only to deprive weaker states and exploit the world wealth and resources, but also suppress any attempts seeking to obtain independence, self-reliance, and development away from the Western umbrella. Likewise, the features of great powers have not changed either (e.g., as hostile, preventive, greedy, and selfish actors). Therefore, the way revolutionary states of the Arab Uprisings respond to the international environment and the existing great powers (especially the US) is based on the orientations and the alignments of the new revolutionary regimes in Egypt and elsewhere in the Arab World. In other words, whether these revolutionary regimes will become hostile to the Western World, and

---

22   Maoz 1989, 1982.

adopt policies (e.g., anti-Western, and anti-Americanism) that are perceived to be a threat to their interests in the region (especially oil and Israel) or not? Or will they adopt socialized policies designed to accelerate the possibilities of integration into the world system? Likewise, whether these revisionist regimes will yield to imposed structural constraints and seize the new opportunities it offered or challenge the status quo and the external pressures?[23]

The preliminary observation of Egyptian foreign policy during the first year following the 2011 revolution confirms that there is a clear tendency of the Egyptian Government to adopt an integrative realist policy. This foreign policy position was based on respect for international laws, norms, and accords, yet it also puts Egypt's national interests (especially security ones) above all other considerations. Furthermore, the government expressed its refusal to tolerate of violation of its autonomy and intervention in Egyptian decision, and practiced intolerance against any transgression of national sovereignty or threat to Egyptian national security. In other words, the new Egyptian foreign policy was a mirror of how the Egyptian revolution had come about; by nonviolent means, which confirmed the accuracy of hypothesis (1) which stated that the way in which changes occurred, defined, and constructed to a great extent the nature of Egypt's revolutionary behavior as the future administration. However, while the Egyptian revolution did not adopt hostile attitudes against other regional or global actors during the first two years of the transition (2011–2013) as well as against it did turn hostile against its own people, in light of the bloody 2013 counterrevolution which resulted in a more oppressive military and authoritarian regime, the nature of Egypt's foreign policy took a radical turn as realism expected.

---

23 In response to the claims that attacked neorealism (structural realism) for its inability to predict the events of the Arab Uprising and whether the structure of international politics helps to determine the future course of Arabian foreign policies after the revolutions? In a personal correspondence with the author shortly after the revolution of 2011 the late Kenneth Waltz argued that: as a theory neorealism may have no role in anticipation the Arab Uprising for two main reasons. The first is that neorealism is a systematic theory (third image theory) in which realists are concentrate on the study of the international structure rather than the behavior of individuals or political leaders (first image variables) or the composition of domestic structure or processes (second image variables). The latter factors were the driving forces and the reasons for the 2011 revolutions. The second reason is that structural realism is not constituted upon predictions or futurology rather seeks to understand (and explain) international conditions. Having said that Waltz also stressed that as a systematic theory in the first-place structural realism confirms that "Structures do not determine outcomes, but they do influence the behaviors that produce those outcomes in one way or another".

Under the new counterrevolutionary regime that seized power after 2013, Egypt's foreign policy became more involved in regional confrontation, and was more inclined to engage with alliance formation and coalitions to confront the revisionist powers and forces in the region. Likewise, it confirmed hypothesis (3) that regional environment represents the biggest challenge revolutionary states face. Away from the historical considerations of regional competition and conflicts, the new confrontations are between revolutionary and non-revolutionary camp. Moreover, the increasing competition between traditional regional powers and rising powers (e.g., UAE, Qatar, and Oman) confirms realist concerns about the possibility of regional conflicts occurring between revisionists and status-quo regimes. These fears emerged as a result of the increasing power of revolutionary regimes, and of being victims of miscalculation and misperceptions about their future intention. In both cases, these attitudes have the potential to drive regional competitors to conflict. From the viewpoint of non-revolutionary actors, such conflicts would be justified through their aims to deter the aggressive actions of the revolutionary regimes against their neighbors.

4.3   *Global Public Opinion Orientations*

In the short term, public opinion and collective image played a crucial role in misleading the international community's attitude towards the Egyptian revolution. This had a significant impact on foreign policy conducted toward the revolutions. At this point, the representations of the 2011 revolution in the international media define to what extent the international community sympathized with or refuted revolution's goals and aspirations. Likewise, it influenced the extent of support or opposition the revolution faced, such as how it dealt with domestic adversaries and external rivals. In return, this representation determined how other countries would react toward the revolution. In the context of the Cold War, the US government celebrated and welcomed right-wing military revolutions which stood against the proliferation of socialism and communism in the developing world. This strategy enabled the US to play a crucial role in demonizing the image of popular independence and liberation revolutions. During the 1950s and 1960s, US officials repeatedly claimed that such revolutions were immoral and illegitimate regimes (as the Secretary of State John Foster Dulles used to describe them) and their leaders were enemies of humanity. This approach legitimized hostile policies adopted by American Presidents Truman, Kennedy, and Johnson against communist and socialist countries such as China, Cuba, Egypt, Congo, and other non-alignment movement members.[24] The US government financed, under the pretext that these revolutions were "red revolutions" instigated by the former Soviet Union, counterrevolutions, and military coups to mobilize people against them. Such attitudes also confirmed the accuracy of hypothesis (1) which argued that correlations existed between the manner of revolutionary change and the nature of global and regional responses towards revolutionary states, at least in the short-term.

The Arab Uprisings took place at a time when the world has become unprecedentedly interconnected and interdependent, where the Egyptian revolution (and the rest of the 2011 Arab Uprisings revolution) has a proponent and advantaged position in global media. The wide-spread availability of media transmission and coverage brought the Egyptian revolution to every connected home in the world. Furthermore, the spontaneously civilized manners of the Egyptian people inside the median, was a critical factor in presenting the revolution positively to the world audiences. The photos of Egyptians cleaning the streets and places of protest, rebuilding and repairing acts of vandalism committed by the opponents of the revolution, as well as not to attack the opponents, and being keen to communicating with all the rest of the world openly, were astonishing and won the hearts and minds of global viewers. This led the leaders of the so-called "free world" to celebrate, welcoming both the revolution and the Egyptian people.[25]

All these factors aside, there is also the impact of common interests between Egypt and other regional powers. Traditionally, Egypt has been (and will always be) one of the key actors of the MENA region and the cornerstone of the Arab World. Any great powers with strategic interests in this region have to seek coordination with Egypt and must establish a dialogue with the Egyptian regime if they want to preserve these interests. Such a geopolitical and geostrategic position means that Egypt holds an indispensable position within the region and cannot easily be replaced with another regional partner. Historical experience of strategic defense interactions since the nineteenth century showed that even when weakened, Egypt cannot be displaced by other rising regional powers, such as Qatar or the UAE, nor with other key players such as Turkey, Iran, or Saudi Arabia. Indeed, in Western eyes, Egypt represents the key to stability and peace in the MENA region. Thus, it is in the interests of Western powers to ensure the stability and security of Egypt in a way which serves and

---

24   Salim 1983; Galal 1987; Abozaid 2009 (Arabic).
25   IDSC 2011; Abrams 2017; Cakmak and Özçelik 2019; Sadiki 2014; Mason 2014; Selim 2013.

protects its interests. If the revolutionary regimes show evidence of contradicting or hostility toward these powers and interests, these great powers (and their regional allies) will repress and abort it, or vice-versa.

If Egypt wants to be strong in the future, rather than the sick man in the region, it must adopt new political orientations (domestically and externally) which reflect public consensus and the interests of most social forces inside the Egyptian society. It is worth mentioning here that the key determinant for foreign policy in the post-revolution era. The revolution has asserted the deterioration of the domestic conditions (especially socioeconomic and sociopolitical conditions) was the key reason behind revolts and popular protests throughout all the regions,[26] as well as the cause of the state's vulnerability. Moreover, the revolutions have shown how those leaders and presidents who believed to enjoy immunity and untouchable impunity, suddenly found themselves isolated, impotent, and powerless. The people proved to be "the black horse" of the political process in the region.[27] All these indicators assert the centrality of domestic factors in constructing and (re)constructing political decisions (internal and external alike) in the future. This confirms the claims that revolutions give priority to domestic issues over external ones in the short and middle run.

Likewise, chaotic domestic developments confirm the hypothesis that reversely links troubling conditions and the efficiency of foreign policy in the post-revolutionary period. With the failure of the political regime that emerged after the revolution in implementing conciliation and concurrence between the previous variants, the future of Egypt's regional role and foreign policy will be bandwagon with both the US and its regional allies such as Israel and the small Gulf States. Eventually, this attitude will drag Egypt to involve in the regional conflicts and competition. In this case, such foreign policy orientation will not reflect or get the support of the public for its high cost (financially and socially), which associated with the regime's failure to satisfy society's demands. This might lead to the adoption of irresponsible or temerity foreign policy to face the pressures posed by both the public opinion and the external allies. Hence, wounded Egypt become unable to lead the region as the revolution expected and wished after 2011.

---

26 Fakhro and Hokayem 2011:19.
27 ibid: 11.

5   Domestic Policy and Post-revolution Foreign Policy

Revolutions per se are not dangerous, the real danger lies in the post-revolution period and the management of this transitional period and laying the general rules for the new regime. This includes how to deal with the international community, or what Waltz called the process of socialization.[28] In general, this chapter has highlighted several unit-level variants that will have a critical impact on the process of decision-making of Egyptian foreign policy in the post-revolutionary period. This claim is based on the realist principle of "every foreign policy is nothing but an extension of domestic policy".[29] However, before dealing with these variants, it is necessary to mention that the future of Egyptian foreign policy will depend on the following hypothesis:

(1) The more social cohesion in the post-revolution period, the more efficient foreign policy becomes.
(2) The more contested the relationship between opposing social forces in Egypt, the more inconsistent the foreign policy decision-making process.
(3) The future of foreign policy depends on social domestic structure.
(4) Efficient and vibrant Egyptian foreign policy in the postrevolutionary period depends on the consolidating of social consensus and unification.

Without underestimating the role and the weight of systematic pressures and restraints, the future of Egypt's foreign policy mainly depends on the domestic transformations which will take place in the post-revolution period (i.e., the transitional period). In fact, the more instability and dislocation of domestic developments, the more external intervention and pressures poses by international structures on Egyptian decisionmakers. In return, this reduces the independence and efficiency of Egyptian foreign policy which was one of the main causes of the revolution in the first place.

As far as the variants are concerned, they are listed below.

5.1   *National Choices*

By national choices I mean "a common understanding among the ruling elites and state's leaders over adopting certain policies, choosing the type of political

---

[28]   Snyder 2000; Mansfield and Snyder 2005; Sharp 2002; Fearon 2011; Carothers 2002; Geddes 1999; Croissant 2004; Schedler 2002; Krastev 2011; Luciani 1989.
[29]   Snyder 1991; Zakaria 1998; Wilkenfeld and others 1980; Alden and Aran 2012; Hill 2003; Holsti and others 1982; Rose 1998.

regime, following a political ideology or specific economic orientation, and foreign policy alignments, aiming to achieve national interest goals that enjoying collective consensus". Such understanding and agreement will have a crucial impact on state foreign policy. On the one hand, it could accelerate the state's integration and adhesion to the world community if these national choices are compatible with the international norms and orientations. Equally, it could lead to a state's isolation and marginalization from the international community and its institutions. in either case, these choices contradict with the prevailing choices on the other hand.

Historically, there is a general tendency between states and great powers towards convergence where they share similar ideologies, national choices, and aims. In fact, states tend to consider those who adopt different choices from theirs as a threat, especially if these choices are revisionists.[30] This is because contradiction and clashes of interests mostly lead to the rise of a security dilemma. Throughout history, national choices adopted by revolutionary countries such as Russia, France, the US, Egypt, and Cuba led to involvement in varied armed conflicts with strong regional powers in their geostrategic arena. This involvement was a result of the overwhelming miscalculation of these powers, and their ruling elite, about how dangerous these choices are, the threat to their security interests, and to regional and international stability in general. In contrast, other domestic developments that took place in other revolutionary states which were compatible with those of Western powers, have led to the expansion of the level of mutual-understanding, economic exchange, and security cooperation.

5.2 National Performance

Andrew Moravcsik defined state performance as a set of comprise a set of fundamental interests that "causally independent of the strategies of other actors, and prior to specific interstate political interactions, including external threats, incentives, manipulation of information, or other tactics".[31] This means that the extent of success or failure of national governments who are emerging from revolutionary changes, in achieving the expectations of the masses, will have a vital influence over post-revolutionary foreign policy. The success of the government in managing the state's affairs, including boosting economic growth and development growth rates, and satisfying citizen's basic needs, will increase the gross domestic product, attract foreign direct investments (FDI),

---

30 Maoz 1990; Ikenberry 2001.
31 Moravcsik 1997: 519.

exports, and achieve self-sufficiency. Hence, the government will be able to smoothly overcome the troubles of the transitional period, allowing it to consolidate and enhance the level of socialization, constructive engagement in international politics and to stimulate its foreign policy.

In contrast, if the national government failed to manage the post-revolution period, the regime's ability to resist the constraints and pressures pose by both domestic and international structures over the process of state-building, and protect its stability, security and survival will be diminished. With the suspension of economic production and the obstruction of governmental services, the regime's ability to confront instability, in the form of protests, increasing demands of the public, reducing the fiscal deficit, and sustaining the national reserve of foreign currency, the state will lose its central sovereignty over its territories and the monopoly of using legitimate violence to guarantee law and order. As a result, armed insurgent groups will emerge to fight the central government and seek regime change by force, or by embroiling the state in a quagmire of trans-regional conflicts. These deficiencies and dysfunctions will have grave repercussions on national performance, which in return will affect foreign policy performance. In sum, these local deteriorating conditions will exaggerate the impacts of constraints and pressures imposed by the international structure, in which great powers try to avoid the spread of instability and disorder.

5.3 *Domestic Policy*

Knowing how domestic policy affects both foreign policy and regional security architecture is crucial to understanding the outcomes of post-revolutionary decisions. For example, neoliberals correctly stressed that the pluralist nature of social structure and domestic policy influences foreign policy orientations by consolidate the motivations toward cooperative and pacifist foreign policies. In this case, compromise, and collective support of adopted and implemented domestic decisions play a critical role in enhancing stability, constancy, and internal cohesion. Likewise, alleviate the acuity of pressures imposed by the conditions and the nature of the domestic political process on decision-makers. In contrast, if the nature of domestic conditions was characterized by violence, competitiveness, divergence, and exclusion of other social forces, it would disrupt and weaken the political process to such an extent that it would abolish the state of national consensus.[32] Consequently, this tussle increases the burdens of pressures posed by the surrounding environments

---

32   Kosek 2005; Stephan and Chenoweth 2008; Karatnycky and Ackerman 2005.

on decision-makers, which have grave repercussions on the outcomes of the foreign policy.

For example, the cohesion of the domestic political process, the clarity of strategic objectives in the minds of decision-makers, and the prevalence of consensus among political elites and their satisfaction with the nature of the policy process, will play an undoubted role, as a catalyst, in adopting an efficient and vibrant foreign policy.

This foreign policy seeks to achieve the aspirations of the people which will reduce the impacts of pressures imposed by domestic structure, processes, and institutions. Therefore, it allows decision-makers to implement efficient foreign policy outcomes which will positively reflect domestic achievements. These improvements increase a state's relative gains which will enhance its position in the international community, improve its image, attract more allies and supporters of its values, principles, and national interests.

Yet, if the nature of the domestic political process is dominated by discord, polarization, and ambiguity, it will discourage other states from establishing strong relations with regimes that struggle from shaky legitimate foundations and overwhelming instability.

Moreover, the repercussions of domestic discord increase the pressures imposed by domestic structure on decision-makers and affect state's perception and assessments (consequently on the outcomes) of foreign policy decisions. Such disputes might induce enmities with other states, where the accumulation of domestic pressures drives decision-makers to take an irrational and reckless policy like embarking on military campaigns (as a form of the so-called omni balancing) as an (ir)rational response to the regime's personal security, to appease secondary domestic adversaries, and divert public awareness of the regime's domestic dysfunctions and failure.[33] According to Steven David:

> It incorporates the need of leaders to appease secondary adversaries, as well as to balance against both internal and external threats in order to survive in power. This theory rests on the assumptions that leaders are weak and illegitimate and that the stakes for domestic politics are very high conditions that are much more common in the Third World than elsewhere. It assumes that the most powerful determinant of alignment is the drive of Third World leaders to ensure their political and physical survival.[34]

---

33 David 1991.
34 ibid: 236.

5.4 Regime Type

Most IR and foreign policy scholars believe there is a strong interlink between domestic regime (i.e., polity) and foreign policy behavior, especially regarding peace and war. Neoliberals, for instance, claimed that there is a reversed relation between the number of democratic governments and the outbreak of conflicts in the world system. In other words, the higher the number of democratic countries, the fewer conflicts and wars occur in the world. Likewise, in contrast to democratic peace theory, most neoliberals believe that non-democratic regimes are more prone to be involved in wars compared to democracies.[35]

In autocratic regimes, where there is a total absence of institutions and organizational structures, the influence of individual decision-makers prevails. Also, the impact of public opinion is indifferent and deeply neglected. There are democratic or representative bodies that enable the public to participate in the decision-making process. A few individuals (e.g., generals, technocrats, businessmen, and former officials) control power positions and the dominant state's resources, the means of production, and tools of popular mobilization (i.e., mass media). More importantly, instead of electoral institutions, the power structure is constructed upon quasi-military foundations, where most of the ruling elite are either from military or security apparatuses. These military elites are more prone to be involved in wars than civilians, which in return makes the probability of involving States in wars much higher.[36]

These assumptions are correct to a large extent. Indeed, the nature of democratic regimes and their internal structures impose several legal and political constraints on decision-makers before waging war. These determinants include: the influence of public opinion on decision-making, the conciliatory and electoral nature of the political process, separation of powers, peaceful settlement of political struggles (e.g., negotiations and compromise, etc.) and the preconditioning of public consent via their representatives in the parliament. Prior to that, the rationality of decision-making is a crucial factor in determining the long-term strategic economic and political interests of the state. These factors empower the mechanisms of oversight, known as checks and balances, in a way that prevents the misuse of power by dragging the country to unnecessary military campaigns which waste the state's economic, human, and soft power resources.

In contrast, if non-democratic regimes emerged after the revolution, it would induce disputes and enmities with other regimes. As mentioned before,

---

35   Ray 1998.
36   Maoz 1996; Russett and Oneal 2001; Maoz and Russett 1993.

most revolutionary states' neighbors hold skeptical perceptions about both non-democratic revolutionary regimes and democratic alike. Since revolutionary regimes tend to adopt expansionist, revisionist, and interventionist foreign policies, they call for dissemination of revolutionary ideologies and principles abroad. Non-democratic regimes generally tend to bully and flex their muscles toward their neighbors and get involved in conflicts with them. Moreover, they are more inclined to engage in foreign adventures to export their revolutionary values with the aim of expanding their ideological hegemony. Through this, states seek to detract distract attention from their repressive, failed, and dysfunctional domestic policies, their inability to rule the country and satisfy the basic needs of their citizens. For all these reasons, these tendencies push other states to deter and contain the revolutions within their territories, by any means necessary.

5.5 Civil-Military Relations

The process of allocating and positioning of political roles between civilians and the military in a post-revolutionary period (i.e., the civil-military relations) is considered one of the most critical indicators of constructing a domestic regime and consequently shaping foreign policy and international relations with the rest of world. The increasing intervention of the military in the (civilian) political process is clearly a sign of militarization of political process and the system in general and transforming the state into a praetorian regime, to use Samuel Huntington's words.[37] Under this regime, generals and high-ranking officers have the upper hand on state power, where they build a new hierarchic structure of power and influence based on norms such as unification, unquestioning loyalty, and chain-command, not diversity, bargains, or negotiations. In contrast with a civil rule, military rule is based on coercion and unilateralism, while civil rule is based on plurality.

Historical records show that the faster a military return to their bases, the better the transition of democracy. Likewise, the more they delay this return, the stronger the desire to re-seize power and abort democratic transition becomes.[38] Throughout the last few centuries, the rise of military rule in the post-revolutionary and transitional periods was associated with a strong tendency to involve states in armed conflicts. For instance, in the Middle East most of the military revolutionary regimes were engaged in wars with their neighbors or in internal conflicts. From Mauritania westward to Afghanistan

---

37   Huntington 1957; Perlmutler 1981.
38   Huntington 1977; Snyder 1984; Herspring 2005.

eastward, from Somalia in the south to Turkey in the north, although some of these disputes were defensive. Moreover, the foreign policy of these regimes was characterized as impulsive, reckless, extremist, aggressive, and hardline in dealing with their neighbors and other great powers. Most importantly, these foreign policy strategies were inconsistent, short-termed in design, and lacked vision.

It became clear that the foreign policy of these military regimes was a primary cause of regional instability and turmoil, threatening the economic and security interests of their neighbors and of the rest of the international powers, and eventually increased the isolation of their state. Such attitudes made regional and great powers either seek alliance against revolutionary regimes to contain them within their borders or delegitimize them by orchestrating and funding a counterrevolution and staging military coups to change these hostile regimes. In fact, the emergence of a military regime in the post-revolution period which adopts the same former authoritarian, repressive, and violent domestic policies toward the citizens, and a unilateral, impulsive, and hostile external behavior, could be the worst-case scenario for any state, like Egypt, that seeks to build a better future.

5.6 *Public Participation*

The most obvious lesson of the Egyptian and the Arab Uprising in general, is that citizens are the cornerstone of the rise or fall of any political regime. Despite systematic policies of marginalization, contempt, and humiliation adopted by despotic Arab regimes against their people, ironically, such oppressed citizens have put the final nail in the coffin of these ruthless regimes.[39] Indeed, behaviorists and political psychologists were correct when they argued that frustration-egress-violence, that violence breeds violence. The accumulation of a population's injustice, frustration, and oppression might culminate in explosion and rage (both physical and emotional), or behavior of a hostile and aggressive manner as a form of liberation from humiliation, injustice, and repression. This psychoanalysis perspective makes us understand what happened in many totalitarian regimes which have ruled the people with an iron fist. In the case of Egypt, in the last two hundred years the Egyptian people have rebelled more than five times, approximately once per generation (30–40 years) as well as a few rebellions, popular uprising, and unfinished revolutions against the autocratic and brutal regimes that suppressed them.[40]

---

39 The leading author in this field is Iranian scholar Asef Bayat, see Bayat 2002, 2000, 1998, 1997.
40 Abul-Magd 2013.

Although these protests were peaceful most of the time, they assert the main hypothesis which states that humans tend to rebel against suppressive circumstances and structures no matter how long they last.[41]

Adopt more humane behaviors that preserve and guarantee the people's dignity, freedom, and respect their humanity, will enhancement state's internal power and cohesion. Moreover, by respecting and protecting its citizen's rights, the state will enhance the level of trust and loyalty to itself and its institutions. Consequently, this will improve citizens' performance, enhance their participation and involvement in the public sphere and political process, and constructive engagement in the public sphere and expand their productivity and positive contribution to society. Indeed, the 'humane' state, as liberals and constructivists argue, is an 'advanced' not 'soft' or 'weak' state as the proponents of authoritarian-based stability theory claim.

As for the role of public participation in post-revolution foreign policy, it must be clear that respecting the citizens' ideas and opinions on foreign policy issues depends on how deep-rooted democratic traditions and values are within the state itself. Hypothetically, in comparison with autocratic governments, the democratic governments give citizens and varied social forces the right to approve or reject approaches and policies adopted by the state's institutions responsible for foreign policy, through the free election and impartial democratic process still decides who be in power and in charge of making and taking state policies. In other words, while foreign policy used to be an "elitist" or a "sovereign" issue, in which citizens had no right to interfere or express their opinion to change it, under democratic and free-elected governments such attitudes and tendencies would not be allowed to dominate–without the people's consent and authorization–under false justifications that pretend to jeopardize the state's national interest.

5.7 *National Strategy*

One can say without hesitation that countries without national 'grand' strategy (i.e., the art of reconciling ends and means) are like a traveler without a compass or guidance. Grand strategy means "the highest level of national statecraft [which] establishes how states, or other political units, prioritize and mobilize which military, diplomatic, political, economic, and other sources of power to ensure what they perceive as their interests". Others defined it as "the collection of plans and policies that comprise the state's deliberate effort to harness political, military, diplomatic, and economic tools together to advance that

---

41 Gurr 2011 [1971].

state's national interest".[42] Accordingly, the existence of a grand strategy is a necessary condition not only to coordinate and direct all the resources of a nation towards the attainment of the political object of the goal defined by fundamental policy, or to calculate and develop the moral resources but also for a national consensus and mobilizing people to incite and push towards the achievement of these expectations, aspirations, and ambitions. Likewise, grand strategy is necessary to ensure dignity, security, and decent living standards, and to foster the people's willing spirit, which often as important as to possess the more concrete forms of power.[43] Yet, if the state operates in a day-to-day manner without any strategic or long-term planning, this will have a prolonged reversed repercussion on its security, stability, and even its survival, as the contemporary Arab revolutionary experience has demonstrated.

Most of modern 'autocratic' Arab regimes are concerned with the past more than the future. There is not a single Arab country that has published or declared its national strategy for the next fifty years, as other developed countries do. Worse than that, in another study claimed that the absence of specialized 'official' institutions interested in the study of futurology and strategic planning in the Arab World, where the Arab states still think about the future as relying on mystic, clairvoyant, and tarot cards readers.[44] These countries still run their affairs based on financial resources (cost-benefit). Hence, no study has been conducted to evaluate or assess the risks, challenges, and necessary requirements to ensure the dignity of the people, and the rate of decay of available resources to secure these values. Likewise, there is no reflection of the state's responsibility in the light of transformations that took place in the regional and global scene, politically, strategically, economically, culturally, technologically, etc. Furthermore, what are the better responses, alternatives, and suggestions to address these transformations? The presence of a national project which mobilizes and unites the public to achieve these national goals and aspirations rising in the milieu of young generations. The lofty goal of such a project/strategy is to rebuild and improve the standards of economic

---

42   Hooft 2017; Feaver 2009. For the debate on Grand Strategy see: Kennedy 1992; Walt 1989; Mastanduno 1997; Layne 1997; Betts 2000; Craig et al. 2023.
43   Hart 1967: 322–323.
44   Perhaps the most influential (and maybe the only) scholarly study of the future of Arab states and society is the project that was initiated organized funded and published (in ten volumes) by the Centre for Arab Unity Studies and supervised by the late economist Ismail Sabry Abdullah with the contributions of dozens of Arab political scientists, sociologists, International Relations scholars, and development scholars in the 1980s and 1990s. For more details see: Abdullah 1999; Haseeb 2002; Abozaid 2014.

development and aggregate power to enable the state to deter other aggressive and hostile states and ensure equal treatment by other actors of international society.

The absence of a national strategy securing public support will decrease the people's trust in the regime's ability and has repercussions on the overall performance of the state. Consequently, this "trust crisis" could lead to a cycle of upheavals, instability, and failure because of the lack of vision which could save the country and prevent it from falling into a disaster. Indeed, one of the biggest challenges facing any revolutionary regime is the inability to construct and promote a national project, mobilization, consolidation and understanding, and to gain the support of the public as the key to hope for a better future for the country and the people.

CHAPTER 4

Counterrevolution

Egypt-Gulf Relations after the Arab Uprising

1   Introduction

Shortly after it prevail, revolutions tend to reject the opposing parties' behavior, but the "socialization" process will force the new revolutionary regime to deal with all countries on the same foundations of international politics: interests and mutual gains. For revolutionary countries like Egypt, in the short and medium term, the relationship between it and other actors and units in the international system will be determined based on their political attitudes towards the 25th of January 2011. There will be a differential approach in dealing with these actors and powers. It is inevitable that the countries that showed support to the revolution, such as the EU, will be preferred and supported by the new regime, and the opposite is true. Countries that were allied with the pre-existing regime, such as China and Russia, will not be favored by the revolutionary regime. In the long term, relations with all other countries will change radically, moving away from personalization and taking a realistic direction, based on bilateral shared interests and expansion of mutual gains. By contrast, non-revolutionary countries, like the GCC countries, will behave differently. The main motivation for and determinants of their foreign policy and external behavior towards their neighbors (both revolutionary and non-revolutionary) will be based on different standards. The main concerns of these countries are the maintenance of their internal security and stability, and prevention of the spread of revolutionary ideas and values across their borders. In addition, assisting "friendly" revolutionary regimes to overcome their economic and social crises is another strategy used by GCC countries. In so doing, non-revolutionary countries could maintain the status quo of regional balance of power, preventing the spread of turmoil and instability and the outbreak of armed conflicts (local and regional) that could have negative repercussions for their security and stability. In short, after revolutions, states and revolutionary systems act in a manner intended to facilitate their support and recognition by the international system; while non-revolutionary states and neighboring countries primarily behave defensively, with the aim of maintaining their internal security and stability and the containment of the revolutions within their national borders.

This chapter first discusses the debate on the correlation between revolution, and the state of regional war and peace. Secondly, the behavior of revolutionary regimes (i.e., Egypt between 2011 and 2013) towards non-revolutionary and counterrevolutionary regimes (i.e., Gulf monarchies), through the lens of balance of power and balance of threat theories. The second parts discuss the behavior from the perspective of non-revolutionary regimes (With Egypt who represent the revolutionary regime and the GCC countries that represent non-revolutionary camp). Especially with the significant alert and transformation of balance of power dynamics and condition in the MENA region that occurred because of the rise of small rich and rich oil-exporting monarchies in the Arabian Gulf region which will be discussed separately in Chapter 5.

Based on the discussion outlined in the previous chapter (Chapter 3), this chapter will analyze five main determinations that will shape GCC foreign policies (i.e., security concerns, threat perception, misperception and miscalculation, foreign aid, stability concerns). At the same time, these factors explain the correlation between revolution and instability and the tensions between revolutionary regimes and their non-revolutionary (conservative) neighbors.

In the case of Egypt, during 2012–2013, the country's relationship with the GCC could be described as a pendulum, swinging between competition and covert conflict. As soon as former president Morsi and the Muslim Brotherhood were overthrown by the army-supported uprising on the 30th of July 2013, relations started to improve. In under twelve months, relations between Egypt and the Gulf Cooperation Countries (GCC) became a formal alliance. As a result of the Arab Uprisings (2011–2021) the group of rich and small monarchies in the Gulf region are facing a new kind of threat that is considered the most dangerous since the fall of the Saddam regime in 2003. In the aftermath of the Arab Uprising, the popular intifada reached Bahrain and Oman in mid-2011, and the Islamic state in Iraq and Syria (ISIS) rose violently in Syria and Iraq. These challenges and threats forced GCC countries to change their foreign policies and approach in dealing with regional crises and conflicts, especially towards countries like Egypt, Yemen, and Syria.

The sources of this major shift in regional dynamics and interactions can be found by assessing certain factors and elements. Regime change is the main element that can encompass the dynamics leading to change. Many scholars have discussed the relationship between types of political regimes and the nature of relations between states. The questions they attempt to answer are: Does the similarity between regimes increase cooperation between states and international units and vice-versa? If there is a link, to what extent would it have an effect? Is the nature of regimes the most critical element that shapes the nature of relations between states at times of turmoil or are there other factors? If so, what are these factors?

The balance of threat and defense-based strategy are the main factors that must be considered to understand and analyze the changes taking place in GCC countries' foreign policy towards Arab Uprising countries like Egypt and other countries within the region. The policies of the GCC towards Egypt since 2011 will be explained within the scope of the factors mentioned. The main element that determines and shapes GCC relations with Egypt is fear of the instability brought by regime change. This started with the revolutions and the emergence of new security threats. This chapter analyses regime changes during the time span from 2011 to 2021, and how regional politics and players were influenced during the rule of the Muslim brotherhood and after their expulsion. The main argument here was that the spread of instability, the rise of extremist, violent radical groups across the region, the gradual withdrawal of the US from the Middle East, and the increasing influence of other great powers like Russia and China, have caused both Egypt and the GCC countries to become the center of regional and global competition on the remaking of the Arab Uprising.

2 Revolution and War and Peace

Most IR scholars tend to see revolutionary changes as acceleratory factors of tension between states to an extent that make the possibility of the outbreaking of wars or slipping into armed conflicts higher than in the absence of revolutions.

Overall, the previous variables contribute to understand the domination of reciprocal sense of mistrust and uncertainty between states, increase the possibility of misperception, and miscalculation of other partners' capabilities and intentions. In addition to these variables, revolution's role in alterations regional and world balance of power in general and allies network also have a critical impact on interstates relation dynamics. Thus, in order to understand post-revolution foreign policy, scholars need to explore the correlations between revolution and war, and most importantly, revealing the role of great powers in this correlation. The next section seeks to reveal these correlations.

The West often perceives nationalist, and revolutionary regimes as a hostile threat to its interests which must be eradicated under the pretext of global security. As such, Western powers repeatedly try to implicate revolutionary regimes in foreign and domestic conflicts. According to this view, the associations between revolution and war need to be understood in the broader global context, i.e., global balance of power, and by understanding to what extent revolutions enhance or restrain great powers' interests. In other words, revolutions are the dependent variable, while war will be the independent variable. One of the primary factors is the mutual misperception, which indicates revolutionary instability is the assumption that great state powers are hostile towards revolutions and the resulting internal upheaval. Consequently, the actions of the revolutionary regime determine how revolutionary leadership assess the level of threat posed by great state powers towards principles, values, and interests of the revolution. Revolutions and revolutionary regimes are often involved in wars, mainly as a means of self-defense, not as expansion or offensive wars as the dominant narrative claims.

In a leading study – that I will expand upon here – Stephen Walt defined five hypotheses which linked revolution to the possibility of war erupting between revolutionary states and their neighbors.[1]

(1) Revolutions increase the levels of threat between revolutionary states and their rivals.
(2) Revolutions encourage both sides to believe that the use of military power is easy and not an expensive strategy to address these threats.
(3) By changing the balance of power status, revolutionary states increase the possibilities of miscalculations and hostility with their rivals, and eventually into a war.
(4) Revolutions amplify the size of overall threats posed by others, hence extends the sense of insecurity.
(5) Revolutions increase the reciprocal sense of vulnerability which drives them to attack or bandwagon with other states, seeking to minimize the extent of the danger posed by other hostile or aggressive states.

However, Walt's argument is flawed for several reasons. Firstly, it presumes an inevitable correlation between revolution and the outbreak of the war. Secondly, even if this argument is valid; the analysis does not show the nature or the type of these wars. For example, are they expansionist, hostile, and offensive wars, or justified, legitimate, and defensive wars? Historically, wars fought in the Global South, particularly the Middle East (the Egyptian experience

---

1 Walt 1992: 332.

precisely), show that revolutionary regimes were involved in these conflicts for the purpose of defense against aggressive neighbors. Thirdly, Walt's argument does not elaborate in the first place on how revolutions change the relationship between states, before jumping to the inevitable conclusion that revolutions cause instability and wars apart of political, cultural, and historical (i.e., colonial and imperial in particular) contexts and interactions.

In contrast with Walt, several studies linked revolution and war based on certain transformations which produced as a result of the outbreak of the revolutions. These transformations are discussed below.

2.1 *The Nature of Revolutionary Organizations and Ideologies*

The foreign policy of revolutionary states is mostly perceived to be ideologically driven. It claims that revolutionary states cause instability and wars because they seek to export their principles and ideological values abroad. The revolution's success in seizing power at home encourages them, under the pretext of the state's moral and ideological superiority, to export these values, unlike other states and movements with non-interventionist natures. In doing so, the revolutionary regime causes other states to evaluate their relationship, which usually concluding that they are "at war with an armed doctrine" to use Edmund Burke's words.[2]

Despite the consensus among realists over this view, in my opinion Burke's phrase presents an incomplete and contested explanation of the link between revolution and war. To the contrary, the historical record shows that revolutionary states tend to behave cautiously, and often portray themselves as victims of other states' attacks rather than being aggressors. Revolutionary France, for instance, played at being a victim when, from 1789 to 1792, its foreign policy was characterized as being passive. This led other European states to lessen their global position. Likewise, in the Middle East, Israel was the aggressor against revolutionary Egypt between 1956 and 1967, and Iraq was the first to wage war against the revolutionary Iranian State in the early 1980s.[3] The ideology of revolutionary states is often more flexible than expected. Instead of depicting it as a demagogic campaign to the outside world, revolutions usually emphasized adopting flexible strategies and tactics which help it obtain its goals. In fact, ideologies play a considerable role in explaining how revolutionary states act and determine the way they are perceived by other countries. However, such states are rarely able to explain the correlation between revolution, instability, and war.[4]

---

2 ibid, p. 335.
3 ibid, p. 326.
4 ibid, pp. 326–327.

2.2 Domestic Repercussions of Internal Changes

The advocates of this view, which links the frequency of domestic and foreign conflicts, claim that domestic conflicts inside revolutionary states encourage them to adopt a hostile foreign policy towards others. The greater the disparity between the elite of the State and the people is obvious, the more bellicose the foreign policy of these states towards its neighbors becomes. This behavior primarily stems from domestic divergences between revolutionary elites, and the contradiction of their tendencies regarding whether to engage in conflicts with other countries in order to ensure their security. An example of this is the French revolutionary wars against Russia, Austria, and Great Britain (1792–1802) to abolish the monarchic regimes threatening its existence at the time.[5] Where the revolutionary regimes sought to wage war with other countries in a bid to avoid the divergences of mobilization and winning people's support of the revolution, as well as to justify domestic repression and distract attention from domestic crisis and challenges This behavior prevailed in other revolutionary countries such as, Iran, Russia and Libya, which demonstrates how to use these attitudes as a pretext to justify mass killing, which followed these revolutions, as a means to overcoming the revolution's rivals.[6]

Despite the cohesion of this view, it is also flawed in its practical application. For instance, it presupposes those revolutionary states are bellicose by nature. This claim contradicts rational logic which asserts that countries that are stuck in a cycle of revolution and domestic chaos cannot be involved in further hostilities which could escalate or restore these threats. In fact, by involving in unnecessary wars with other strong neighbors, revolutionary regimes are jeopardizing the value of their domestic victory. Although revolutionary states might lead to the eruption of tension between states to consolidate its domestic legitimacy, nonetheless it seeks to avoid getting involved in external wars by any means necessary. For example, revolutionary China adopted such an attitude towards the Korean war where Mao Tse-tung sought to avoid exposing Chinese national interests by involving China an unnecessary military confrontation with the US. Today, revolutionary regimes are more inclined to rapprochement and sympathizing with their probable enemies to gain time to protect domestic assets.[7]

---

5   ibid, p. 327.
6   Ibid.
7   ibid, p. 328.

2.3 The Type of Revolutionary Regimes and Leadership

The supporters of this view argue that the leaders of revolutionary regimes usually display personal characteristics such as self-confidence, suspiciousness, stubbornness, and cruelty. These personality features make it difficult to coerce or deter them from taking irrational and irresponsible foreign policy decisions. Accordingly, such leaders tend to act irresponsibly and are unable to see things in a comprehensive way, either because of being convinced by the unquestionable correctness of their actions, or tending to achieve a revolutionary, heroic, unprecedented performance. All these tendencies lead to miscalculation, misperception, and a suspicion of other intentions.[8]

This view is considered the most accepted among scholars, yet its supporters have omitted the foreign policy influence on revolutionary leaders. The primary flaw of this view is the absence of any theoretical link between the existence of the foreign policy and the personality of revolutionary leaders. For example, Walt argued that, by admitting that revolutionary leaders have distinguished personalities, it cannot help in identifying their options and alternatives before them in critical and brinkmanship situations. In fact, revolutionary elites mostly disagree over foreign policy orientations. Likewise, the dominant stereotyped images of revolutionary figures as irrational and reckless are neither coherent nor accurate. Several studies revealed that the claims about reckless revolutionary leaders in countries such the former Soviet Union, China, North Korea, Pakistan, and Iran (who possess WMD) were not accurate. For example, Waltz showed that revolutionary leaders, either in revolutionary, conservative, democratic, or non-democratic states, behaved with the same measure of rationality and caution like Western democratic countries, on the edge of war.[9]

For realists, the key role that revolutions have over foreign policy (and international politics in general) depends on their influence on the global balance of power, and power relations. As such, it will be useful to elaborate more on the relationship between revolutions and theories of global balance, i.e., the balance of power, the balance of threat, and what I called the balance of values. While the first two have been extensively discussed, I will briefly outline them again and expand more on the latter.

Balance of power theory states that: in a realist world order, while nation-states are similar in terms of functions and needs, they differ in capabilities. The position of the state is determined based on what it possesses by means of

---

[8] ibid, pp. 328–329; Jervis 1976.
[9] Waltz 1981; Sagan and Waltz 1995.

power capabilities (distribution of capacities). Due to the disparity of balance of power inside the state, the possibilities of cooperation or conflict, and of relying on other countries is reduced due to the fear that others could achieve relative gains at their expense.[10] The system of power balance appears when the gap between the main actors in the system and their rivals expands in such a way that one side becomes stronger than the other. This drives the other side to act to prevent their rival from becoming dominant and gaining a position that allows it to impose its will over other states. In this case, in order to protect their security and ensure their survival, other states have two options, either to balance against the strongest state (i.e., allies) or to bandwagon with it. Under this anarchic, self-help system, the primary purpose of most actors' foreign policies is to seek to maximize either their security (defensive realism) or their power (offensive realism).[11]

According to balance of power theory, revolutions mostly cause wars and instability for two reasons. The first is that revolutionary states alert the status quo and offer opportunities for states to increase the size of its power capabilities. For example, if revolutions contribute to the growth of relative capabilities in favor of the revolutionary side, the revolutionary regime will try to take advantage of these new conditions and attack others. Likewise, if other countries sensed that revolution reduced the capabilities of revolutionary states, they would try to maximize their capabilities and that of their allies. The second reason why revolutions cause wars and instability is that revolutions increase the likelihood of mistakes and uncertainty, which make it more difficult to predict the outcome of a conflict stemming from major political upheaval.[12]

Balance of threat theory argues that in order to protect their survival and ensure their security, the central goal of the nation-state is to balance against regional powers (not bandwagon as balance of power stresses). Under these conditions, the alliance is not against the strongest state, but against the state(s) that poses more threat to other actors in the system. This threat can be identified and is tangibly based on several indicators. According to Walt, it is important to consider all the factors that will affect the level of threat that states may pose. This is because balancing and bandwagoning are more accurately viewed as a response to threats that occurred when nations with a significantly greater combined power allied against the recognized threat.

---

10 Waltz 1979; Kaufman, Little and Wohlforth 2007; Little 1999; Paul, Wirtz, and Fortmann 2004.
11 Waltz 1959; Mearsheimer 2000.
12 Walt 1997: 331.

These factors are: 1) aggregate power; 2) proximity; 3) offensive capability; and 4) offensive intention.[13] Nation-states acting under the overwhelming fear of threat resort to adopting all possible strategies, whether legitimate or not, to restore regional balance. They achieve this either by forming coalitions with other actors to defy the threat, or by unifying to confront any external enemies.[14]

In short, from the point view of both balance of power and balance of threat theories, revolutions have a great impact on both balance of power and balance of threat due to the fact that every part (revolutionary and status-quo states alike) tends to perceive the other as a source of defiance and danger. Yet, none of them can determine the extent of the danger represented by the other. The lack of precise information about the extent of threats which must be overcome means both parties tend to be suspicious and are inclined to self-interest. This is especially when such suspicions are confirmed. Each part is intimidated by the other, and both believe in state capability to abolish the threat imposed by the other, thereby putting an end to it easily and cheaply. In fact, the perception of how weak and vulnerable the enemies of revolutionary state are, heightens the calls in favor of preventative actions, and perhaps pre-emptive actions, as was seen with Israel and Egypt in 1956 and 1967.[15] Furthermore, while the revolutionary state's power rises and its external appeal increases, non-revolutionary and hostile states perceive this new state as a serious threat which requires containing regionally and beyond. Mostly revolutionary states give non-revolutionary states the impression of self-confidence and have more freedom of action, sometimes in an exaggerated way, which can lead them to triumph over their adversaries.

Not surprisingly, history is full of such inaccuracies and assumptions. For instance, the heightened fervor of the French revolution was the catalyst which pushed Britain into war against France in 1793. Then- Prime Minister Pitt was convinced that "a war was inevitable and the sooner it was begun the better". His view was that if Great Britain did not surround revolutionary France within its territory, France would surround the whole continent imminently. The eighteenth-century logic of imperial Britain continued to govern the actions of another imperial power in the twentieth century. Following the conclusion of World War Two, the US government and its regional proxies kept intervening (both preventively and pre-emptively) in the Third World to

---

13 Walt 1987, 1985: 9–15.
14 Walt:1996; Little 1999; Paul, Wirtz, and Fortmann 2004.
15 Walt 1992: 356.

repress and contain the revolutionary regimes, stopping them from destabilizing the interests of the US and its allies, in proxy conflicts in Egypt, Iran, Yemen, Algeria, Chile, Nicaragua, Cuba, Argentina, Vietnam, and many other countries.[16] Furthermore, the vulnerability of revolutionary states makes other countries at the stake and therefore more inclined to attack and put an end to the danger revolutionary regimes produce. The lack of self-confidence in waging a war to ensure security and stability at home, results in a new form of social structure, which prevent other states from intervening and manipulating the decisions of revolutionary states.

3 Revolution from the Perspective of 'Balance of Values' Theory

While balance theories claim that revolutionary states seek to protect their survival, states tend to maximize their power in confrontation with other powers, or to balance against sources of threatening powers. In return, I am claiming that in the Global South, states do exist in an anarchic world, yet seek to achieve central values, and are more interested in protecting their values and in obtaining non-material goals such as independence and dignity.[17] In principle, due to their military and economic weaknesses, nation-states in the Global South prioritizing normative goals such as independence and autonomy from oppressive states in the international arena. In a competitive, anarchic international system, states are driven by their national interests and maximize their security, which depends on their economic capabilities, experience in the international arena, and the adaptation of their domestic structure. However, this logic is not prevalent in the Global South, where states disadvantaged by their limitations including military and economic weaknesses, their [lack of] experiences dealing independently with other great powers, and the incomplete state formation process whereby many Global South states are considered primitive by Western standards. Moreover, compared to liberal democratic governments in the West, many of these states are still governed by either authoritarian or

---

16 Gaddis 1982; McDougall 1997; Bacevich 2016; Gendzier 1997; McPherson 2016; LaFeber 1993.

17 Many of classical realistic thinkers like Carr and Morgenthau were interesting in studying the role of the "normative" aspects of national power. Carr focuses on ideology and political beliefs. Hans Morgenthau focuses on the role of ideology and sociological motivates that determine and shape National Interest, which he defined it in term of Power, here, I mean by values, "national interest in the term of political values, like autonomy, independence, sovereignty, not moral or religious terms". See: Carr 1964; Morgenthau [1948] 1973.

patriarchal regimes, which has meant that they are unable to adopt policies compatible with norms and practices that govern Western democratic states.[18]

In the Global South, ideological tendencies have a significant impact on the regional political competitions.[19] The interests, values, and alliances of these states shift in accordance with changes to ideologies and belief system of the autocratic leadership, where specific democratic mechanisms that organize and coordinate these changes are absent. In other words, it can be argued that if Western democratic states determine their policies based on national interest calculations, states in the Global South determine their national interests based on their policies. While the policies of the former are united and sustainable, the policies of the latter are temporary and varied according to the ideological orientations of the ruling regimes.

On that basis, the link between revolutions and national instability depends on the presence of a national strategy. For many countries this strategy is based

---

18   According to Stein Rokkan's model of the development of European Societies since the federation era, many of the Third World countries still in the first stage of that model "State Formation", where central government still under construction, resources monopoly does not mobilize by taxation, arms still under organize, and internal order establish by coups and revolutions, guard by military not police. Even the source of regime legitimacy, still adopt its roots from a traditional bases like monarchies, succession and other form of what Max Weber consider it as a "traditional" source of legitimacy. See: Rokkan 1975; 562–500; Weber 1947.

19   Shortly after the end of the Cold War, leading realist scholars such as John Mearsheimer and others underestimate the role that ideology, ideals, and norms will have on international interactions. In contrast, I argued that the role of not only ideology but also other normative (non-material) factors in the Global South in the post-Cold War world is still crucial and maybe even bigger than the Cold War itself. The role of the so-called "universal Jihadism" may represent the most explicit example of the role of ideology and norms in the Arab-Islamic World. Interestingly, almost 30 years after Mearsheimer's famous paper "Back to the Future", Mearsheimer's last paper "Bound to Fail" reasserts the same argument about the liberalism-based international system and argued that "liberal international order, erected after the Cold War, was crumbling by 2019. It was flawed from the start and thus destined to fail". Once again, I am arguing that Mearsheimer's new argument is also false, on the one hand, because of the rise of global right-wing ideology (i.e., populism and hyper-nationalism), and the state-centric, and illiberal ideology of the Chinses global power which will trigger (if not already) the conservative, nationalist, and realist ideology of the US foreign policy to stop the rise of China on the other hand. Likewise, in the Global South, the considerable expansion of ultra-right-wing nationalism in India, the Arab-Islamic World, Africa, and South America, besides the growth of xenophobic tendencies and neo-Nazism parties in Europe. All these indications refer to one thing, ideology here to stay. As in the past two centuries, ideological-driven clashes between nation-states will determine the future of the international system as did before. See: Mearsheimer 2019; Vukovich 2018; Zakaria 1997; Ikenberry 2014; Barma and Ratner 2006; Barma, Chiozza, Ratner, and Weber 2009; Evans 2012.

on specific values in the revolutionary leadership, combined with an awareness of threats and challenges posed to the state. Predominately, idealist revolutionary leadership determine their relations with their neighbors based on the compatibility in adopting the same values and norms. Such compatibility denotes standards which determine the intensity of a state's relationship in the first few years after a revolution. Accordingly, IR scholars should focus on addressing the lack of understanding around the motives and ideological foundations that drive revolutionary decision-makers and construct their priori decisions.[20] Having said that, nonetheless, in the absence of such motives and ideologies, the behavior of both revolutionary and non-revolutionary states in the Global South can be understood by adopting realist models such as balance of power theory, balance of threat theory, hegemonic stability and other Western models.

The previous discussion of revolution and war has shown that Waltz was correct in arguing that revolutionary states are no different from any other states in the international system. For Waltz, the constraints imposed by the international structure deter revolutionary states of joining the fold of international community. Since the emerging of Westphalian state system, not a single state has managed to deviate from the orbit of the international system and its governing mechanisms. States might challenge the structure, but they cannot leave it. For almost 400 years a system of international statehood has existed. What has been challenged is the behavior of nation-states, revolutionary and non-revolutionary alike, to work within the system rather than without. Therefore, the main reason for the link between revolutions and wars is determined by a state's success or failure to priorities its national stability (internally and externally), above any other consideration. This chapter argues that the links between revolution, national instability, and the possibility of warfare revolves around five vital variables, listed below.

3.1 Security Concerns

As the realists believe, in an anarchic system, the main objective of nation-states is to protect their security and stability, to preserve their physical survival as a sovereign entity, and to defend their central values. According to Stephen Walt, during revolutionary periods, wars rarely occur as a result of ideological claims that demand the export of values and principles. On the other hand, besides these "external" factors, the "domestic" factors play a vital role in escalating the tension between the revolutionary regimes and their neighbors, in order to

---

20   Singer 1960.

protect and preserve their security and stability. During the French revolution, for example, whenever the internal factors were dominant on the scene, the decision to go to war stemmed from the fear of domestic enemies (aristocrats and clergy) and their external conspirators, who were calling for the return of the old regime. Due to the nature of the international system, revolutionary regimes seeking to ensure their security will clash with other countries which are trying to ensure their own security. Hence the so-called "security dilemma" between revolutionary nations and their neighbors will emerge. This situation may lead to war because of the way leaders perceive other countries' actions. The likelihood of miscalculation and misperception increases because of the lack of information and communication with other parties, who (on the other side) are dominated by suspicion, mistrust, and uncertainty as to other countries' intentions.[21]

3.2   *Threat Perception*

These perceptions emerge from both systemic and unit levels. These threats mainly emerge as a result of alerting the balance of threat perception, changing the distribution of capabilities, and increasing the sense of threat caused by the revolutions. This in turn increases the revolutionary leaders' feeling of vulnerability and the temptation to believe that attack strategy is the easiest means to confront these threats. The problem here is the high degree of uncertainty regarding other factors (e.g., domestic developments, ideological tendencies, socio-political and socioeconomic conditions) and mechanisms that encourage both parties to perceive each other as a competitor, a rival, and as an enemy. Since revolutionary states operate in an anarchic and competitive system, governed by the mechanism of self-help, and where conflict and war are permanent and inevitable features, their endeavors to secure national security clash with the efforts of other countries. The status-quo states consider the efforts of revisionist states to protect their security an attempt to reduce their security. Hence, a security dilemma between revolutionary and non-revolutionary states, and their neighbors, arises. This tension could escalate to war depending on how other state's perceive threats that other countries pose on the one hand. Likewise, due to the miscalculations and misperceptions which emerge because of the lack of information and the miscommunication with revolutionary states. The latter in return become under an overwhelming sense of suspicion and distrust of their neighbors. These indications could

---

21   Herz 1950; Jervis 1978; Glaser 1997.

lead either toward counterrevolution attempts or external interventions which seek to change revolutionary regimes and the restoration of the old regimes.[22]

3.3 Misperception and Miscalculations

Usually, status-quo states perceive revolutionary states to be a potential source of danger which incite conflicts at the regional level, and which require allies to contain them within their borders in response. For example, during the Cold War and its aftermath, states with conservative (non-revolutionary) political principles (e.g., the United States and Western Europe) often found it difficult to believe that revolutionary regimes were not efficient in managing their internal affairs and foreign relations. This perception has a systematic/structural effect on their attitudes toward revolutionary regimes. For instance, the United States perceived communist regimes in the Third World as illegitimate and immoral ideological governments for a long time. Consequently, any regime which adopts this ideology has since been considered by the US Government as an enemy of the State. Such predisposition explained the American foreign policy attitude towards the Chinese Revolution of 1945, the Egyptian Revolution of 1952, the Cuban Revolution of 1959, and other Third World revolutions. Both US and the Western Governments repeatedly claimed that these regimes were proxies of the Soviet Union and must be contained. Nevertheless, the US Governments deliberately decided to overlook the fact that none of these revolutionary regimes were hostile to the US and the West *per se*, they still posed a threat since they could spread to other countries. In fact, these regimes were mainly seeking to protect their sovereignty and fulfil their basic economic and political interests, for which they were formed, according to the balance of values theory arguments.

3.4 Foreign Aid

Revolutionary regimes tend to cooperate and constructively engage with foreign parties who financially contribute to and support the democratic transition, reconstruction, reform of domestic institutions, and strengthening of democratic movements, groups, and civil society, but only when this support involves no political agenda, compulsory procedures, or specific form of governmentality opposed to national interests or stability.[23] In the case of the Arab

---

22   Herz 1950; Jervis 1978; Glaser 1997.
23   Ikenberry, 2002; Walt, 1987. Carapico, 2002; Pace, 2015. For more details see the special issue of *Mediterranean Politics Journal* on "The Politics of Foreign Aid in the Arab World: The impact of the Arab uprisings", Challand, 2014; Heydemann, 2014; Amin, 2014; Isaac, 2015.

Uprising, there is evidence to support this assumption. Relations of Egypt, Yemen, Bahrain, Libya, and Tunisia with GCC countries (like Saudi Arabia and UAE) were very close due to the amount of aid they donated, compared with their relationships with other countries who had been considered their greater supporters and donors in the past, like France and the United States.

3.5 *Stability Concerns*

Realistically, nation-states tend towards rapprochement and cooperation (even bandwagoning) with great powers that support their stability and security. On the other hand, they tend towards balance and against revisionist powers that seek to change the regional balance of power, thus threatening regional and domestic stability.[24] Consequently, revolutionary regimes and their neighbors in the post-revolution period become deeply sensitive and vulnerable to any attempt to destabilize or promote turmoil in the surrounding environment due to the repercussions of these actions for the stability of the region. These repercussions may slow attempts to rebuild and reconstruct the society and the states once again. Instability could escalate and lead to war if the revolutionary regimes fail to achieve any domestic progress or restore stability and maintain security within the state. Accordingly, this will lead other countries to form a bloc against these parties in order to defend their interests, values, and principles, and above all their security and stability.

In summary, the previous discussion addressed the gap in current literature on the International Relations of the Global South, played out through the relationship between revolutions and foreign policy. The debate between the three canonical schools in International Relations on the role of revolutions, reveals how liberalism can explain security challenges in the Western countries (the center), but not in the Global South (peripheries).[25] In addition, the discussion of the correlation between revolutions and foreign policy shows that the most influential determinants (in descending order) are psychological factors

---

24 Ikenberry 2002; Walt 1987.
25 In comparison with Western democratic countries, most of the Global South countries are still suffering from severe legitimacy, participation crises, and other forms of internal fragmentation, and developmental and institutional weakness. Ironically, all aspects of modernization in the Third World are "false". According to Peter Flora: "modernization in general sense can describe how increasing (1) education, science, and technology, (2) organizational capacities, and (3) social mobilization led to greater levels of industrialization, urbanization, and bureaucratization of society". All these elements are not easy to be found in almost all the third countries. (Flora and Heideneimer 1981: 17–33). For more details about the evolution of the states in the Third World see: Buzan 1983; Jackson 1990; Migdal 1988.

(i.e., first image variables); the relationship between the state and the society (i.e., second image variables) and last the international interactions (i.e., third image variables). The analysis displayed shows that within the neighborhood of revolutionary states, the tendencies of misperception have prevailed among decisionmakers within non-revolutionary states, who believe that radical changes within revolutionary territories will have serious repercussions in the future. These transformations make those neighbors firmly fear, caution, and intimidated by the new revolutionary regimes, regardless of their orientations. Moreover, non-revolutionary states are becoming more inclined to monitor the actions (internal and external) of revolutionary regimes, which in return determine the ways to address and interact with these revolutionary regimes.

To overcome the shortcomings of both Realism and Liberalism's lack of understanding and inability to articulate the post-revolution foreign policy, this study proposes an alternative to address these limitations, based on the Realist-Constructivist approach.[26] For example, the absence of domestic consensus and cohesion among different social forces in Egypt, has become difficult to explain given the complexity of domestic conditions in the Global South. The Realist-Constructivist alternative, primarily based on looking at international politics not as an inevitable anarchic structure but as a structure that is constructed through different stages of the development of the social system, represents a more suitable approach which could provide better explanations for these conditions. The case of the Arab Uprising represents a serious challenge to the realist approach, specifically with cases such as Egypt and other Arab countries. For instance, looking at the number of societal variables (the unit level) in a comparative perspective with Western countries, in which internal functional cohesion and consensus dominant and constitute the relationship between the state and the society, these conditions do not exist at the same level or intensity. In the Arab countries, the relationship between the state and society (i.e., Muslims, Copts, Nubians, Bedouins, etc.) and sociopolitical forces (i.e., liberals, nationalists, conservatives, and extremists) can be characterized and identified through political tensions and unrest. In such a sphere, competition and conflict between the states and these forces widening the level of contentiousness and divergence of the political process. Thus, clearly, realism cannot explain these internal (sub-state) interactions and dynamics.

---

26 Barkin 2020, 2010, 2003; Barkin and Sjoberg 2019; Jackson et al. 2004.

Constructivism, on the other hand, understands and explains the link between revolutions (as a form of change in identities, ideas, interests, preferences, and ideals within a certain state), foreign policy, and international relations primarily through a conceptual framework. This framework claims that states exist in an environment that is constructed by identities, norms, and ideals that govern the collective behavior of individuals and groups. These variables construct (and reconstruct) state perceptions of the world. In the case of the Arab Uprising, such transformations have occurred in several Arab countries since 2010, where researchers have focused on understanding how individuals and groups perceive and articulate the nature of their surrounding environment and their perceptions of other actors in the international system. Following this understanding, I argue that Egyptian foreign policy is determine and shape based on three key variables:

- The first variable is societal force, and the way political identities and values are constructed, including how these forces interact with other domestic groups and actors.
- The second variable is the state as a unit of analysis. which sees the state not as a utility, but as a multidimensional unit. Furthermore, constructivists do not consider the state the only actor in international politics, rather as a key actor among several. Therefore, to understand the external (or internal) behavior of nation-states, one must consider other variables such as the role of domestic, regional, and international institutions, and the nature of interactions between these actors, and how they perceive each other.
- The third variable is the decision-making process, which refers to the process of constructing and formulating the foreign and external behavior of certain states. In other words, constructivists perceived foreign policy not only as a product of the interactions, constraints, and power relations within material structural but also of normative. Constructivists stress the role of agency and in particular the identities, values, motives, and ideals of individuals and non-state actors. The agent-structure debate concentrates on two main problems, what are the political and societal implications of foreign policy on the first-image variables (the societal forces), and how do these behaviors affect the process of constructing the identities and motives of societal forces? Thus, the processes of constructing the culture, interests, norms, preferences, and ideals of social forces determines the official decision-making process and the orientation of state's external behaviors and relations with other actors (either states or non-state actors) in the international system.

Accordingly, I claim that the future of Egyptian foreign policy, according to the constructivist perspective, can be anticipated by understanding the causal relationship between these three variables. Moreover, by defining the hierarchies within the perception of the decision-makers who ultimately determine the national priorities of both foreign and domestic policies. The future of Egyptian foreign policy can be anticipated based on the outcomes of interrelations between three variables. For instance, if the relations are positive, i.e., adopting a Kantian conception of the international order, where harmony and convergence prevalence between the various social forces within the state. These outcomes make it possible to predict the changes that revolutionary states may undergo in the future. Thus, contributing to the process of (re)formation the collective culture, interests, norms, and values of these countries in a way that leads to positive foreign policies towards other states and actors in the international system. Under this state of anarchy, the state's values, identities, and norms play a vibrant constructive, and dynamic role that contributes to the processes of constructing national policies, initiatives, and preferences that the state adopts and implements. Conversely, the negative outcomes of relations between the three variables (i.e., the adoption of Hobbesian conception of anarchy), are driving revolutionary states to hostile positions prone to engage in armed conflicts with their neighbors (regionally and internationally). In such Hobbesian system, the prevalence of divergence between the various social forces, the deterioration of formal policies that fail to coincide and fulfil the aspirations and needs of the people, forced revolutionary states to adopt realistic, egoistic, and self-help foreign policy that emphasizes more on relative gains rather absolute gains.

4 Regional Balance of Power in the Middle East after the Arab Uprisings

Each nation-state seeks to achieve security and survival, but how can this be attained? The answer mainly depends on decision-makers' perceptions, and on how they understand the balance of power status, how they evaluate their national capabilities in relation to other powers in the system, and above all how they perceive the nature of the international structure.[27] Any theory, according to Waltz and others, is trying to provide 'explanations' not 'expectations' of a certain phenomenon, and if it tells us 'Whether' something

---

27 Singer 1960:461; Lobell Ripsman and Taliaferro 2009.

will happen, it does not, and should not, say 'when' or 'how' it will happen.[28] Accordingly, in international politics, states coexist in an anarchic international system (where there are no higher authorities above states), dominated by uncertainty and competition, ruled by self-help mechanisms, and depending only on their capabilities and sources of power (primarily military and economic) to ensure their security. For small states, like most of the GCC countries, because of the imbalance of power and capabilities between them and larger, stronger, and more aggressive neighbors, these countries tend to follow strategies such as Balancing, Bandwagoning, Appeasement, and Neutrality, as well as other strategies, in order to confront external threats imposed by other powers.[29] For neorealists like Mearsheimer, if you are not a predator in an anarchic system, you will be prey.[30]

Regarding the small states (such as most of the GCC countries), realists believe that the main criterion that determines their external behavior is the threat to their security and survival (or: is it vulnerable?) Given the fact that the international system does not discourage aggressive behavior, in the case of lack of capabilities to protect their security and sovereignty, small states can be pushed to concentrate on pursuing, maintaining, and adopting realistic strategies to protect their core values and preserve their position in the balance of power.[31] In international politics, it is survival that is the most important value for all states, not cooperation or potential profit.[32]

---

28 Mearsheimer and Walt 2013: 434–435; Mearsheimer 2009: 242–243.
29 Kenneth Waltz defines Balancing behavior as "joining with the weaker side to prevent hegemonic bids" while he defined the behavior of Bandwagoning as "joining the stronger coalition" (Waltz 1979: 126). Likewise, Stephen Van Evera defines Balancing as "aligning against the greatest threat to a state's independence" and Bandwagoning as "to give in to threats" (Van Evera 1990/1991:20). As for the definition of Appeasement while Paul Kennedy defined it as "the policy of settling international (or for that matter domestic) quarrels by admitting and satisfying grievances through rational negotiation and compromise thereby avoiding the resort to an armed conflict which would be expensive bloody and possibly very dangerous" (Kennedy 1976:195) Daniel Treisman defined it as "the policy of making unilateral concessions to a challenger or potential challenger in the hope of avoiding or delaying conflict" [which] "does not require any rational negotiation or compromise. On the contrary the concessions envisioned are unilateral" (Treisman 2004:347). Finally, Neutrality means "impartiality or non-belligerency" or as Pertti Joenniemi defined it "a policy designed to restrict and regulate the use of force in international relations. It creates political space for states wishing to differentiate themselves as neutrals in a power political arena while maintaining their connection with states willing to engage in war" (Joenniemi 1993:289).
30 Mearsheimer 2013: 74.
31 Mearsheimer 2009: 243–244.
32 Glaser 2003; Powell 1991.

These conditions oblige small and rich Gulf States to submit to the security and defense umbrella of friendly great powers, which the Gulf leaders believe to be the sole protectors of their sovereignty and security. This tendency illuminates why most of the Third World countries formed deep relations and bandwagon with the US during the Cold War and its aftermath, despite relinquishing many aspects of their sovereign rights and independence. Obviously, the GCC countries realize that in the case of an outbreak of an armed conflict between themselves and their neighbors (or even civil war), the European Union with its current institutional structure (which is driven by principles rather than interests) does not have the capacity or will to intervene to protect them. In contrast, US policy is driven more by interests than by principles and relies more on bilateral alliances than on international institutions. Given their grievous international and regional experiences, the GCC states learned that the most important value is to protect their survival, not to realize gains, as liberals argue. In fact, GCC countries admire the EU economic and political model, but because these states coexist with an anarchic and hostile world, their regimes prefer to join the Western camp.

Since they gained their independence in the late 1960s, the newborn regimes in the Gulf seek to maximize oil's utility by using great powers' needs and dependency on oil to supply arms, to rely upon its defensive umbrella to protect autocratic pro-Western regimes, and to protect sovereignty that might be threatened by revisionist neighbors.[33] Clearly, the less democratic the state, the more likely it is to adopt Realist policies. This means that these states prefer to establish bilateral relations with great powers to ensure their security and survival, rather than to build multilateral relations with other great powers, even if the benefits of multilateral relations would exceed the gains of bilateral relations with the pacifier.[34] For small states, security and defense considerations undoubtedly are a matter of life or death.

In the last few decades, the Gulf regional order has witnessed more than three wars, with the average rate of warfare in the Gulf being one war per decade (1980, 1990, and 2003). Consequently, these conditions pushed small and rich GCC countries to seek long-term security commitments and ensure the provision of a defense umbrella from friendly great powers. This could explain the deep relations and bandwagoning of Third World countries with the US in the post-Cold War order, despite the intervention and exploitation of independence and sovereignty of these countries by the US.[35] Small GCC states

---

33 Layne 2009.
34 Hook and Niblock 2015; Fürtig 2007; Al Shayji 2014.
35 Cordesman 2004; Ramazani 1988.

realized that in the event of an outbreak of conflict between them and their larger neighbors (or even of internal civil war), the EU, with its current institutional structure driven by principles rather than interests, has neither the capabilities nor the will to intervene and protect GCC states' sovereignty and security. By contrast, US policy in the Middle East region is driven by interests rather than principles and relies on bilateral alliances rather than international institutions. Based on their international and regional experience, the GCC countries believe that the most important goal is ensuring their survival, not realizing gains, as liberal theorists argue.

In brief, neorealism may offer only partial prospects of understanding and illuminating the origins, motivations, and role of social forces and ideational and non-material variables in constructing nation-states' policies and strategic choices. Nevertheless, it certainly still has the ability to provide a rigorous analysis of strategic and political options and explain the mechanisms of survival in the international system, especially in prone-to-conflict and hot zones such as the Middle East and the Arabian Gulf. Such fields are better addressed and discussed by both neoliberal institutionalists and the English School.

5 Between Morsi and Sisi: Regime Change and Egypt-GCC Relations

The complexity of the unprecedented deteriorating security situation in the region since 2011 jeopardizes the stability and security of the GCC states on broad and multiple fronts and levels. Understanding the political, economic, and social situation within the GCC countries is essential in order to analyze the repercussions of revolutions and regional instability for the domestic situation within the GCC.

5.1 *Locally*

According to Human Development Reports, GCC countries are the most advanced of the MENA region in terms of economic and developmental growth. They are top of the list of Arab developed countries, preceding some Western developed countries. According to UNDP Human Development Report (2014), Qatar ranked no. 31 globally, while Saudi Arabia ranked 34, UAE ranked 40 and Kuwait 46. In per capita income, GCC countries occupy the world's high-income scale. According to World Bank reports, income in Qatar registers at $119,029, Kuwait $85,820, UAE $58,068, and Saudi Arabia $52,109, compared to $10,440 in Tunisia, $10,400 in Egypt, and $3,945 in Yemen[36] (see Table 4.1).

---

36   UNDP 2014 2011; The World Bank 2014.

TABLE 4.1   GCC countries by GDP per capita (by US dollar) (2013–2014)

Country	2013	2104	World ranked 2014	HDI rank
Saudi Arabia	21,430	52,109	34	Very high human development
UAE	42,293	58,068	40	Very high human development
Qatar	77,987	119,029	31	Very high human development
Kuwait	47,935	85,820	46	Very high human development
Bahrain	21,345	32,072	44	Very high human development
Oman	25,330	42,191	56	High human development
Egypt	5,547	10,400	110	High human development
Tunisia	8,258	10,440	90	High human development
Yemen	2,060	3,945	154	Low human development

SOURCE: UNDP 2014: 160–162; 2013: 162–164

Despite this advanced status, increased oil revenues, and the relative stability of the GCC compared to other Middle Eastern states, GCC countries still face domestic, social, and political issues. The relative absence of democracy is the main reason behind this unrest along with the political exclusion of a large segment of the population, monopolization of power, and lack of openness and transparency in some of these countries. This, in part, creates and spreads extremist ideas within Gulf societies, especially in Saudi Arabia. According to a recent poll, the popularity of extremist groups such as Al-Qaida and ISIS is growing among Saudi citizens. Another study shows that most ISIS and other radical violent groups' fighters in Iraq, Syria, Yemen, etc., come from certain Gulf countries. If this problem remains unsolved, it may be a platform for potential instability in the GCC.

5.2   *Regionally*

This level of analysis considers regional conflicts as the biggest source of threat that GCC countries have faced recently. Inter- and intra-relations between GCC countries (particularly between Qatar, the United Arab Emirates, and Saudi Arabia) are muddled by inconsistent policies on approaching regional crises. This is reflected in the growing media war between these three countries. Such differences lead to an unprecedented tension point in the record of Gulf countries' relations. Saudi Arabia, UAE, and Bahrain are temporarily freezing their relations with Doha and withdrawing their ambassadors: an action interpreted by some experts and pundits as a sign of failure of the regional integration model over the last five decades.

The tension between GCC countries and other regional players, such as Iran and Turkey, is known to be characterized by tension and unpredictability. The long and continued hostility between Iran specifically and Saudi Arabia, and as a result, its GCC allies, is well-known. As for Turkey, UAE announced in 2013 the freezing of its 12-billion-dollar investments in Turkey because of the latter's policy towards Arab countries such as Egypt and Syria.[37] As the regime change resulting from revolutions restructured foreign policies and changed regional players, the tension between those countries has been alleviated in some cases.

It is also worth mentioning the threat posed by the Islamic State (ISIS) group to the GCC countries. The dominance of this violent extremist group in Iraq and Syria represents a regional and international threat. A map published by IS recently shows Kuwait as within the territorial ambitions of the Islamic State. In Saudi Arabia, Saudi fighters affiliated with the Islamic State have executed many terrorist attacks in the last 15 months (Mackay 2014). Due to the internationalization and regionalization of the conflict in Syria, Iraq, Yemen, and elsewhere, the dangers from ISIS could be more complicated and harder to contain in the short term, especially if the GCC's discordant policies continue.

6   Egypt–GCC Relations Issues

Implicitly, the Arab Uprising constituted a big challenge to GCC countries' regional stability and security. We disagree with most of the predictions that argue that, because of their historical attitudes towards revolutions and revolutionary regimes in the region since the sixties, the GCC countries might take hostile decisions against Egypt and its people. Due to the GCC's close relations with the Mubarak regime and its dissatisfaction with the way he was treated after he stepped down, as well as what some called "Egypt's rapprochement with Iran" and the Muslim Brotherhood regime's appeasement by the Iranian regime, Gulf relations with Egypt will become more divided, and even conflictual, in the coming years. All these predictions are reductive and oversimplified arguments; they ignore facts about the historical, economic, cultural, and long-term political and strategic partnership between the two parties since the mid-1970s.

---

37   Makahleh 2015; Hurriyet 2013; Arabian Business 2013; Al-monitor 2013.

There are many major issues between Gulf Cooperation Council countries and Egypt: from economic aid to political and strategic cooperation, fighting terrorism, maintaining, and preserving Gulf security and regional stability, the situation in Syria and Libya, and of course the violent military conflict in Yemen, and other regional issues. But due to the length limits of this chapter, we choose to discuss just five major issues that will shed light on how relations between the two parties have developed and changed since 2011.

7   Bilateral Relations

Relations between the GCC and Egypt will be discussed according to the nature of both regimes. The change in foreign policies starting from 2011 will be analyzed in terms of the change in regimes. However, there will be more emphasis on the relations between Saudi Arabia and Egypt, as the Saudis are the determinant for the most part due to its greater influence in the regional arena. During the course of events in Egypt following the Arab Uprising, the foreign policies of Saudi Arabia were more direct and influential. This is due to the structure of the Saudi system as one of the major regional players in the Arab World, in addition to Iran. Whereas relations between Egypt and Saudi will be the focus of the topic, there will also be some emphasis on the change of relations amongst Egypt and the GCC countries the UAE and Qatar. To analyze the dynamics of the relationship between Saudi Arabia and Egypt, it is essential to provide some historical background on Saudi, as it also provides the platform for the dynamics of the relationship between Egypt and the GCC.

"Saudi Arabia stands at the center of many critical issues and crises which are confronting the Middle East, the Islamic World and the wider global order today".[38] To understand the influence of Saudi Arabia, developments within the country will be a condition of analysis of the pattern of international relations in the 21st century. The country's significance emerges from the global dependence on Saudi Arabian oil and gas, and the critical role of the country regarding security issues in the GCC and the Middle East – specifically on issues of radical Islamism and international terrorism.[39]

The substantial economic importance of Saudi Arabia will be central to understanding the issue. According to 2002 figures, Saudi Arabia holds 25%

---

38   Niblock 2006.
39   ibid.

of the world's remaining oil reserves.[40] While worldwide oil reserves are estimated at 1,050 billion barrels, Saudi's reserves are proven to be 260 billion, given that 65% of oil reserves are situated in the Middle East. In addition, Saudi Arabian oil is relatively cheaper than that from elsewhere, which makes it more attractive in the global market. This shows an aspect of the regional and global importance of Saudi Arabia.

What is essential to know about the start of Saudi Arabian state formation is the religious and traditional legitimacy that characterizes it. This influences the other important dimension of Saudi significance, which is its stance on radical Islamism and international terrorism. This is certainly due to Saudi Arabia containing Islam's two most holy sites, which attract millions of pilgrims every year. This necessitates the critical religious character of the country; thus, any government must emphasize its role as the protector of the holy sites and Islam.

Another dimension is the Saudi Arabian influence on regional issues in the Gulf and the Middle East due to the country's strategic position and importance. The critical dimension in which the policies of Saudi Arabia become more direct, and complex is that of the Gulf Wars and the issues with revolutionary Iran (1979). During the Iraq-Kuwait war, Saudi Arabia's invitation to the US to deploy troops was a critical event, which later impacted on the dynamics of the Middle East. It was also divisive within the country itself, as it triggered extremist movements such as Al-Qaida to react violently against this incident. The invitation to American troops was regarded by those extremist movements as a betrayal of Islam, as Saudi Arabia allowed foreign troops to deploy their movements in Islam's holiest lands. Therefore, it was a radicalizing turning point which marked the beginning of a campaign against the Arab leaderships.[41]

The strategic security issues posed by radical Islamism played on regional issues, clearly instigating fears of these issues' socioeconomic and strategic impact on oil production. These events triggered the need for a new approach from which to secure Saudi interests. This point will be crucial in explaining the dynamic that shaped Saudi interactions with the changing political regime in Egypt, especially with the Muslim Brotherhood's ascent to power.

8 The GCC and the Arab Uprising in Egypt

The acute social tensions plaguing the Arab countries, with an emphasis on radical Islamism, in addition to the governments' efforts to achieve economic

---

40   ibid.
41   Baxter and Akbarzadeh 2008.

and political development amidst these crises, were certain to bring the events to a climax. According to the author Tim Niblock, the attempt of Arab countries to tackle these issues by putting forward the image of democracy "while unwilling to risk their future to electoral processes" was destined to cause political conflict.[42] Niblock predicted the escalation of this conflict in 2008, stating that if the failure of political elites, or an ill-considered intervention by external powers, were to take place, the Middle East could become an arena of conflict. This described the events that occurred specifically in 2011, that is, the Arab Uprising, which had critical consequences for security within the Middle East, in addition to a considerable rise in extremist movements.

The Islamic character of Saudi Arabia, along with its stance towards extremism, establishes a platform on which its reaction to the Muslim Brotherhood can be understood. The removal of the Muslim Brotherhood by the military establishment triggered two reactions within the GCC. While Qatar was sympathetic to the Muslim Brotherhood, the UAE and Saudi Arabia were united in their opposition to its regime. Primarily, this can be explained by the aspirations of the Muslim Brotherhood, which threaten the sovereignty of countries, specifically monarchies in the GCC. The aspirations of such groups are towards "*Khilafa*", which means the unification of all Arab countries under one Islamic Republic. While Saudi was not concerned about this eventuality, it was more apprehensive about the destabilizing effect of the Muslim Brotherhood in the region.[43] That would be the appeal of the cause to some groups, given the extremism in the Middle East and the transnational connections between them. In other words, the threat that Saudi Arabia and the GCC countries faced from the Muslim Brotherhood was existential in nature.

9 Egypt and Saudi Arabia

During the age of Arab nationalism, primarily employed by the Egyptian president Jamal Abdel Nasser in the 60s, the relation between Egypt and Saudi Arabia was competitive. With Egypt's ideological and charismatic influence in the Arab World, Saudi has bristled at its role within the region. In respect of Egypt's size and history, it has played a significant role on the Arab stage. For example, the Arab League was established in 1945 in Cairo. Although Saudi Arabia was among the founding members of the League, it was largely based in

---

42 Niblock 2006: 7.
43 Hellyer 2015.

Egypt. During Saudi Arabia's rise in the 1970s oil boom, the expulsion of Egypt from the Arab league due to its peace treaty with Israel caused a temporary change. However, Egypt continued to maintain its dominant role in the organization in 1989, with Amr Moussa as secretary general.[44]

Nevertheless, over the past decade, Egypt's influence in the regional arena has diminished and Saudi Arabia has filled the gap. It could be said that the competition between Egypt and Saudi for the leadership of the Arab World turned in Saudi's favor. With the economic, political, and social downturn in Egypt during Mubarak's reign, Saudi Arabia enjoyed rising status due to its financial prowess and rising oil prices. However, certain events influenced the establishment of stronger ties between Egypt and Saudi Arabia despite the political rivalry of the previous decades.

From 2004 until the revolution, according to the Egyptian Minister of Trade and Labour, bilateral trade between the two countries increased by 350%. Saudi Arabia was Egypt's "largest Arab export destination and source of imports".

> Cairo's exports to Saudi Arabia reached USD926 million (up from USD600 million in 2007), while imports from the kingdom totaled USD2.6 billion. Saudi exports to Egypt are on track to surpass USD3 billion in 2009. Taken together, this USD3.5 billion in 2008 bilateral trade represents more than a third of Egypt's commerce in the Arab world.[45]

In addition, there were various investment projects undertaken by Saudi Arabia in Egypt. For example, in 2008, the Construction Project Holding Company (CPC) was established with an investment of USD 120 million. Furthermore, the kingdom provided more opportunities for Egyptian labor. This shows the strong economic ties between the two countries, which aimed to establish a political alliance. It also raises questions such as: How did the pre-existing rivalry between the two countries over the leadership of the Arab World transform to an alliance between them? The answer to this question lies within the regional dynamics of the countries surrounding the Gulf. With Iran's ascendance as a regional player, the dynamics influenced the Sunni, pro-US authoritarian regime to seek alliances for balance of power purposes. Therefore, Saudi Arabia's economic assistance to Egypt and the mutual benefits between the two countries were efforts to strengthen their influence within the region and so to counter Iran's strength. It is also noteworthy that, given the power

---

44   Schenker and Henderson 2009.
45   ibid: 2.

vacuum in Iraq, Iran's influence was growing because of Shiite domination in Iraq. Furthermore, Syria was and still is allied with Iran. Hence, the regional dynamics of the situation pushed Saudi Arabia to seek alliances within the region to strengthen its influence.

However, with the Arab Uprising occurring in 2011, there was even more change in regional dynamics. First, although the nature of authoritarian regimes remained the same in the Arab World, there was more emphasis on alliance building as the rivalry between Saudi Arabia and Iran became increasingly apparent. With the power vacuum in both Syria and Iraq, the transnational extremist and terrorist movements, and the ascension of the former president Morsi of the Muslim Brotherhood to the presidency, the situation became further complicated for Saudi Arabia.

The history of the relationship between the Muslim Brotherhood and Saudi Arabia is an unpleasant one. As instability was brought about by the Iraq-Kuwait war in 1991, the Muslim Brotherhood supported Saddam Hussein against the Gulf monarchies. Hence, the Brotherhood was an instigating factor for the instability of that period. In addition, their general aspiration to form an Islamic caliphate totally defied the sovereignty of the Gulf monarchies. Nevertheless, during their ascension to the presidency, there was still an effort by Saudi Arabia to reconcile with the Brotherhood so as to avoid confrontation. For example, during President Morsi's visit to Saudi Arabia on July 11th, 2012, the Saudis provided Egypt with around USD 2 billion in financial and economic assistance.[46]

Nevertheless, when the Muslim Brotherhood were ousted from power by the Egyptian military, Saudi Arabia, and the UAE both showed their strong support for that move by sending huge amounts of monetary aid. Saudi's economic aid to Egypt after the ouster of President Morsi in July was around USD 5 billion. The United Arab Emirates provided Egypt with USD 2 billion in economic aid.

This shows their firm support for the new government and for the expulsion of the Brotherhood from power. It also shows the importance of Egypt to the GCC. When Egypt was spiraling out of control during the Muslim Brotherhood's ascension to power and it was clear that they were unable to control the country, Saudi Arabia and the UAE sensed an undeniable threat emerging from the situation. This is evident from their support for the new regime and their alliance with President Abdel-Fattah El-Sisi.

In sum, the regional dynamics of Saudi Arabia and the changes within its political system during the 1960s have shaped its reactions to the regime change

---

[46] Ottaway 2015.

in Egypt. Furthermore, the changes within the balance of power, mostly caused by Iran's stronger influence in regional politics due to the power vacuum in Iraq, also caused Saudi to seek alliances within the Middle East to counter its force. Nevertheless, the religious character of Saudi Arabia and its reactions against extremist movements caused tension in its relations with Egypt due to the Muslim Brotherhood's ascension to power. However, the removal of the Muslim Brotherhood from power and the ascension of President Sisi has led to a strong alliance between the two countries, as Egypt is dependent on Saudi Arabia for economic aid. Thus, the influence of Saudi Arabia within Egyptian domestic politics is highly evident.

10   Economic Aid

Amidst this tempestuous situation of regional revolutions and popular uprisings in the Arab World, it has become clear that, consequently, the coming change from the west (Tunisia and Egypt) will extend to the rich monarchies in the east, sooner or later.[47] If radical change occurs in these countries, especially Saudi Arabia, it will have tremendous impacts on the entire region, if not the world, by freeing citizens and vast wealth from waste, investing instead in real development projects throughout the entire region.[48] This is why GCC regimes feared the spread of the revolution's "virus" into its territories. When the revolution promised to break out in countries like Bahrain and Oman, the other GCC countries (especially Saudi Arabia and United Arab Emirates) made efficient efforts to curb and extinguish it quickly.

These monarchies have a huge amount of wealth, accumulated over the years from oil revenues (after the oil embargo of 1973), that helped to guarantee the loyalty of their own citizens. Through a series of incentives, grants, and tenders, with the aim of avoiding the destiny of countries like Egypt, Libya, Tunisia, and others, the GCC countries hope that these steps will raise living standards, create more jobs, improve the level of public services, etc. All these steps could gradually ease the severity of internal political tension and unrest. The rich Gulf monarchies pumped around $45 billion into avoiding the outbreak of revolution within GCC borders. Saudi Arabia, for example, gave Bahrain 5 billion and Oman 5 billion, in addition to similar actions by Kuwait, Qatar and the United Arab Emirates. Hopefully, these monarchies think that

---

47   Davidson 2012: 2.
48   Heikal 1992.

redistribution (albeit slight) of wealth and oil revenues can contribute greatly to calming these kingdoms and absorbing their domestic unrest.[49]

On their side, GCC countries have responded to these announcements by providing more than twenty billion dollars in financial support to help the Egyptian regime recover from economic losses and damage caused by the revolution; this includes $3 billion from the United Arab Emirates, $4 billion from Saudi Arabia, and $5 Billion from Kuwait.[50] Later indicators show that these countries have exploited their funding and aid to control the path of democratization, designing and directing Egyptian politics (internal and external) in such a manner as to preserve and maintain their own national interests, rather than Egyptian interests.

11 Political Support

Since the revolution of 1952, and even before that, the Egyptian regime has looked to the Gulf States as an integral part of Egypt's national security system. Traditionally, Egypt has been at the forefront of actors interested in Gulf affairs. The Egyptian regime tried to resolve their crises and conflicts during the second half of the twentieth century and to deter attempts at domination by regional and international aggressive and hostile parties, from the Shah of Iran to Saddam Hussein, and recently the Islamic Republic of Iran.[51]

Even after the outbreak of the 25th of January, and despite its weakness and vulnerability, the new regime in Cairo has kept its commitment to do so. From day one, it was clear that the Egyptian revolution was rooted in pan-Arab and nationalistic trends, and in the belief that the security of Egypt depended, not only on that of its sovereign borders, but also on that of the Arab countries. This perspective emerged from Egyptian geographic and strategic thinker and scholar Gamal Hamdan, who once wrote that: "Egypt's national security in its wide circle begins from the Taurus mountains in the north, passing through the Arabian Gulf into the east, until the headwaters of the Nile in the south, and to the Strait of Gibraltar in the west[52]" – which means that the new decision-makers of Egyptian foreign policy would put the interests of the Arabian cycle (and especially the GCC countries) at the top of its priorities.

---

49 Dadush and Dunn 2011.
50 Reuters 2015.
51 On Egypt's relations with the Gulf countries since the late sixties, see Kerr 1971.
52 Hamdan 1982.

Egypt's first prime minister after the revolution, Essam Sharaf, visited Gulf countries in his first foreign trip after Sudan, where he placed emphasis on the deep relations between Egypt and the Arab Gulf countries and Egypt's commitment to their security and stability. Mr. Sharaf said, "there is no doubt that the Egyptian Gulf relations [are] characterized by a high degree of excellence and continuity. It builds on solid foundations of strong conviction, where Egypt believes that the security of the Gulf is a red line".[53]

Similarly, the minister of foreign affairs, Dr. Nabil Al-Arabi, announced that the "Arab Gulf region represents a strategic depth to Egyptian national security, maintains stability in the Gulf, represents a national commitment and a strategic necessity at the same time". Also, he asserted that "Egypt's commitment to the unity, stability and territorial integrity of each country in the Gulf, is considered one of the fundamentals of Egyptian foreign policy principles, which believe that the security, stability, and identity of the Arab Gulf States are a red line". On another occasion, Mr. Al-Arabi declared, "Egypt relations with Iran won't be at the expense of Egypt's relations with the Arab Gulf, or [at the] expense of [Gulf States'] security and stability".[54]

The assumption that the GCC countries would jeopardize their strategic, political, and economic partnership with Egypt for a single person is illogical. As conservatives, the leaders of these countries might have objections to and make observations about what happened to Mubarak; however, these leaders are also known for their pragmatic and realistic actions when it comes to national security or their own survival. For strategic and security considerations, GCC leaders know that their relations with Egypt (the society and the state) are more essential than their personal relationships with Mubarak (or other leaders), which means that they will be compelled to accept the provisions issued by the Egyptian judiciary against Mubarak and his family.

12 Regional Stability

When the Supreme Council of the Armed Forces (SCAF) was in power, it was aware of all attempts at provocation and entanglement by other regional (Iran, Turkey, Israel) and international (United States and the European Union) powers that were trying to embroil the revolution in order to provoke it and display SCAF as incapable of running or controlling the situation inside the country, or

---

53 Arabiya 2011; Ezzat 2011; Farouk 2014.
54 Toumi 2011; Al Arabiya 2011; Daily News Egypt 2011.

as acting hostilely toward specific countries, or being biased in favor of other countries. The SCAF has successfully survived all these attempts, whether through reaffirming the commitment to respect peace agreements with Israel signed by the former regime or allowing the transit of Iranian military ships through the Suez Canal for the first time since the Iranian revolution of 1979. Such actions must be seen and understood in the overall context and time frame in which they took place (domestically in particular) rather than projecting them onto results, which will prove to be faulty after the new regime stabilizes.

13   Conclusion

To recap, following the theoretical analysis of revolutions, a pattern across the ways neighboring countries deal with revolutionary regimes can be assessed. Revolutionary regimes pose a threat to regional security and stability, as their ability to spread across countries and even continents is very powerful. It is noteworthy that the sense of threat that is felt by the GCC countries is the more powerful due to their regime structure as monarchies. In addition, the social divisions that characterize Middle Eastern society further increase the risk of political upheavals.

It is important to understand the factors that shape the foreign policy and external behavior of GCC countries towards their neighbors. These factors primarily emerge from these countries' concern about security, stability and the conflicts that can be caused by the possible spread of revolutionary ideas across their own borders. However, another strategy that was employed by these countries was a "friendly" attempt to assist the revolutionary regimes to overcome social and economic crises. This strategy is pursued to contain the conflict as much as possible and prevent its escalation. One situation in which this can be observed is Morsi's visit to Saudi Arabia in 2012, when Egypt received USD 2 billion in foreign aid. This was an attempt by the Saudis to contain the tensions between the two countries. However, when the regime was ousted, Saudi Arabia and the UAE provided even larger amounts of aid, which proved their opposition to the Muslim regime in spite of their attempts at reconciliation with it. Therefore, GCC countries are mainly concerned with maintaining the status quo of the regional balance of power and prevent the spread of turmoil and instability.

Within this pattern, accordingly, the relation between Egypt's revolutionary regime and the GCC countries can be explained. During Morsi's ascendancy to power, the tension between Egypt and the GCC countries, specifically the UAE and Saudi, was apparent. The sources of this tension can mostly be found within Saudi's stance on extremist movements. The approach adopted by Saudi in dealing with this can be traced in its history, specifically the 1970s. Events relating to Al-Qaida and the Gulf Wars are essential to understanding Saudi's stance on this matter. Furthermore, the threat also emerges from the aspirations of groups like the Muslim Brotherhood, which seek the establishment of "Khilafa": the unification of all Muslim states under a single leadership.

When Morsi and the Muslim Brotherhood regime were ousted from power, Saudi Arabia and the UAE sent a substantial amount of aid to Egypt. This shows their approval and support of the military removal of the Muslim Brotherhood from power. Now, the relation between Egypt and Saudi Arabia can be characterized as a formal alliance. This is due to the nature of the regimes being more compatible. Hence, the alliance can be characterized as both an economic and a military alliance. Finally, the influence of Saudi Arabia in particular is very apparent within Egyptian politics.

CHAPTER 5

Undesired Revolution

Power Transition in the Arab World

Structural realism claims to explain international political phenomena, whether of conflict or cooperation, but in fact it places emphasis on great power politics. This raises the question of whether structural realism offers the right lens through which to understand and explain behavior and relations between small states. Its explanation of these phenomena lies in its arguments, concepts, and perceptions as to the nature of international politics, which then are used to interpret these states' behavior.

Kenneth Waltz, the founding father of structural realism, argued that since the emergence of nation-states and even since the Peloponnesian war between the Greek city-states (Athens and Sparta), the international system has had the following characteristics. (1) It is an anarchic system, containing no higher authority above states (the only unit of analysis), which maintain the right to direct and impose their will on others. This system is also (2) a self-help system, in which nation-states rely only on themselves to protect their security and maintain their survival. (3) The quest for survival is the main driving force for their external behavior towards the remaining units and members of international society; therefore, (4) states seek to strengthen their power and expand their security positions. (5) Nation-states are rational instruments that achieve their goals by adopting a rational approach; and their actions are not random but are subject to complicated (cost-benefit) calculations.[1]

According to structural realism, these principles shape states' external behaviors; therefore, countries are essentially interested in preserving their security and survival, and the only way to achieve these goals is through self-reliance and removal of sources of threat by deterring other strong and aggressive states. States tend to build their national capacity, coalitions, and alliances with other great power/s to cope with common threats (as balance of power and threat theories suggest). Choosing between these two patterns depends on leaders' perception and estimation of power distribution, identification of source of threats, and choice of protectors and pacifists.

---

1 Waltz 1979, 2000.

Even though structural realism, as Waltz has repeatedly stated, has been widely recognized as a theory of international politics that explains the behavior of great powers in the international system, rather than a theory of foreign policy that explains certain state behaviors, I argue that structural realism is still able to provide an explanation for states' policies and strategic choices, independently of their size.[2] Moreover, structural realism does not deal with bilateral relations, but with general patterns of international interactions; in addition, it is a theory for "great powers" rather than one for "small states" or a general theory of International Relations. Some scholars have argued that both Waltz and proponents of his theory intentionally neglect the study and analysis of small states,[3] which is an accurate deficiency.

Substantially, structural realism may have partial prospects when it comes to understanding and illuminating the origins, motivations, role of social forces, ideational and non-material variables in constructing nation-states' policies and strategic choices. Nevertheless, it certainly still can provide a rigorous analysis of strategic and political options and explain the mechanisms of survival in the international system, especially in prone-to-conflict and hot zones such as the Middle East and Arabian Gulf. In general, these claims are partly correct. Reconsideration of the main assumptions of Waltz's theory shows that he partly touched on or dealt with small states' behavior, despite having acknowledged that he constructed his theory based on the actions of major powers, as the largest and most important actors in international politics.[4] For example, Waltz focused on maintaining security and survival in general, but did not indicate how to achieve it, even by great powers. Waltz also argued that structural realism does not aim to explain the foreign policy of a particular state, but instead to clarify the general principles that govern the conduct of all actors in international politics.[5]

Every nation-state seeks to achieve security and survival, but how can this be done? The answer mainly depends on decision-makers' perceptions, and how they understand the balance of power status, evaluate their national capabilities along with those of other powers in the system, and above all on how they perceive the nature of the international structure.[6] Any theory, according to Waltz and others, is trying to provide "explanations" not "expectations" of a certain phenomenon, and if it indicates "whether" something

---

2 Waltz 1996; Elman 1996; Telhami 2002; Fearon 1998.
3 Telhami 2003.
4 Waltz 1979: 97–98.
5 Elman 1995; Ayoob 2002; Ingebritsen et al. 2006.
6 Singer 1961: 461. Lobell, Ripsman and Taliaferro 2009; Starr 2006; Rose 1998.

will happen, it does not, and should not, say "when" or "how" it will happen.[7] Accordingly, in international politics, states coexist in an international anarchic system where there are no higher authorities above states, dominated by uncertainty and competition, ruled by self-help mechanisms, depending only on their own capabilities and sources of power (primarily military and economic) to ensure their security. Small states, like most of the GCC countries, because of the imbalance of power and capabilities between themselves and other larger, stronger, and more aggressive neighbors, tend to follow strategies such as Balancing, Neutrality, Bandwagoning, Appeasement, and Dependency, as well as other strategies for confronting external threats imposed by other powers.[8] For [offensive] neorealists like Mearsheimer, if you are not a predator in an anarchic system, you will be prey.[9]

Contrary to this view, political scientist Randall Schweller argues that for nation-states in peacetime, when there are no explicit security dilemmas and apparent grave threats, secondary goals such as acquiring more power, maximizing relative gains, and living in peace and tranquility become primary goals.[10] Given that survival has been ensured, states will seek to enhance the level of cooperation and integration, and to maximize their relative gains. As a result, great powers will appreciate small states' support for their own interests by not obstructing, restraining, or de-legitimizing the latter's actions. Furthermore, small states will bandwagon with a larger state in case they fail to curb a potential hegemony and/or have to deter aggression from neighbors that threaten their survival.[11]

According to other realists (defensive realism in particular,), the main criterion that determines small states' external behavior is the threat to their security and survival (or: is it vulnerable?). Because the international system does not discourage aggressive behavior, in the case of inadequate capability to guard their security and sovereignty, small states can be pushed to concentrate on pursuing, maintaining, and adopting realistic strategies to protect their core values and preserve their position in the balance of power.[12] In international politics, it is survival that is the most important value for all states, not cooperation or gains.[13]

---

7   Mearsheimer and Walt 2013: 434–35; Mearsheimer 2009: 242–243.
8   Walt 1987: 21–22.
9   Mearsheimer 2013: 74.
10 Schweller and Priess 1997: 8–9.
11 Ibid; Walt 1985; Schweller 1994.
12 Mearsheimer 2009: 243–244.
13 Glaser 2003, 1997; Powell 1991.

Neorealist explanations of nation-state behaviors prevail when national interests that have an impact on the national security of X state are linked to or dependent on natural resources owned by other states.[14] The clear example of this is the case of GCC countries' relations with great powers such as Great Britain (before 1968) and the United States.[15] Conventionally, most of the great powers in the current international system (i.e., the US, China, India, Brazil, and others), due to their dependence on GCC oil, compete with each other for national security considerations such as control of the production capacity and oil prices, in order to maintain their supremacy and keep the status quo of the world balance of power in their favor.[16]

1 Structural Realism and International Relations of the GCC Countries

According to structural realism, the GCC countries are just small, rich, and vulnerable states, surrounded by hostile larger powers, living in a permanent state of tension and instability resulting from the deep imbalance of regional power. Since the British "East of Suez" withdrawal of 1968, these countries have continued to bandwagon with great powers that assure their security and survival, and the persistence of ruling tribal regimes. In return, the newborn Gulf countries pledged to provide these friendly great powers (the protectors) with privileges and preferential treatment such as reasonable oil prices and acceptance of a military presence on their territories.[17] In summary, due to inability to deter powerful and aggressive neighbors, the GCC small states have become "pawns" and "subordinates" in the hands of great powers that provide a defense umbrella and ensure the security of the sheikhdoms.

Some might claim that this perspective is oversimplified and minimizes the role and importance of these countries outside the realm of oil and relations with great powers. Most Middle East experts are aware that, from a political-strategic perspective in economic terms, the Gulf regional order is an "American Gulf" and "Gulf of Oil" or "World's oil-artery". Emirati political scientist Abdulkhaliq Abdullah correctly argues that "outside these two factors, there is no significant contribution to the Arabian Gulf countries".[18]

---

14   Donnelly 2000; Porter 2016.
15   Gause 2010; Macris and Kelly 2012; Kemp 2012.
16   Luciani 2016; Price-Smith 2015; Duane 2009; Chapman and Khanna 2006 2004; Marafi 2009; David and Gagné 2007; Homer-Dixon 1991; Ullman 1983.
17   Gause 2010; Almezaini and Rickli 2017.
18   Abdullah 2011: 15; Al-Rumaihi 1996 2001; Naqīb 1990.

However, this factor does not diminish the importance of the GCC countries in the international arena. On the contrary, due to their possession of the largest oil reserves and their geopolitical significance, the GCC countries exert unparalleled influence over the global economic system that has existed since the end of the Second World War.[19] For instance, according to many studies, the Kingdom of Saudi Arabia is considered the pivotal state of the Arab World, as well as the cornerstone of the international economic system.[20] Proponents of this view suggest that, given its enormous oil reserves and production capacity, any tension or instability within the kingdom (the world's oil bank) would trigger a new global "great depression" like the one that hit the world in the 1930s, or even worse.[21] Because of Saudi Arabia's influential position, some experts believe that it has as much power as the US, the founder of the world economic system, if not more.

> Saudi Arabia is not only the world's largest oil producer and the holder of the world's largest oil reserves, but it also has a majority of the world's excess production capacity, which the Saudis use to stabilize and control the price of oil by increasing or decreasing production as needed. Because of the importance of both Saudi production and Saudi slack capacity, the sudden loss of the Saudi oil network would paralyze the global economy, probably causing a global downturn at least as devastating as the Great Depression of the 1930s, if not worse.[22]

2   The Characteristics of the Arabian Gulf Regional System

To understand the rise of Gulf States, and the interstate and regional relations with each other and other actors in international society, it is crucial to be comprehensively cognizant of the regional and inter-relational contexts of these states, known as the Gulf Regional System (GRS). According to Abdulkhaliq Abdullah, GRS is the geographical area that includes "all the gulf contiguous and coastal countries, [which] are considered, because of their interactions, linkages, and conflicts, a distinct regional unit".[23] This sub-regional system is distinct from the Arab Regional System. Also, the GRS is not the GCC. The GCC

---

19   Ulrichsen 2016.
20   Miller 2016; The Middle East Institute 2009; Kechichian 1999; Pollack 2003.
21   Pollack 2003: 3–4.
22   ibid: 4.
23   Abdullah 2011: 15.

includes all member states of the GRS except Iraq and Iran and was mainly established to deter and contain these two larger regional powers.[24] Certainly, the international relations of these countries cannot and should not be studied and explained apart from Iraq, Iran and even Yemen. These "outcast" neighbors are still an indispensable part of the context that determined and formed the GCC's internal-external behaviors.

Given the lack of capabilities to protect their security and sovereignty and the existence of many sources of threat, small states are compelled to pursue and adopt realistic strategies. To protect their core values even at the expense of greater economic gains, strategic rentier resources and significant geostrategic location, small GCC countries are expected to strengthen their security and expand their influence in international forums through tools and means such as multilateralism, strategic hedging, appeasement, and soft power diplomacy. GCC countries strongly believe that in international politics survival is the most important value, not cooperation or economic gains.[25]

Theoretically speaking, neorealist explanations of nation-states' behavior prevail when national interests that have an impact on the national security of X state are linked to or dependent on natural resources owned by other states. The obvious example of this case is the GCC countries' relations with great powers. Traditionally, most great powers, because of their dependence on oil, have competed with each other and tried to impose control over raw materials. This would allow them to keep their supremacy and maintain the status quo of the world balance of power in their favor. In turn, small states usually exploit great powers' oil needs for the sake of maximizing the resulting benefits, supplying, and purchasing more arms and military technology to protect and defend their sovereignty when it might be threatened by revisionist neighbors, and to bolster the defensive umbrella protecting the autocratic pro-Western monarchic regimes. At first glance, this relationship seems to be reciprocally beneficial for both parties, even if it comes at the expense of small states' independence and sovereignty.

Apparently, the less democratic the small states' regimes, the higher the likelihood that they will adopt realistic policies, which means that they would prefer to establish bilateral relations with great powers that protect and defend their security and survival, than to form multilateral relations with other great powers, even if the returns and the benefits of the latter policy would surpass

---

24 ibid.
25 Waltz 1979; Mearsheimer 2001.

the gains of bilateral relations with their pacifier. Security and defense considerations for small states are a matter of life or death.

Although the GCC countries are part of the MENA region, there are many characteristics that distinguish them from other countries in the region, especially in military and security terms. The first characteristic is that this area has always been a "Tripolar" sub-regional system. Since the end of the Second World War and after the end of Cold War, there have always been three major players: Iran, Iraq (until 2003) and Saudi Arabia.[26] Secondly, in this area, conflict (not peace) has been the dominant norm. Rivalries between major players never stop, whether they occur between Saudi Arabia and Iran, Saudi Arabia, and Iraq, Iran, and Iraq, or between the Gulf's newborn small states (Bahrain, Qatar, UAE, Oman, and Kuwait) and Saudi Arabia or Iran.[27] The third characteristic is that GCC states have always felt vulnerable and exposed, either to Iran and/or Iraq, who have sought to control the Gulf region since the end of the British presence in the region. The behavior of these two powerful countries is permanently identified by GCC countries as aggressive and expansionist. Iran tried to invade Bahrain in 1971, and to this day it occupies the three Emirates islands (Abu Musa and the Greater and Lesser Tunbs), while Iraq tried to engulf Kuwait in 1990.

The fourth characteristic is that in order to preserve their security and survival, these nations have always been in a state of alliance and under the defensive umbrella of one of the great powers since the Cold War (Great Britain, and the US after the British withdrawal from the East of Eden in 1971). The fifth characteristic is that, for the Arabian part of the Gulf, the dominant actor has always been the Saudis. Saudi Arabia established its own "Pax Saudica" or "sphere-of-influence" in the Arabian Gulf in the 1950s, when Al-Saud designed a military and strategic policy in this area of the Middle East that prevented the rise of any competitors and ensured that the Arabian part of the Gulf became mare nostrum, a Saudi lake.[28]

The "GCC Unity myth" is the sixth characteristic of the GCC conglomerate. Despite all the signs of cooperation and convergence between the six members of the Gulf Cooperation Council organization, many observers have argued that among them there are many salient fears and trepidations. For example, Kenneth Pollock argued that because of deep disputes among the tribes over historical territories in the pre-state era, the Qatari's US military bases were established not to shield them from Iran or Iraq but rather to deter Riyadh

---

26   Kechichian 1999: 233.
27   Gause 2010.
28   Kechichian 1999: 249.

from invading Doha. Bahrain also wants an advanced defensive missiles program, not to turn itself into an effective member of the Peninsula Shield Force (PSF), but to reinforce its preventive capabilities against Qatar should it ever feel the need to do so (Peterson 2011). Moreover, while the alliance between Saudi Arabia and the UAE is getting stronger, reports claim that Riyadh had started to complain about the growing power of Abu Dhabi as early as 2011.[29]

The seventh characteristic is that this region is a fundamentally off-balance system. The GCC countries suffer from a structural imbalance of power. According to balance of power theory, the Gulf region is divided into two camps: a powerful "Goliath" camp, which includes Iran, Iraq and Saudi Arabia, and a "David" camp, weak and small, that includes the GCC city-states (Qatar, Bahrain, Kuwait, UAE, and Oman). There is a great power disadvantage between the two camps in all aspects of capability and possibility (political, military, economic, etc.). For example, while the size of Saudi Arabia is about 2.2 million sq. km (about 49 percent of the GRS total area) and Iran's is about 1.6 million sq. km (about 35 percent of the Gulf region), the total area of UAE (77,000 sq. km), Qatar (11,000 sq. km), Bahrain (600 sq. km) and Kuwait (17,000 sq. km) does not exceed 2.4 percent of the total size of GRS. Due to the fear of threats, the small Gulf States thus seek to protect their security and stability, either through alliances with great powers from outside the region or via military build-up, coalitions, and counterbalancing against their hostile larger neighbors. This spiral model (to use Jervis's analogy) leads to a permanent state of tension and instability in the region.[30]

Lastly, this area can be characterized as a trajectory system. Interestingly, most of the Arab Gulf States were established through outside agencies, the British and Americans in particular. This artificial and abnormal process of state formation makes the GRS a fundamentally externally-oriented-system, whose trajectory comes from abroad to compensate for the lack of internal mechanisms for managing one's own affairs. Since all great powers are in a permanent struggle over oil reserves, the external relations of GCC countries with these powers are always those of subordination. The internal and external political behaviors of GCC countries have been formed according to the arrangements of great powers. GCC countries cannot make any arrangements (political, diplomatic, or defensive) that would be incompatible with the interests of the hegemonic powers. For example, when in the early fifties the Iranian Prime Minister Mosaddegh tried to nationalize oil companies, the

---

29   Davidson 2012.
30   Jervis 1976.

United States and Britain revolted against him and removed him from power. Likewise, when Saddam Hussein sought to impose Iraqi hegemony over the Gulf, the US did not hesitate to strike him in 1990.[31]

Aforementioned features confirm arguments of structural realism regarding both small states' alignments, their behavior towards great powers, and the supremacy of security, defense, and survival considerations above any other concerns. Structural realism argues that as small, rich, and vulnerable states, GCC countries would be primarily inclined to ally (bandwagon) with those great powers which would be willing and able to protect and defend their security and survival, as well as to deter any source of domestic and external threats. On the other hand, as previously noted, given that these states exist in an anarchic, self-help international order, and are located in one of the most prone-to-war regions, surrounded by a hostile, malicious and antagonistic environment, the GCC countries will likely pay attention to enhancing their relations with the US more than with any other great powers, as the US has demonstrated an apparent will and ability to protect and defend these monarchies.

3 The Small States in the Arabian Gulf: an Outline

The foremost objective of this study is to elucidate how in certain periods the strategic situation could be a tool of implementing vibrant and ambitious external activities. The question here is: why the UAE and Qatar succeed in expanding foreign polies despite their small size, while the other small [and larger] Gulf countries fail to act the same? Which social forces are most linked to the Emirati and Qatari external effectiveness, and what are the conditions that create incentives for these social forces to use economic and financial resources as a tool to control and confront their local political rivalries and to strengthen the state's political power? How do these social forces succeed in implementing this polices domestically? Furthermore, the study seeks to provide a conceptual and analytical connection between local political struggles, sociopolitical and sociopolitical mobilization, and the rise and growth of external influence of small Arab Gulf States such as the UAE and Qatar.

Since the creation of the modern Arab Regional System (ARS) after World War II, this is the first time where the small Gulf States occupy this prominent status. In the last seven decades, large and middle size regional powers such as Egypt, Syria, Iraq, and the Kingdom of Saudi Arabia (K.S.A.) were the key actors

---

31 Heikal 1992.

in the region. But since the early 2000s, small and even micro-states such as the United Arab Emirates (U.A.E.) and Qatar have become some of the key players and central actors of this regional system. With the outbreak of the Arab Uprisings in 2011 and their aftermath, both countries have become the most influential players in the region (economically, diplomatically, and politically). The Gulf (or the Khaleeji) power triangle that includes Saudi Arabia, the UAE, and Qatar dominant the region, where the power structure in the region have shifted tremendously.

The chapter concerns on investigating the process of socioeconomic and sociopolitical transformation, which allows these newborn, tribal, and underdeveloped city-states to become vibrant economies, some of the most powerful actors in the Middle East, and vital stockholders of the international economic system in less than fifty years. I concentrate on examining the impacts of nation-building and formation process, capacity-building measures, power shifting and transition (domestically and regionally), the correlation between social and political mobilization and the growth of external power and influence of small states.

If there is an affirmative law in international politics, it is the fluctuation of power, which leads to the rise and fall of great powers. Today's superpowers could be tomorrow's sick-man of world order. From the Pharaohs, Persians, Greeks, Romans, to the Islamic empire, through European imperial powers, and recently to the US unipolar domination, the game of power politics of the international system is an infinite cycle of rising and falling. In the modern Middle East, the major regional powers concentrated on countries like Egypt, Iraq, Syria, and Saudi Arabia, along with Iran, Turkey, and Israel as non-Arab regional powers. Except for Israel, the large geographic and population size, massive natural resources, significant geopolitical location, and the considerable size of militaries gave these states a relative advantage in the regional balance of power compared with small and 'vulnerable' neighbors. In the Arab World too, Egypt was the strongest regional power for more than three decades. Since the mid-1970s, Iraq and Syria shared the domination over the Eastern part of the Arab World until the US invasion of Iraq in 2003. Meanwhile, Saudi Arabia was the regional hegemon of the area that contains the six members of the Gulf Cooperation Council (GCC) organization and Yemen. Lately, for nearly a decade and half, there has been notable evidence referring to the emerging changes and new developments that occur in the region, especially in terms of the traditional regional balance of power and soft power diplomacy, where the power transits from old regional powers like Egypt, Syria, and Libya to the hands of new small rising powers in the Gulf region, in particular the UAE and Qatar.

These transformations include the retreat of classical regional (Arab) powers, due to the fundamental changes in the distribution of power among Arab countries, the accumulation of oil revenues, the completion of nation-building process in the Gulf States, the increasing regional influence of Iran, the changing balance of power in favor of the Gulf Arab States, especially Saudi Arabia. As well as the enormous flourishing of Khaleeji economic development, cultural inspiration, strategic ambition, changing political identities, and the increasing of political and diplomatic leverage of the Gulf monarchies.

Perhaps the most important pillar of the Emirati and Qatari rising is their financial and economic capabilities, which are inevitable outcomes of the accumulation of oil revenues that associated manufacturing industries during the past four decades. These two countries succeeded in reinventing their posture by investing and employing their wealth in establishing durable economic and development base, which became the foundation of their economic, political, and diplomatic strength. The second pillar is stability, which contributed to the resilience of political regimes and improves the concentration on realizing economic, social, and political development that relies on the achievement of social justice, welfare, respect citizens' rights, and securing their basic needs. The third pillar is the multilateral dynamic diplomacy approach. Both countries declare their firm commitment of constructive interaction with other countries, abide by the rules of international law, support the rights of other nations, promote multilateralism through international organizations such as the United Nations and the Arab League. Likewise, concentrate on cultural activities, robust participation in the peacekeeping missions, humanitarian activities, development aids, and promoting international dialogue.

Apparently, these approaches improve the UAE's and Qatar's images and inspired them engage further in international activities. Both UAE and Qatar have succeeded in proper exploitation and reinvestments of their national (economic and political) capabilities to construct their foreign policies and using it to expand their global weight. In fact, small Arab Gulf countries re-emphasized the assumption that internal stability strengthening the influence and engagement on the international arena.[32] These pillars are manifested in three fundamental facets, economically, politically, and culturally. As a result, Abu Dhabi and Doha have become the political, diplomatic, economic, and cultural gravity centers of the Arab World and Middle East and North Africa (MENA) region since the early 2000s. This radical change in the regional power

---

32 Mastanduno, Lake, and Ikenberry, 1989.

dynamics is still overlooked by most of the region's experts and has not been investigated systematically or in depth.

Notably, most of IR theories had failed to address the trends and forms of change in the Middle East since the end of the Cold War. Therefore, this study argues that the main reason for these changes finds its roots in the process of not only power shift that occurred in the region since the Iraq War of 2003, and the outbreak of the Arab Uprisings of 2011. Instead, it argues that the origins of these changes are fundamentally lying on several sociopolitical and socioeconomic transformations that have taken place within the Gulf region since the early 2000s.

To understand the changing status and the foreign policies of both the UAE and Qatar, the chapter will substantially concentrate on the interplay between material and ideational variables of small states' foreign policy and external role. The increasing external influence, the assertiveness of their foreign policies, regional power projection and expansion of both the UAE and Qatar were artefact by the dialectic relations between ideational and material variables. The material variables include the process of nation-building, state formation, institution capacities, power-structure, authority building, social mobilization, economic diversification, and the transformation from oil-based economy to knowledge-based economy (or from a rentier state into post/new rentier state), while the ideational variables include the role of identity, norms, and other non-material factors, e.g., branding, soft power, and cultural diplomacy. Simultaneously, the chapter will take into consideration the interlaced role of domestic-international nexus and the impact of the complexity of international political/economic structure, the balance of power consideration, and the distribution of capabilities over the development of small states' foreign policy.

The literature on small states in the Gulf region focuses on three main topics: International politics of the Gulf States, their foreign and security policies, and that to which an increasing attention has been paid, to the study of growing accumulative power and influence of small Gulf States recently, especially the UAE and Qatar after the outbreak of the Arab Uprising of 2011.

Since the beginning of the 21st century the Arab Gulf region is still neglected or under-researched. According to Onn Winckler, "only two books had been written on this country prior to the early 2000s and I doubt if there was any full academic course in any university outside the Gulf on Qatar until recent years".[33] This chapter investigates the rise of small states in the Arabian Gulf

---

33 Winckler, 2015: p. 159.

region, which includes the six-member states of the Gulf Cooperation Council (GCC) organization, plus Iran, Iraq, and Yemen. This nine-member-order contains five small states (Bahrain, Qatar, UAE, Yemen, and Kuwait). Most of the literature deals with these different actors in a semi-unified category under the wider umbrella of Middle East studies,[34] Persian Gulf Studies,[35] or the GCC umbrella.[36] Other studies combined these divergent countries under the umbrella of rentier economies,[37] or oil-based economy societies.[38] Therefore, as Karen Young correctly pointed out, to understand diverse trends in the Gulf States, IR and foreign policy scholars should avoid the common mistake of most of "typology" of the Gulf States based on the false assumption of a shared model of governance, culture, and traditions.[39]

Because of methodological considerations, this chapter is not interested in this analytical direction, although the author believes that the Arab Gulf States have many similarities (historically, economically, culturally, and socially). On the contrary, the author believes that despite these similarities, each Gulf country has its unique historical and developmental experience, where the process of nation-building, and foreign policy orientation was basically manufactured and produced individually through distinct socioeconomic and sociopolitical features. Likewise, yet justifiably, it was necessary to eliminate cases of other small states in the Gulf region such as Bahrain, Oman, and Kuwait. Bahrain lacks the financial and economic capabilities of the UAE and Qatar. As for Kuwait, which is considered to be one of the richest countries in the region and in the world (in term of GDP per capita), it does not share the same vision as the UAE or Qatar, and it also does not adopt the same assertive or ambitious foreign policy trend of these two states.[40] Finally, under the longstanding rule of Sultan Qaboos Bin Said, the Sultanate of Oman with its moderate finance and economic capabilities conducts and adopts a genuinely different foreign policy and strategic choices (neutrality, non-intervention, and reconciliation) than Abu Dhabi and Doha and the rest of the GCC members.[41]

---

34   Kornay and Dessouki, 2010; Hinnebusch and Ehteshami, 2014.
35   Kamrava 2011; Moghaddam, 2009; Gause, 2010.
36   Legranzi, 2011; Ulrichsen, 2017; Young, 2017.
37   Ulrichsen, 2016.
38   Foley, 2010, Ross, 2013.
39   Young, 2017: p. v.
40   Al-Ebraheem, 1984 [2016].
41   Al-Khalili, 2009.

4 How to Study Small States: A Historical Sociology Perspective

The chapter mainly concerns measuring the nature and forms of change within small states by emphasizing such features as state formulation process, authority building mechanism, state-society relations, state-capacity and institutional development, etc. On the regional level, it investigates the role and impacts of power dynamics, the rise and fall of regional power in the Arab World, war, identity formation processes, evolving institutional structure of the region and ways in which it relates to the case of small Arab Gulf States.

In order to understand the rise of small states in the Arab Gulf region as a form of change, I claim that Historical Sociology (HS) as the main methodological framework.[42] Basically, HS refers to "a subfield of Sociology studying the structures and processes that have shaped important features of the modern world, including the development of the rational bureaucratic state, the emergence of capitalism, international institutions and trade, transnational forces, revolutions, and warfare".[43] According to Fred Halliday, HS mostly investigates "the core components of a political and social order, state, ideology, and society, and focuses specifically on how institutions, be they political or social/religious power, are established and maintained".[44] These institutions include coercion, disciplinary and appropriation institutions that had been established in the modern times and the role and impacts of both domestic variables such as ever-changing, non-state social forces and systemic variables such as global structures of power and imperial/capitalist competition.[45]

Basically, HS is an attempt to pave the way for greater engagement between IR and Sociology, since the central core of this subfield aims to understand large-scale historical change and identify transformative moments that reshaped social structures and institutions and revealed hidden social structures that frustrated or advanced human aspirations.[46] Unfortunately, most of the HS studies emphasis on system and sub-system level of analysis and less attention had been given to the study of small states or individual cases. Within the field of International Relations, the relevance of HS has been disputed due to the underestimation of the importance of history and historical analysis in this filed. IR theories consider history as superfluous or exogenous to the subject matter of the discipline.[47]

---

42 Hobson, 1998.
43 Pula and Stivachtis, 2017: p. 1.
44 Halliday, 2005: p. 36.
45 ibid, 72–73.
46 Pula and Stivachtis, 2017: pp. 1–2.
47 ibid, p. 3.

In general, mainstream IR theorists employ an "instrumentalist" approach of history, where they only used it as a tool to confirm theories of the present, not to rethink the present.[48] In contrast to this instrumental and functionalist use of history, historical sociologists such as John Hobson called for a "constitutive" reading of history. According to Hobson, the constitutive reading of history "examine[s] history not simply for its own sake or to tell us more about the past, nor simply as a means to confirm theorizing of the present, but rather as a means to rethink theories and problematize the analysis of the present, and thereby to reconfigure the International Relations research agenda".[49]

Neorealists either assume that history is repetitive nothing ever changes because of the timeless presence of anarchy,[50] or that history takes on the form of repetitive great power/hegemonic cycles, each phase of which is essentially identical, with the only difference of great power either rising or declining.[51] Consequently, neorealists either assert that world politics has always been governed by timeless and constant logic of anarchy or argue that balance of power politics has been practiced for over millennia.[52] As Waltz claimed, the utility of historical-sociological inquiry is dismissed.[53]

From HS perspective, mainstream IR theories appear to be caught within two modes of ahistoricism: "chronofetishism" and "tempocentrism". According to Hobson, chronofetishism represents the assumption that the present can be adequately explained only by examining the present.[54] In sum, by presenting international history as a static entity that operates according to a constant and timeless logic, tempocentrism ignores the fact that there has not been one international system but many, all of which are quite different. Likewise, the HS declines the neoliberals' perspective on the process of change and state formation in international system. Neoliberals believe that historical progression has occurred from a world divided into states to the one in which the non-state (transnational) has become significant, and that change and growth in the international system over time can be characterized as a linear process over time.[55] As proponents of critical school, historical sociologists argue that neoliberal assumptions reflect the Anglo-Saxon assumption and Eurocentric

---

48   Rosecrance, 1973; Cox, 1986; Barnett, 2002.
49   Hobson, 2002, p. 5.
50   Waltz, 1979.
51   Gilpin, 1981.
52   Waltz, 1986, p. 341; Kaufman, Little, and Wohlforth, 2007.
53   Waltz, 1979, pp. 43–49.
54   Hobson, 2002: p. 6.
55   Keohane and Nye, 1977; Keohane 1989.

experience intentionally neglecting and overlooking other forms of organizations, governance, development, and administration produced by other communities and nations outside the West.[56]

Regarding Constructivism, and despite the similarities with HS, there are a few differences between HS and constructivist approaches. Many historical sociologists believe that Constructivism tends to swap external, imposed categories from the vantage point of regional actors. Moreover, Constructivism deliberately overlooks the role and impacts of material factors in favor of ideational and normative factors. For historical sociologists, when it comes to the Middle East, Constructivism is considered to be old-fashioned deception and a self-delusional analytical frame.[57]

The main questions regarding HS are related to political power, state formation process, social change, and improvement of human conditions by unmaking and remaking human institutions that play a crucial role within societies since industrialization in 18th and 19th centuries Europe.[58] Further, HS challenges assumptions of linear development of history and the interpretation of modernity as an evolutionary process with roots in Western Europe. Moreover, it questions the validity of noncritical theorizing of structures of power organized around such conceptual and analytical categories such as class, gender, race, and completely neglecting the concept of the state.[59] In contrast, the HS understand modernity, the rise of the modern state and other events, as a product of transformative historical events such as wars, revolutions, and structures of social inequality, or what Charles Tilly called "big structures, long processes, huge comparisons".[60]

5   Historical Sociology and the Rise of Small Arab Gulf States

Historical Sociology perspective, as a co-constitution of the inter/transnational and the state levels, that traces the impact of long-term macro transformations, path-dependency, variegated regime types,[61] could help us illuminate the parameters of the state formation process, and authority-building paths leading to the rise of small states in the Arab Gulf region. Given

---

56   Halliday, 2005; 255–257.
57   ibid, pp. 32–33.
58   Gellner, 1988; Elias, 1994.
59   Skocpol, 1979; Moore, 1966; Tilly, 1975, 1978, 1981; Wallerstein, 1974.
60   Polanyi, 1957; Tilly, 1984.
61   Hinnebusch, 2013: p. 137.

the fact that states in the Middle East are operating in "a quasi-autonomous fashion",[62] it makes the analysis of Middle Eastern politics into a convoluted process. Fred Halliday suggests that HS provides an analytical framework that could "combine an awareness of that margin of independence ... in the face of all theories of total foreign control of events, with a study of the factors that do constrain and shape a state's foreign policy".[63]

In contrast with the widely accepted presumption of "the ruler decides" model of understanding the policies of Arab and Gulf States, historical sociologists believe it is a false argument. They argue that the leaders of Middle Eastern countries operate within a variety of domestic and external restrictions such as bureaucratic interests, public opinion, state capacity (including economic, demographic, and geographic factors), norms (nationalism, revolution, Islamism), and a more developed, prosperous aggressive external world.[64] For instance, analyzing the Middle Eastern states and societies through Historical Sociology, Fred Halliday emphasizes four main analytic frames, which include military conflict, modern ideologies, transnational actors, and international political economy.[65] Others, like Raymond Hinnebusch and Adham Saouli, believe that the status of small states of the Arab Gulf (and almost all members of the Arab Regional system) can be explained and understood by the context and process of state formation and state-capacity building.[66]

Raymond Hinnebusch argued that state's status pathways in the Middle East are mainly a product of how state-builders address three fundamental challenges: nation-building, economic development and authority building.[67] These strategies were shaped through negotiation of environmental opportunities and pressures on the domestic level (balance of class power, wealth, political culture), on the regional level (war, oil, ideology, identity), and on the international level (international structure, deepening globalization). According to Hinnebusch, the outcomes of these strategies depend on sufficient congruence of a regime's strategy with its environment incentives, and/or the ability to resist its restraints.[68]

Hinnebusch claimed that to understand the process of state formation, building state-capacity and power transition it is important to understand

---

62   Hurd, 2005: p. 245.
63   Halliday, 2005: p. 43.
64   ibid, pp. 69–70.
65   ibid, 197–302.
66   Saouli, 2012; Hinnebusch, 2015, 2010.
67   Hinnebusch, 2010: p. 201.
68   ibid.

the process of nation-building and regime types in the Middle East and the Gulf region and to illuminate the dialectical relations between identity and territory, which could enhance or inhibit unity and seize legitimacy. In the Middle East, there was a prevalent incongruence between territory (state) and identity (nation) or between norms of sovereignty (sub-state) and the norms of supra-state identities, i.e., Islam and Arabism; the Dawla [state] and the Umma [nation].[69] The balance between these ideological regimes has affected state cohesion, integration, and determined policies and strategic outcomes through the last six decades.[70]

To understand and analyze the process of change in the international system, HS gives great attention to the process of state formation. For the Middle Eastern case, historical sociologists stress the role of external forces and internal developments factors such as imperial competition, colonialism, the creation of modern state institutions, forging of national identity, secularization process, and the emergence of ideological movements after the end of the First World War.[71] Historical records show that the rise of the modern state (even in the Middle East and the Arab Gulf regions) involves the process of producing and the promoting of ideology, nationalism, legitimization of this division.[72] Consequently, historical sociologists are perspicacious in asserting this argument as a springboard for advancing our understanding of change processes in the Middle East, and the rise of the small Arab Gulf States, respectively.

Future studies should emphasis the connection between porous boundaries of state-society relations and the persistent of structural power factors, e.g., global financial system, balance of power, climate of ideas, and the character of technology for both state and non-state actors. For example, Hurd suggests broadening the framework of analysis to encompass the discussion on traditional and modern methods of governance, the ability to understand the transformation in the Middle East in will augmentative.[73] This kind of study could enhance our understanding of how small states such as the UAE and Qatar look at their relations with larger neighbors such as Saudi Arabia and Iran, and to each other. Rather than the narrow lens of realist-neoliberal dichotomy of national interests, security considerations, balance of power calculations, and economic interdependence, HS analysis emphasizes deconstruction of the tribal, religious, ethnic, and communal genesis of these states, and ways in

---

69   Eyadat, Corrao, and Hashas, 2018; Al-Barghouti, 2008; Tibi, 2009; Ayubi, 1995; Zubaida, 1989.
70   Hinnebusch, 2010: p. 200; Barnett, 1995, 1993.
71   Halliday, 2005: pp. 79–82; Buzan, and Gonzalez-Pelaez, 2009.
72   Halliday, 2005: p. 257.
73   Hurd, 2005.

which these variables effect the process of state-formation, boundary-making, foreign policy, and interstate relations. After all, the Arab Gulf States, like most of the Middle East countries, are still just "tribes with national flags" in the words of Bassam Tibi.[74]

6 A Three-Level Model

Why (and how) do certain small states become strong and emerge as a power on the international stage, while others do not? Neorealists and neoliberals argue that international politics is an eternal field of struggle and competition between big countries, how small states grow such influence over other larger, stronger, and more powerful countries. The essence of this section is to understand the constitutive process of "the rising power of small states in international politics".

I am interested in understanding the genesis of small states' power in world politics rather than explaining the way small states act in international politics or explaining their power and how they implement it. Therefore, the dilemma this study is trying to deconstruct is: where does the power of small states come from? How is it manifested, produced, and projected? I am interested in the study of the source of power, not its implications, origins or outcomes.

My critique of the IR mainstream theories addressing this problematique emphasizes not only the absence of questioning the origins of power of small [Arab Gulf] states, but also explores how we know what we think we know about these small states. Historical Sociology, especially John Hobson's and Stephen Hobden's works on neorealism and neoliberalism, suggests that traditional IR theories construct our mind and knowledge of IR phenomenon.[75] With all its fallacies and shortcomings (e.g., chronofetishism and tempocentrism) that had been based on the Western experience and understanding of international political dynamics.[76] Annette Baker Fox's classic study, *The Power of Small States* [1959], and Matthias Maass's *Small States in World Politics* [2017] reflect the most obvious (and dominant) examples of this fallacy. If the case studies of these works were small states in Africa, Latin America, Asia, or the Middle East, with all historical and colonial experiences of these regions and societies, can the results and findings of such studies be the same? Clearly, the answer is no. Nevertheless, despite the attractiveness and promise of such

---

74 Tibi 1997; Ayubi, 1996; Glass, 1990; Khoury and Kostiner, 1990; Ajami, 1991.
75 Hobden and Hobson, 2002; Hobson, 1998.
76 Hobson, 2002: pp. 6–15.

argument and the critique of IR theory it offers, these kinds of questions and inquiries are outside the scope of this study. What this section is trying to investigate is how and why certain small states become strong and powerful.

If IR scholars understand how the power of small states is established, they can explain the way the small states act in world politics, shape their foreign policies. However, how to modify the theories that deal with the actions and foreign policies of small states, and states in general. To dissolve this puzzle, I claim that the process of small states' rising in international politics find its roots in a few variables which are embodied in the three levels of analysis, i.e., individual level, state level, and system level (see Figure 5.1). However, it comprises several ideational and material variables, which are usually being neglected or/and overlooked. These variables do not encompass traditional realist and neoliberal material sources of power, e.g., military power, economic power, natural resources, population size, etc.

Based on the second law of dialectical materialism that predicts that "qualitative changes – in a manner exactly fixed for each individual case – can only occur by the quantitative addition or quantitative subtraction of matter or motion",[77] I explore the essence of small states' rising process on domestic, regional, and international scales (see Figure 5.2).

Apparently, the relationships between these levels are overlapping, interconnected, and cannot be separated. A full understanding of the phenomenon of small states' rising should incorporate an understanding of the dialectic of interconnectivity and mutual influence of these variables and indicators, and how they constitute and affect each other. The variables of these three levels of analysis (as inputs) play a crucial role in the process of small states rising (the outputs) through their interactions and the relational dynamics within the surrounding domestic and external environments (see Figure 5.3). On the individuals' level (or the leadership level), variables such as legitimacy challenges, leadership style and persona, strategic choices, learning, authority building, and leadership identity are crucial elements to understanding of the micro-foundations of the process of small states' rising. On the state level, several variables play an essential role in formulating and constituting the rise of small states. These variables include regime type, power structure, national ambitions, the level of development, soft power, the level of modernization, state-society relations, domestic social ruling alliance, social mobilization, institution capacity and professionalism, foreign aid, economic liberalism and clear definition of national interests, objectives, and vision. Finally, on the

---

77   Engels, 1987: p. 356.

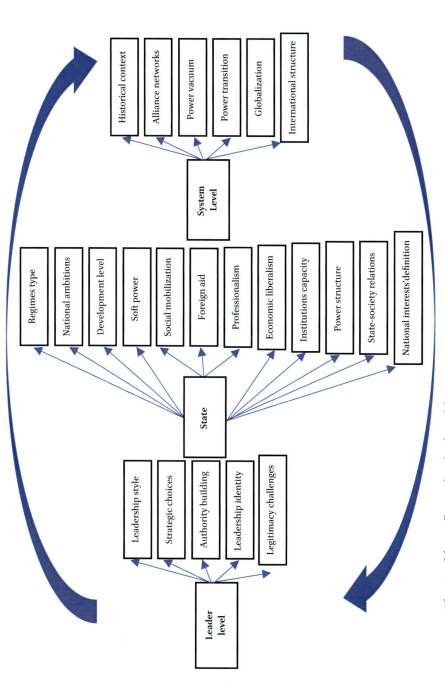

FIGURE 5.1 The rise of the small state: three levels model
SOURCE: THE AUTHOR

FIGURE 5.2 Materialist dialectics of change
SOURCE: THE AUTHOR

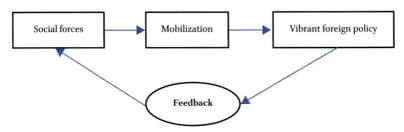

FIGURE 5.3 Systematic process of small states' rise
SOURCE: THE AUTHOR

system level, historical context plays a vital role in the process of small states' rising, international structure (polarity), alliance networks, power vacuum, power transition, and the relative power of great and regional powers, i.e., great powers fatigue and exhausting, the retreat of regional powers.

Neorealists and Neoliberals believe that every foreign policy is a product of strategic considerations and geopolitics, where nation-states mainly seek to improve their positions in the region to balance and confront foes and rivals. Despite the fundamental role systemic (structural) variables plays in determining the status and the position of states in international politics, the variables of state and individuals' level of analysis are the most important for understanding the process of small states rising in international politics. Evidently, when it comes to the case of small states, the relation between domestic social forces is the most influential one.

Several studies argue that assertive, ambitious, and even aggressive, foreign policy of small states is a result of power change, domestic political struggles, leadership personalities and strategic motivations that demonstrate what the leaders are aiming to obtain through adopting certain foreign policy programs.[78] Likewise, Robert Gilpin argues that any attempt to measure the change in the international system and how it relates to influence depends on two main variables. First is an extent to which the domestic social structure is

---

78   Lawson, 1992: pp. 26–29.

efficient. The second is when the profits of national activities start to accumulate and grow in the favor of private sector for the public good interest.[79] Gilpin stated that the tendency of a society to seek changes in the international system depends "not only on decreased costs but also on domestic factors that influence the capacity and willingness of a society to pay these costs".[80]

In the case of the Arab Gulf States, while the UAE and Qatar have not been historically the most efficient regimes (comparing with Iraq, Kuwait, Bahrain, Oman, and Saudi Arabia) they are the only two [small] regimes that adopt such assertive and ambitious foreign policies. These tendencies are still ambiguous and vague. There are five main types of mobilization and transformations, which took place in the UAE and Qatar in the last four decades and which lead to the rise of these two countries. Similarly, the failure of other small countries in the Gulf region to cope is a result of the insufficiency of these transformations. In contrast with Abu Dhabi and Doha, others small Arab Gulf States failed to address modernization crisis, i.e., economic demands for a big industrial base away from the rentier economy model, establishment of more flexible and efficient administrative apparatuses, and maintenance and strengthening of state-society relationships (public sphere, business elites and civil society). These transformations contain: 1) social mobilization: transforming from tribe-based society into modernism; 2) economic mobilization: converting from fishing to oil into post-oil economy; 3) political mobilization: developing from tribe and ruling family into nation-state; 4) security and defense mobilization: revolutionizing from protection rackets into independence; 5) foreign policy mobilization: moving from dependency to engagement, into leading and primacy, which is a result of high level of professionalism and institutionalization of foreign policy decision making process (see Table 5.1).

To recap, as the foreign trade exchange, diplomatic relations, international engagement and intervention tendencies of the UAE and Qatar grow, so does their political role and obligations to maintain peace and stability of their neighborhood and beyond. These small states have been known for their policies of international institutionalism, constructive engagement, and belief in the achievement of peace through multilateral dialogue within the respective international institutions, most notably the United Nations.[81] The ascension of the significance of the UAE and Qatar in the global economy is further

---

79 Lawson, 1992: p. 30.
80 Gilpin, 1981: p. 96.
81 Al-Mashat 2010.

TABLE 5.1 Mobilization type in small Arab Gulf States

Type of mobilization	Details
Social	from tribal-based society into modernism
Economic	from fishing to oil into post-oil economy
Political	from Tribe to family, into nation-building
Security/Defense	from protection rackets into independence
Foreign Policy	from dependency to engaging, into leading and primacy

SOURCE: THE AUTHOR

underlined by the fact that these are Arabic and Islamic countries with modern institutions and therefore are well placed to be key players between the East and the West.

The emerging power of the GCC countries, notably the UAE and Qatar, synchronizes with the deterioration of the political and economic conditions of the rest of the classical regional powers. The growing political and economic power and influence of these small countries is a product of increasing economic growth that was achieved by the oil high prices and the resilience of political and social systems of these countries reflected in a constant increasing level of stability, public satisfaction, confidence, and content with the performance of the governments. Likewise, it was a product of the process of dynamic economic development, regional megaprojects, and tremendous foreign direct investment (FDI). Furthermore, the proliferation of political and diplomatic activities these states enjoyed finds its roots in their abilities to anticipate the instability in the region, which have led to expansion of their external involvement in regional crises and disputes, as well as successes in managing and resolving some of the region's recent conflicts. The growing significance of the small states in the Arab Gulf region further lies in the diversity of their economic prosperity continues to attract. These countries have become hubs for different cultures and people of diverse backgrounds. Bringing these groups together is nevertheless a considerable task. Both UAE and Qatar have been able to hold the internal affairs sound and secured so far. Nevertheless, one of the main concerns here is to examine how can the UAE and Qatar keep external factors, as well as internal affairs under control, and how can they consolidate their power and external influence?

All these reasons compel to assume that, in the first half of the twenty-first century, the small states of the GCC organization will have the upper hand in determining the future's course of the Middle East.[82] Foreseeably, the events of the Arab uprisings, the deterioration of the situation in both Egypt and Syria, the disintegration of Iraq under the yoke of occupation and Iran's dominance, dealt to the Arab political arena blow and created a tremendous regional power shift and strategic vacuum in the MENA region. The pattern of external attitudes of both the UAE and Qatar since 2011 show their intention and determination to fill that vacuum and lead the region.

In sum, as mentioned above, I argued that the phenomenon of the increasing power of small Arab Gulf States finds its roots in the changing nature of certain ideational variables i.e., identity, norms, institutions, and interests, as much in material variables such as the balance of power, economic development, and security considerations. Therefore, the rise of the small Arab Gulf States is a product of the large-scale historical change in the social and institutional structures of both the UAE and Qatari societies.

To elaborate further, in order to expand our understanding and adding value to our knowledge about such phenomenon, future studies should investigate, interrogate, and examine various hypotheses, i.e.:

1) As the long-term power of the small states increases, the state will increase its external mobilization/extraction. In other words, as the long-term level of modernization and internal mobilization increases, the small state will expand its external extraction and validation.
2) As the nation-building and legitimacy-building process being consensual and socially rooted, the state will pursue external validation and engage in international affairs. Meaning, the more peaceful the state-building process, the more likely small states will focus on adopting external strategies, and vice versa.
3) Ambitious leaders of small states will rely on international strategies to greater extent than other small states leaders. Conversely, moderate/conservative leaders of small states will rely on domestic strategies to a greater extent than ambitious leaders.
4) There are no direct correlations between small States' possession of natural resources, financial and economic capabilities and the external influence and effective foreign policy. Namely, the possession

---

82   Abdullah 2012.

of strategic and significant natural resources (e.g., oil and gas) does not necessarily guarantee that a small state would be internationally powerful or influential.

5) Domestically strong states will emphasis external strategies more than will domestically weak small states. In other words, as long-term domestic stability increases, the small state will increase its external extraction and allocate resources to engage in the international arena.

6) If national identity is clear and lucidly defined, the small state will adopt an efficient foreign policy. In other words, if the differentiation between the Dawala (the state) and the Umma (the nation) is clear, the foreign policy of small states will be unchained and energetic.

7) As the long-term professionalism and institutionalization level of the decision-making process of the small states increases, the external involvement of small states will increase.

8) And, last but not least, as the greater scale of large and middle powers' burdens and fatigue increases, the small states will increase their engagement in the regional neighborhood and in international affairs. In other words, the weaknesses of regional and international powers increase the possibilities of small states' external extraction and allocation of resources for the purpose of engaging in the international arena.

7 Welcome to "The Khaleeji Age"

What was "really" new about the Arab Regional System? Lynch and others were completely correct to argue that the fundamental change that altered the regional balance of power was the rise of the Gulf States.[83] The rise of wealthy small states with tremendous "Money, media empires, and a central position in robust transnational networks or international business [that] have allowed them to exercise soft power" on the one hand, and with "extremely well-equipped and well-trained militaries, supplemented by well-compensated mercenaries" on the other hand, is considered "the fundamental change in the region". These rising powers can "project far more hard power into areas such as Libya and Yemen than the traditional Arab powers ever could".[84]

---

83   ibid; Miller 2016; Young 2017.
84   Lynch 2018: 20.

Undeniably, this is the new transformation in the Arab Order since its creation after World War II. It is the first time in the history of the modern Arab Regional System (ARS) that the Small Gulf States have held this prominent and leadership status. Throughout the last six decades, big and middle powers such as Egypt, Syria, Iraq, and Saudi Arabia, were the dominant and key actors in the region. However, since the early 2000s, small and even micro-states (such as the UAE and Qatar) have been among the key players and central actors in the region. With the outbreak of the Arab Uprisings in 2011 and their aftermath, the two countries became the most influential actors in the region (economically, diplomatically, and politically). The Gulf (or the Khaleeji) power triangle that includes Saudi Arabia, Qatar and UAE dominates the region, where the power structure had shifted and been transferred from the traditional regional powers (Egypt and Syria) to the states of the Gulf region.[85] This is what most studies misinterpreted and even still deny.

Misreading the dimensions, consequences, and manifestations of the Gulf Moment phenomenon (as the Emirati Scholar Abdulkhaliq Abdullah called it) led these experts to describe the current moment as a state of disorder, chaos, and quagmire.

This new situation, which had emerged before the Arab Uprising and culminated in its manifestations afterwards, did not make states "… view every event in the region as both an index of power and a potential threat: no state could afford to opt-out. Whether out of a desire to spread power or a defensive interest in preventing rivals from doing the same, almost every regime has found itself drawn into civil wars and other power games".[86] On the contrary, this moment was mainly an attempt to reshape the region on the basis of the new distribution of power, which leaned in favor of the rising Gulf States. This has been the case in international politics for centuries. The historical record shows that it was the case in Europe with the rise of Napoleon at the beginning of the nineteenth century and with the rise of Hitler after the end of the First World War, as well as in the Middle East with the rise of Muhammad Ali in the early 1800s and with the rise of Nasser after the Second World War. International (and regional) systems (according to Hans Binnendijk) tend to last for two to three generations and are established and destroyed by large-scale conflicts.[87] Therefore, the current situation in the region is no exception, and certainly will not prove to be.

---

85   Beck 2015.
86   Lynch 2018: 21.
87   Gilpin 1981; Binnendijk 1999.

These regional rivalries have existed for more than a decade, but the Arab Uprisings pushed them to the forefront, because of the political vacuum that lasted from the fall of Saddam Hussein in 2003 to the fall of Mubarak in 2011. This is not a "security dilemma" so much as a new round of the "struggle for regional hegemony". The main game-changing element in the Arab World was the power shift (and power diffusion and even power transition) that the Arab Uprisings produced. Those shifts allowed some countries, based on new realities, potentialities, and promises, to reconstruct the region and revive their power and influence over it. However, this round of regional competition is now taking place because the main actors or players are small countries (the UAE and Qatar in particular). This is not only the "new" fact about the Arab order but also the foundation of several regional rivalries.

As the trade relations of the United Arab Emirate (UAE) grow, so do its political role and obligations to maintain peace and stability in its neighborhood in particular and in the world in general. The UAE has always been known for its policy of international institutionalism and its belief in the achievement of peace through multilateral dialogue within the respective international institutions, most notably the United Nations. The ascension of UAE's importance in the global political economy is further underlined by the fact that it is an Islamic country with modern institutions and therefore is well placed to be a key player between the East and the West. This could be of particular value in the context of recent struggles in the Middle East. The growing importance of the UAE in the Gulf region further lies in the increasing diversity that its economic prosperity continues to attract. The country is a meeting point for different cultures and people of varied backgrounds. From professionals to academics to migrant workers, all these groups have found their place in the UAE today. Bringing them together is nevertheless a considerable task.

If there is a significant law in international politics it would be that of the fluctuation of power, which often leads to the powers' rise and fall. Today's superpower could be an example of how, since the Pharaohs, Persians, Greeks, Romans, the Islamic civilization, European imperial powers and recently US unipolar domination of the international system, international politics remains an eternal game of snakes and ladders.

In modern Middle East history, the major regional powers were centered on Egypt, Iraq, and Syria, along with Iran and Turkey, because their large geographical size, weight of population, natural resources, geographical location, and substantial size of militaries gave them a relative advantage in the regional balance of power compared to their small and "vulnerable" neighbors. Egypt, for example, was the major regional and North African power. On the other hand, Iraq, and Syria shared domination over the Eastern part of the region until the recent US invasion of the former. Lately, for nearly a decade, one could observe emerging changes and new developments occurring in the area, especially in the traditional regional balance of power. The emerging power of Gulf Cooperation Council (GCC) countries, notably Saudi Arabia, United Arab Emirates, and Qatar, then the rest of the GCC countries (Kuwait, Bahrain, Oman), synchronized with the deterioration in political and economic conditions of the rest of the traditional regional powers due to political and social unrest.

The increasing political power of the GCC countries, resulting from efforts towards sustainable development and increased economic growth realized by high oil prices, along with the state of political and social stability in these countries, was reflected in the constant increase in public satisfaction and contentment with their governments' performance. Furthermore, they have enjoyed an increase in the scope of their soft power and diplomatic activities, leading to the expansion of their involvement in regional crises and disputes as well as success in management and resolution of some of the recent conflicts in the region.

All these reasons compel one to assume that, in the first half of the twenty-first century, the GCC countries will have the upper hand in determining the course and the future of the Middle East, especially the Arabian Gulf region. The events of the Arab Uprising, the deterioration of the situation in both Egypt and Syria, the displacement of Iraq under the yoke of occupation, all these struck a blow to the Arab political sphere and created a power shift. The pattern of GCC countries' external behavior shows their intention and determination to fill that vacuum and proves their serious intention to lead the region in the future.

This chapter explores such aspects of the GCC countries as their rise, pillars, and objectives, the challenges that face them in the future, and what we may hope to expect from the rise of the Gulf States and the whole Arab World.

8   The Pillars of the GCC Rise

Perhaps the most important pillar of the GCC rise is financial and economic power, thanks to the accumulation of oil revenues and associated manufacturing industries during the past four decades. These countries succeeded in reinvesting their wealth in the establishment of durable economic and development bases, which became the support base of their economic strength. According to Arabian Monetary Fund (AMF) reports, the share of GCC countries in Arab foreign trade is about 40 percent ($473 billion out of a total of

$1.7 trillion), and the proportion of Gulf exports exceeded 23 percent of the total Arab exports in 2010, which amounted to $726 billion dollars. All the GCC countries showed a large surplus in their annual budgets; these surpluses were spent on improving living standards and development at home, while strengthening their status and influence abroad (i.e., in the Arabian Gulf region).

The second pillar is stability, which contributed to their secure political regimes focusing mainly on economic, social, and political development that relies on the achievement of social justice, welfare, respect for citizens' rights, and fulfilment of all their basic needs. These factors led, most importantly, to a gradual strengthening of political participation by various social forces in a manner corresponding to the traditional characteristics of the Gulf States. This situation helped the GCC states to expand their constructive engagement in international activities. Hence, the GCC countries reemphasized the assumption that internal stability helps to strengthen the size of influence and engagement on the international front.

The third element is the GCC states dynamic diplomacy, comprising a commitment to positive interaction, adherence to the rules of international law, support for the rights of nations, stimulation of multilateral work through international organizations (like the United Nations and the Arab League), focus on humanitarian and cultural activities, active participation in the peacekeeping missions and humanitarian relief, foreign aid programs, promotion of dialogue between civilizations, and other forms of public and cultural diplomacy, etc. These approaches improve the GCC image in the eyes of other nations, attracting and inspiring them towards engagement in international activities. The GCC had succeeded in recruiting and exploiting its national resources (natural and human) and sources of national power (economic and political) to build up their foreign policy and renew and expand their external influence.

9 The Aspects of the GCC Rise

The shifting size of GCC political and economic power produced effects on its external behavior in all fields. At the economic level, Gulf cities like Dubai and Abu Dhabi in the UAE, Riyadh and Jeddah in Saudi Arabia, Doha in Qatar, and other cities, became attractive places for huge foreign direct investment (FDI), as their open encouragement of a positive economic climate became a catalyst for free-market activity and investment. These conditions persisted and helped to attract foreign capital. The volume of investments in one of the seven emirates such as Dubai is equal to (or even higher than) the volume of foreign investments in one of the strong regional powers such as Egypt (which is several times larger in geographical, demographic, and human resources than Dubai). The political stability in the GCC, the constructive and liberal economic and public policies stimulating and encouraging investment, the ease of business regulation and open economic activities (with GCC countries ranking at the top of Arab countries according to the Heritage Foundation and Dow Jones index of economic freedom), favorable legal terms and serious anti-corruption measures – seen to be working in Kuwait's successful and bloodless demand for the resignation of the prime minister amid corruption allegations – show that GCC states are leading by example. Such measures and laws increased economic returns and expanded the GCC's economic and financial influence, which benefitted from the accumulation of their revenues to increase the volume of foreign investments in Arab countries. According to the GCC General Secretariat, the amount of foreign investment in the Gulf States was about $135 billion, with the UAE having $54 billion (40 percent), Saudi Arabia $40 billion (30 percent), Qatar and Kuwait $16 billion (12 percent), Bahrain $8 billion (5.6 percent), and the Sultanate of Oman an estimated one billion dollars.

The GCC states allocate a significant part of their economic wealth to support Arabian causes and help other poor Arabian countries. For example, the democratic transformation that occurred in Egypt, Tunisia, and Bahrain during the so-called "Arab Uprising" had a negative impact on the national economy and the living conditions of citizens in these countries, which prompted the Gulf countries to provide urgent and unconditional financial aid. Saudi Arabia helped Egypt with $4 billion, the UAE with $5 billion, Qatar provided $10 billion, and Kuwait provided aid of about $3 billion. The same aid was provided to Tunisia and Bahrain. Certainly, the increasing size of GCC countries' economic power leads to a commensurate strengthening and enhancement of their political and strategic capabilities.

At the political level, the GCC countries, especially the UAE, Qatar, and Saudi Arabia, have become the most effective and influential actors involved in the management of Arab conflicts and crises. Qatar and UAE have played an unprecedented role in the defense and protection of Libyan people through nonviolent involvement in the conflict in Libya. In addition, both countries are now trying to follow the same strategy in relation to Syria, where the regime in Damascus has turned against its own people.

At the diplomatic level, the GCC states' influence was clear in crises and conflicts before the start of the Arab Uprising. In the Arab Israeli conflict, for example, the diplomatic initiative presented by His Majesty King Abdullah Bin Abdul-Aziz of Saudi Arabia in 2003, known as the "Arab Peace Initiative", is still considered one of the most viable among other Arabian and Western initiatives. It won acceptance by all parties in the international community as an historic milestone in the efforts to resolve the Arab Israeli conflict. At the same time, the role of Prince Hamad bin Khalifa Al Thani, Emir of Qatar, by far one of the most active and influential leaders in the region, proved vital in the reconciliation between the Palestinian Liberation Authority (PLA) and the Islamic Resistance Movement (Hamas) that aimed to strengthen the unity of Palestinian people in the face of the Israeli occupation. To this can be added His Highness's role in signing the peace agreement between the central Sudanese government and the Sudan Liberation Movement (which currently rules the now separated South Sudan), and his serious attempts to resolve the political conflict in Yemen.

The UAE, led by His Highness Sheikh Khalifa Bin Zayed Al Nahyan (who passed away in May 2022), is still pursuing the course of action initiated by the late HH Sheikh Zayed bin Sultan Al Nahyan, which calls for and works to achieve a strengthened mutual Arab cooperation, rapprochement between Arab views, and help for all Arab countries unconditionally and without limits. This is reflected in the fact that the UAE was the first country to intervene to peacefully resolve the political crisis in Egypt during the early days of the revolution of 2011. His Highness Sheikh Abdullah bin Zayed, the energetic UAE foreign affairs minister, was the first Arab foreign official figure to visit Egypt during the conflict. The daring diplomatic and non-combatant military assistance from the UAE to the Libyan conflict is also well noted. On the international level, the UAE is considered one of the leading members in encouraging and supporting multilateralism and international cooperation, as well as championing environmental awareness; this was manifested in the establishment of the International Renewable Energy Agency (IRENA) in Abu Dhabi in 2009, and the UAE's initiative in and ongoing call for clearing weapons of mass destruction (WMD) out of the Middle East. In charitable and worldwide humanitarian activities, the most notable faces and figures were those from the GCC, such as His Highness Sheikh Mohammed bin Rashid Al Maktoum, Ruler of Dubai, his daughters, Sheikha Maitha and Sheikha Manal; also, from Qatar there is Her Highness Sheikha Mozah, the wife of former Emir of Qatar who is considered one of the most influential international figures in contributions to humanitarian and charitable work. Gulf leaders topped the international calls to save lives in areas of humanitarian disasters and calamities such as Sudan, Somalia, Pakistan, and other regions. Numerous contributions from the Gulf States funded activities to deal with natural disasters which struck other nations, such as the floods in Pakistan, the earthquake in Turkey, and the tsunamis in Southeast Asia, Japan and elsewhere.

The GCC's cultural attractiveness and rise is reflected in artistic, literary, media, and intellectual activities, in which cities like Kuwait, Manama, Muscat, Sharjah, Abu Dhabi, and Dubai (with the largest number of regional radio stations, television and media companies being based in Dubai Media City, DMC), besides hosting major Multinational Corporations (MNCs) in telecommunications and information technology, have become the Arabs' new cultural capitals, similar to and competitive with Cairo, Baghdad, Beirut and other centers of classical Arabic literature. Exhibition halls, museums, theatres, art centers and academies of art and science overlook the Gulf. These countries have become host cities for seminars, conferences, art exhibitions, film and theatre festivals, and book fairs throughout the year. Such activities increase the countries' attractiveness, so that they become models at both the regional and global levels. Nowadays, every Arabian citizen wishes to live and work in cities like Dubai, Abu Dhabi, Jeddah, Doha, or Muscat, where the lifestyle and other attractions are becoming irresistible.

Thanks to the creativity and vision of the rulers and princes of the GCC countries – mostly known for their status as poets and thinkers (one need only mention His Highness Sheikh Mohammed bin Rashid Al-Maktoum as a poet, and Sheikh Sultan Al Qassimi as an author and historian) and for their practical and valuable spending on science, art and culture – the UAE became a cultural and Knowledge Lake producer, exporting thought to the rest of the Arab World more extensively than any other Arab country. In the media field, the GCC states own the largest and most powerful media groups (both electronic and print) in the region. According to a recent study published by the University of Maryland, the most viewed and influential TV channels in the Arab World are based in the Gulf; such stations comprise Al-Jazeera, Al-Arabia, Abu Dhabi TV, and Saudi's MBC Group. In print media, the most influential Arabian newspapers are *Al-Sharq Al-Awast* and *Al-Hayat*. Notably, all these media projects are GCC owned and located. Gulf States have become the force that constitutes the Arabian collective consciousness (culturally, politically, intellectually, etc.).

Furthermore, the GCC countries provide the greatest support and funding for Arab intellectual and literary activities. For example, UAE have the largest number of awards that help to provide recognition, encouragement, and stimulation for work in the fields of science, the arts, and literature. Abu Dhabi offers the most prestigious Sheikh Zayed Book Award, as well as the Arab Booker Prize, the most important form of recognition in the field of literary writing. There is also the Shaer Al-million (Prince of Poetry) award for the best Arabian poet, sponsored by His Highness Sheikh Mohammed bin Zayed Al Nahyan, Crown Prince of Abu Dhabi. In Dubai, Sheikh Mohammed Bin Rashid

Al Maktoum provides the Dubai International Prize of the Holy Qur'an for prominent Islamic figures, scientific institutions, and the best Islamic advocacy organizations. Qatar also offers the biggest prize in the field of social sciences, known as the Arabian Social Sciences and Humanities Prize. Saudi Arabia has been known for decades as the source of the King Faisal International Prize that supports scientific research, Islamic studies, Arabic literature, medicine, and science, the last given to the best Muslim contribution to science. There is also King Abdullah Bin Abdul Aziz's prize for translation. Beside these awards and awardees and grants made to science and scientists, some Gulf countries, like the UAE, Kuwait, and Bahrain, have allocated their national day to the celebration of science and scientists, naming it "Science Day".

This development has put the Gulf States on the path to revival of some of the intellectual fields such as calligraphy, alchemy, and mathematics literature, which were all once led by Arabs and Muslims.

The GCC states may seem overwhelmed with the expansion in construction of urban facilities, entertainment, consumer outlets, industrial activities, and service industries (the Concert Revolution), but they have not neglected the nourishment of people's minds and the enhancement of facilities for scientists and researchers. The rulers' foresightedness made possible a vision that connected development with knowledge, which was best applied in the spread of universities, scientific institutes, technical institutions, and public libraries in every city in the Gulf States.

10   The Objectives of the GCC Rise

Arguably, the growing external influence of GCC countries, due to the benefits from Arab states in general and the GCC states, is an indispensable part of the Arab and Islamic Umma. The peoples and rulers believe that what is in the interest of Arabs is definitely in the interest of the GCC and its people, and vice versa.

The GCC considers its growing potential and external influence as a fund held in reserve for all the Arab states. The people of the Gulf hope that their economic growth, development, political power, and diplomatic influence will help to achieve many national and regional goals, such as:

- Attaining and maintaining the security and stability of the Arab states and protecting their citizens from exposure to any kind of internal or external threat, especially from hostile regional powers.
- Supporting and encouraging all forms of collective action among Arab States and other regional actors, in ways that serve and contribute

to the acceleration of voluntary unity among Arab countries, as a first step towards achieving economic integration between the Arab economies.
- Achieving regional peace and stability by expanding the volume of trade, investment, and economic cooperation.
- Rejecting the use of force in resolving conflicts between the Arab States and their neighbors and declining to intervene in the internal affairs of other countries.
- Creating opportunities for economic growth and building a real economic development base, which will improve the living conditions of all Arab citizens and societies.
- Reconstructing the Arab scientific, technological and knowledge renaissance, by working to accelerate the pace of knowledge production, raising, and improving the levels of education, building the knowledge-based economy, encouraging innovation and financing renaissance projects in all fields in different Arab countries in order to restore them to their former glory and raise their status as competitors of great powers, rather than imitators or consumers of their knowledge.

11 Challenges and Obstacles to the GCC Rise

The course of the GCC rise was not easy or smooth, and nor, of course, will its future be. Despite all their achievements, these countries still face many difficulties and challenges (internally and externally) which may prevent the continuation of progress and advancement of the Gulf countries. Perhaps some of the most important challenges to the GCC rise are:

Demographic challenge: This occurs because of the imbalance of the demographic map within the GCC states. On one side, there is the imbalance between citizens and immigrants, with a severe decline observed in the numbers of local citizens, especially in UAE and Qatar. This may threaten stability, security, and economic growth in the future if serious political crises should occur involving immigrants' home countries. On another side, there is the demographic imbalance between Arabian Gulf States and their neighbors (especially Iran), which leads to the continuing situation of imbalance of power and a permanent security dilemma in the Arabian Gulf. While the total number of the Arab population in the six Gulf countries is about 40 million, the number of Iranian people exceeds 80 million. Even Yemen, the poor neighbor of GCC, has a population equivalent to that of the GCC countries minus Saudi Arabia. This population weakness may induce other countries to attack and threaten the GCC, as Saddam Hussein did in 1990.

Economic challenge: The Gulf regional system is based on oil, whether exported as raw material or for the industries associated with it. Oil revenues are the main, or even the only, source of GCC national income, and the financer of its massive governmental spending. In the light of increasing international demand for energy and the decreasing size of oil reserves in the GCC countries, these countries need to look for alternatives to oil with which to confront the predicted end of the oil age.

Military challenge: The paradox of the geographical and geopolitical characteristics of the GCC as small countries surrounded by a group of strong powers and, at the same time, as rich countries, makes them envied and vulnerable to attack from their aggressive neighbors. These facts forced the GCC to look for an external umbrella to protect them from attacks by hostile and aggressive neighbors. But this strategy imposed an enormous economic burden on the GCC, with emerging political troubles, and still did not provide protection. During the last three decades (1980–2003) the GCC engaged in three bitter wars (the Gulf Wars) which killed millions of Arab people and wasted billions of dollars. If these sums were spent on development activities, the living standards and developmental status of the Arabian Gulf countries and the entire Arab World would become higher than those prevailing in the Organization for Economic Cooperation and Development (OECD) countries.

Historical experience shows that external powers are not always able to provide protection to their allies. The 2011 events in the Kingdom of Bahrain showed GCC countries that without their own military intervention with GCC forces, they would have lost a valued member. The complex strategic and political calculations of the United States (the traditional protector of the GCC) could have led to chaos in the Bahraini Kingdom. While the scale of the crisis was not large enough for the United States to intervene on the country's behalf, it was nearing the condition of a destabilizing factor in the hard-earned development described above. Hence, the GCC unilaterally took the decision to intervene and sent a military task force to protect the kingdom without waiting for approval from outside. This was the right and acceptable solution for the GCC countries as well as to the strategic challenge that would have catapulted the region into a major political crisis. Realistically, besides its national armed forces, the permanent and natural ally for the GCC will not come from outside powers, but from within the Arab nation, at least so long as the conflict has not reached global level. This explains why GCC states insisted on helping other Arab countries and displayed in practice their belief that the security of the Arab states will only be achieved with Arab forces first before any foreign intervention by major allies.

12 Great Expectations?

The historic transformation wrought by the Arab revolutions will affect the GCC, but not as strongly as their weaker economic neighbors. The people of the Arabian Gulf are not Egyptians, Tunisians, or Libyans. The percentage of public satisfaction and support for governmental performance in the Gulf countries is very high. In the UAE, for example, Lieutenant General Dahi Khalfan said in an interview that public satisfaction with and support for government exceeded 85 percent, which is considered an unusual rate for any regime, and foretells peaceful and stable times ahead. The leaders of the GCC countries were intelligent and wise enough to absorb and thoroughly study the revolutions, consequently taking preventive steps to meet popular demands for the exercise of political and social rights. The success of the UAE September municipal election is a notable example. Leaders worked hard to meet their citizens' demands, gradually rather than radically, as they believe that revolutionary methods are ill-fated and may lead to chaos after so much hard work to build stable, thriving economies. As His Highness Sheikh Mohammed bin Rashid said, "Let's start step by step ... then we'll see the results and compare our performance with others in the future".

The Gulf States gave assistance to the weak Arabian countries to save their relations with the people and elected governments, regardless of their political and ideological trends, and to expand trade and economic cooperation, cultural exchange, and political integration with these countries. With these projects in hand, they can try to unite the Arab front in fighting all nations' ever-present enemies such as poverty, terrorism, unemployment, underdevelopment, and the knowledge gap. These problems are the sparks that ignited revolutions across the region. Such a position could provide an incentive for a united front between the population and leaders against any future threat from such long-standing traditional adversaries as Iran and Israel.

In recent international roles played by NATO, much was said about the transformation of traditionally military alliances into catalysts for democracy. The GCC in this sense is a model. To strengthen what the GCC has begun, the Arab populace and governments have a historic opportunity to compensate for their failure by rejoining the march towards progress and modernization, through strengthening and supporting the people's hopes for freedom, democracy, human rights, and social justice, and for that purpose harnessing and exploiting national resources (human, financial and natural). Now, the GCC countries have the chance and the objective circumstances to move out of the back seat into the driver's seat. Let's hope that the GCC's leading role in the Middle East in the twenty-first century takes Arabs to the shore of safety, peace, stability, freedom, dignity, and justice for all.

Overall, the study has claimed that neorealism presents a comprehensive lens through which to articulate the nature and prospects of the changing dynamics of regional rivalries and hostilities, which could enable a more consistent understanding of the current crisis within the GCC organization and the clash of interests between its leading members. For instance, the study finds that it is hard to neglect the obvious deficit and stagnation of the GCC organization. Such a finding adds value to the credibility of the neorealist interpretation and claims that signify the limitations of international organizations in both regional and international crisis negotiations, if their role(s) should conflict with security concerns, or what nation-states perceive as or consider an issue of national security or its constitutive institutions (to use the terminology of the English School) such as sovereignty and security.

This international crisis (so designated, as it contains more than two international actors) reflects the contested leadership question in the Arabian Gulf System as well as in the Arab Regional System since the outbreak of the Arab Uprising(s) in 2011 and their aftermath. In other words, this international crisis (so designated as it contains more than two international actors) reflects the contested leadership question in the Arabian Gulf System as well as in the Arab Regional System since the outbreak of the Arab Uprising(s) in 2011 and their aftermath. Day after day, it becomes clearer that the dispute over foreign policy orientations and trends between the contestant parties is the genesis of the current crisis. From this perspective, each actor adopts a particular perception of the future of the region, the form of security arrangements, dynamics of the alliances (and the identification of rivals) and agenda-sitting for Gulf and Arab collective actions in general.

Regarding the role of the great and external powers, the study claimed that this role remains ambiguous. In fact, their attitude is strongly consistent with neorealist and neoliberal arguments that emphasize power and interests, and inconsistent with the arguments of the English School and Regional Security Complex (RSC) theory. Likewise, the role of regional powers is complicated and remains a puzzle. Interestingly, the role of regional powers such as Iran, Turkey, Egypt, and others, can be appropriately explained and illuminated through any of the three perspectives (neorealist, neoliberal institutionalism, and the English School). In fact, the crisis could be deconstructed and explained differently based on the position and the stance (strategic, economic, or normative) that a researcher(s) adopts. This finding indicates how complex and difficult it is to study or to understand the phenomenon of the international relations of the Arab Gulf region and the Middle East in general, as the late Fred Halliday pointed out.[88]

Nonetheless, one of the shortcomings of such macro-level strategic and orthodox security studies is that they deliberately neglect the role of the social construction of regional security architecture, which is considered a crucial element in the process of formulating the official discourse of national security strategies and threat perceptions in the current crisis in the Arabian Gulf region and among the main actors, as the English School persuasively argued.

Likewise, accordingly, neorealist explanations overlooked the human and societal consequences of such military and strategic rivalries. For instance, in the case of the current GCC crisis, the social repercussions of online and social media contentions had ruined and poisoned the relationships between the Qataris, Saudis, Emiratis, and Bahrainis (and other societies beyond the Arabian Gulf region) for unknown periods. Such antagonisms and overtly malignant activities, with both sides funding and producing adverse and aggressive media products (e.g., songs, documentaries, propaganda, and international defamation campaigns, etc.) escalated the level of misunderstanding and hatred between the conflictual actors and their people, and led to the failure of various mediation and arbitration efforts carried out by both the Sultan of Oman (Qaboos bin Said) and the emir of Kuwait (Sabah Al-Ahmad Al-Jaber Al-Sabah). In contrast to the neorealist belief that the reason the mediation efforts failed was that neither Oman nor Kuwait had enough power or influence over the parties to the crisis to push them towards reconciliation or trigger de-escalation and defuse the tension among them, the English School correctly demonstrates that such claims are genuinely reductionist, since neorealists had overlooked these aspects: not only because it is a system-level theory but also because of the fallacies in its state-centric and hard-threats emphasis. This emphasis eventually undermines its capability to accurately indicate and address the essence of such disputes, on both societal and cultural levels.

Furthermore, clearly, there is a separation between political and security divergences on the one hand, and economic interests on the other. Since the outbreak of the crisis in 2013, the effects on economic relations and interests

---

88   Halliday 2007: 7.

have been modest. The study finds that security concerns still prevail over institutional and normative ones, and even over gains and potential gains. On the economic level, strategy and security-based studies cannot explain the factors that kept the damages mainly at the micro-level, and why the other macro-level economic interests (such as the Qatari gas supplies to the UAE and Dubai in particular) were kept away from the tension and outside the radar of the proxies of the media cold war between Qatar, UAE and Saudi Arabia, where numerous public Khaleeji, Arabic, European, and American figures, officials, academics, pundits, and commentators in newspapers, TV channels, radios, social media platforms (e.g., Facebook, Twitter, and Snapchat, etc.) were involved in, engaged in, and recruited for deceptive, furious, and hateful correspondence collusions to extend the divergence between the collusive parties. The last seven years witnessed unprecedented propaganda campaigns from both parties, in which fake news was spread, and rumors and mutual accusations were manufactured and leaked on a vast scale.

At the beginning of 2020, two crucial events happened in the region, which the experts claim will have critical impacts on the crisis and relations between the Arab Gulf States. The first event was the death of Sultan Qaboos bin Saeed of Oman, whose contributions to the maintenance of stability in the Gulf and reduction in the intensity of rivalries between states were highly respected worldwide.[89] The new Sultan of Oman is the cousin of sultan Qaboos, Haitham bin Tariq, who previously served as the minister of Heritage and Culture and chairman of the national census committee.[90] Even before the official coronation, bin Tariq's candidature as the new Sultan was well received in most Khaleeji, Arab, and international diplomatic circles. Most of the Gulf States' leaders visited Muscat to express their condolences over the death of Sultan Qaboos and to congratulate the new Sultan. However, there was no sign of rapprochement, behind-closed-doors or arranged "pop-in" meetings between the rival leaders. These visits indicated desperate attempts by the parties to bring Oman onto their side and push it to abandon the neutrality and non-interference policy launched by the late Sultan Qaboos.

From his very first days in power, Sultan Haitham called for reconciliation, unification, and peaceful resolution of disputes between Gulf family members, which demonstrated that the role of the Sultanate would not change.[91] As expected, however, these efforts neither drove the crisis towards a settlement,

---

[89] Baabood 2017; Abozaid 2020b: 129.
[90] *The Economist* 2020; France 24 2020; Aljazeera 2020; BBC Arabic 2020.
[91] DW 2020.

nor ended the estrangement between the parties. Moreover, in the foreseen future Sultan Haitham's ruling strategy may show a greater inclination towards isolation and prioritization of internal affairs. The Sultan's first hundred days indicate that most of his decisions were mainly related to economic and development matters, and were primarily concerned with solving potential causes of domestic unrest such as high unemployment, budget deficits, and dwindling oil reserves, as well as with measures such as Omanization (nationalization), empowerment of women and youth, and institutional reform, to turn the Sultanate into an investment-friendly environment that "would propel rapid growth and urgently needed job creation while dealing with the heavy load of debt Oman had assumed over the past four years".[92] In a speech to the nation on February 23, 2020, Sultan Haitham pledged to "take the necessary measures to restructure the state's administrative apparatus" to "achieve good governance, performance, integrity and accountability".[93]

Nonetheless, there were several speculations that Oman was interested in joining the UAE-led alliance (with Saudi Arabia, Bahrain, and Egypt) because of Sultan Haitham's friendship with the Crown Prince of Abu Dhabi, and his previous business partnerships with Emirati business circles. Therefore, unlike the reclusive Qaboos, the new Sultan may be more receptive to alignment with Emirati objectives.[94] In addition, both the UAE and Saudi Arabia exhibit a strong willingness to pursue geostrategic schemes and expand their regional influence. Finally, as a result of the Emirati and Saudi lobby and pressure groups in Washington D.C., the Omani position lacks the support of Trump's administration. Therefore, with domestic instability in Oman, the new Sultan has been under enormous pressure to review the Sultanate's alignments and foreign policy orientations.[95]

It is still too early to predict the new Sultan's foreign policy; however, based on his decisions during the last six months, Oman will not invest all its diplomatic efforts in solving the Gulf crisis. Until now (July 2020), there have been no indications of a possibility of dialogue among the parties involved in the dispute, despite the growing number of calls for it from the public and the elites, which received attention neither from the leadership nor from the media.[96]

---

[92] Sievers 2020.
[93] Mostafa 2020.
[94] Sheline 2020.
[95] ibid; Tsukerman 2020.
[96] Al-Khatib 2020; Abozaid 2020:131.

The second event is the COVID-19 pandemic. Work towards combatting and preventing the virus on a global scale could increase tendencies towards international rapprochement, multilateralism, and cooperation, which have led several experts to predict that the pandemic could push the Gulf crisis towards a solution.[97] This optimism is a result of increasingly frequent talks and meetings among all members of the GCC organization, which are being held to discuss repercussions of the COVID-19 crisis for the Gulf States. Since March 2020, the GCC has witnessed a vibrant interaction of experts in sectors such as health and disease prevention. More than three meetings of GCC health ministers have been held (including the Qatari minister of health Dr. Hanan Al-Kuwari), and more than 70 meetings of executive committees. During the meetings, the GCC health ministers' decisions were reviewed, experiences and protocols were exchanged, and guidance on preparation for and response to pandemics was unified.[98] However, such cooperation did not exceed specific protocols and formal frameworks of the health field, and the countries have not witnessed rapprochement in spheres unrelated to the pandemic. This situation proved that the current Gulf crisis is primarily a security crisis deeply rooted in the fanatical, egoistic, and short-sighted leadership which prevents any possibility of dialogue or intervention by third parties from putting an end to it.

In sum, the Gulf crisis had begun as a "chicken game" of testing which party would retract and give up on its strategy first. After almost seven bitter years of embargoing and isolating Qatar, freezing the work of the GCC organization, and curbing integration attempts, this "chicken game" strategy has turned into a "shoot yourself in the foot" strategy, whereby the actors in the crisis show zero interest in the effects of their rivalry on the rest of the Khaleeji states. Sooner or later a solution will be found;[99] the question is at what expense and who will pay for it. Moreover, even if a solution is found, the crisis will have already left the whole Khaleeji society in a state of deep political, economic, and social fermentation. Regrettably, such critical questions remain insignificant for the competitive parties.

---

97 Khoja 2017; Abouzeid 2018; Telji 2020; Abozaid 2020b: 131.
98 GCC 2020; Ministry of Public Health 2020; Albayan 2020; CNN Arabic 2020.
99 After almost 7 years, the crisis was managed and temporary settled on 4th of January 2021 under the so-called Al-Ula Summit agreement. On Al-Ula agreement see: Abozaid 2022; Gulf countries sign accord, Qatar embargo ends. DW 2021; CNN Arabic 2021a, 2021b; Alyami 2021.

Conclusion

Much Ado about Nothing: [Eurocentric] Theories of International Relations and the Study of Arab Uprisings

To understand the current wave of democratization in the Arab World – regardless of the setbacks that have occurred – the book indicated that scholars should be moving away from the positivist (state-centric) perspectives that define international relations and foreign policy in terms of the pursuit of "national" interests, which is defined with reference to power by sovereign states, and towards a more critical approach that places human beings at the center of analysis. A critical or emancipation-based perspective, in turn, claims that International Relations should become a tool for achieving people's goals of ending fear and oppression and expanding freedom and justice beyond sovereign territories. Interestingly, as noted earlier, this is done not only by the state but also through other non-state actors, such as individuals, social movements, and civil society organizations. The emancipation of international politics and foreign policy projects aims to create and establish a "people-centric model" that does not recognize the separation between the internal and external spheres of the state's actions.

According to Ole Waever, territorially defined borders do not apply to foreign policy in today's world, or emancipatory foreign policy in particular. For countries like Germany, "emancipation" refers to "a new sense of self-esteem, independence, and follow[s] enlightened self-interest".[1] For China, emancipation is considered an anti-hegemonic attitude,[2] and for other countries such as Egypt and the Arab Uprising countries, the claims of emancipation during the first wave of the Uprising of 2011 were based on both understandings, including seeking independence, countering hegemony, and restoring national self-esteem. Therefore, since emancipation meant freeing people from physical and human constraints (e.g., violence, war, poverty, oppression, and other material and normative constraints) which prevent them from carrying out what they would freely choose to do, it also means that scholars should first concentrate on individual human beings, not the state, and secondly on achieving people's ends and not those of the state.

---

1 Forsberg 2005.
2 Waever 1994.

It is interesting to note that critical theory is not the only approach that emphasizes the notion of emancipation and freedom. Liberalism is built on similar ideas. However, while critical theory shares some traditions and practices of freedom and equality with the liberal school, its boundaries and prospects are wider than the latter's. In other words, while liberalism largely seeks to achieve individual freedom, critical theory seeks human emancipation. Furthermore, even though liberalism (and neoliberal institutionalism in particular) purports to have an interest in bringing about change, its presuppositions also purport to have such an interest.[3] In other words, the neoliberal change is contained within the system, and does not extend to questioning the world state system itself, which means justifying the Western domination of non-European societies and keeping order. Consequently, it likewise displays a system-maintenance bias, which means that this type of change is profoundly not radical or structural. Hence, this change, as Shapcott stated, becomes "more predictable but still not subject to critical reasoning".[4]

Contrary to such an adaptive-functionalist perspective, which in essence reflects and represents a latent intention to preserve and sustain the status quo of inequality and exclusion, critical school propositions call for change in the global system itself. For instance, in contrast with Neoliberal institutionalists, Cox persuasively argued that the global hegemonic class is disseminating and consolidating its ideology through different international organizations and bodies (e.g., the World Bank, the International Monetary Fund, the G8, and the United Nations) that expand and manifest its domination by drafting global norms and controlling the global structures of accumulation, division of labor, and internationalization of production that enforce the structurally unequal development and complex dependency between the North and the Global South (or the core and periphery, in other words). In turn, this leads to an empowerment of transnational forces (e.g., MNCs and Transnational Corporations (TNCs)) that accelerates and catalyzes the formation of a nascent global civil society, which then exerts pressure on peripheral states to adopt the accumulation strategies of the hegemonic state(s). In the final analysis, these weak states become what Cox called "transmission belts" between the hegemonic bloc/s and their domestic societies. This situation could result in the resurgence of resistance and create new forces for anti-hegemonic struggles against such structures, or could become part of the hegemonic world system, such as the 19th century Pax Britannica and the 20th and 21st century Pax Americana.[5]

---

3   Keohane 1988.
4   Shapcott 2008: 332–333; Teschke 2014:28; Hobson 2007.
5   Cox 1989; Van der Pijl 1984; Gill and Law 1988; Gill 1993; Yalvaç 2015.

CONCLUSION

Nevertheless, the Arab Uprising(s) without question was a genuinely emancipatory effort, in a Linklaterian view. Andrew Linklater defines emancipation as "powers of self-determination and the ability of initiate actions",[6] while Richard Ashley defines it as: "[A]n interest in securing freedom from unacknowledged constraints, relations of domination, and conditions of distorted communication and understanding that deny humans the capacity to make their future through full will and consciousness".[7] Another scholar defines it as: "autonomy, freedom of action, security and freedom of individuals and nations from domineering and repressive structures and elimination of restrictive social grounds and contexts which are conducive to injustice, and redefinition and reconfiguration of justice and equality in the international system".[8] According to these definitions, emancipation is considered a revolutionary-revisionist concept that requires not only changing the domestic and internal structures of oppression, but also changing the international structures of power. This is because norms and values, and the hegemonic and oppressive structures they create, are the main sources of injustice, inequality, and authoritarianism in the world.

Consequently, critical theory projects in the field of traditional IR – that is, in its principles – is considered the theoretical approach that most closely addresses the Arab Uprising(s), due to its having been perceived as an instrument of the powerless with which to advance more equitable types of global relations, by illuminating and highlighting possibilities of liberation and emancipation. Nevertheless, its presence in the mainstream debates and spaces is still marginalized. Therefore, to push its research agenda to occupy wider space, the book suggests that proponents of the critical theory of IR should re-evaluate the Eurocentric and Enlightenment-based-Modernity foundations which produce several cognitive fallacies. Moreover, some critical theorists need to abandon their dogmatic, anti-academic, and cognitive supremacist claims, to become less demagogic, equivocal, elitist, and isolationist, and more inclusive and open to the contributions of Southern voices.

In fact, such deficiencies (and others) have been transcendent, penetrating and proliferating in most of the critical studies, through which critical theory has become marginalized and unwelcome within academia and among the young generations of IR scholars, outside the isolated micro-archipelagic European academic elitist cycles. Finally, it needs to depart from its ivory tower and transform its theoretical claims and statements into practical projects

---

6   Linklater 1990: 135.
7   Ashley 1981: 227.
8   Abadi 2008.

more related to the realworld (rather than the lifeworld), which will allow its proponents not only to engage but also to join the masses in their struggle and fight for emancipation. In so doing, the critical theory of IR will be able to change not only the field of IR but its real-world outcomes as well.

To sum up, since the aim of critical theory is "to understand how these (realistic) socially created constraints upon the freedom of human subjects (emancipation) could be reduced and, where possible, eliminated",[9] and by focusing on Critical IR studies of foreign policy, revolution, and the correlations between a failed revolution and the inability to achieve human emancipation, this book has tried to explore the main reasons behind the failure of emancipatory projects in non-Western societies, by showing and explaining how anti-progressive countries used and employed emancipation as an instrument for preventing it. These counterrevolutionary and anti-emancipatory policies and projects have been drafted, supported, and designed by problem-solving theories. These theories must be tamed and challenged. In the end, the previous analysis has highlighted the theoretical and practical potentialities diverse critical theories of IR enjoy, which could accelerate the realization of these objectives; but only if critical theorists overcome the fallacies and deficiencies the book has indicated and specified.

1 Towards New Imagination: On Decolonizing the Study of the Arab World

By using the term "Arab World" I am distancing myself from colonial, Imperial, and Neo-colonial terms such as "The Middle East", "MENA", "The Greater Middle Eastern", and other problematic terms such as Middle East, Caucasus, and Central Asian Studies (MECCAS), that forcibly integrate varied regions, nations, ethnicities, and communal, religious, and racial communities within a unified and homogeneous "imaginary" constituent and study it as one area. This academic and political fixation (and cognitive form of violence) overlooks and neglects the deeply embodied complexity and richness of these regions, while failing to acknowledge the rights of other communities that different forms of coloniality have suppressed and silenced. Therefore, I am using the term "Arab World" to refer to most Arabic speaking countries, which means – first – the excluded countries (communities and cultures) such as Pakistan, Afghanistan, Iran, Turkey, Israel, Central Asian countries, and the rest of the

---

9 Linklater 1990: 1.

Islamic World. Moreover, secondly, this term does not claim (either implicitly or explicitly) to represent other communities in the Arab World (e.g., Kurds, Nubians, Black Arabs, Armenians, and others). I do not deny that these communities have their distinct character, languages, identities, belief systems, histories, etc. that are not necessarily a part of the region called the Arab World. On the contrary, I do believe that the experiences of the modern Arab States (since the late nineteenth century) demonstrate that local (and indigenous) communities have suffered (and still suffer) from a double-edged coloniality comprising the external form (European colonialism) and the internal form (Arab Nationalism). There is ongoing contestation and controversy over the naming, belonging, and identities of local communities in the Global South. Such a topic is culturally and politically sensitive and needs to be re-appraised and re-perceived away from all forms of colonial heritage, hegemony, and violently imposed (from above) academic frameworks that deny the rights of others.

In the case of Egypt, for instance, scholars need to avoid and give up the previously mentioned centrality of some regions of Upper Egypt within Egyptian and Western academia. For instance, while most studies of the revolution in Upper Egypt were dealing with two main cities (Luxor and Aswan), the role of other parts of the Sa'îd (e.g., the Red Sea and Al-Wadi Al-Gadeed governorates in particular) in the 2011 revolution is still an enigma, or a black hole strikingly overlooked by most of these studies. In fact, shockingly, we do not know what happened in these two governorates either in 2011 or in the aftermath. Also, scholars need to be aware of the danger of dealing with Upper Egypt as a single bloc or unbroken unity. However, this proposition does not negate the existence of common ground and features among the Sa'îd components. For instance, besides shared customs, traditions, geographical proximity, and continuity, etc. between the governorates of Upper Egypt (and among the peasants in general), the tendency to cling to the agricultural lands is one of the most evident variables. As an example, Saker al-Nur presented a premium contribution that elucidated how the so-called tenancy law of 1992 had unified the Egyptian peasants (al-Fellaheen and as-Sa'îdiyya alike), prompting them to revolt and disobey the law and the authority that aimed to expel them from their farms. Likewise, interestingly, the release of law no. 1 of 2020, known as the Construction Violations Reconciliation Law, represents strong evidence for such claims.[10] Firstly, it shows that Sa'îd sometimes can speak as a single, cohesive bloc to a large extent; secondly, it shows the centrality of agricultural

---

10 Daily News Egypt 2020.

lands in the life of as-Sa'îdiyya and their willingness to stand and challenge authority if the latter encroaches on or tries to uproot them from or seize their land coercively.

For instance, while writing the final draft of the book's chapter on Upper Egypt, despite the state of emergency and the exceptional conditions caused by the COVID-19 situation, a series of protests spread all over Upper Egypt for the first time since 2011, as a reaction to the construction violations reconciliation law. Several clashes between the police forces and Sa'idi people occurred in Luxor, Qina, Al-Minya, Sohag and elsewhere. In October 2020, in the city of Al-Awamiyah, which is part of the province of Luxor, there were clashes between security forces and residents of the city because of the assault on a resident of the city by the security forces during the arrest of his brother, who objected to the implementation of the law. The man, Aweys Al-Rawi, was killed by the police. To make it worse, after killing him, the police started shooting and letting off bombs, which prompted the people of the city to respond by attacking the police, so that exchange fire between the two parties continued. For more than two weeks following the death of Al-Rawi (who became a martyr – shahid al-shahama, "the martyr of magnanimity"), the city of Al-Awamiyah witnessed demonstrations and protests police brutality, the land law, and overall malignant conditions. Several cities and villages in the Sa'îd and elsewhere witnessed similar events and protest activities against the law and the police forces. The confrontations between the police and the people of the city turned into a national event after the posting of videos of the confrontations, protests, and police brutality. Also, the solidarity on social media platforms with the city and its people was enormous, to the extent that activists started a Twitter hashtag to compare and associate what happened to the young Sa'idi man (Al-Rawi) at the hands of the Egyptian forces with what happened to the African American man (George Floyd) whose murder was the spark that ignited the Black Lives Matter movement.

Also, every time I went back to the field (after 2015) I noticed that the tendencies and trajectories of anger and frustration had grown considerably. For instance, I noticed a clear change in the language and the reasons given by interviewees when expressing their anger over the economic and political conditions. There was a tendency for s'ab al-deen (sinful cursing, with the use of forbidden religious words) to become more common and normal among ordinary and poor men (old and young alike) as a variant way of expressing their anger and frustration over illegal tributes, unemployment, poverty, and the insane increases in the price of basic needs. This is unusual, either before or since the 2011 revolution.

In future studies, more comparative interviews on revolution and social mobilization in the Sa'îd are needed. By interviewing groups drawn from different points on the age, gender, class, and religion scale, it will be possible to investigate and illuminate how these identities affect political attitudes and behavior. Also, in future studies, and based on the results of this study, I will be able to focus my enquiries on the topics raised in preliminary interviews, and to spend more time in the field, in turn enabling me to compare the results with those gleaned from other Sa'idi cities and villages.[11]

Moreover, I intend to strengthen my knowledge of the Sa'idi society, and to investigate the genesis of the identity construction process, state-society relations, and the role of social and power structures. In addition, I will explore the dialectical relationships (from below) between the Authority (i.e., security, police, military, and disciplinary apparatuses in general) and the citizens; the penetration of society by these apparatuses; and the role of ideological, discursive, and pedagogical techniques, forming the apparatus – in Gramsci's and Althusser's words – that exists in symbiosis with the oppressive apparatus of the state.[12] Furthermore, I aim to expand my understanding so as to pave the way for exploration of these isolated, peripheral societies, which will reveal what is hidden and unsaid about political behavior in modern Egypt, since focus on and concerns about these kinds of societies are still insignificant.[13] Such investigations are needed to reveal the articulation between these structures, and to identify the continuation and disruption of power relations, subjection methods and forms of displacement and confiscation in Sa'îd and other local communities in Egypt, and elsewhere in MENA region.

In the end, academics who work in such fields (i.e., marginalized, and isolated societies) need to reflect on their research agendas and cognitive biases, both inherent and invisible. The case of the study of Upper Egypt demonstrates how such societies and human groups are not represented or made visible on the radar of the mainstream academic and research agenda, due either to initial cognitive and methodological deficiencies, or to deliberate exclusion of these topics by the dominant research and academic institutions. Although Upper Egypt is inhabited by more than 30 different ethnic, communal, and religious groups, we find hardly any study of communities such as Al-jmaseh, Al-Halab, Al-Bajah, or other invisible subalterns. The question is no longer about whether the so-called "subaltern" can speak;[14] the question now is whether the

---

11   Abu-Lughod 2012.
12   Gramsci 1957: 180–183; Buci-Glucksmann 1980: 357–361.
13   Hobsbawm 1973.
14   Spivak 1988; Morris 2010.

very presence of these human beings will be acknowledged and recognized, and whether their right to be fairly represented will be gained. Such distortion and epistemic neglect are still in dire need of correction and erasure.

In addition, the problem is not only representation or recognition but also the need to get rid of the stereotypes and clichés that characterize area studies. For instance, these fields suffer from several deficiencies and shortcomings such as the compulsive inclination towards totality, subjugation, displacement, containment, distortion, and acquisition of small communities and their forcible annexation under colonial, hegemonic, and politically loaded academic frameworks. While these regions include varied ethnic, religious, national, racial, etc. groups and nations, the frameworks imposed from above tend to integrate and homogenize these different communities under one illusionary and imaginary umbrella based on shared religious, national, linguistic etc. features. Examples include Middle East, Central Asia, and Caucasus Studies (MECACS); the Middle East and North Africa (MENA); the Greater Middle East that extends from the boundaries of India in the East to the Atlantic beaches in the West; and other programs that encompass distinct societies and diverse cultures under anomalous frameworks such as Oriental Studies or Oriental and African Studies. These programs genuinely ignore the fundamental differences not only between de-homogenized states and societies but also between groups within a singular country (e.g., Upper Egypt and Nubia in Egypt, Kurds, Yazidis, Assyrian, Turkmen, Chaldean-Syriac communities in Iraq, among other examples). Interestingly, such tendencies are not exclusive or limited to Middle Eastern studies; they control studies of other areas of the Global South such as Eastern Europe (studied as part of so-called Slavic, East European, and Eurasian Studies, or SEEES), and Latin America, traditionally examined as a part of Spanish or Portuguese studies. Within this framework, Latin American societies, the Caribbean, and other societies are treated mainly as a part of "colonial" Spanish culture. Overall, these contested "macro" frameworks are too broad, ambiguous, and problematic, as within them local (micro) communities, native, and indigenous communities are lost and coercively integrated and unified, leading to several tensions and ruptures, as well as to systematic epistemic and moral contestation. These epistemic impositions need to be seriously and openly addressed, encountered, and remedied.

Finally, on the ontological and self-level, as researchers we are all required to reflect on and pay more attention to the question: Whom do we write our research for? and for what purposes? Are we writing for purely academic and cognitive purposes, or to contribute to institutions, policymakers, or the communities we study? Most importantly, how do we write? Researchers belonging to the Global South should be always on the alert regarding their positionalities

CONCLUSION

and epistemological and methodological choices. Likewise, academia and journals should be encouraged to support critical investigations that aim at decolonizing the knowledges of Non-Western societies (e.g., Middle Eastern studies) that have been produced and (re)produced in Eurocentric and Western academic circles. These societies have their own historical, cultural, political, and modernity-related experiences that are distinct from the dominant Western experiences which systemically overlook and violently silence other "Southern" voices. To explicitly rupture and break the Western monopoly of representation of others and demolish the hegemonic knowledge system that seeks to silence voices that challenge its interpretations of the world, different kinds of knowledges and the oppressed "local" voices must be represented and have the chance to express their own experiences.

Bibliography

Abadi, S. (2008) Emancipating Foreign Policy: Critical Theory and Islamic Republic of Iran's Foreign Policy. *The Iranian Journal of International Affairs*, 20(3): 1–26.

Abaza, M. (2013) 'Intimidation and Resistance: Imagining Gender in Cairene Graffiti', *Jadaliyya*. Available: https://www.jadaliyya.com/Details/28858 (consulted 29 December 2017).

Abdalla, N. (2016a) Youth Movements in the Egyptian Transformation: Strategies and Repertoires of Political Participation. *Mediterranean Politics*, 21(1): 44–63.

Abdalla, N. (2016b) The Labor Movement in the Face of Transition. In: S. Lacroix and B. Rougier (eds) *Egypt's Revolutions: Politics, Religion, and Social Movements*. New York: Palgrave Macmillan, 197–211.

Abdalla, N., and Wolff, J. (2019) From Driver of Change to Marginalised Actor: Organised Labour in Post-Revolutionary Egypt from a Comparative Perspective. *The Journal of North African Studies*, 25(6): 918–938.

Abdelrahman, M. (2014) *Egypt's Long Revolution: Protest Movements and Uprisings*. Abingdon: Routledge.

Abdullah, A. (2012) The Arab Gulf Moment. In: D. Held, and K. Ulrichsen (eds.) *The Transformation of the Gulf: Politics: Economics and the Global Order*. London: Routledge, 106–124.

Abdullah, A. (2010) *Contemporary socio-political issues of the Arab Gulf moment*. Kuwait Programme on Development, Governance and Globalisation in the Gulf States, 11. The London School of Economics and Political Science, London, UK.

Aboul Gheit, M. (2012) 'al-fa'ez al-akbar fi intekhabat al- Sa'id' (The Biggest Winner in the Upper Egypt Elections), *Al-Shorouk*, (17 January 2012). Available: https://www.shorouknews.com/columns/view.aspx?cdate=17012012&id=913e8ecb-a432-4395-8a63-0db43fa6c0aa (consulted 30 December 2017).

Abozaid, A. (2022) *Counterterrorism Strategies in Egypt: Permanent Exceptions in the War on Terror*. New York: Routledge.

Abozaid, A. (2020a) Counterterrorism strategy and human rights in Egypt after the Arab uprising: A critical appraisal. *Aggression and Violent Behavior*, 51(1): 1–15.

Abozaid, A. (2020b) Bitter Years Qatari Crisis and the Future of GCC Countries. *Contemporary Arab Affairs*, 13(4): 108–137.

Abozaid, A. (2014) 'Lemazha lam yathor al-Sa'id?' [Why did Upper Egypt not rebel?]. *Jadaliyya*, (7 March 2014). Available: https://www.jadaliyya.com/Details/30325 (consulted 29 December 2017).

Abozaid, A. (2013) 'al-syasiha fi al- Sa'id 2–2' [Politics in Upper Egypt 2–2], *al-Watan*, (2 April 2013). Available: https://www.elwatannews.com/news/details/157965120 (consulted 29 December 2017).

Abozaid, A. (2009) *shaykhukha mubakerah: 'adam al-inhyaaz fi alam mutghayeer* [Non-alignment in changing world]. *Weghat Nazar*, 11(128): 40–47.

Abu-Lughod, L. (2012) Living the "Revolution" in an Egyptian Village: Moral Action in a National Space. *American Ethnologist*, 39(1): 21–25.

Abu-Lughod, L. (2007) *Dramas of Nationhood: The Politics of Television in Egypt*. Illinois: Chicago University Press.

Abul-Magd, Z. (2013) *Imagined Empires: A History of Revolt in Egypt*. Berkeley; California University Press.

Acharya, A. (2018) *Constructing Global Order: Agency and Change in World Politics*. New York: Cambridge University Press.

Acharya A., and Buzan B. (2019) *The Making of Global International Relations: Origins and Evolution of IR at its Centenary*. New York: Cambridge University Press.

Achcar, G. (2016) *Morbid Symptoms: Relapse in the Arab Uprising*. Stanford: CA: Stanford University Press.

Achcar, G. (2013) *The People Want: A Radical Exploration of the Arab Uprising*. London: Saqi Books.

Adams, J. (1957) Culture and Conflict in an Egyptian Village. *American Anthropologist*, 59(2): 201–235.

Adams, R. (2000) Evaluating the Process of Development in Egypt, 1980–97. *International Journal of Middle East Studies*, 32(2): 255–275.

Adams, R. (1985) Development and Structural Change in Rural Egypt, 1952 to 1982. *World Development*, 13(6): 705–723.

Adib-Moghaddam, A. (2009) *The International Politics of the Persian Gulf: A Cultural Genealogy*. New York: Routledge.

Adorno T., and Horkheimer, M. (1972) [1944] *Dialectics of Enlightenment*. Translated by John Cumming. New York: Herder and Herder.

Ahmed, S., and Malik, M. (2013) hamelet "la le-tahmeesh al-Sa'id" tabda' gama' tawqeeat le takhasees nesbat min mukhtat al-tanmiyat be mawad al-dostur ('No more marginalization of Upper Egypt' campaign begins collecting signatures to allocate a percentage of the development plans inside the constitution) *al-Watan*, (29 September 2013). Available: https://www.elwatannews.com/news/details/331771 (consulted 29 December 2017).

Ajami, F. (1995) The Sorrows of Egypt. *Foreign Affairs*, 74(5): 72–88.

Ajami, F. (1991) *The Arab Predicament: Arab Political Thought and Practice Since 1967*. Cambridge: Cambridge University Press.

Akhbar al-yom (2020) Al-ihessha, taragooh moa'del al-oumeyyha fem asr, w al-minya a'laah al-muhafazat [CAPMS: The rates of illiteracy has decreased in Egypt, and Al-Minya is the highest], *Akhbar el-yom*, https://akhbarelyom.com/news/newdetails/3109794/.

BIBLIOGRAPHY

Akhbar al-yom (2016) be al-arqaam ... narsod arqaam w era'dat w ihessa't fi masr (In numbers: Figures, revenues and statistics of tourism in Egypt), *Akhbar al-yom*, https://akhbarelyom.com/news/newdetails/590574.

Al-Abnoudi, A. (2017) *Complete Works*. Cairo: Al-ha'yh al-masriyya al-a'amha le ak-ketab.

Al-akhwan al-mslmoun yahseloun ala 235 maqa'ad fi majles al-shaab (The Muslim Brotherhood gets 235 seats in the Parliament), *France24*, (21 January 2012). Available: https://www.france24.com/ar/20120121-egypt-muslim-brotherhood-winner-parl iamentarian-elections (consulted 29 December 2017).

Al-Anani, K. (2016) *Inside the Muslim Brotherhood: Religion, Identity, and Politics.* New York: Oxford University Press.

Al-Aswany, M. (2015a) 'lemazha yoshareek al-Sa'id fi thawra la ta'nee la'ho shaian' (Why is Upper Egypt participating in a revolution that means nothing to it? 2–2) *Rose Al-Youssef*, (28 January 2015). Available: https://www.rosaelyoussef.com/-12920 (consulted 30 December 2020).

Al-Aswany, M. (2015b) 'Lemazha yoshareek al- Sa'id fi thawra la ta'nee la'ho shaian' (Why is Upper Egypt participating in a revolution that means nothing to it? 1–2), *Rose al-Youssef*, (25 January 2015). Available: https://rosaelyoussef.com/-12909 (consulted 30 December 2017).

Al-Ayoubi, N. (1989) *Al-dawlah almrkziah fi msr* [The Central State of Egypt]. Beirut: Center for Arab Unity Studies.

Al-Barghouti, T. (2008) *The Umma and the Dawla: The Nation-State and the Arab Middle East*. London: Pluto Press.

Al-Ebraheem, H. (1984) [2016] *Kuwait and the Gulf: Small States and the International System*. Croom Helm Ltd.

Al-Husseini, D. (2020) 'Kamel al-Wazir le 'sout alomma': azmet mahtet Bashteel mufta'ilha wln yafla'h mn asha'el neraanha' [Kamel al-Wazir to 'Sout al-omma': the crisis of the Bashteel station is fabricated and those who created it will not succeed], *Sout al-omma*, (5 September 2020). Available: http://www.soutalomma.com/Article/938 844/ (consulted 30 December 2021).

Al-ihessha, taragooh moa'del al-oumeyyha fem asr, w al-minya a'laah al-muhafazat [CAPMS: The rates of illiteracy have decreased in Egypt, and Al-Minya is the highest], *Akhbar el-yom* (8 September 2020). Available: https://akhbarelyom.com/news /newdetails/3109794/ (consulted 29 December 2021).

Al-Iskandarani, I. (2013) 'al-shamal al-tha'er w al-ganoob al-saaket' (Egypt: the rebellious North and the silent South!) *al-Akhbar*, (27 April 2013). Available: https://al -akhbar.com/Arab/50090 (consulted 30 December 2017).

Al-Khalili, M. (2009) *Oman's Foreign Policy: Foundation and Practice*. Westport: CT; Praeger.

Al-Khatib, A. (2020) Muthaqafoon w akadeimeoon khaleejoon ya'daun le-wefaq yaqudoh ahl al-hikmah. *The New Arab*. Accessed July 10, 2020. https://www.alaraby.co.uk/%D9%85%D8%AB%D9%82%D9%81%D9%88%D9%86-%D9%88%D8%A3%D9%83%D8%A7%D8%AF%D9%8A%D9%85%D9%8A%D9%88%D9%86-%D8%AE%D9%84%D9%8A%D8%AC%D9%8A%D9%88%D9%86-%D9%8A%D8%AF%D8%B9%D9%88%D9%86-%D9%84%D9%88%D9%81%D8%A7%D9%82-%D9%8A%D9%82%D9%88%D8%AF%D9%87-%22%D8%A3%D9%87%D9%84-%D8%A7%D9%84%D8%AD%D9%83%D9%85%D8%A9%22.

Al-Mashat, A. (2010) Politics of Constructive Engagement: The Foreign Policy of the United Arab Emirates. In: B. Korany, and A. Dessouki (eds.) *The Foreign Policies of Arab States: The Challenge of Globalization*. Cairo: American University in Cairo Press, 457–480.

Al-Masry al-youm (2009) *Al-Sa'id bain ehmaal al-dawla w iftr'aat al-deramah* (Upper Egypt: Between State Neglect and the Fabrication of the Media), *al-Masry al-youm*, https://www.almasryalyoum.com/news/details/66161.

Al-Mezaini, K., and Rickli, J. (eds.) (2017) *The Small Gulf States: Foreign and Security Policies Before and After the Arab Spring*. New York: Routledge.

Al-Rafi'i, A. (1946) *Thourah 1919 ttarikh msr alkoumi mn snah 1914 ili 1921* [The Revolution of 1919: A National History of Egypt from 1914 to 1921] Cairo: Maktabet al-Nahda al-Masryyia.

Al-Rumaihi, M. (1996) *alkhlij lis nfta* [The Gulf is not only Oil]. Kuwait: New Dar.

Al-Sa'id bain ehmaal al-dawla w iftr'aat al-deramah (Upper Egypt: Between State Neglect and the Fabrication of the Media), *al-Masry al-youm*, (consulted 19 September 2009). https://www.almasryalyoum.com/news/details/66161.

Al-seyah'a al-masriyyha tohaqeeq era'dat kea'sseyha fi 2019 (Egyptian tourism achieves record revenues of $13 billion in 2019), *Al-Arabiya*, (31 March 2020). Available: https://www.alarabiya.net/en/aswaq/travel-and-tourism/2020/03/31/ (consulted 29 December 2021).

Al-seyah'a fi masr (Tourism in Egypt), *Al-Assema'h Center for Economic Research and Studies* (19 December 2019). Available: http://ccsr-eg.com/news/news.aspx?id=7966# (consulted 29 December 2021).

Al-Shayji, A. (2014) The GCC-US Relationship: A GCC perspective. *Middle East Policy*, 21(3): 60–70.

Alatas, S. (1977) *The Myth of the Lazy Native: A Study of the Image of the Malays, Filipinos and Javanese from the 16th to the 20th Century and Its Function in the Ideology of Colonial Capitalism*. London: Frank Cass.

Alexander, A., and Bassiouny, M. (2014) *Bread, Freedom, Social Justice: Workers and the Egyptian Revolution*. London: Zed Books Ltd.

Alexandrani, I. (2016) Sinai: From Revolution to Terrorism. In: S. Lacroix and B. Rougier (eds.) *Egypt's Revolutions: Politics, Religion, and Social Movements*. New York: Palgrave Macmillan, 179–96. 90.

Ali, T. (2013) Between past and future. Reply to Asef Bayat. *New Left Review* 80: 61–74.

Ali, Y. (2013a) 'la le-tahmeesh al-Sa'id fi al-dostur" ftotaleeb be tazeeh al-wezarat ala al-muhfazat' (No more marginalization of Upper Egypt in the constitution calls for the distribution of ministries equally among the governances), *Al Bawabh News,* (9 September 2013). Available: https://www.albawabhnews.com/138239 (consulted 29 December 2017).

Ali, Y. (2013b) mataleb "la le-tahmeesh al-Sa'id" tantazer saferht tanmiyat al-janoob al-mansi (The demands of "No more marginalization of Upper Egypt" await the sign of developing the forgotten south), *al-mandara,* (10 October 2013). Available: https://bit.ly/43eaYXk (consulted 29 December 2017).

Alkadry, M. (2002) Reciting Colonial Scripts: Colonialism, Globalization and Democracy in the Decolonized Middle East. *Administrative Theory & Praxis*, 24(4): 739–62.

Almezaini, K., and Rickli, J. (eds.) (2016) *The Small Gulf States: Foreign and Security Policies Before and After the Arab Spring*. New York: Routledge.

Alqus Yaqoub, H. (2012) *Sarkhet dam a'layeh: Shohada mazbahet Maspero* [A Loud Shout of Blood: The Martyrs of the Maspero's Massacre]. Alexandria: Deer Al-Shaheed Al-Azeem Marmina Al-Ajibi.

Alterman, J. (2000) Egypt: Stable, but for How Long? *Washington Quarterly*, 23(4): 107–118.

Althani, M. (2012) *The Arab Spring and the Gulf States Time to embrace change*. London: Profile Books.

Alyami, H. (2021) *qamet al-Ula tewahhed qadet al-khaleej wa tewaahed sefofhim* [Al-Ula Summit embraces the Gulf leaders and unites them]. *Al-Watan,* https://www.alwatan.com.sa/article/1065389.

Amer, S. (2015) 'mahtet Bashteel ta;'sta'ed le isteqbal qetarat al-Sa'id be taklefat 1.5 milyar dollar' [Bashteel's station prepares to receive Sa'idi trains, at a cost of $1.5 billion], *al-Watan*, (7 February 2015). Available: https://www.elwatannews.com/news/details/657190 (consulted 30 December 2017).

Amin, S. (2016) *The Reawakening of the Arab World: Challenge and Change in the Aftermath of the Arab Spring*. New York: Monthly Review Press.

Amin, S. (2011) An Arab Springtime? *Monthly Review* Available: https://bit.ly/2BaZuMo (consulted 5 November 2017).

Anderson, K. (2017) The Egyptian Labor Corps: Workers, Peasants, and the State in World War I', *International Journal of Middle East Studies*, 49(1): 5–24.

Anievas, A. (2010) On Habermas, Marx and the Critical Theory Tradition: Theoretical Mastery or Drift? In C. Moore and C. Farrands (eds.) *International Relations Theory and Philosophy: Interpretive Dialogues*. Abingdon: Routledge, 144–156.

Anievas, A. (2005) Critical Dialogues: Habermasian Social Theory and International Relations. *Politics* 25(3): 135–143.

Anis, M. (1981) The Role of Egyptian Peasants in the 1919 Revolution. In: C. Agüero (ed.) *Peasantry and National Integration*. Mexico City: Colegio de Mexico, 257–270.

Ashley, R. (1981) Political realism and human interest. *International Studies Quarterly* 25(2): 204–236.

Ashley, R., and Walker, R. (1990) Speaking the Language of Exile. *International Studies Quarterly* 34(3): 367–416.

'Ashmawi, S. (2001) *Alflahoun walsltah: A'la dhou'a alhrkat alflahiah almsriah 1919–1999* [The Peasants and Power in the Light of the Egyptian Peasant Movements 1919–1999: A Historical Study] Cairo: Merritt House.

Atkinson, P., and Hammersley, M. (1998) Ethnography and Participant Observation. In: N. Denzin, and Y. Lincoln (eds.) *The Sage Handbook of Qualitative Research*. Thousand Oaks: Sage, 110–136.

Awal rad min as-Sa'idiyya ba'ad krar manaeh qitar al-Sa'id min dekhoul mahetet ramsis [as-Sa'idiyya's first reaction to the decision to prevent Sa'id's trains from entering Ramses railway station], *YouTube*, (23 August 2020). Available: https://bit.ly/3Mjq eMD (consulted 30 December 2017).

Ayeb, H. (2010) *La crise de la société rurale en Egypte ou la fin du fellah?* [The Crisis of Rural Society in Egypt or the End of the Fellah?]. Paris: Karthala.

Ayeb, H., and Bush, R. (2019) *Food Insecurity: Revolution in the Middle East and North Africa*. New York: Cambridge University Press.

Ayeb, H., and Bush, R. (2014) Small Farmer Uprisings and Rural Neglect in Egypt and Tunisia. *MERIP*, 272: 2–10.

Ayubi, N. (1995) *Over-stating the Arab State: Politics and Society in the Middle East*. London: I. B. Tauris.

Ayubi, N. (1991) *The State and Public Policies in Egypt Since Sadat*. Reading: Ithaca Press.

Ayubi, N. (1989) *al-dawala al-markazyya fi misr* [Central State in Egypt]. Beirut: Centre for Arab Unity Studies.

Ayubi, N. (1981) *Bureaucracy and Politics in Contemporary Egypt*. London: Ithaca Press.

Baabood, A. (2017) Oman and the Gulf Diplomatic Crisis. *Gulf Affairs*, 3(3): 30–31.

Baaz, M., Lilja, M., and Vinthagen, S. (eds.) (2018) *Researching Resistance and Social Change: A Critical Approach to Theory and Practice*. London: Rowman & Littlefield.

Badrawi, M. (2000) *Political Violence in Egypt, 1910–1924*. Richmond; Surrey: Curzon Press.

Baker Fox, A. (1959) *The Power of Small States: Diplomacy in World War II*. Illinois: University of Chicago Press.

Bakr, H. (1996) *Ala'nf al-syasi fi masr* [The Political violence in Egypt 1977–1993]. Cairo: Dar al-Mahrousa.

Barnett, M. (2002) Historical sociology and constructivism. In: S. Hobden, and J. Hobson (eds.) *Historical sociology of international relations*. Cambridge, U.K.: Cambridge University Press, 99–119.

Barnett, M. (1995) Nationalism, Sovereignty, and Regional Order in Arab Politics. *International Organization*, 49(3): 479–510.

Barnett, M. (1993) Institutions, Roles, and Disorder: The Case of the Arab States System. *International Studies Quarterly* 37(3): 271–296.

Baxter, B., and Akbarzadeh, S. (2008) *US Foreign Policy in the Middle East: The Roots of Anti-Americanism*. New York: Routledge.

Bayat, A. (2017) *Revolution without Revolutionaries: Making Sense of the Arab Spring*. California: Stanford University Press.

Bayat, A. (2010) *Life as Politics: How Ordinary People Change the Middle East*. Netherlands: Amsterdam University Press.

Bayat, A. (2009) *Life as Politics: How Ordinary People Change the Middle East*. Stanford: Stanford University Press.

Bayat, A. (1997) Un-civil society: The Politics of the informal people. *Third World Quarterly*, 18(1): 53–72.

BBC Arabic. (2020) Haitham bin Tariq Al Saeed sultanan le oman khalafan le qaboos. Accessed July 10, 2020. https://www.bbc.com/arabic/middleeast-51076164.

Be al-arqaam ... narsod arqaam w era'dat w ihessa't fi masr (In numbers: Figures, revenues and statistics of tourism in Egypt), *Akhbar al-yom*, (16 November 2016). Available: https://akhbarelyom.com/news/newdetails/590574 (consulted 29 December 2017).

Beck, M. (2015) The End of Regional Middle Eastern Exceptionalism? The Arab League and the Gulf Cooperation Council after the Arab Uprisings. *Democracy and Security*, 11(2): 190–207.

Bellin, E. (2012) Reconsidering the Robustness of Authoritarianism in the Middle East Lessons from the Arab Spring. *Comparative Politics* 44(2): 127–149.

Berger, R. (2015) Now I See It, Now I Don't: Researcher's Position and Reflexivity in Qualitative Research. *Qualitative Research*, 15(2): 219–234.

Bhabha, H. (1994) *The Location of Culture*. London: Routledge.

Binnendijk, H. (1999) Back to Bipolarity. *The Washington Quarterly*, 22(4): 5–14.

Blackman, W. (2000) [1927] *The Fellahin of Upper Egypt*. Cairo: The American University in Cairo Press.

Booth, K. (2008) The human faces of terror: Reflections in a cracked looking-glass. *Critical Studies on Terrorism* 1(1): 65–79.

Booth, K. (1991) Security and Emancipation. *Review of International Studies* 17(4): 313–326.

Bradley, J. (2008) *Inside Egypt: The Land of The Pharaohs on the Brink of a Revolution.* New York: Palgrave Macmillan.

Brincat, S. (2018) Critical International Relations Theory. In: Best, B., Bonefeld, W., and O'Kane, C. (eds.) *The SAGE Handbook of Frankfurt School Critical* Theory. Calif: SAGE, 1436–1449.

Brincat S (2012) On the Methods of Critical Theory: Advancing the Project of Emancipation beyond the Early Frankfurt School. *International Relations* 26(2): 218–245.

Bronner, S. (2011) *Critical Theory: A very short Introduction.* New York: Oxford University Press.

Brooks, S. and Wohlforth W. (2008) *World Out of Balance: International Relations and the Challenge of American Primacy.* New Jersey: Princeton University Press.

Brooks, S., and Wohlforth, W. (2002) American Primacy in Perspective. *Foreign Affairs* 81(4): 20–33.

Brown, N. (1990) *Peasant Politics in Modern Egypt: The Struggle against the State.* New Haven: Yale University Press.

Brynen, R. (1991) Review: Peasant Politics in Modern Egypt: The Struggle against the State. Nathan J. Brown. *Canadian Journal of Political Science*, 24(2): 410–412.

Buci-Glucksmann, C. (1980) *Gramsci and the State.* London: Lawrence & Wishart.

Bull, H. (1977) *The Anarchical Society: A Study of Order in World Politics.* London: Macmillan.

Burns, D. (2018) An Arab Spring Autopsy. *The American Interest.* Accessed September 14, 2018. https://www.the-american-interest.com/2018/04/05/arab-springautopsy/.

Bush, R. (2011) Land, Politics and Agrarian Reform in Egypt. *British Journal of Middle Eastern Studies*, 38(3): 391–405.

Bush, R. (2002) *Counter-Revolution in Egypt's Countryside: Land and Farmers in the Era of Economic Reform.* London: Zed Books.

Bush, R. (2001) Civil Society, and the Uncivil State: Land Tenure Reform in Egypt and the Crisis of Rural Livelihoods. UNRISD. Available: http://www.unrisd.org/unrisd/website/document.nsf/(httpPublications)/752BA19D99154FF1C1256EC300429549?OpenDocument (consulted 29 December 2017).

Bush, R., and Ayeb, H. (2012) *Marginality and Exclusion in Egypt.* London: Zed Books.

Bush, S (2017) Varieties of International Influence and the Middle East. *Political Science & Politics* 50(3): 668–671.

Bustos, R. (2017) The Arab Spring changes under the prism of international relations theory. In: I, Szmolka. (ed.) *Political Change in the Middle East and North Africa: After the Arab Spring.* Edinburgh: Edinburgh University Press, 38–60.

Buzan, B., and Gonzalez-Pelaez, A., (eds.) (2009) *International Society and the Middle East: English School Theory at the Regional Level.* New York: Palgrave MacMillan.

Buzan, R., and Jones, J., (eds.) (1981) *Change and the Study of International Relations: The Evaded Dimension.* New York: St. Martin's Press.

Calhoun, G. (2004) A World of Emergencies: Fear, Intervention, and the Limits of Cosmopolitan Order. *Canadian Review of Sociology/Revue canadienne de sociologie,* 14(4): 373–395.

Campbell, J. (2004) *Institutional Change and Globalization.* Princeton, NJ: Princeton University Press.

CAPMS (2016) Estimated Census of Provinces and Sheikhs (online) (Cairo: Central Agency for Public Mobilization and Statistics). Available: http://www.capmas.gov.eg/Pages/IndicatorsPage.aspx?page_id=6156&ind_id=4575 (consulted 29 December 2017).

Cherkaoui, M. (2001) Relative Deprivation. In: N. J. Smelser, and P.B. Baltes (eds.) *International Encyclopedia of the Social & Behavioral Sciences.* Netherlands: Elsevier.

Chomsky, N. (2012) *Making the Future Occupations, Interventions, Empire and Resistance.* New York: Penguin.

Choucri, N. (1980) International Political Economy: A Theoretical Perspective. In: O. Holsti, R. Siverson, and A. George, (eds.) *Change in the international system.* Boulder, Colo.: Westview Press, 103–129.

CNN Arabic. (2020) be musharaket qatar: faerous korona yagma' Wazara al-seha al-khaleejeen fi leqa '"eftradi' abar al-vedeo. Accessed July 10, 2020. https://arabic.cnn.com/health/article/2020/03/14/gcc-health-ministers-met-videoconference-coronavirus.

Coleman, I. (2011) '"Blue bra girl" rallies Egypt's women vs. oppression', *CNN.* Available: http://www.cnn.com/2011/12/22/opinion/coleman-women-egypt-protest/ (consulted 29 December 2017).

Cox, R. (2012) For someone and for some purpose. In Brincat, S., Lima, L., and Nunes, J. (eds.) *Critical theory in international relations and security studies: Interviews and reflections.* Abingdon: Routledge, 15–34.

Cox, R. (2001) The Way Ahead: Toward a New Ontology of World Order. In Wyn Jones, R. (ed.). *Critical Theory and World Politics.* Boulder, CO: Lynne Rienner, 45–60.

Cox, R. (1996) Gramsci, Hegemony and International Relations: An Essay in Method. In Cox, R., and Sinclair, T. (eds.) *Approaches to World Order.* Cambridge: Cambridge University Press, 124–143.

Cox, R. (1995) Critical Political Economy. In: Hettne, B. (ed.). *International Political Economy: Understanding Global Disorder.* London: Zed Books Ltd, 31–45.

Cox, R. (1992) "Towards a post-hegemonic conceptualization of world order: Reflections on the relevancy of Ibn Khaldun. In: J. Rosenau, and E. Czempiel (eds.) *Governance without Government: Order and Change in World Politics*. New York: Cambridge University Press, 132–159.

Cox, R. (1989) Production, the State and Change in World Order. In E.O. Czempiel and J.N. Rosenau (eds.) *Global Changes and Theoretical Challenges: Approaches to World Politics for the 1990s*. Lexington, MA: Lexington Books, 37–50.

Cox, R. (1987) *Production, Power, and World Order: Social Forces in the making of history*. New York: Columbia University Press.

Cox, R. (1986) Social Forces, States and World Orders: Beyond International Relations Theory. In: Keohane, R. (ed.) *Neorealism and Its Critics*. New York: Columbia University Press, 204–254.

Cox, R. (1983) Gramsci, Hegemony and International Relations. *Millennium* 12(2): 162–175.

Cox, R. (1981) Social Forces, States and World Orders: Beyond International Relations Theory. *Millennium* 10(2): 126–155.

Cox, R., and Jacobson, H. (1974) *The Anatomy of Influence*. New Haven, Yale University Press.

Cox, R., and Sinclair, T. (1996) *Approaches to World Order*. Cambridge: Cambridge University.

Craig, C., Friedman, B., Green, B., Logan, J., Brooks, S., Ikenberry, G., and Wohlforth, W. (2023) Debating American Engagement: The Future of U.S. Grand Strategy. *International Security*, 38(2): 181–199.

Dabashi, H. (2015) *Can Non-Europeans Think?* London: Zed Books.

Dabashi, H. (2012) *The Arab Spring: The End of Postcolonialism*. London: Zed Books Ltd.

Dadush, U., and Dunn, M. (2011) American and European Responses to the Arab Spring. *Washington Quarterly*, 34(4): 131–145.

Daily News Egypt (2011) Gulf Arab rulers tense over Egypt's policy shifts. *Daily news Egypt*, accessed April 2015 http://www.dailynewsegypt.com/2011/04/28/gulf-arab-rulers-tense-over-egypts-policy-shifts/.

Darwich, M. (et al.) (2021) The Politics of Teaching International Relations in the Arab World: Reading Walt in Beirut, Wendt in Doha, and Abul-Fadl in Cairo, *International Studies Perspectives* 22(4): 407–438.

David, S. (1991) *Choosing Sides: Alignment and Re-Alignment in the Third World*. Baltimore; MD: John Hopkins University Press.

Davidson, C. (2016) *Shadow Wars: The Secret Struggle for the Middle East*. London: Oneworld Publications Ltd.

Davidson, C. (2012) *After the Sheikhs: The Coming Collapse of the Gulf Monarchies*. London: Hurst & Co.

Davidson, C. (2010) *The Persian Gulf and Pacific Asia: From Indifference to Interdependence*. New York: Columbia University Press.

Davidson, C. (2005) *The United Arab Emirates: A Study in Survival*. Boulder, CO: Lynne Rienne.

De Lellis, F. (2019) Peasants, Dispossession and Resistance in Egypt: An Analysis of Protest Movements and Organisations Before and After the 2011 Uprising. *Review of African Political Economy*, 46(162): 582–98.

Deutsch, K. (1968) *The Analysis of International Relations*. Englewood Cliffs, NJ: Prentice-Hall, Inc.

Devetak, R. (et al.) (2013) *An Introduction to International Relations*. New York: Cambridge University Press.

Devetak R. (1995) Critical Theory. In: Burchille, S., and Linklater, A. (eds.) *Theories of International Relations*. New York: St. Martin's Press, 159–182.

Diamond, L. (2010) Why Are There No Arab Democracies? *Journal of Democracy* 21(1): 93–112.

Dunne, T., Kurki, M., and Smith, S. (eds.). (2013) *International Relations Theories: Discipline and Diversity*. New York: Oxford University Press.

DW. (2020) Thawabet siyaset oman fi ahad qaboos hal tastamer fi ahad khalafh Haitham? Accessed July 10, 2020. https://p.dw.com/p/3W2NO.

Eckersley, R. (2008) Ethics of Critical Theory. In: Reus-Smit, C., and Snidal, D. (eds.) *Oxford Handbook of International Relations*. New York: Oxford University Press, 346–58.

Eckstein, S. (1982) The Impact of Revolution on Social Welfare in Latin America. *Theory and Society*, 11(1): 43–94.

Egypt's George Floyd: A young man shot dead by police in Luxor, *Egypt Watch* (2 October 2020). Available: https://egyptwatch.net/2020/10/02/egypts-george-floyd-a-young-man-shot-dead-by-police-in-luxor/ (consulted 29 December 2021).

Egypt Today (2021) TV presenter Tamer Amin suspended for remarks on Upper Egypt: read the full story, *Egypt Today*. https://www.egypttoday.com/Article/1/98809/TV-presenter-Tamer-Amin-suspended-for-remarks-on-Upper-Egypt.

El-Hamalawy, N. (2011) Arab exceptionalism? A case study of Egypt's regime breakdown. Bachelor Degree, Lund University, Department of Political Science. https://lup.lub.lu.se/luur/download?func=downloadFile&recordOId=2199099&fileOId=2205137.

Elias, N. (1994) *The Civilising Process*. Oxford: Blackwell.

Elman, M. (1995) The Foreign Policies of Small States: Challenging Neorealism in Its Own Backyard. *British Journal of Political Science* 25(2): 171–217.

El-Nour, S. (2015) Small Farmers and the Revolution in Egypt: The Forgotten Actors. *Contemporary Arab Affairs*, 8(2): 198–211.

El-Sayed, G., and Soliman, M. (2021) 'Tamer Amin TV show suspended over "offensive" comments against Upper Egyptian parents', *Al-Ahram online* (19 February 2021).

Available: https://english.ahram.org.eg/NewsContent/1/64/404401/Egypt/Politics-/Tamer-Amin-TV-show-suspended-overoffensive-commen.aspx (consulted 30 December 2022).

Engels, F. (1987) [1873–82] Dialectics of Nature. In: K. Marx, and F. Engels. *Collected Works*. Moscow: Progress Publishers, 313–590.

Evans, P. (2012) *Embedded Autonomy: States and Industrial Transformation*. New Jersey: Princeton University Press.

Eyadat, Z., Corrao, F., and Hashas, M. (eds.) (2018) *Islam, State, and Modernity: Mohammed Abed al-Jabri and the Future of the Arab World*. New York: Palgrave Macmillan.

Fakhro, E., and Hokayem, E. (2011) Waking the Arabs. *Survival*, 53(2): 21–30.

Farouk, Y. (2014) More Than Money: Post- Mubarak Egypt, Saudi Arabia and the Gulf. GRC *Gulf Papers*, accessed May 2015 http://grc.net/data/contents/uploads/Egypt_Money_new_12-05-14_4667.pdf.

Fearon, J. (1998) Bargaining, Enforcement, and International Cooperation. *International Organization*, 52(2): 269–305.

Ferreira, M. (2015) Critical Theory. In: McGlinchey, S., Walters, R., and Scheinpflu, C. (eds.) *International Relations Theory*. 49–55. Available: https://www.e-ir.info/publication/international-relations-theory/ (consulted 5 November 2017).

Fierke, K. (2007) *Critical Approaches to International Security*. Cambridge: Polity Press.

Fierke K., and Jabri, V. (2019) Global conversations: Relationality, embodiment and power in the move towards a Global IR. *Global Constitutionalism* 8(3): 506–535.

Fine, R., and Smith, W. (2003) Jürgen Habermas's theory of cosmopolitanism. *Constellations* 10(4): 469–487.

Finefter-Rosenbluh, I. (2017) Incorporating Perspective Taking in Reflexivity: A Method to Enhance Insider Qualitative Research Processes', *International Journal of Qualitative Methods*, 16(1): 1–11.

Finlay, L. (1998) Reflexivity: An Essential Component for All Research? *British Journal of Occupational Therapy*, 61(10): 453–456.

Foley, S. (2010) *The Arab Gulf States: Beyond Oil and Islam*. Boulder: Lynne Rienner.

Fontana, A., and Frey, J. (2005) The Interview: From Neutral Stance to Political Involvement. In: N. Denzin, and Y. Lincoln, (eds.) *The Sage Handbook of Qualitative Research*. Thousand Oaks: Sage, 695–727.

Fontana, A., and Frey, J. (1994) On Interviewing. In: N. Denzin and Y. Lincoln (eds.) *The Sage Handbook of Qualitative Research*. Thousand Oaks: Sage, 361–376.

Foran, J. (1997) *Theorizing Revolutions*. New York: Routledge.

Foreign Policy. (2009) The Failed States Index. *Foreign Policy*, (173): 80–84.

Forsberg, T. (2005) German Foreign Policy and the War on Iraq: Anti-Americanism, Pacifism or Emancipation? *Security Dialogue* 36(2): 413–431.

Foucault, M. (1980) *Society must be defended: Lectures at the Collège de France, 1975–76*. New York: Penguin.

Fukuyama, F. (1992) *The End of History and the Last Man*. New York: Free Press.
Fuller, G. (2014) *Turkey and the Arab Spring: Leadership in the Middle East*. N. P., Bozorg Press.
Fürtig, H. (2014) *Regional Powers in the Middle East New Constellations after the Arab Revolts*. New York: Palgrave Macmillan.
Gause, G. (2011) Why Middle East Studies Missed the Arab Spring: The Myth of Authoritarian Stability. *Foreign Affairs* 90(4): 81–90.
Gause, F. G. (2010) *The International Relations of the Persian Gulf*. Cambridge: Cambridge University Press.
Gellner, E. (1988) *Plough, sword and book: The structure of human history*. London: Collins Harvill.
George, A., and Bennett, A. (2007) *Case Study Research: Principles and Practices*. New York: Cambridge University Press.
George, A., and Bennett, A. (2005) *Case Studies and Theory Development in the Social Sciences*. Boston: MA; MIT Press.
George, J. (1989) International Relations and the Search for Thinking Space: Another View of the Third Debate. *International Studies Quarterly* (33): 269–79.
Germain, R., and Kenny, M. (1998) Engaging Gramsci: international relations theory and the new Gramscians. *Review of International Studies* 24(1): 3–21.
Ghazal, O. (2020) 'Al-wazir: naql qetarat qebli ela Bashteel le takhfeef al-daghad ala Ramses, w aqol le as-Sa'idiyya "ma'teza'loosh"' [The Minister: moving Said's trains to Bashteel is to decrease the pressure on Ramses. I say to as-Sa'idiyya: 'Do not be sad'], *al Dostor*, (1 September 2020). https://www.dostor.org/3191190 (consulted 30 December 2020).
Ghimire, K. (2002) Social Movements and Marginalized Rural Youth in Brazil, Egypt and Nepal. *Journal of Peasant Studies*, 30(1): 30–72.
Gill, S. (2003) *Power and Resistance in the New World Order*. London and New York: Palgrave Macmillan.
Gill, S. (ed.) (1993) *Gramsci, Historical Materialism, and International Relations*. Cambridge: Cambridge University Press.
Gill, S., and Law, D. (1988) *The Global Political Economy: Perspectives, Problems and Policies*. New York: Harvester.
Gilpin, R. (1981) *War and Change in World Politics*. Cambridge: Cambridge University Press.
Glaser, C. (1997) The Security Dilemma Revisited. *World Politics*, 50(1): 171–201.
Glass, C. (1990) *Tribes with Flags: A Dangerous Passage Through the Chaos of the Middle East*. Washington: Atlantic Monthly Press.
Goldberg, E. (1992) Peasants in Revolt: Egypt 1919. *International Journal of Middle East Studies*, 24(2): 261–80.

Goldstone, J. (2011) Understanding the Revolutions of 2011: Weakness and Resilience in Middle East Autocracies. *Foreign Affairs*, 90(3): 8–16.
Goldstone, J. (1997) Revolution, War, and Security. *Security Studies* 6(2): 127–151.
Goldstone, J., Gurr, T., and Moshiri, F. (eds.). (1991) *Revolutions of the Late Twentieth Century*. Boulder; CO: Westveiw Press.
Gough, K. (1974) Indian Peasant Uprisings. *Economic and Political Weekly*, 9(23/24): 1391–412.
Gramsci, A. (2011) *Prison Notebooks: Volume 2*. Edited by Buttigieg, J. New York: Columbia University Press.
Gramsci, A. (1971) *Prison Notebooks*. London: Lawrence and Wishart.
Gramsci, A. (1957) *The Modern Prince and Other Writings*. London: Lawrence & Wishart.
Gurr, R. (1970) *Why Men Rebel*. Princeton: Princeton University Press.
Guzansky, Y. (2014) *The Arab Gulf States and Reform in the Middle East: Between Iran and the Arab Spring*. New York: Palgrave.
Haas, M., and Lesch, D. (2017) *The Arab Spring: The Hope and Reality of the Uprisings*. Boulder, Colo.: Westview.
Habermas, J. (2015) *The Lure of Technocracy*. Malden: Polity.
Habermas, J. (2012) *The Crisis of the European Union: A Response*. Cambridge: Polity Press.
Habermas, J. (2009) *Europe: The Faltering Process*. Cambridge: Polity Press.
Habermas, J. (2006) *The Divided West*. Cambridge: Polity.
Habermas, J. (2003) Toward a cosmopolitan Europe. *Journal of Democracy* 14(4): 86–100.
Habermas, J. (2001) *The Postnational Constellation: Political Essays*. Cambridge: MIT Press.
Habermas, J. (1998) *The Inclusion of the Other: Studies in Political Theory*. Cambridge: MIT Press.
Habermas, J. (1996) *Between Facts and Norms: Contributions to a Discourse Theory of Law and Democracy*. Cambridge, MA: MIT Press.
Habermas, J. (1992) *The Structural Transformation of the Public Sphere: Inquiry into a Category of Bourgeois Society*. Cambridge: Polity Press.
Habermas, J. (1979) *Communication and the Evolution of Society*, trans. T. McCarthy. Boston, MA: Beacon.
Hafez, S. (2014a) The Revolution Shall Not Pass Through Women's Bodies: Egypt, Uprising and Gender Politics. *Journal of North African Studies*, 19(2): 172–85.
Hafez, S. (2014b) Bodies That Protest: The Girl in the Blue Bra, Sexuality and State Violence in Revolutionary Egypt. *Signs*, 40(1): 20–28.
Halliday, F. (2005) *The Middle East in International Relations: Power, Politics and Ideology*. New York: Cambridge University Press.
Halliday, F. (1999) *Revolution and world politics: the rise and fall of the sixth great power*. Basingstoke: Macmillan.
Halliday, F. (2007) The Middle East in an age of globalization: states, revolts and cultures. *RUSI Journal*, 152(1): 53–57.

Hamdan, J. (1982) *istrategiat al-istammar wa al-tahrir* [Strategies of Colonialism and Liberation]. Cairo: Dar El-Shorouk.

Hamdan, J. (1967) *Shakhsiah masr: Derasah fa a'bkriah almakan* [The Character of Egypt: A Study in the Genius of Place]. Cairo: Dar Al-Hilal.

Hamid, S. (2014) *Temptations of Power: Islamists and Illiberal Democracy in a New Middle East*. New York: Oxford University Press.

Hammad, H. (2017) Sexual Harassment in Egypt: The Old Plague in the New Revolutionary Order. GENDER– *Zeitschrift für Geschlecht, Kultur und Gesellschaft*, 9(1), 44–63.

Hamzawy, A. (2013a) 'Sa'id masr' (Upper Egypt), *al-Watan*, (31 March 2013). Available: https://www.elwatannews.com/news/details/15680592 (consulted 29 December 2017).

Hamzawy, A. (2013b) 'al-syasiha fi al- Sa'id 1–2' [Politics in Upper Egypt 1–2], al-Watan (2 April 2013). https://www.elwatannews.com/news/details/157323 (consulted 29 December 2017).

Haseeb, K. et, al. (2002) *mustaqbal al-umma al-arabiya: al-tahdiyyat wa al-kheyarrat: mashrou isteshraf mustaqbal al-watan al-araby* [The Future of the Arab Nation: Challenges and Alternatives]. Beirut: Centre for Arab Unity Studies.

Heikal, M. (1992) *Illusions of Triumph: An Arab View of the Gulf War*. London: Harper & Collins.

Hellyer, H. (2015) The new Saudi king, Egypt and the MB. *Al-Monitor*, accessed May 2015, http://www.al-monitor.com/pulse/originals/2015/03/saudi-arabia-new-egypt-muslim-brotherhood.html.

Henderson, E. (2013) Hidden in plain sight: racism in international relations theory. *Cambridge Review of International Affairs* 26(1): 71–92.

Herspring, D. (2005) *The Pentagon and the Presidency: Civil-military Relations from FDR to George W. Bush*. Lawrence: University Press of Kansas.

Hinnebusch, R. (2015a) Change and continuity after the Arab Uprising: the consequences of state formation in Arab North African states. *British Journal of Middle Eastern Studies* 42(1): 12–30.

Hinnebusch, R. (2015b) Conclusion: Agency, Context and Emergent Postuprising Regimes. *Democratization* 22(2): 358–374.

Hinnebusch, R. (2013) Historical Sociology and the Arab Uprising. *Mediterranean Politics* 19(1); 137–140.

Hinnebusch, R. (2010) Toward a Historical Sociology of State Formation in the Middle East. *Middle East Critique*, 19(3): 201–216.

Hinnebusch, R., and Ehteshami, A. (eds.) (2014) *The Foreign Policies of Middle East States*. New York: Lynne Rienner.

Hinnebusch, R. (2015) Conclusion: Agency, Context and Emergent Postuprising Regimes. *Democratization,* 22(2): 358–374.

Hobden, S., and Hobson, J. (2010) *Historical Sociology of International Relations*. New York: Cambridge University Press.

Hobden, S., and Hobson, J. (2002) *Historical Sociology of International Relations*. New York: Cambridge University Press.

Hobsbawm, E. (1973) Peasants and politics. *Journal of Peasant Studies*, 1(1): 3–22.

Hobson, J. (2012) *The Eurocentric Conception of World Politics*. Cambridge: Cambridge University Press.

Hobson, J. (2011) *The Eurocentric Conception of World Politics: Western International Theory 1760–2010*. Cambridge: Cambridge University Press.

Hobson, J. (2007) Is critical theory always for the white West and for Western imperialism? Beyond Westphilian towards a post-racist critical IR. *Review of International Studies* 33(1): 91–116.

Hobson, J. (2002a) What's at Stake in—Bringing Historical Sociology back into International Relations? In: Hobden, S., and Hobson, J. (eds.). *Historical Sociology of International Relations*. Cambridge: Cambridge University Press, 3–41.

Hobson, J. (2002b) The Two Waves of Weberian Historical Sociology in International Relations. In: S. Hobden, and J. Hobson (eds.) *Historical sociology of international relations*. Cambridge, U.K.: Cambridge University Press, 63–81.

Hobson, J. (1998) The Historical Sociology of the State and the State of Historical Sociology in International Relations. *Review of International Political Economy* 5(2): 284–320.

Hobson, J., Lawson, G., and Rosenberg, J. (2010) Historical sociology. In: R. Denemark (ed.) *The International Studies Encyclopedia, vol. VI*. Oxford: Wiley-Blackwell, 3357–3375.

Hobson, J. (2002) What's at Stake in —Bringing Historical Sociology back into International Relations? pp. 3–41, in: Hobden, S., and Hobson, J. (eds.). *Historical Sociology of International Relations*. Cambridge: Cambridge University Press.

Hoffman, M. (1991) Restructuring, reconstruction, reinscription, rearticulation: Four voices in Critical International Relations Theory. *Millennium* 20(2): 169–185.

Hoffman, M. (1987) Critical Theory and the Inter-Paradigm Debate. *Millennium* 16(2): 231–49.

Hoffmann, S. (1977) An American Social Science: International Relations. *Daedalus* 106(3): 41–60.

Holsti, O., Siverson, R., and George, A. (eds.) (1980) *Change in the International System*. Boulder, Colo.: Westview Press.

Hopgood, S. (2000) Reading the Small Print in Global Civil Society: The Inexorable Hegemony of the Liberal Self. *Millennium* 29(1): 1–25.

Hopgood, S., and Horkheimer, M. (1992) *Critical Theory: Selected Essays*. New York: Continuum Press.

Hopkins, N., and Saad, R. (eds.) (2004) *Upper Egypt: Identity and Change*. Cairo: American University of Cairo Press.

Howell, A., and Richter-Montpetit, M. (2020) Is securitization theory racist? Civilizationism, methodological whiteness, and antiblack thought in the Copenhagen School. *Security Dialogue* 51(1): 3–22.

Huntington, S. (1991) *The Third Wave: Democratization in the Late Twentieth Century*. Norman: University of Oklahoma Press.

Huntington, S. (1999) The Lonely Superpower. *Foreign Affairs*, 78(2): 35–49.

Hurd, E. (2005) A Political Sociology of the Middle East. *International Studies Review* 7(3): 445–448.

Hutchings, K. (2001) The Nature of Critique in Critical International Relations Theory. In: Wyn-Jones, R. (ed.), *Critical Theory and World Politics*. Boulder: Lynne Rienner, 79–90.

Ikenberry, J. (2001) *After Victory: Institutions, Strategic Restraint, and the Rebuilding of Order after Major Wars*. Princeton: Princeton University Press.

Ikenberry, J., Mastanduno, M., and Wohlforth, W. (eds.) (2011) *International Relations Theory and the Consequences of Unipolarity*. New York: Cambridge University Press.

Inayatullah, N., and Blaney, D. (2004) *International Relations and the Problem of Difference*. Abingdon: Routledge.

Ingebritsen, C., Neumann, I., Gstohl, S., and Beyer, J. (eds.) (2006) *Small States in International Relations*. Seattle: University of Washington.

Isaac, S. (2015) A Resurgence in Arab Regional Institutions? The Cases of the Arab League and the Gulf Cooperation Council Post-2011, pp. 151–167, in: E. Monier (ed.) *Regional Insecurity After the Arab Uprisings: Narratives of Security and* Threat. New York: Palgrave.

Isaacman, A. (1990) Peasants and Rural Social Protest in Africa. *African Studies Review*, 33(2):1–120.

Ismail, K. (2011) 'Al-Saʿid w al-thawra' [Upper Egypt and the Revolution], *Al-hewar al-mutamaden*, (2 December 2011). Available: https://www.ahewar.org/debat/show.art.asp?aid=285799 (consulted 29 December 2017).

Ismail, S. (2012) The Egyptian Revolution against the Police. *Social Research* 79(1): 435–462.

Jabri, V. (2013) *The Postcolonial Subject: Claiming Politics/Governing Others in Late Modernity*. Abingdon: Routledge.

Jackson, P., Nexon, D., Sterling-Folker, J., Mattern, J., Lebow, R., and Barkin, J. (2004) Bridging the Gap: Toward a Realist-Constructivist Dialogue. *International Studies Review*, 6(2): 337–352.

Jackson, R. (2008) The ghosts of state terror: Knowledge, politics and terrorism studies. *Critical Studies on Terrorism* 1(3): 377–392.

Jackson, R. (et al.) (2009) *Critical Terrorism Studies: A New Research Agenda*. Abingdon: Routledge.

Jackson, R.H. (2000) *The Global Covenant: Human Conduct in a World of States*. Oxford: Oxford University Press.

Janesick, V. (1994) The Dance of Qualitative Research Design: Metaphor, Methodolatry, and Meaning. In: N. Denzin and Y. Lincoln (eds.) *The Sage Handbook of Qualitative Research.* Thousand Oaks: Sage, 209–219.

Jesse, N., & Dreyer, J. (eds.) (2016) *Small states in the international system: At peace and at war.* Lanham: Lexington Books.

Joenniemi, P. (1993) Neutrality beyond the Cold War. *Review of International Studies,* 19(3), 289–304.

Johnson, C. (1962) *Peasant Nationalism and Communist Power.* Stanford: Stanford University Press.

Johnston, A. (1990) Altered States: Structural Change in Contemporary International Relations. *Theoria: Journal of Social and Political* Theory 76 (3): 45–65.

Jones, B. (2006) *Decolonizing International Relations.* Lanham: MD; Rowman & Littlefield.

Jones, M., Porter, R., and Valeri, M. (eds.) (2018) *Gulfization of the Arab World.* Berlin, London: Gerlach.

Joseph, J. (2008) Hegemony and the Structure-Agency Problem in International Relations: A Scientific Realist Contribution. *Review of International Studies* 1(34): 109–28.

Joyce, M. (2012) *Bahrain from the Twentieth Century to the Arab Spring.* New York: Palgrave Macmillan.

Kamrava, K. (2013) *Qatar: Small State, Big Politics.* Ithaca, New York: Cornell University Press.

Kamrava, K. (ed.) (2011) *The International Politics of the Persian Gulf.* New York: Syracuse University Press.

Kandil, H. (2012) Why did the Egyptian Middle-Class March to Tahrir Square? *Mediterranean Politics* 17(2): 197–215.

Karatnycky, A., and Ackerman, P. (2005) *How Freedom Is Won: From Civic Resistance to Durable Democracy.* Washington, D.C.: Freedom House.

Katz, M. (2014) The International Relations of the Arab Spring. *Middle East Policy* 22(2): 76–84.

Katzenstein, P. (1990) *Analyzing change in international politics: The new institutionalism and the interpretative approach.* A guest lecture atthe MPI für Gesellschaftsforschung. Köln: Max-Planck-Institut für Gesellschaftsforschung. https://citeseerx.ist.psu.edu/document?repid=rep1&type=pdf&doi=2b12eecbca931 d675dbddeodaocd58ad4e74c2d1.

Katzenstein, P., and Keohane, R. (2006) *Anti-Americanisms in World Politics.* Ithaca: Cornell University Press.

Kaufman, S., Little, R., and Wohlforth, W. (eds.) (2007) *Balance of Power in World History.* New York: Palgrave Macmillan.

Kazemi, F. (1980) *Poverty and Revolution in Iran: The Migrant Poor, Urban Marginality, and Politics.* New York: New York University Press.

Keck, Z. (2012) Realism and the Arab Spring. *The Majalla*, (July 3, 2012). Available: https://bit.ly/3fv9E97 (consulted 5 November 2017).

Kemp, G. (2012) *The East Moves West: India, China, and Asia's Growing Presence in the Middle East.* Washington D.C.: Brookings Institution Press.

Keohane, R. (1998) Beyond Dichotomy: Conversations between International Relations and Feminist Theory. *International Studies Quarterly* 42(1): 193–197.

Keohane, R. (1989) *International Institutions and State Power: Essays in International Relations Theory.* Boulder, Colo.: Westview.

Keohane, R. (1988) International Institutions: Two Approaches. *International Studies Quarterly* 32(4): 379–396.

Keohane, R. (1969) Lilliputians' Dilemmas: Small States in International Politics. *International Organization* 23(2): 291–310.

Keohane, R., and Nye, J. (1977) *Power and interdependence: World politics in transition.* Boston: Little, Brown.

Kerr, M. (1971) *The Arab Cold War: Gamal 'Abd al-Nasir and His Rivals, 1958–1970.* New York: Oxford University Press.

Khouri, R. (2011) Drop the Orientalist Term 'Arab Spring'. *The Daily Star.* Available: https://bit.ly/3oVmZ6H (consulted 5 November 2017).

Khoury, P., and Kostiner, J. (eds.) (1990) *Tribes and State Formation in the Middle East.* London: I.B. Tauris.

Kilomba, G. (2010) *Plantation Memories: Episodes of Everyday Racism.* Münster: UNRAST-Verlag.

Kissinger, H. (2009) The Chance for a New World Order. *The New York Times.* https://www.nytimes.com/2009/01/12/opinion/12iht-edkissinger.1.19281915.html.

Korany, B., and Dessouki, A. (eds.) (2010) *The Foreign Policies of Arab States: The Challenge of Globalization.* Cairo: American University in Cairo Press.

Krauthammer, C. (2002/3) The Unipolar Moment Revisited. *The National Interest* 70: 5–18.

Krauthammer, C. (1990/91) The Unipolar Moment. *Foreign Affairs*, 70(1): 23–33.

Kurki, M. (2012) The Limitations of the Critical Edge: Reflections on Critical and Philosophical IR Scholarship Today. *Millennium* 40(1): 129–146.

LaFeber, W. (1993) *Inevitable Revolutions: The United States in Central America.* New York: W.W. Norton.

Lawson, F. (1992) *The Social Origins of Egyptian Expansionism during the Muhammad 'Ali Period.* New York: Columbia University Press.

Lawson, F. (1981) Rural Revolt and Provincial Society in Egypt, 1820–1824. *International Journal of Middle East Studies*, 13(2): 131–53.

Layne, C. (2009) America's Middle East grand strategy after Iraq: The moment for offshore balancing has arrived. *Review of International Studies*, 35(1): 5–25.

Le Melle, T. (2009) Race in International Relations. *International Studies Perspectives* 10(1): 77–83.

Legranzi, M. (2011) *The GCC and the International Relations of the Gulf: Diplomacy, Security and Economic Coordination in a Changing Middle East*. London: I.B. Tauris.

Leysens, A. (2008) *The Critical Theory of Robert W. Cox: Fugitive or Guru?* New York: Palgrave MacMillan.

Lilja, M., Baaz, M., Schulz, M., and Vinthagen, S. (2017) How Resistance Encourages Resistance: Theorizing the Nexus Between Power, 'Organised Resistance' and 'Everyday Resistance'. *Journal of Political Power*, 10(1): 40–54.

Linklater, A. (2011) *The Problem of Harm in World Politics: Theoretical Investigations*. Cambridge: Cambridge University Press.

Linklater, A. (2010) Global civilizing processes and the ambiguities of interconnectedness. *European Journal of International Relations* 16(2): 155–178 24.

Linklater, A. (2007) Towards a sociology of global morals with an emancipatory intent. *Review of International Studies* 33(1): 135–150.

Linklater, A. (2004) Norbert Elias, the civilizing process' and the sociology of International Relations. *International Politics* 41(1): 3–35.

Linklater, A. (2002) The problem of harm in world politics: Implications for the sociology of states systems. *International Affairs*, 78(2): 319–338.

Linklater, A. (2001) The Changing Contours of Critical International Relations Theory. In: Jones, R. (ed.). *Critical Theory and World Politics*. Boulder: Lynne Rienner Publishers, 23–43.

Linklater, A. (2000) *International Relations: Critical Concepts in Political Science*. Abingdon: Routledge.

Linklater, A. (1998) *The Transformation of Political Community: Ethical Foundations of the Post-Westphalian Era*. Cambridge: Polity Press.

Linklater, A. (1996) The Achievement of Critical Theory. In: Smith, S., Booth, K., and Zalewski, M. (eds.) *International Theory: Positivism and Beyond*. Cambridge: Cambridge University Press, 279–298.

Linklater, A. (1990) *Beyond Realism and Marxism: Critical Theory and International Relations*. London: MacMillan Press. Athens Journal of Social Sciences April 2021 149.

Linklater, A. (1982) *Men and Citizens in the Theory of International Relations*. London: MacMillan Press.

Linklater, A. (1980) Rationality and Obligation in the States-system: The Lessons of Pufendorf's Law of Nations. *Millennium* 9(3): 215–228.

Linklater, A., and Suganami, H. (2006) *The English School of International Relations: A Contemporary Reassessment*. Cambridge: Cambridge University Press.

Lobell, S., Ripsman, N., & Taliaferro, J. (eds.) (2009) *Neoclassical realism, the state, and foreign policy*. New York: Cambridge University Press.

Luciani, G. (1989) Economic Foundations of Democracy and Authoritarianism: The Arab World in Comparative Perspectives. *Arab Studies Quarterly*, 10(4): 457–476.

Lynch, M. (2018) The New Arab Order: Power and Violence in Today's Middle East. *Foreign Affairs*, 97 (5): 116–26.

Lynch, M. (2016) *The New Arab Wars: Uprisings and Anarchy in the Middle East*. New York: Public Affairs.

Lynch, M. (2014) *The Arab Uprising: The Unfinished Revolutions of the New Middle East*. New York: Public Affairs.

Lynch, M., and Ryan, C. (2017) Symposium: The Arab Uprisings and International Relations Theory. *Political Science & Politics* 50(3): 643–646.

Maass, M. (2017) *Small States in World Politics: The Story of Small State Survival, 1648–2016*. Manchester: Manchester University Press.

Mackay, D. (2014) ISIS militants in Iraq proclaim new Islamic state and pose threat to 'all countries'. *The Mirror*, accessed May 20, 2015 http://www.mirror.co.uk/news/world-news/isis-militants-iraq-proclaim-new-3790221.

Madbouly, M. (2021) Remembering Nubia's Past: Space, Generations and Memorial Practices. *Middle East Critique*, 30(4): 373–389.

Madbouly, M. (2019) 'Al-nashedyah al-nubeyya fi masr: A'layyat al-tataoor w al-ta'teer' [Nubian Activism in Egypt: Evolution and Framing Mechanisms], in D. El-Khawaja (ed.) *The First Report on Societal Activism: Overlapping Meanings and Domains*. Beirut: The Asfari Institute for Civil Society and Citizenship, 38–47.

Magagna, V. (1991) Peasant Politics in Modern Egypt: The Struggle against the State. Nathan J. Brown, *The Journal of Politics*, 53(3): 920–922.

Maghazi, A. (2013) 'Al- Sa'id da'eman w abadan. le al-fakr dor' (Upper Egypt is always and forever: Poverty has been returned) *al-Masry al-youm*, (23 January 2013). Available: https://www.almasryalyoum.com/news/details/285704 (consulted 30 December 2017).

Malla, M. (2020) 'na'eb ya'tared ala karar al naql' [An MP objects to the transfer decision], *al-Masry al-youm*, (20 August 2020). Available: https://www.almasryalyoum.com/news/details/2015672 (consulted 30 December 2021).

Mamdani, M. (1996) *Citizen and Subject: Contemporary Africa and the Legacy of Late Colonialism*. New Jersey: Princeton University Press.

Maoz, Z. (1996) *Domestic Sources of Global Change*. Ann Arbor; MI: University of Michigan Press.

Maoz, Z., and Abdolali, N. (1989) Regime Types and International Conflict: 1816–1976. *Journal of Conflict Resolution*, 33(1): 3–35.

Maoz, Z., and Russett, B. (1993) Normative and Structural Causes of Democratic Peace 1946–1986. *American Political Science Review*, 83(3): 624–638.

Mason, R. (2016) *Egypt and the Gulf: A Renewed Regional Policy* Alliance. Berlin: Gerlach Press.

Mason, R. (2014) *The International Politics of the Arab Spring: Popular Unrest and Foreign Policy*. New York: Palgrave Macmillan.

Masr: era'dat al-seyah'a 7.6 milyar dollar (Egypt: tourism revenues are 7.6 billion dollars), *Sky News*, (31 March 2013). Available: https://www.skynewsarabia.com/business/165696 (consulted 29 December 2017).

Mastanduno, M., Lake, D., and Ikenberry, G. (1989) Toward a Realist Theory of State Action. *International Studies Quarterly* 33(4): 457–474.

Matta, A. (2020) 'Min George Floyd ela Owis al-Rawi' (From George Floyd to Owais Al-Rawi), *Daaarb*. Available: https://bit.ly/3nQsocB (consulted 29 December 2021).

Mattar, J, and Dessouki, A. (1982) *al-Nizam al-iqlimi al-`Arabi* [Arab Regional System]. Beirut: Centre for Arab Unity Studies.

Maxwell, J. (2005) *Qualitative Research Design: An Interactive Approach*. 2nd edition. London: Sage.

Maxwell, J. (1996) *Qualitative Research Design: An Interactive Approach*. Thousand Oaks: Sage.

Mearsheimer, J. (2013) Structural Realism, pp. 71–82, in: T. Dunne, M. Kurki, & S. Smith (eds.). *International Relations Theories: Discipline and Diversity*. Oxford: Oxford University Press.

Mearsheimer, J. (2009) Reckless states and realism, *International Relations*, 23(2): 242–243.

Mearsheimer, J. (2000) *The Tragedy of Great Power Politics*. New York: Norton.

Mearsheimer, J. (1995) The False Promise of International Institutions. *International Security* 19(3): 5–49.

Migdal, J. (1988) *Strong Societies and Weaken States: State–Society Relations and State Capabilities in the Third World*. Princeton; N.J.: Princeton University Press.

Mignolo, W. (2012) *The Darker Side of Western Modernity: Global Futures, Decolonial Options*. Durham: Duke University Press.

Mignolo, W., and Walsh, C. (2018) *On Decoloniality: Concepts, Analytics, Praxis*. Durham: Duke University Press.

Miller, C. (2004) Between Myth and Reality: The Construction of a Sa'idi Identity. In: N. Hopkins, and R. Saad (eds) *Upper Egypt: Identity and Change*. Cairo: American University of Cairo Press, 25–54.

Miller, R. (2016) *Desert kingdoms to global powers: the rise of the Arab Gulf*. New Haven, CT, and London: Yale University Press.

Misr: eshtibkat be al-luxor ba'd maqtal mowaten masri be rosaas dahbet shrtah (Egypt, clashes in Luxor after the killing of an Egyptian citizen by bullets of a police officer), *Italian News* (1 October 2020). Available: http://www.alitaliyanews.com/2020/10/news-egitto.html (consulted 29 December 2021).

Moghaddam, A. (2009) *The International Politics of the Persian Gulf: A Cultural Genealogy*. New York: Routledge.

Moore, B. (1966) *Social origins of dictatorship and democracy: Lord and peasant in the making of the modern world*. Boston: Beacon.

Moravcsik, A. (2008) The New Liberalism, pp. 234–254, in: Reus-Smit, C., and Sindal, D. (eds.): *The Oxford Handbook of International Relations*. New York: Oxford University Press.

Moravcsik, A. (1997) Taking Preferences Seriously: A Liberal Theory of International Politics. *International Organization,* 51(4): 513–553.

Morgenthau, H. [1948] 1973. *Politics among Nations: The Struggle for Power and Peace*. New York: Alfred Knopf.

Mostafa, R. (2020) 'Video: resa'lah ghadeba'h min as-Sa'idiyya le wazeer al naql' [Video, An angry message from as-Sa'idiyya to the Minister of Transportation], *al Watan*, (24 August 2020). Available: https://www.elwatannews.com/news/details/4961061 (consulted 30 December 2021).

Moyo, L., and Mutsvario, B. (2018) Can the Subaltern Think? The Decolonial Turn in Communication Research in Africa. In: B. Mutsvairo (ed.) *The Palgrave Handbook of Media and Communication Research in Africa*. New York: Palgrave, 41–54.

Murphy, C. (1994) *International Organization and Industrial Change: Global Governance since 1850*. Oxford, Oxford University Press.

Murphy, C. (1990) Freezing the North-South Bloc (k) After the East-West Thaw. *Socialist Review* 20(3): 25–46.

Naples, N., and Sachs, C. (2000) Standpoint Epistemology and the Uses of Self-Reflection in Feminist Ethnography: Lessons for Rural Sociology. *Rural Sociology*, 65(2): 194–214.

Niblock, T. (2006) *Saudi Arabia: Power, Legitimacy and Survival*. New York: Routledge.

Obadele, I. (1978) People's Revolt Against Poverty: An Appeal and Challenge. *The Black Scholar*, 9(8–9): 35–39.

Onar, N. (2015) IR and Middle East studies: Speaking Truth to Power in a Multipolar World. In: Lynch, M. (ed.). *International Relations Theory and a Changing Middle East,* 36–39. Available: https://bit.ly/3d5hDb6 (consulted 5 November 2017).

Osman, T. (2010) *Egypt on the Brink: From Nasser to the Muslim Brotherhood*. New Haven: Yale University Press.

Ottaway, D. (2015) New Era of Relations Between Egypt and Saudi Arabia? *The Wilson Center.* https://www.wilsoncenter.org/new-era-relations-between-egypt-and-saudi-arabia.

Owen, R. (2012) *The Rise and fall of Arab Presidents for Life: With a New Afterword*. Boston: MA; Harvard University Press.

Paul, T. V., Wirtz, J., and Fortmann, M. (eds.). (2004) *Balance of Power: Theory and Practice in the 21st Century*. New Jersey; CA: Stanford University Press.

Payne, R., and Samhat, N. (eds.) (2004) *Democratizing Global Politics: Discourse Norms, International Regimes, and Political Community*. New York: SUNY Press.

Perlmutler, A. (1981) *Political Roles and Military Rules*. London: Frank Cass and Company.

Perry, E. (1978) The politics of China's peasant revolution. *Bulletin of Concerned Asian Scholars*, 10(3): 44–47.

Peterson, J. E. (2011) Sovereignty and boundaries in the Gulf States: Settling the peripheries, pp. 21–49, in: Kamrava, M. (ed.): *The International Politics of the Persian Gulf*. Syracuse: Syracuse University Press.

Pierson, P. (2003) Big, Slow Moving and Invisible: Macro Social Processes in the Study of Comparative Politics. In: J. Mahoney and D. Rueschemeyer (eds.) *Comparative Historical Analysis in the Social Sciences*. Cambridge: Cambridge University Press, 177–207.

Pillow, W. (2003) Confession, Catharsis, or Care? Rethinking the Uses of Reflexivity as Methodological Power in Qualitative Research. *International Journal of Qualitative Studies in Education*, 16(2): 175–196.

Pinker, S. (2018) *Enlightenment Now: The Case for Reason, Science, Humanism, and Progress*. New York: Viking.

Pinker, S. (2011) *The Better Angels of Our Nature: Why Violence Has Declined*. New York, NY: Viking.

Polanyi, K. (1957) *The Great Transformation*. Boston: Beacon.

Pollack, K. (ed.) (2011) *The Arab Awakening: America and the Transformation of the Middle East*. Washington D. C.: Brookings Institution Press.

Pollack, K. (2003) Securing the Gulf. *Foreign Affairs*, 82(4): 2–16.

Porter, P. (2016) Taking Uncertainty Seriously: Classical Realism and National Security. *European Journal of International Security*, 1(2): 239–60.

Powell, R. (1991) Absolute and Relative Gains in International Relations Theory. *The American Political Science Review*, 85(4): 1303–1320.

Power, T., and Morton, T. (2020) Relative Deprivation and Revolt: Current and Future Directions. *Current Opinion in Psychology*, 35(4): 119–124.

Price, R., and Reus-Smit, C. (1998) Dangerous Liaisons? Critical International Theory and Constructivism. *European Journal of International Relations* (4)3: 259–294.

Pula, B., & Stivachtis, Y. (2017) Historical Sociology and International Relations: Interdisciplinary Approaches to Large-Scale Historical Change and Global Order. DOI: 10.1093/acrefore/9780190846626.013.90 (consulted 30 March 2018).

Qura'h w modun manseyyha fe zakat al-thawrha al-masriyyha [Forgotten villages and cities from the memory of the Egyptian revolution], *al-Araby al-Gadded*, (25 January 2018). Available: https://www.alaraby.co.uk/ (consulted 29 December 2017).

Ragab, E., and Colombo, S. (eds.) (2017) *Foreign Relations of the GCC Countries: Shifting Global and Regional Dynamics*. New York: Routledge.

Ramadan, T. (2012) *Islam and the Arab Awakening*. New York: Oxford University Press.

Ramani, S. (2017) Israel and the Gulf. *The Jerusalem Post*. Accessed February 20, 2018. https://www.jpost.com/Opinion/Israel-and-the-Gulf-520092.

Ramazani, R. (1988) *The Gulf Cooperation Council: Record and analysis*. Charlottesville: The University Press of Virginia.

Rashid, A. (2000) *Taliban: Militant Islam, Oil and Fundamentalism in Central Asia*. London: I. B. Tauris.

Ray, J. (1998) Does Democracy Cause Peace. *Annual Review of Political Science*, (1): 27–46.

Reclaiming their Voice: New Perspectives from Young Women and Men in Upper Egypt, *The World Bank,* (2012). Available: http://documents.worldbank.org/curated/en/514301468233333500/Reclaiming-their-voice-new-perspectives-from-young-women-and-men-in-UpperEgypt (consulted 30 December 2017).

Reconciliation of construction violations thorny but important for Egypt: Prime Minister, *Daily News Egypt,* (9 September 2020). Available: https://dailynewsegypt.com/2020/09/09/reconciliation-of-construction-violations-thorny-but-important-for-egypt-prime-minister/ (consulted 29 December 2021).

Reed, S. (1993) The battle for Egypt. *Foreign affairs* 72(4): 94–107.

Rengger, N., and Thirkell-White, T. (2007) *Critical International Relations Theory after 25 Years*. Cambridge: Cambridge University Press.

Reuters (2015) Egypt got $23 bln in aid from Gulf in 18 months –minister. *Reuters*, accessed May 2015 http://www.reuters.com/article/2015/03/02/egypt-investment-gulf-idUSL5N0W41XL20150302.

Risse, T. (2000) Let's Argue! Communicative Action in World Politics. *International Organization* (54)1: 1–39.

Roach, S. (2013) Critical Theory. In: Dunne, T., Kurki, M., and Smith, S. (eds.) *International Relations Theories: Discipline and Diversity*. New York: Oxford University Press, 171–186.

Rose, G. (1998) Neoclassical Realism and Theories of Foreign Policy. *World Politics*, 51(1): 144–172.

Rosecrance, R. (1973) *International Relations*. New York: McGraw-Hill.

Rosenberg, J. (2006) Why Is There No Historical Sociology? *European Journal of International Relations* (12)3: 307–40.

Ross, M. (2013) *The Oil Curse: How Petroleum Wealth Shapes the Development of Nations*. Princeton: N.J.: Princeton University Press.

Roussillon, A. (2014) *Je suis le peuple* [I am the People]. France: Hautlesmains Productions.

Roy, G. (2016) Copts, and the Egyptian Revolution: Christian Identity in the Public Sphere. In: S. Lacroix and B. Rougier (eds) *Egypt's Revolutions: Politics, Religion, and Social Movements*. New York: Palgrave Macmillan, 213–27.

Runciman, W. (1966) *Relative Deprivation and Social Justice*. London: Routledge and Kegan Paul.

Rutherford, B. (2008) *Egypt after Mubarak*. New Jersey: Princeton University Press.

Saad, R. (2018) Qura'h w modun manseyyha fe zakat al-thawrha al-masriyyha [Forgotten villages and cities from the memory of the Egyptian revolution], *al-Araby al-Gadded*. https://www.alaraby.co.uk/.

Saad, R. (2016) Before the Spring: Shifting Patterns of Protest in Rural Egypt. In: A. Ghazal and J. Hanssen (eds.) *The Oxford Handbook of Contemporary Middle Eastern and North African History*. New York: Oxford University Press, 554–571.

Sabaratnam, M. (2020) Is IR Theory White? Racialised Subject-Positioning in Three Canonical Texts. *Millennium*. 49(1): 3–31.

Sagan, S., and Waltz, K. (1995) *The Spread of Nuclear Weapons: A Debate*. New York: W. W. Norton.

'Sa'idi youhadeed al-Sisi w baseb Amr Adib' (A Saidi man threatens Sisi and insults Amr Adib) *YouTube*, (21 October 2016). Available: https://www.youtube.com/watch?v=tSobt43mRYw (consulted 30 December 2017).

Said, E. (1994) *Culture and Imperialism*. New York: Vintage.

Saikal, A. (2016) *The Arab World and Iran: A Turbulent Region in Transition*. New York: Palgrave Macmillan.

Samhat, N., and Payne, R. (2004) Critical Theory, Habermas, and International Relations. In: Samhat, N., and Payne, R. (eds.). *Democratizing Global Politics: Discourse Norms, International Regimes, and Political Community*. New York: State University of New York Press, 9–25.

Samir, H. (2013) *mazbahet Maspero: Asra'r w kwalees* [The Secrets of Maspero's Massacre]. Cairo: al-Hureyya House.

Saouli, A. (2012) *The Arab State: Dilemmas of Late Formation*. New York: Routledge.

Saul, S. (1974) African Peasants and Revolution. *Review of African Political Economy*, 1(1): 41–68.

Schenker, D., and Henderson, S. (2009) Paradoxes of Egyptian-Saudi Relations. *The Washington Institute for Near East Policy*. https://www.washingtoninstitute.org/policy-analysis/paradoxes-egyptian-saudi-relations.

Scheuerman, W. (2006) Critical Theory after Habermas. In: Dryzek, J., Honig, B., and Phillips, A. (eds.) *The Oxford Handbook of Political Theory*. Oxford: Oxford University Press, 85–105.

Schmid, D. (2018) The poverty of Critical Theory in International Relations: Habermas, Linklater and the failings of cosmopolitan critique. *European Journal of International Relations* 24(1): 198–220.

Schweller, R. (1994) Bandwagoning for Profit: Bringing the Revisionist State Back In. *International Security*, 19(1): 72–107.

Schweller, R., and Priess, D. (1997) A Tale of Two Realisms: Expanding the Institutions Debate. *Mershon International Studies Review*, 41(1): 1–32.

Scott, J. (1992) *Domination and the Arts of Resistance: Hidden Transcripts*. New Haven: Yale University Press.

Scott, J. (1985) *Weapons of the Weak: Everyday Forms of Peasant Resistance.* New Haven: Yale University Press.

Scott, J. (1989) Everyday Forms of Resistance. *Copenhagen Papers,* 4(89): 33–62.

Scott, J. (1979) Revolution in the Revolution: Peasants and Commissars. *Theory and Society,* 7(1–2): .97–134.

Selim, G. (2013) The United States and the Arab Spring: The Dynamics of Political Engineering. *Arab Studies Quarterly,* 35(3): 255–272.

Shanin, T. (1966) The Peasantry as a Political Factor. *The Sociological Review,* 14(1): 5–10.

Shapcott, R. (2008) Critical Theory. In: C. Reus-Smit, and D. Snidal (eds) *The Oxford Handbook of International Relations.* York: Oxford University Press, 327–345.

Shapcott, R. (2004) IR as practical philosophy: defining a — classical approach. *British Journal of Politics and International Relations* 6(3): 271–91.

Shawky, H. (2011) '15.8 zeyadh'a fi era'dat al-seyh'a al- masriyyha' (A 15.8 per cent increase in Egyptian tourism revenues), *Al-Masry Al-Youm,* (17 January 2011). https://www.almasryalyoum.com/news/details/108882 (consulted 29 December 2017).

Sheline, A. (2020) Oman's Smooth Transition doesn't Mean its Neighbors won't Stir Up Trouble. *Foreign Policy,* January 2 3. Accessed July 10, 2020. https://foreignpolicy.com/2020/01/23/omans-smooth-transition-saudi-arabia-uae-mbsstir-up-trouble/.

Shilliam, R. (2021) *Decolonizing Politics: An Introduction.* Cambridge: Polity Press.

Shilliam, R. (2020) Race and racism in international relations: retrieving a scholarly inheritance. *International Politics Reviews* 8(3): 152–195.

Sievers, M. (2020) Sultan Haitham Makes a Strong Start by Addressing Economic Challenges. *Atlantic Council,* June 1 1. Accessed July 10, 2020. https://www.atlanticcouncil.org/blogs/menasource/sultan-haitham-makes-a-strong-start-byaddressing-economic-challenges/.

Sikkink, K. (2008) From International Relations to Global Society. In: Reus-Smit, C., and Snidal, D. (eds,) *The Oxford Handbook of International Relations.* Oxford: Oxford University Press, 62–83.

Silva, M. (2005) Critical theory in international relations. [In Portuguese] *International Context* 27(2): 249–282. Available: https://bit.ly/3e3fFtn. (consulted 5 November 2017).

Sindjoun, L. (2001) Transformation of International Relations: Between Change and Continuity. *International Political Science Review* 22(3): 219–228.

Singer, D. (1960) International Conflict, Three Levels of Analysis. *World Politics,* 12(3): 453–461.

Sinha, A. (2018) Building a Theory of Change in International Relations: Pathways of Disruptive and Incremental Change in World Politics. *International Studies Review* 20(2): 195–203.

Skocpol, T. (1979) *States and Social Revolutions.* Cambridge, U.K.: Cambridge University Press.

Smith, L. (2012) *Decolonizing Methodologies: Research and Indigenous Peoples*. London: Zed Books.

Smith, L. (1999) *Decolonizing Methodologies: Research and Indigenous Peoples*. London: Zed Books.

Smith, S. (2002) The United States and the Discipline of International Relations: Hegemonic Country, Hegemonic Discipline. *International Studies Review* 4(2): 67–85.

Spivak, G. (1988) Can the Subaltern Speak? In: C. Nelson, and L. Grossberg (eds.) *Marxism and the Interpretation of Culture*. Basingstoke: Macmillan, 271–313.

Stadnicki, R. (2016) An Urban Revolution in Egypt? In: S. Lacroix and B. Rougier (eds), Egypt's *Revolutions: Politics, Religion, and Social Movements*. New York: Palgrave Macmillan, 229–44.

Steans, J. (et al.) (2010) *An Introduction to International Relations Theory: Perspectives and Themes*. Abingdon: Routledge.

Sterling-Folker, J. (2002) Realism and the Constructivist Challenge: Rejecting, Reconstructing, or Rereading. *International Studies Review*, 4(1): 73–97.

Streeck, W., and Thelen, K. (eds.). (2005) *Beyond Continuity: Institutional Change in Advanced Political Economies*. Oxford: Oxford University Press.

Susser, A. (2009) *Challenges to the Cohesion of the Arab State*. New York: Syracuse University Press.

Talani, L. (2014) *The Arab Spring in the Global Political Economy*. London: Palgrave McMillian.

Tantawi, A. (2003) *Al-mohamshoon fi Sa'id misr: A'liyat al-saytarha w al-ghodooh* [The Marginalized of Upper Egypt: Mechanisms of Control and Submission]. Cairo: Merit House.

Taylor, L. (2012) Decolonizing International Relations: Perspectives from Latin America. *International Studies Review* 14 (3): 386–400.

Telhami, S. (2003) An Essay on Neorealism and Foreign Policy, pp. 105–119, in A. Hanami (ed.): *Perspectives on Structural Realism*. New York: Palgrave Macmillan.

Telji, I. (2020) Tadaiyat jaehat faerous korona al-mustagad fi al-khaleej: Al-tahdeyat wa al-soubaat. Doha: Arab Center for Research and Policy Studies. Accessed July 10, 2020. https://www.dohainstitute.org/ar/PoliticalStudies/Pages/The-Implicationsof-Covid-19-in-the-Gulf-Challenges-and-Constictions.aspx.

Teschke, B. (2014) IR theory, historical materialism, and the false promise of international historical sociology. *Spectrum: Journal of Global Studies* 6(1): 1–66.

Teschke, B. (2008) Marxism. In: Reus-Smit, C., and Snidal, D. (eds.) *The Oxford Handbook of International Relations*. Oxford: Oxford University Press, 163–187.

The World Bank (2012) Reclaiming their Voice: New Perspectives from Young Women and Men in Upper Egypt, *The World Bank* [Online]. https://documents.worldbank.org/en/publication/documents-reports/documentdetail/514301468233333500/reclaiming-their-voice-new-perspectives-from-young-women-and-men-in-upper-egypt (accessed 30 December 2017).

Thorhallsson, B. (ed.). (2018) *Small States and Shelter Theory: Iceland's External Affairs.* New York: Routledge.

Thorhallsson, B. (2000) *The Role of Small States in the European Union.* New York: Routledge.

Thorhallsson, B. (2000) *The Role of Small States in the European Union.* Aldershot, U.K.: Ashgate.

Tibi, B. (2009) *Islam's predicament with Modernity.* Abingdon: Routledge.

Tibi, B. (1997) *Arab Nationalism: Between Islam and the Nation-State.* Basingstoke: Macmillan Press.

Tilly, C. (1984) *Big Structures, Long Processes, Huge Comparisons.* New York: Russell Sage Foundation.

Tilly, C. (1981) *As Sociology meets History.* New York: Academic Press.

Tilly, C. (1978) *From Mobilization to Revolution.* Reading, MA: Addison-Wesley.

Tilly, C. (1975) *The formation of national states in Western Europe.* Princeton, NJ: Princeton University Press.

Tohamy, A. (2016) *Youth Activism in Egypt: Islamism, Political Protest and Revolution.* New York: I.B. Tauris.

Totten, M. (2016) The New Arab–Israeli Alliance. *World Affairs* 179 (2): 28–36.

Tsukerman, I. (2020) Why Oman's Confiscation of Al Shehhi Property threatens the Integrity of the GCC. *Small Wars Journal.* Accessed July 10, 2020. https://smallwarsjournal.com/jrnl/art/why-omans-confiscation-al-shehhi-propertythreatens-integrity-gcc.

TV presenter Tamer Amin suspended for remarks on Upper Egypt: read the full story, *Egypt Today*, (19 February 2021). Available: https://www.egypttoday.com/Article/1/98809/TV-presenter-Tamer-Amin-suspended-for-remarks-on-Upper-Egypt (consulted 30 December 2021).

Ullman, R. (1983) Redefining Security. *International Security*, 8(1): 129–153.

Ulrichsen, K. (2017) Foreword. *Gulf Affairs* 2(7), IV–V.

Ulrichsen, K. (2016) *The Gulf States in International Political Economy.* London and New York: Palgrave Macmillan.

Ulrichsen, K. (2015) *Insecure Gulf: The End of Certainty and the Transition to the Post-Oil Era.* New York: Oxford University Press.

Ulrichsen, K. (2014) *Qatar and the Arab Spring.* London: Hurst Publishers.

United Nations Development Programme (1990–2019) Human Development Reports 1990–2019. New York: United Nations. Available: https://bit.ly/2Bg97Zy (consulted 15 November 2020).

UNDP. United Nations Development Programme, Human Development Report 2019. *Beyond income, beyond averages, beyond today: Inequalities in human development in the 21st century.* New York: United Nations Development Programme.

UNDP. United Nations Development Programme, Human Development Report. (2014). *Sustaining Human Progress: Reducing Vulnerabilities and Building Resilience*. New York: United Nations Development Programme.

Valbjørn, M. (2017) Strategies for Reviving the International Relations/Middle East Nexus after the Arab Uprisings. *Political Science & Politics* 50(3): 647–651.

Van der Pijl, K. (2013) The Financial Crisis and the War for Global Governance, Anti-capitalist Initiative. Available: https://bit.ly/3e4hQwM (consulted 5 November 2017).

Van der Pijl, K. (2011) Arab Revolts and Nation-State Crisis. *New Left Review* 70: 27–49.

Van der Pijl, K. (1984) *The Making of an Atlantic Ruling Class*. London: Verso.

Vincent, R. (1983) Review: Change and International Relations. *Review of International Studies* 9(1), 63–70.

Vishwanath, L. (1990) Peasant Movements in Colonial India: An Examination of Some Conceptual Frameworks. *Economic and Political Weekly*, 25(2): 118–122.

Vitalis, R. (2015) *White World Order, Black Power Politics: The Birth of American International Relations*. Ithaca, NY, Cornell University Press.

Wæver, O. (1994) Resisting the Temptation of Post-foreign policy analysis. In: Carlsnaes, W., and Smith, S. (eds.) *European Foreign Policy: The EC and Changing Perspectives in Europe*. London: Sage, 238–273.

Wakeman, F. (1977) Rebellion and Revolution: The Study of Popular Movements in Chinese History. *The Journal of Asian Studies*, 36(2): 201–237.

Wallerstein, I. (1974) *The Modern World-System*. New York: Academic Press.

Walt, S. (2011) Is IR still 'an American social science'. *Foreign Policy*, Available: https://foreignpolicy.com/2011/06/06/is-ir-still-an-american-social-science/ (consulted 30 December 2017).

Walt, S. (1997) *Revolution and War*. Ithaca: Cornell University Press.

Walt, S. (1992) Revolution and War. *World Politics*, 44(3): 321–368.

Walt, S. (1987) *The Origins of Alliances*. Ithaca; New York: Cornell University Press.

Waltz, K. (1986) Reflections on Theory of International Politics: A Response to My Critics. In R. Keohane (ed.) *Neorealism and its Critics*. Princeton: NJ; Princeton University Press, 322–346.

Waltz, K. (1979) *Theory of International Politics*. Reading: Mass; Addison-Wesley.

Wane, N. N., and Todd, K. (2018) *Decolonial Pedagogy: Examining Sites of Resistance, Resurgence, and Renewal*. New York: Palgrave Macmillan.

Weber, C. (2001) *International Relations Theory: A Critical Introduction*. London: Routledge.

Weber, M. (1947) *The Theory of Social and Economic Organization*. London: Oxford University Press.

Welch, C. (2009) Camponeses: Brazil's Peasant Movement in Historical Perspective (1946–2004). *Latin American Perspectives*, 36(4): 126–155.

Welch, C. (2006) Keeping Communism Down on the Farm: The Brazilian Rural Labor Movement during the Cold War. *Latin American Perspectives*, 33(3): 28–50.

Wiarda, I., and Wiarda, H. (1967) Revolution or Counter-Revolution in Brazil? *The Massachusetts Review*, 8(1): 149–165.

Winckler, O. (2015) Qatar: Small State, Big Politics. *Middle Eastern Studies* 51(1): 159–162.

Winegar, J. (2011) Egypt: A Multi-Generational Revolt, *Jadaliyya*, Available: http://www.jadaliyya.com/Details/23721/Egypt-A-Multi-Generational-Revolt (consulted 11 December 2019).

Wittes, T. (2008) *Freedom's Unsteady March America's Role in Building Arab Democracy*. Washington, D.C.: Brookings Institution Press.

Woertz, E. (2017) Agriculture and Development in the Wake of the Arab Spring. In: G. Luciani (ed.) *Combining Economic and Political Development: The Experience of MENA*. Geneva: Graduate Institute Publications, Boston: Brill-Nijhoff, 144–169.

Wohlforth, W. (1999) The Stability of a Unipolar World. *International Security* 24(1): 5–41.

Wyn-Jones, R. (2001) *Critical Theory and World Politics*. Boulder, Colo.: Lynne Rienner.

Wyn-Jones, R. (1999) *Security, Strategy, and Critical Theory*. Boulder: Lynne Rienner.

Yalvaç, F. (2015) Critical Theory: International Relations' Engagement with the Frankfurt School and Marxism. *Oxford Research Encyclopedias of International Studies*. Available: https://bit.ly/3hvkOMM. (consulted 5 November 2017).

Yazbak, M. (2000) From poverty to revolt: economic factors in the outbreak of the 1936 rebellion in Palestine. *Middle Eastern Studies*, 36(3): 93–113.

Yilmaz, S. (2016) China's Foreign Policy and Critical Theory of International Relations. *Journal of Chinese Political Science* 21(1): 75–88.

Yossef, A., and Cerami, J. (2015) *The Arab Spring and the Geopolitics of the Middle East: Emerging Security Threats and Revolutionary Change*. New York: Palgrave Macmillan.

Young, K. (2017) Foreign Policy Trends in the GCC States. *Gulf Affairs* 2(7): IV–V.

'Young People in Upper Egypt: New Voices, New Perspectives', *The World Bank*, (6 September 2012). Available: https://www.worldbank.org/en/news/feature/2012/09/06/young-people-in-upper-egypt (consulted 5 November 2017).

Zakaria, F. (2007) *The Future of Freedom: Illiberal Democracy at Home and Abroad*. New York: W. W. Norton.

Zinn, H. (1980) *A People's History of the United States: From 1492 to the Present*. New York: HarperCollins.

Zubaida, S. (1989) *Islam, the people and the state*. London: I.B. Tauris.

Zvobgo, K., and Loken, M. (2020) Why Race Matters in International Relations. *Foreign Policy*. Available: https://foreignpolicy.com/2020/06/19/why-race-matters-international-relations-ir/ (consulted 30 April 2021).

Index

12 February 2011 60, 94, 102
1919 revolution 84
1919 uprising 83, 88
1952 coup 88
2013 coup 61
25 January revolution 92, 93
25 January 2011 92, 93, 94, 96, 97, 103

a'daa al-watan ('enemies of the country') 91
Abd al-Khaliq Abdullah 53, 174, 175, 197
Abd al-Malik, Anwar 41, 57
Abdelhai, Walled 52
Abdelrahman, Maha 84
Abdo 70, 103
Abdullah, Ismail Sabry 136
Abdullah, Nadine 85
Abdul-Jalil Al-Marhoun 54
Abdullah Al-Otaibi 54
Abid al-Jabri 54
Abou Samra, Amira 50
Abu Al-Fadl, Mona 54
Abu Dhabi 178, 181, 183, 193, 200, 202, 203, 211
Abu Dhabi TV 203
Abu-Lughod, Lila 86, 101, 102
Abu Musa 177
Abu Qurqas 90, 96, 102
Achcar, Gilbert 31, 34
Adams, Richard 88
Adaptive authoritarianism 34
Afghanistan 22, 133, 216
Africa 21, 81, 83, 111, 148, 189
African American 218
Agent-structure debate 154
Ahistoricism 40, 44, 185
Ahl al-balad [the natives] 64
Akher al nahar (TV talk show) 63
Alexandria 62, 64, 76, 79, 96, 100
Algeria 24, 54, 55
Algerian 53, 55
Algerian Encyclopedia of Political Science 53
Ali, Hassan Hajj 54
Ali, Tariq 31
Alternatives: Global, Local, Political (journal) 5

Althusser, Louis 219
Al-Abnoudi, Abdul-Rahman 89, 98
Al-Ahram Center for Political and Strategic Studies 57
Al-Ansari, Muhammad 54
Al-Arabi, Nabil 168
Al-Arabia 91, 203
Al-Arabiya 91
Al-Ard Center for Human Rights 94
Al-Assad, Bashar 41
Al-Atas, Syed Hussein 49
Al-Awamiyah (city) 108, 218
Al-Awqaf (Islamic Endowments) 90
Al-Azhar 90
al-Bajah 111, 219
Al-Bloshi, Hamad 52
Al-Delta 63, 64, 85, 95
Al-Fawreyka 97
Al-Fellaheen 64, 84, 88, 107, 217
Al-Fikriyya city 72, 80, 96, 97, 98
Al-Gheit (the land) 71, 91
Al-Halab 64, 111, 219
Al-Hayat 203
Al-Hizb al-watani 102
Al-Jama'ah al-Islamiyyah 11, 103
Al-Jazeera 91, 203
Al- Jazeera Sport 91
Al-Jmaseh 64, 111, 219
Al-Kheder, Moutaz 54
Al-Kuwari, Hanan (Qatari minister of health) 212
Al-Mashat, Abdel Moneim 57
Al-Minya (governate) 61, 66, 67, 84, 90, 93, 94, 95, 97, 101, 105, 218
Al-Moddara'h (an armoured fighting vehicle) 87
Al-Mustafa, Hamza 54
Al-Mustaqbal Al-Arabi 55
Al-Naqib Khaldoun 54
Al-Noaimi, Haya 56
Al-Qaida 10, 159, 162, 170
Al-Rashdi, Aisha 56
Al-Romaihi Mohamed 53
Al-Sayed, Wafa 54
Al-Sayyid, Mustapha Kamel 54

INDEX

Al-Sharq Al-Awast 203
Al-Shaji, Abdullah 54
Al-Siyassa Al-Dawliya 55
Al-Ula agreement 212
Al-Ula Summit 212
Al-Wadi al-Gadeed 79, 93, 217
Al-Wafd 80
Al-wasla (a monthly subscription) 91, 105
Al-Zubairi, Fatemah 54
American Anthropologist 96
American foreign policy 151
American Gulf 174
American Journal of Political Science 49
American troops 162
Amin, Samir 31, 48
Amin, Tamer 63
Anarchic system 149, 156, 171, 173
Anglo-Saxon 7, 47, 48, 49, 50, 51, 52, 53, 54, 58, 185
Anievas, Alexander 43
Anti-Americanism 124
Anti-elections protests 28
Anti-emancipatory policies 216
Anwar, Tasniem 54
Appeasement 156, 160, 173, 176
Arab academy 56
Arab-Arab Conflicts (book) 53
Arab Booker Prize 203
Arab citizens 33, 36, 38, 205
Arab countries 12, 31, 34, 35, 41, 54, 56, 89, 94, 153, 154, 160, 162, 163, 167, 181, 201, 202, 205, 207
Arab dictators 34
Arab economies 205
Arab exceptionalism 36
Arab foreign trade 199
Arab-Islamic World 148
Arab Israeli conflict 201, 202
Arab Journal of Political Science 55
Arab Journal of Sociology 55
Arab leadership 162
Arab League 56, 163, 164, 200
Arab nation 31, 163, 207, 217
Arab Nationalism 163, 217
Arab Peace Initiative 202
Arab People 28, 32, 35, 37, 39, 51, 206
Arab Political Regimes (book) 53
Arab political thought 47

Arab regimes 33, 35, 134, 136
Arab Regional System (ARS) 11, 175, 179, 187, 196, 197, 208
Arab Regional System (book) 53
Arab revolutions 122, 202
Arab scholars 47, 54, 55, 57
Arab societies 34. 36, 39
Arab States 9, 10, 11, 34, 35, 39, 41, 136, 181, 204, 205, 207, 217
Arab Uprising 1, 2, 3, 4, 5, 6, 8, 9, 10, 12, 13, 15, 20, 22, 23, 28, 29, 32, 33, 34, 35, 36, 38, 59, 60, 61, 66, 67, 71, 79, 84, 85, 86, 87, 90, 93, 96, 105, 105, 122, 124, 134, 138, 139, 140, 153, 154, 160, 161, 162, 163, 165, 182, 197, 199, 201, 208, 213, 215
Arab Uprisings 1, 3, 4, 5, 11, 12, 24, 26, 31, 32, 37, 38, 39, 40, 54, 120, 121, 122, 123, 126, 139, 151, 155, 180, 182, 195, 197, 198, 213
Arab World 3, 6, 7, 10, 11, 14, 16, 36, 41, 45, 48, 49, 51, 52, 53, 54, 56, 57, 58, 123, 126, 136, 151, 161, 163, 164, 165, 166, 171, 175, 180, 181, 184, 198, 199, 203, 206, 213, 216, 217
Arab youth 122
Arabian foreign policies 125
Arabian Gulf 3, 14, 120, 139, 158, 162, 167, 172, 174, 175, 177, 179, 182, 199, 200, 205, 206, 207, 208, 209
Arabian Gulf countries 3, 174, 206
Arabian Gulf region 14, 139, 199, 200, 209
Arabian Gulf Regional System 175
Arabian Gulf System 208
Arabian Monetary Fund (AMF) 199
Arabian poet 203
Arabian Social Sciences and Humanities Prize 204
Arabic knowledge 47, 48
Arabic literature 203, 204
Arabic speaking countries 216
Arabic textbooks 52
Arabic texts 53
Arabism 32, 33, 188
Arabs 44. 47, 48, 64, 203, 204, 208, 217
Argentina 147
Armenians 217
'Asabiyat 41
Asfour 70, 100, 103
Ashley, Richard 24, 33, 215
Asia 23, 81, 189, 202

Asl (heritage)   63
Assad, Hafez   32
Assiut   48, 56, 84, 90, 93, 94, 95, 105
Assyrian   111, 220
as-Sa'idiyya   59, 60, 61, 62, 63, 64, 66, 67, 74, 76, 81, 84, 86, 88, 89, 91, 92, 93, 94, 98, 99, 104, 105, 106, 107, 108, 109, 110
Aswan   62, 79, 84, 89, 92, 93, 94, 95, 101, 105, 106, 217
Athens   23, 171
Atlantic   23, 46, 111
Austria   117, 143
Authoritarian-based stability theory   135
Authoritarian-stability nexus   11, 36
Aweys Al-Rawi   108, 218
Ayubi, Nazih   53

Baaz, Mikael   77
Badran, Wadoda   48
Baghdad   56, 203
Bahrain   24, 31, 36, 38, 54, 55, 122, 139, 152, 159, 166, 177, 178, 183, 193, 201, 204, 206, 211
Bahraini Kingdom   206
Balance of Power   14, 16, 36, 114, 115, 123, 138, 139, 140, 141, 144, 145, 146, 149, 152, 155, 156, 164, 166, 169, 171, 172, 173, 174, 176, 178, 180, 181, 182, 185, 188, 195, 196, 198, 199, 205
Balance of Threat theory   14, 139, 140, 144, 145, 148, 149
Balance of Values Theory   144, 147, 151
Balancing   120, 145, 156, 173
Bandwagon   37, 120, 127, 138, 141, 145, 152, 156, 157, 173, 174, 179
Bashteel (southern part of Greater Cairo)   62
Bayat, Asef   93
Baylis, John   53
Bedouins   63, 64, 153
Beirut   203
Beni Suef   93, 95
Bhabha, Homi   51
Binnendijk, Hans   197
Biopolitics   29
Bishara, Azmi   54
Black Arabs   217
Black Lives Matter movement   49, 110, 218

Bolshevik Revolution in 1917   123
Bolsheviks   115
Bonaparte, Napoleon   19, 197
Booth, Ken   38
Boutros-Ghali, Boutros   53, 57
Brazil   21, 99, 174
Brexit   46
Brincat, Shannon   42
British authorities   98
British colonial authorities   64
British despotism   88
British hegemony   19
British occupation   82
Brown, Nathan   77, 83, 84, 88, 97
Brynen, Rex   82
Burchill, Scott   53
Bureaucratization   152
Burke, Edmund   142
Bush, Ray   80
Bustos, Rafael   29

Cairo   23, 56, 57, 62, 64, 76, 79, 84, 86, 93, 96, 100, 101, 103, 163, 167, 203
Cairo University   54
Cairoian   96
Caribbean   111, 220
Carr, E. H.   147
Catalonian-Spanish protests   28
Categorization   63, 66
Caucasus   111, 216
Central Agency for Public Mobilization and Statistics (CAPMS)   95, 96, 101
Central Asian countries   216
Centre for Arab Unity Studies   136
Chaldean-Syriac   111, 220
Chile   147
China   18, 21, 46, 83, 117, 125, 138, 140, 143, 144, 148, 174, 213
Chinese global power   148
Chinese peasant rebellions   83
Chinese Revolution of 1945   151
Chomsky, Noam   31
Choucri, Nazli   17
Chronofetishism   40, 44, 185, 190
Civil society   2, 6, 8, 15, 26, 45, 61, 67, 80, 87, 151, 193, 213
Civil war   10, 41, 87, 157, 158, 197
Civil-Military Relations   133

INDEX

Clash of civilizations   21, 22
Cognitive fallacies   215
Cold War   16, 17, 19, 21, 22, 23, 28, 125, 148, 151, 157, 177, 182
Collective memory   62, 85
Colonial powers   85
Color Revolutions   28
Communicative action   40, 42, 45
Comparative Politics   2, 17, 41, 50, 57, 90
Concert Revolution   204
Confucian   83
Congo   125
Construction Project Holding Company (CPC)   164
Constructivism   3, 4, 13, 36, 39, 43, 50, 58, 114, 154, 186
Constructivists   135, 154
Coptic Church   80
Copts   85, 90, 153
Counterbalancing   36, 37, 178
Counterinsurgency   87
Counterrevolution   1, 6, 8, 14, 106, 118, 119, 121, 122, 123, 124, 125, 126, 134, 138, 139, 151
Counterrevolutionary forces   38, 66
Counterrevolutionary regimes   1, 14, 122, 139
Counterterrorism   61, 67, 87
Coup d'état   31, 121, 122
COVID-19   108, 212, 218
Cox, Robert   25, 26, 39, 40, 214
Coxian critical project   39
Crisis Management and Conflict Resolution (book)   53
Critical International Relations (CIR)   5, 6, 28, 29, 32, 42
Critical school   4, 23, 24, 26, 36, 40, 42, 50, 58, 185, 214
Critical Security Studies (CSS)   24
Critical Theory   1, 3, 4, 5, 6, 23, 24, 25, 28, 37, 214, 215, 216
Critical Theory of International Relations (CTIR)   5, 28
Crown Prince of Abu Dhabi   203, 211
Crusade   22
Cuba   117, 125, 129, 147
Cuban Revolution of 1959   123, 151

Dabashi, Hamid   31, 57
Dahl, Robert   52

Dairut (city)   84, 90
Damanhur   96
Damascus   201
Darwich, May   48
David, Steven   131
Dawla (state)   41, 188, 196
Dayr-Mawas   84, 97
Decision-makers   31, 100, 119, 120, 128, 132, 154, 196
Decision-making process   100, 128, 132, 154, 196
Decoloniality   51, 58
Decolonizing   12, 49, 57, 58, 59, 77, 216, 221
deep state   106, 107
Defensive realism   145, 173
Democratic peace theory   132
Democratization   2, 6, 7, 14, 31, 32, 33, 35, 36, 37, 39, 167, 213
Dependency   35, 157, 173, 193, 194, 214
Deutsch, Karl   52
Devetak, Richard   53
Dialectical materialism   190
Dialogical   44, 51
Doha   160, 178, 181, 183, 193, 200, 203
Double-edged coloniality   217
Dougherty, James   52
Dow Jones index   201
Dubai   200, 202, 203, 204, 210
Dubai International Prize of the Holy Qur'an   204
Dubai Media City (DMC)   203
Dunne, Tim   53
Dutch empire   19

East European   111, 220
East of Eden   177
East of Suez   174
Eastern Europe   23, 111, 220
Ebid, Hana   55
Economic Aid   33, 161, 165, 166
Egypt   1, 2, 3, 9, 11, 12, 13, 14, 24, 31, 34, 35, 36, 39, 48, 54, 55, 56, 59, 60, 61, 62, 63, 64, 65, 71, 76, 80, 81, 82, 83, 84, 85, 86, 87, 88, 89, 90, 91, 92, 93, 94, 95, 96, 98, 99, 100, 101, 102, 103, 104, 105, 106, 107, 108, 110, 11, 114, 120, 121, 122, 123, 125, 126, 127, 128, 129, 134, 138, 139, 140, 142, 146, 147, 152, 153, 158, 159, 160, 161, 162, 163, 164,

Egypt (cont.)
    165, 166, 167, 168, 169, 170, 171, 179, 180,
    195, 197, 198, 199, 200, 201, 202, 208, 211,
    213, 217, 218, 219, 220
Egypt-GCC relations   120, 140, 158, 160
Egypt's foreign policy   13, 124, 125, 128
Egypt's revolutionary regime   169
Egyptian foreign policy   13, 113, 120, 124, 128,
    154, 155, 167, 168
Egyptian national security   124, 168
Egyptian revolution   2, 121, 123, 124, 125, 126,
    151, 167
Egyptian Revolution of 1952   123, 151
Egyptian School   54
Egyptians   62, 79, 86, 93, 102, 126, 207
El-Bernoussi, Zaynab   54
El-Feki, Mustafa   120
El-Nour, Saker   84, 93, 94, 107
El-Sisi, Abdel-Fattah   63, 80, 158, 165, 166
Emancipation   4, 6, 8, 24, 27, 36, 37, 38, 42,
    45, 83, 213, 214, 215, 216
Emir of Kuwait   209
Emir of Qatar   202
English School   158n, 208, 209
Enlightenment   12, 39, 42, 43, 45, 50, 57, 215
Enlightenment-based-Modernity   215
Environmental protests   28
Epistemic Fallacy   39
Epistemological fallacy   12
EU   31, 46, 122, 138, 157, 158
Eurasia   23
Eurasian Studies   111
Eurocentric   19, 42, 43, 47, 49, 50, 58, 185, 213,
    215, 221
Eurocentric-Capitalism   12
Eurocentric Fallacy   39, 42
Eurocentrism   42, 57
Euromodernism   49
Europe   23, 40, 45, 46, 81, 148, 186, 197
European colonialism   217
European empires   19
European imperial powers   180, 198
*European Journal of International
    Relations*   49
European Union   33, 46, 157, 168
Everyday life resistance   76, 97
Everyday resistance   77
Ezbet al-fawreyka (village)   97

Fabrique   97
Facebook   62, 73, 102, 210
Faculty of Economics and Political
    Science   54
Farag, Anwar   54
Fatimah Ahmed Abdul-Ghafar   89
Fayoum   95
Fayz Farahat, Mohamed   55
Flora, Peter   152
Fontana, Andrea   66
Foreign Aid   13, 38, 139, 151, 169, 190, 200
Foreign Direct Investment (FDI)   129,
    194, 200
Foreign Policy Analysis (book)   53
Former Soviet countries   28
Foucault, Michel   33
Fouda, Ezzeldin   52
Fox, Annette Baker   189
France   117, 129, 142, 146, 152
Frankfurt School   3, 5, 29, 42
Freedom House   35
French Revolution of 1789   117
French revolutionary wars   143
Frey, James   66
Fukuyama, Francis   53

G8   214
Garr, Ted Robert   60
GCC (Gulf Cooperation Council)   1, 8, 9, 12,
    13, 14, 33, 38, 39, 120, 138, 139, 140, 152,
    156, 157, 158, 159, 160, 161, 162, 163, 165,
    166, 167, 168, 169, 173, 174, 175, 176, 177,
    178, 179, 180, 183, 194, 195, 199, 200, 201,
    203, 204, 205, 206, 207, 208, 209, 212
General theory of international
    relations   172
George Floyd   110, 218
#George_Floyd_of_Egypt   108
George, Jim   5
Ghalioun, Burhan   54
Ghimire, Krishna   74
Gill, Stephen   34
Gilpin, Robert   53, 192, 193
Giza   62, 64
Global IR   51
Global civil society   29, 214
Global Database of Events, Language and
    Tone Project (GDELT)   29

INDEX

Global political community 44
Global right-wing ideology 148
Global South 5, 10, 13, 21, 27, 42, 43, 45, 47, 48, 49, 51, 58, 79, 88, 111, 114, 141, 147, 148, 149, 152, 153, 214, 217, 220
Global war on terror 22, 87
Globalization 6, 18, 22, 26, 37, 39, 53, 187
Google Maps 97
Goudjili, Sid 54, 55
Gough, Kathleen 82
Gramsci, Antonio 26, 110, 219
Grand strategy 135, 136
Great Britain 143, 146, 174, 177
Great Depression 175
Great powers 10, 18, 19, 20, 21, 23, 118, 122, 123, 126, 127, 129, 130, 134, 140, 141, 147, 152, 157, 172, 173, 174, 176, 177, 178, 179, 180, 192, 205
Greater Middle East 3, 22, 111, 220
Greater Tunbs 177
Greek city-states 171
Greeks 171, 180, 198
Green movement in Iran 23, 28
Gulf cities 200
Gulf crisis 211, 212
Gulf leaders 157, 202
Gulf Moment 197
Gulf monarchies 14, 139, 165, 166, 181
Gulf of Oil 174
Gulf region 8, 14, 18, 139, 168, 177, 178, 180, 182, 183, 184, 186, 188, 193, 194, 197, 198, 199, 200
Gulf Regional System 175, 206
Gulf States 9, 14, 19, 54, 86, 89, 120, 127, 157, 167, 168, 171, 175, 178, 179, 181, 182, 183, 184, 186, 187, 188, 189, 193, 194, 195, 196, 197, 199, 200, 201, 202, 203, 204, 205
Gulf Wars 14, 18, 162, 170, 206

Habermas, Jürgen 31, 40, 43, 45, 46
Habermasian-Linklaterian model 44
Habermasian project 3, 5, 6, 32, 39, 40, 42, 44, 45, 46, 58
Halim Barakat 54
Halliday, Fred 184, 187, 209
Hamchi, Mohamed 55
Hamdan, Gamal 167
Hammad, Khairy 52

Hamzawy, Amr 91, 92, 95
Hanafi, Sari 54
Hassan 70, 101, 102
Hassan, Hassan Bakr 53
Hayajneh, Adnan 54
Hegemonic stability 149
Heraji al-Kot 89
Heritage Foundation 201
Hezbollah 10
High Dam 89
Hilal Dessouki, Ali 11, 52, 53, 57
Hinnebusch, Raymond 187
Historical Sociology (HS) 17, 184, 185, 186, 187, 188, 189
Hitler, Adolf 197
Hobbesian system 155
Hobden, Stephen 189
Hobsbawm, Eric 31, 81
Hobson, John 40, 42, 44, 185, 189
Hong Kong protests 28
Horkheimer, Max 27
Houthi 10
Human Development Reports 158
Huntington, Samuel 22, 53, 133
Hurd, Elizabeth 188
Hussein, Saddam 32, 38, 139, 165, 167, 179, 198, 206
Hyper-nationalism 148

Ibrahim, Saad 54, 57
Illiteracy 61, 62, 95, 104
India 21, 46, 111, 148, 174, 220
Industrialization 152, 186
Institute of Arab Research and Studies (IARS) 56
International Critical Theory (ICT) 4
International Law (book) 53
International Monetary Fund (IMF) 11
International Organization (journal) 49
International Organizations (book) 53
International Political Economy (book) 53
International Political Sociology (journal) 5
International Politics 1, 3, 6, 7, 13, 15, 16, 19, 20, 21, 28, 36, 48, 55, 124, 130, 138, 144, 153, 154, 156, 171, 172, 173, 176, 180, 182, 189, 190, 192, 197, 198, 213
International Relations (IR) 1, 2, 3, 4, 6, 7, 8, 14, 15, 16, 17, 18, 20, 24, 25, 26, 28, 36, 40,

International Relations (IR) (*cont.*)
    42, 48, 49, 50, 52, 53, 54, 58, 114, 115, 133, 136, 152, 154, 156, 161, 172, 174, 176, 184, 185, 209, 213
International Relations Theories: Discipline and Diversity (book)   53
International Security (journal)   49
International structures   25, 45, 128, 130, 215
International Studies (journal)   5
International Studies Association (ISA)   48
International Studies Perspectives (journal)   48
International system   19, 20, 21, 23, 39, 115, 138, 147, 148, 149, 150, 154, 155, 156, 158, 171, 172, 173, 174, 180, 185, 188, 192, 193, 198, 215
Interventionist foreign policies   133
IR Theories in the 19th and the 20th Centuries (book)   53
Iran   9, 23, 28, 117, 126, 143, 144, 147, 160, 161, 162, 165, 167, 168, 176, 177, 178, 180, 181, 183, 188, 198, 205, 207, 208, 216
Iranian bombs   9
Iranian military ships   169
Iranian people   205
Iranian power   8
Iranian Prime Minister   178
Iranian regime   160
Iranian revolution   123, 169
Iranian rivalry   14, 18
Iranian scholar   134
Iranian State   142
Iraq   8, 10, 22, 28, 38, 54, 55, 89, 111, 117, 139, 142, 159, 160, 162, 165, 166, 176, 177, 178, 179, 180, 182, 183, 193, 195, 197, 198, 199, 220
Iraq war of 2003   182
Iraq-Kuwait war   162, 165
Iraqi hegemony   179
ISIS (Islamic State in Iraq and Syria)   11, 38, 139, 159, 160
Islam   41, 43
Islamic constitutionalism   34
Islamic empire   180
Islamic militant groups   87
Islamic movements   103
Islamic revolution (1979)   11
Islamic State (IS)   11

Islamic terror   90
Islamicate period   41
Islamists   106, 115
Islamization of knowledge   54
Israel   9, 33, 124, 127, 142, 146, 164, 168, 169, 180, 207, 216
Israeli existential fears   9
Israeli occupation   6, 202
Israeli pressure   9
Ittihad (party)   97
Izab (villages)   93

Jackson, Richard   58
Janissaries   41
Japan   202
'Je suis le people'   102
Jeddah   200, 203
Jervis, Robert   178
Jihadism   29, 148
Joenniemi, Pertti   156
Johnson, Chalmers   82
Johnson, Lyndon   125
Johnston, Alexander   20
Jordan   12, 54
Jordanian   52
Julião, Francisco   83
Journal of Democracy   44
Journal of Political Science   55
Journal of Social Affairs   55
Journal of Social Sciences   55
Journal of Strategic Research   55

Kafuor (villages)   93
Kantian   155
Kennedy, John   125
Kennedy, Robert   53, 156
Khaleeji Age   196
Khaleeji countries   103, 105
Khaleeji society   212
Khaleeji states   212
Khalfan, Dahi   207
Khalifa, Sally   54
Khawana'h ('traitors')   90
Khilafa   163, 170
Khufara   97
Kilomba, Grada   7, 47
King Abdullah Bin Abdul-Aziz   201, 204
King Faisal International Prize   204

INDEX

Kissinger, Henry   23
Korany, Bahgat   48, 57
Korean war   117, 143
Kurds   111, 217, 220
Kurki, Milja   53
Kuwait   9, 52, 54, 55, 56, 158, 159, 160, 162, 165, 166, 167, 177, 178, 183, 193, 199, 201, 203, 204, 209
Kyiv   23

La le-tahmeesh al-Sa'id   106
Lajnat al-khamseen   106
Laroui, Abdullah   54
Latin America   28, 111, 189, 220
Latin American revolutions   31
Latin American societies   111, 220
Law no. 1 of 2020, known as the Construction Violations Reconciliation   61, 217, 218
Lebanon   10, 24, 55, 56
Lesser Tunbs   177
Liberalism   3, 13, 25, 31, 36, 50, 58, 114, 148, 152, 190, 191, 214
Liberalization   33, 34, 37, 89
Liberals   130, 132, 135, 153, 157, 185, 189, 192
Libya   24, 31, 35, 36, 86, 89, 94, 122, 143, 152, 161, 166, 180, 196, 201
Lifeworld   78, 79, 91, 216
Lilja, Mona   77
Linklater, Andrew   4, 25, 31, 40, 41, 43, 44, 45, 46, 53, 215
London   23
Long Peace   43
Lorde, Audre   58
Luxor   79, 92, 93, 95, 101, 102, 105, 108, 217, 218
Lynch, Marc   9, 196

Maass, Matthias   189
Madbouly, Mayada   85
Madinat Al-Fikriyya (city)   13, 60, 61, 72, 80, 96, 97, 98
Madrid   23
Magagna, Victor   83
Magued, Shaimaa   54
Mahatet Masr (Ramses Station)   62
Makled, Ismail Sabri   53
Mallawi   84, 90
Mamlūki   41
Mamlūks   64, 98

Man, the State and War (book)   52
Managed democracy   34
Manama   203
Mansheyat al-Fikriyah   67
Mao, Tse-tung   83, 143
Maoz, Zeev   117, 118
Marginalization   61, 79, 81, 86, 89, 92, 104, 106, 111, 129, 134
Marginalized communities   85, 105
Marx, Karl   4, 24
Marxism   4
Marxist   39, 45, 83
Matar, Jamil   53
Mauritania   133
Maxwell, Joseph   65
MBC Group   203
Mearsheimer, John   53, 148, 156, 173
Mediterranean   23
Mediterranean Politics Journal   151
Middle East   3, 5, 8, 9, 10, 21, 33, 38, 43, 48, 49, 58, 81, 88, 111, 120, 123, 133, 140, 141, 142, 155, 158, 161, 162, 163, 166, 172, 175, 177, 180, 182, 186, 187, 188, 189, 195, 197, 198, 199, 202, 208, 209, 216, 220
Middle East/North Africa (MENA)   5, 12, 14, 18, 37, 126, 139, 158, 177, 181, 195, 216, 219, 220
Middle East, Central Asia, and Caucasus Studies (MECACS)   220
Middle East countries   189
Middle Eastern States   159, 187
Middle Eastern studies   1, 2, 3, 7, 37, 47, 48, 50, 54, 81, 111, 220, 221
Militant Islamic rebellions   97
Militarization fallacy   12, 39
Military juntas   31
Millennium (journal)   5
Miller, Catherine   63
Miscalculation   13, 120, 125, 129, 139, 140, 141, 144, 150, 151
Misperception   13, 125, 139, 140, 141, 144, 150, 151, 153
MNCs (Multinational Corporations)   203, 214
Mobilization   29, 32, 39, 67, 71, 74, 76, 80, 83, 88, 89, 94, 95, 96, 105, 110, 132, 137, 143, 152, 179
Modern Political Analysis (book)   52

Modernity   12, 39, 40, 42, 43, 45, 57, 60, 186, 215, 221
Modernity/Enlightenment Fallacy   12, 39, 43
Modernization   50, 88, 89, 152, 190, 193, 195, 208
Moghul government   82
Mohamed   70, 72, 98, 103
Monological   7, 47
Monologic Fallacy   39, 44
Moravcsik, Andrew   129
Morgenthau, Hans   52, 147
Morocco   54, 56
Morsi, Mohamed   106, 139, 158, 165, 170
Mosaddegh, Mohamed (Iranian Prime Minister)   178
Moussa, Amr   120, 164
Mozambique   83
Mubarak, Hosni   41, 59, 60, 72, 80, 84, 87, 93, 94, 98, 100, 102, 103, 104, 106, 160, 168, 198
Mubarak's regime   35, 61, 67, 84, 85, 94, 100, 104
Muhammad Ali (Pasha)   197
Multinational Corporations (book)   53
Munsha'iat Al-Fikriyya (village)   13, 60, 61, 67, 80, 96, 98
Mura'jat al-dirasat al-dawliya (journal)   55
Muscat   203
Muslims   21, 47, 90, 153, 204
Muslim Brotherhood   80, 95, 103, 105, 106, 139, 140, 160, 163, 165, 166, 170
Muslim culture   36
Muslim states   170
Mustafa, Nadia   54
Mut'khalefeen (backward)   63

Napoleon I (Napoleon Bonaparte)   19, 197
Nasser, Gamal   32, 89, 98, 99, 163, 197
Nasserist   89
Nation-building   180, 181, 182, 183, 187, 188, 194, 195
National Democratic Party (NDP)   80, 102
National interest   6, 7, 15, 36, 124, 131, 143, 147, 148, 151, 167, 174, 176, 188, 190, 213
National Strategy   136, 137, 148
NATO   207
Nazif, Ahmed   74
Nazism parties   148
Nedjar, Mekia   54

Nejou'h (villages)   93
Neoconservative   44
Neo-Gramscian   5, 29, 39, 38
Neoliberal institutionalist   6, 158, 214
Neoliberalism   4, 6, 23, 29, 36, 39, 43, 189
Neoliberals   130, 132, 185, 189, 192
Neorealism   5, 6, 20, 37, 39, 116, 120, 124, 158, 189, 208
Neorealist   6, 20, 29, 36, 37, 174, 176, 208, 209
Nepal   99
Neutrality   156, 173, 183, 210
New York   22
Niblock, Tim   163
Nicaragua   117, 147
Nile   92, 167
Nile Cinema   91
Non-alignment movement   126
Non-governmental organizations (NGOs)   80
Non-revolutionary actors   84, 125
Non-revolutionary camp   14, 125, 139
Non-revolutionary countries   36, 37, 138
Non-revolutionary regimes   14, 139
Non-revolutionary states   1, 116, 138, 146, 149, 153
Non-Western knowledges   7, 47, 48, 50
Non-Western societies   47, 216, 221
North Africa   111
North Korea   144
North-South relationships   31
Nubia   111, 220
Nubian activism   85
Nubians   63, 64, 85, 153, 217
Nuclear proliferation   29
Nye, Joseph   53

Occupy Wall Street movement   28
Offensive realism   145
Oil boom   88, 164
Oil and International Relations (book)   53
Oil-based economy   182, 183, 205
Oil-exporting monarchies   14, 139
Oman   9, 38, 125, 139, 159, 166, 177, 178, 183, 193, 199, 201, 209, 210, 211
Omanization   211
Omni balancing   131
On Political Science (book)   53
Open-door policy   89
Oriental Studies   111, 220

INDEX

Orientalist 1, 3, 41, 44
Organization for Economic Cooperation and Development (OECD) 206
Organized resistance 76, 77, 81, 93, 97, 98
Ottomans 20, 64
Over-stating the Arab State (book) 53
Owens, Patricia 53

Pacifist foreign policies 130
Pakistan 144, 202, 216
Palestinian Liberation Authority (PLA) 202
Pan-Arab ideology 33
Pan-Arabism 56
Paris 23
Paul, Pierson 18
Pax Americana 214
Pax Britannica 214
Pax Saudica 177
Peasants 12, 59, 60, 63, 64, 77, 81, 82, 83, 84, 87, 88, 89, 93, 94, 97, 98, 103, 107, 217
Peasant Leagues 83
Pedagogical fallacy 12, 39, 48
Penguin Dictionary of International Relations 52
Peninsula Shield Force (PSF) 178
People-centric model 2, 7, 8, 15, 213
People's History 78
People's revolution 122
Persians 180, 198
Persian Gulf 14, 18, 31, 183
Pfaltzgraff, Robert 52
Pharaohs 180, 198
Pitt the Younger, William (Prime Minister) 146
Pivot to East Asia 9
Polarization 131
Police brutality 108, 218
police state 31, 87, 106, 107
Political Behavior 50
Political elites 23, 46, 131
Political participation 13, 113, 200
Political philosophy 54
Political Science 17, 48, 52, 53, 54, 56, 81
Political Theory 50
Political thought 54
Political Violence in the Arab Political Systems (book) 53
Politicization 92
Politics Among Nations (book) 52

Pollock, Kenneth 177
Populism 17, 148
Portuguese empire 19
Postcolonial 4, 12, 40, 41, 56, 85, 87, 90
Post-cold war 16, 148, 157
Post-revolution foreign policy 120, 128, 135, 140, 153
Post-revolutionary period 127, 128, 133, 149
Predominance 16, 138
Prince Hamad bin Khalifa Al Thani 202
Professionalism 190, 193, 196
Pro-US authoritarian regime 164
Pro-Western regimes 157
Proxy conflicts 8, 147
Prussia 20, 117
Psychoanalysis perspective 134
Public opinion 13, 92, 113, 119, 125, 127, 132
Public Participation 61, 67, 80, 134

Qaddafi, Muammar 41
Qatar 1, 9, 55, 125, 126, 158, 159, 161, 163, 166, 177, 178, 179, 180, 181, 182, 183, 188, 193, 194, 195, 197, 198, 199, 200, 201, 202, 204, 205, 210, 212
Qatar embargo 212
Qatari 14, 179, 181, 195, 210, 212, 218
Qatari-Emirati relations 8
Qina (governate) 93, 94, 97, 105

Radical Islamism 161, 162
Ragab 70, 72, 98
Rajab, Eman 54
Realism 3, 4, 13, 19, 25, 26, 27, 36, 50, 58, 114, 120, 124, 145, 153, 171, 172, 173
Realist 19, 36, 114, 122, 124, 125, 128, 144, 148, 149, 153, 157
Realist Constructivism 114
Red Sea 79, 217
Reflexivity 48, 76, 77, 78
Regime change 13, 114, 115, 117, 118, 123, 130, 139, 140, 158, 160, 165
Regional powers 8, 14, 115, 125, 126, 129, 145, 176, 179, 180, 192, 194, 197, 198, 199, 200, 204, 208
Regional Security Complex (RSCs) theory 208
Rengger, Nicholas 23
Responsibility to Protect (R2P) 6
Revisionist neighbors 157, 176

Revolution and War (book)   114
Revolution in Nicaragua 1979   117
Revolutionary countries   36, 37, 38, 113, 115, 117, 123, 129, 138, 143
Revolutionary France   142, 146
Revolutionary ideologies   118, 133
Revolutionary leaders   116, 120, 122, 144, 150
Revolutionary regimes   14, 37, 115, 116, 118, 119, 122, 123, 125, 127, 133, 134, 139, 140, 141, 142, 143, 144, 147, 149, 150, 151, 152, 153, 160, 169
Revolutionary states   13, 114, 115, 118, 119, 120, 123, 125, 126, 129, 133, 141, 142, 143, 145, 146, 147, 149, 150, 151, 153, 155
right of return   85
Riyadh   177, 178, 200
Roach, Stephan   32
Rokkan, Stein   148
Romans   180, 198
Rome   23
Rotana Cinema   91
Rotana Zaman   91
Roussillon, Anna   102
rule of law   32, 34, 35, 36, 37, 39
Ruler of Dubai   202
Russia   20, 21, 46, 117, 129, 138, 140, 143

Sa'îd   12, 217, 218, 219
Sa'idi   59, 61, 62, 63, 65, 66, 67, 74, 80, 81, 86, 89, 90, 91, 92, 93, 94, 95, 96, 98, 99, 102, 105, 106, 110, 218, 219
Saad, Reem   84
Sadat, Anwar   87
Saddiki, Said   56
Saeed, Muhammad al-Sayed   53
Said, Abdel Moneim   57
Salafi TV channels   91
Salafists   95, 106
Salamé, Ghassan   41
Saleh, Ali   41
Salem, Ahmed Ali   54
Salim, Muhammad   62
Salloukh, Bassel   58
Saouli, Adham   187
Saraya (the palace)   88
Saudi Arabia   1, 8, 9, 31, 54, 56, 126, 152, 158, 159, 160, 161, 162, 163, 164, 165, 166, 167, 169, 170, 175, 177, 178, 179, 180, 181, 188, 193, 197, 199, 200, 201, 204, 206, 210, 211

Saudi Iranian rivalry   14, 18
Sayigh, Yezid   41
Sayyidah   72, 98, 102
Schmid, David   5, 28
Schweller, Randall   173
Science Day   204
Scott, J. C.   76, 77, 82, 97
Second World War   7, 19, 23, 43, 47, 175, 177, 197
Sectarianism   92
Security dilemma   129, 150, 198, 205
Security-stability nexus   2, 10
Selectivity fallacy   12
Selectivity & Positionality Fallacy   39
Self-help system   145, 171
Selim, Mohamed El Sayed   53
Shabab Abu-Qurqas   102
Shaer Al-million (Prince of Poetry)   203
Shafiq, Ahmed   106
Shah of Iran   167
Shahid al-shahama ("the martyr of magnanimity")   218
Sharaf, Essam   168
Sharjah   203
Sharshoub Hamam   67
Sheikh Abdullah bin Zayed   202
Sheikh Khalifa Bin Zayed Al Nahyan   202
Sheikh Mohammed bin Rashid Al-Maktoum   202, 203, 207
Sheikh Mohammed bin Zayed Al Nahyan   203
Sheikh Sabah Al-Ahmad Al-Jaber Al-Sabah   209
Sheikh Sultan Al Qassimi   203
Sheikh Zayed bin Sultan Al Nahyan   202
Sheikh Zayed Book Award   203
Sheikha Maitha   202
Sheikha Manal   202
Sheikha Mozah   202
Shiite   165
Shilliam, Robbie   50
Shisha   71
Sinai   11, 85
Sinha, Aseema   16, 17, 19
Sino-Russian threat   22
Six-Day War of 1967   33
Siyasaat Arabia (journal)   55
Slavic   111, 220

INDEX 265

Slavic, East European, and Eurasian Studies (SEEES)   111, 220
Small farmers   94
Small states   14, 18, 19, 39, 156, 157, 171, 172, 173, 174, 176, 177, 179, 180, 182, 183, 184, 186, 187, 188, 189, 190, 192, 193, 194, 195, 196
Small States in World Politics (book)   189
Smith, Steve   53
Snapchat   210
Social forces   1, 25, 26, 29, 34, 117, 121, 127, 128, 130, 135, 153, 154, 155, 158, 172, 179, 184, 192, 200
Social media networks   37, 39
Social mobilization   67, 88, 105, 110, 152, 182, 190, 193, 219
Social movements   2, 6, 8, 15, 27, 37, 80
Social non-movements   93
Social Theory of International Politics (book)   53
Socialization   13, 116, 128, 130, 138
Sociology   2, 17, 54, 65, 184
Soft Power (book)   53
Sohag   93, 94, 95, 105, 218
Somalia   8, 117, 134, 202
Songs Channels   91
Souad   70, 99
South Africa   21
South America   148
South Sudan   202
Southeast Asia   202
Southern Egypt   63
Southern voices   215, 221
Sovereign democracy   34
Soviet Union   21, 22, 28, 126, 144, 151
Spanish culture   112, 220
Spanish empire   20
Sparta   171
Spiral model   178
State-building   130, 195
State-centric   6, 7, 14, 42, 148, 209, 213
State-society relations   13, 60, 61, 67, 74, 110, 184, 188, 190, 193, 219
State of anarchy   155
Statism & Militarization Fallacy   12, 39
Status-quo regimes   125
Status-quo states   146, 150, 151
Strait of Gibraltar   167
Strategic Studies (journal)   55
Structural change   3, 19, 20, 21, 44
Structural realism   27, 124, 171, 172, 174, 179
Students protests   28
Subaltern Studies   77
Sudan   8, 24, 31, 34, 54, 64, 122, 168
Sudan Liberation Movement   202
Suez   96
Suez Canal   169
Sulta (authority)   41
Sultan Haitham bin Tariq   210, 211
Sultan of Oman   209, 210
Sultan Qaboos Bin Said   183, 209, 210, 211
Sunni   8, 164
Supreme Council of the Armed Forces (SCAF)   168, 169
Supreme Council for Media Regulation   63
Syria   24, 31, 35, 36, 38, 54, 56, 122, 139, 159, 160, 161, 165, 179, 180, 195, 197, 198, 199, 201

Tabaqet al-mou'zafeen (employees' class)   89
Tahrir Square   93, 96, 101, 102
Takfiri   90
Tanzania   83
Taurus mountains   167
Tempocentrism   40, 44, 185, 189
Tenancy law of 1992   107, 217
Terrorism   10, 61, 67, 87, 161, 162, 207
Teschke, Benno   39, 40
The Analysis of International Relations (book)   52
The Contending Theories of International Relations (book)   52
The Future of Power (book)   53
The Globalization of World Politics (book)   53
The Gulf Regional System (book)   53
The Lazy Native (book)   49
The Lazy Natives   57
The New Arab War (book)   9
The Power of Small States (book)   189
The Rise and Fall of Great Powers (book)   53
The Tragedy of Great Power Politics (book)   53
Theories of Foreign Policy (book)   53
Theories of International Relations (book)   53
Third World countries   22, 27, 32, 148, 157

Third World revolutions 151
Thirkell-White, Tristram 23
Threat Perception 13, 139, 150
Tibi, Bassam 189
Tik-Tok 62
Tilly, Charles 186
TNC (Transnational Corporation) 214
Tohamy, Ahmed 85
Treisman, Daniel 156
Tribalism 92
Tribe-based society 193, 194
Tripolar system 177
Truman, Harry 125
Tunisia 23, 24, 34, 35, 36, 56, 94, 121, 152, 158, 159, 166, 201
Turkey 117, 126, 134, 160, 168, 180, 198
Turkish despotism 88
Turkmen 111, 220
Twin Towers 21
Twitter 108, 210, 218

UAE 1, 9, 31, 48, 54, 55, 125, 126, 152, 158, 159, 160, 161, 163, 165, 169, 170, 177, 178, 179, 180, 181, 182, 183, 188, 193, 194, 195, 197, 198, 200, 201, 202, 203, 204, 205, 207, 210, 211
UK 49
'Um'al al-Yawmiya 101
'Umdah 97
Umma 188, 196, 204
UN Human Development Index 35
UNDP Human Development Report 158
unipolar moment 28
Unit of analysis 220, 244
United States (US) 8, 9, 10, 11, 20, 21, 22, 28, 29, 31, 33, 35, 83, 87, 91, 101, 117, 122, 123, 125, 126, 127, 129, 140, 143, 146, 147, 148, 151, 152, 157, 158, 159, 162, 164, 168, 174, 175, 177, 179, 180, 198, 199, 206
University of Assiut 48, 56
University of Maryland 203
Upper Egypt 3, 11, 12, 13, 48, 56, 59, 60, 61, 62, 63, 64, 65, 76, 81, 85, 86, 87, 88, 89, 90, 91, 92, 93, 94, 95, 96, 98, 99, 100, 101, 102, 103, 104, 105, 106, 107, 108, 111, 217, 218, 219, 220
Upper Egyptians 102
'Urabi's revolt 84, 88

Urbanism & Privileged Fallacy 12, 39
Urbanization 60, 64, 152
US invasion of Iraq 28, 180

Valbjørn, Morten 50
Van der Pijl, Kees 31, 34
Van Evera, Stephen 156
Vietnam 117, 147
Vincent, R.J. 16
Vinthagen, Stellan 77
Vitalis, Robert 50
Vulnerability 42, 118, 119, 120, 127, 141, 147, 150, 167

Waever, Ole 213
Wafdist candidate 97
Walker, R.B.J. 24
Wall Street 23
Walt, Stephen 49, 115, 116, 118, 121, 141, 142, 144, 145, 149
Waltz, Kenneth 52, 115, 124, 128, 144, 149, 155, 156, 171, 172, 185
War and Change (book) 53
War on Terror 22, 23, 87
Wasfa 70, 72, 100, 103
Washington 22, 23, 211
Wazir, Kamel 62
Weapons of Mass Destruction (WMD) 9, 144, 202
Weber, Max 148
Wendt, Alexander 53
Weskheen (dirty) 63
Western camp 157
Western democratic states 148
Western developed countries 158
Western domination 214
Western Europe 151, 186
Western Governments 151
Western hegemonic 1, 7
Western International Relations (IR) 1, 42
Western IR theories 11, 42, 58
Western knowledge 7, 47, 48, 51
Western norms 44
Western Positivism 12
Western powers 22, 27, 31, 33, 35, 43, 44, 126, 129, 140
Westphalian state 149

INDEX

Westphalianism 50
WhatsApp 72
Winckler, Onn 182
Winegar, Jessica 96
Women's rights movements 28
World Bank 35, 62, 81, 94, 103, 158, 214
World's oil-artery 174
World War I 19, 188, 197
World War II 7, 19, 23, 39, 43, 47, 146, 175, 177, 179, 197
World Wrestling Entertainment (WWE) 71, 91

Yalvaç, Faruk 44
Yassin, Syed 57
Yazidis 111, 220
Yemen 8, 10, 12, 22, 24, 31, 34, 35, 36, 122, 139, 147, 152, 158, 159, 160, 161, 176, 180, 183, 196, 202, 206
Young, Karen 183
Youssef, Ahmed 53
Youth bulge 97
YouTube 62

Printed in the United States
by Baker & Taylor Publisher Services